Weaving a Malawi Sunrise

Weaving a Malawi Sunrise

ROBERTA LAURIE

A Woman, A School, A People

The University of Alberta Press

Published by

The University of Alberta Press
Ring House 2
Edmonton, Alberta, Canada T6G 2E1
www.uap.ualberta.ca

Copyright © 2015 Roberta Laurie

LIBRARY AND ARCHIVES CANADA
CATALOGUING IN PUBLICATION

Laurie, Roberta, 1965-, author
     Weaving a Malawi sunrise : a woman,
a school, a people / Roberta Laurie.

Includes index.
Issued in print and electronic formats.
ISBN 978-1-77212-086-8 (paperback). —
ISBN 978-1-77212-113-1 (EPUB). —
ISBN 978-1-77212-114-8 (MOBI). —
ISBN 978-1-77212-115-5 (PDF)

     1. Chazeza, Memory. 2. Women—
Education—Malawi. 3. Women—Malawi—
Social conditions. 4. Education—Malawi.
5. Schools—Malawi. 6. Malawi—Social
conditions. 7. Malawi—Politics and
government. I. Title.

LC2475.8.L39 2015   371.822
C2015-905830-9
C2015-905831-7

Index available in print and PDF editions.

First edition, first printing, 2015.
Printed and bound in Canada by Houghton
Boston Printers, Saskatoon, Saskatchewan.
Copyediting and proofreading by Kirsten Craven.
Map by Wendy Johnson.
Indexing by Adrian Mather.

The University of Alberta Press is committed
to protecting our natural environment. As part
of our efforts, this book is printed on Enviro
Paper: it contains 100% post-consumer recycled
fibres and is acid- and chlorine-free.

The University of Alberta Press gratefully
acknowledges the support received for its
publishing program from the Government of
Canada, The Canada Council for the Arts, and
the Government of Alberta through the Alberta
Media Fund.

Government of Canada   Gouvernement du Canada   Alberta Government

Canada Council for the Arts   Conseil des Arts du Canada

For my daughters Nastassja and Nicola: the sun that gives me life and the moon that shines in the darkness.

Contents

Preface

IT MAY SOUND TRITE to say I'm grateful to have had the chance to write this book, but it's true. Throughout the process I have been reminded of the single opportunity this book represents. Beginning in 2007, I travelled to Malawi on several occasions, and each time I've been accepted with generosity and kindness into the lives and homes of ordinary Malawian people. I have asked probing, and sometimes inappropriate, questions, and I've received nothing but considerate, good-natured responses from everyone I've interviewed. I have come to know some extraordinary people: Christie Johnson, Memory Chazeza-Mdyetseni and her husband Henry, along with Grace, Memory's sister—who I have grown to love and care for—and many others. So while this book has been a long, exacting undertaking, it has been worth every minute.

This was a difficult project. Over the past few years, I've stepped beyond my comfort zone on many occasions. I've pushed past my limitations as a writer and grown immeasurably in the process. One week I would become an expert on Malawi's primary education system, and the next I'd need to learn the ins and outs of IMF policy and the effect it has on developing nations. It's with the utmost humility that I say, *I hope I got it right.*

Throughout this project I have consulted with many individuals: Memory, her husband Henry, her sisters Lucy and Grace, and other Malawian men and women; Agness, Eunice, Basimati, Chidothi, and the other CEAG girls; many of APU's students including Lucita, Patience, Blandina, and Chifundo; Chuck Morrison and other school supporters; Gordon Poultney, founder of the Simon Poultney Foundation; Leslie Vermeer, my mentor and friend; and, of course, Christie Johnson, without whom this book would not have been possible.

I also consulted and worked with Ken Haywood, one of the school's most passionate supporters. Ken passed away in 2011. The following year, his ashes were flown to Malawi and spread at the base of a newly planted baobab tree on the school grounds.

All of these people have been unendingly helpful to me throughout this process, but it's important for me to make this distinction: any mistakes or misinterpretations I have made in this book are mine and mine alone.

It should also be noted that while all the place names are accurate, to protect their privacy, I have changed many of the names of the individuals in this book, and CEAG is a fictitious acronym for a real school. However, Memory, Henry, and Christie, along with the book's other major characters, retain their names, and you can learn more about them, as well as the school, *Atsikana Pa Ulendo*, by visiting the website www.malawigirlsonthemove.com.

Their story is not over.

Acknowledgements

I RECALL LANDING AT THE KAMUZU AIRPORT. It was the colours that I noticed first—reds and blues and greens—saturated and vibrant. And the air, I can almost smell the air: hot and humid and full of life. The airline had lost my luggage, so on my first day in Malawi, I was without the little comforts: toothpaste, toothbrush, clean underwear.

We arrived in Malawi on the same day Memory and Henry moved into their house in Lilongwe's bustling Area 25. They had been evicted from their old house a few days before, learning they were without a home when the new owners knocked on the door and told Henry they were moving in. Memory was nine months pregnant. It was amidst this upheaval that seven jet-lagged Canadians landed on Malawian soil. Yet Memory, Henry, and Grace welcomed us into their home without hesitation. A bit of lost luggage seemed trivial by comparison.

From that moment to this day, Memory, Henry, and Grace have been helpful, kind, and encouraging. Although we are separated by half a world, I think of them often and am ever grateful for their many kindnesses. Without them, this book could not have been written.

I vividly remember the moment Christie Johnson said, "I'm travelling to Malawi this spring with a group of Pearson College students. You should come with us." I doubt she thought I would take her up on her offer, but I did. Throughout the years, and throughout her own struggles, she has given her unconditional support to this project.

I recall mentioning Christie's offer to my husband at the time, Jeff, and I recall his response: "You should do it." For his ongoing support, I'm forever grateful.

It is a thrill and an honour to have the University of Alberta Press publish this book. My thanks to Peter Midgley, for his support, his belief, and his confidence, along with Linda Cameron, Alan Brownoff, Cathie Crooks, Monika Igali, Duncan Turner, and Kirsten Craven.

To the many Canadians who sat with me and shared their words, their thoughts, and their experiences: Audrey Kaplan, Gordon Poultney, Chuck Morrison, Leslie Vermeer, and Timothy Anderson, as well as Ken Haywood, who I will remember always for his compassion, understanding, and encouragement, thank you.

And, finally, I am filled with gratitude to the dozens of Malawians who, in some cases, spent hours sharing their insights and allowing me to gain a glimpse into their lives and their realities: Lucy, Bodwin, Anna, Enala, Esther, Valentina, Maness, Blandina, Grace, Florence, and the many others whose contributions—both large and small—helped me along the way.

It is impossible to mention the countless individuals who made this book possible. This project was very much a collaboration. Without the innumerable Malawians and Canadians who gave their support, opinions, knowledge, and experiences, this book could not have been written.

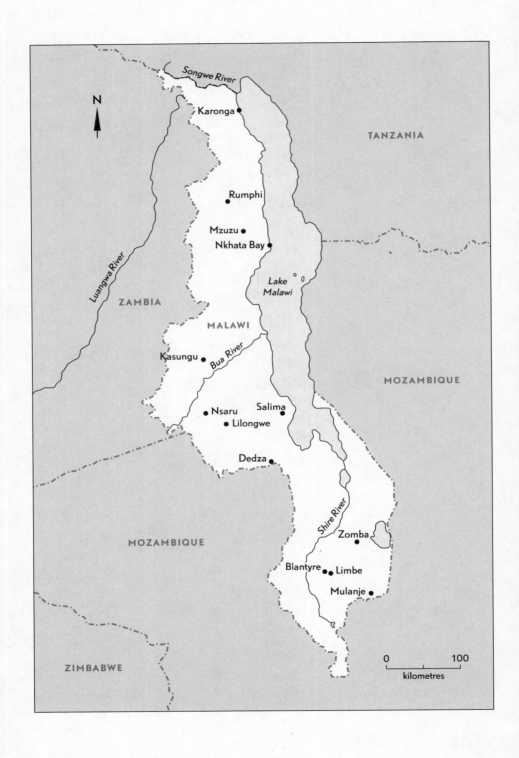

N

Songwe River

Karonga

TANZANIA

Rumphi

Mzuzu
Nkhata Bay

Lake
Malawi

Luangwa River

ZAMBIA

MALAWI

Kasungu   Bua River

MOZAMBIQUE

Nsaru   Salima
Lilongwe

Dedza

Shire River

MOZAMBIQUE

Zomba

Blantyre Limbe

Mulanje

ZIMBABWE

0   100

kilometres

Introduction

The world is for the stubborn.

—*Memory Chazeza-Mdyetseni*[1]

WITHOUT CHRISTIE JOHNSON, I would not have met Memory Chazeza-Mdyetseni. Without Memory Chazeza-Mdyetseni, I could not have written this book. *Weaving a Malawi Sunrise* is their story. It is also the story of Malawian women, all Malawian women. Not just women who were able to fight the bonds of tradition and gain independence through education and determination, but those who were not.

I met Christie Johnson in 2003. She came to speak at our weekly Rotary Club breakfast meeting in Stony Plain, Alberta. So while digesting a full stomach of scrambled eggs, pancakes, and sausage, I listened to her stories of poverty, hunger, and—yes—hope from a far away country whose name I hardly recognized and whose location I couldn't begin to find on a map.

Christie was at the meeting to raise awareness of the challenges facing young girls in Malawi, Africa. She was also seeking funds to help with their education. Christie told us stories about the success of twenty-two Canadian-sponsored girls. Many of the girls were now in trade school. A few would soon be on full scholarships at university. They were all working hard to make a better life for themselves and their families. Some of the girls were in tailoring school and needed materials. We were asked to contribute fabric, needles, thread—anything Christie could squeeze into her duffle bag and take to Malawi on her next trip. I dutifully went home that day and rooted through boxes of half-finished projects. I gathered up bolts of fabric, handfuls of buttons, and an assortment of outdated appliqués. The next week, I lugged my box of cast-offs to the Rotary meeting. I was pleased with myself. I had contributed to a worthy cause. I took my sense of self-satisfaction and went home, but Christie's words followed me. I was haunted by the images from her presentation. I was haunted by the image of Ivy.

Christie often saw Ivy squatting in a field across from the school where she taught. Ivy was just an ordinary fourteen-year-old Malawian girl who came with her brothers to pick termites for her family to eat. Ivy had been expelled from primary school because she was pregnant, and Ivy wasn't married. Christie had heard the gossip and the rumours. The rumours told a tale of sorrow: Ivy had been impregnated by her teacher. It isn't uncommon for girls of Ivy's age to be sexually exploited by male teachers or to sell their bodies for the price of a meal. It is a story that is tragic in its frequency.

During her presentation, Christie had shown us a photo of Ivy and her brothers. In the photo, Ivy doesn't look like a teenager. She looks small and sad and vulnerable, a child herself. She sits on the baked earth between two little boys, her belly pushing against a grubby flowered blouse. Not long after the photo was taken, Christie heard Ivy's screams from the nearby village. They lasted for many hours and went on into the night. Ivy died in childbirth.

Christie Johnson travelled to Africa in 2000 to volunteer teach for a Canadian-funded girls' school in rural Malawi. Canadians Educating African Girls (CEAG) had been founded with the best of intentions, but by the time Christie arrived at the small, two-class school, it was facing a multitude of problems. Christie hadn't known the magnitude of the problems the school was experiencing when she left Canada, but she soon found out. The school closed less than a year later. But by then, Christie had become committed to her students' education. They were no longer faceless statistics; they were girls she had come to love. She couldn't return to Canada and continue with life as before. She knew what lay ahead for girls who lacked an education.

Without an education, Malawian girls are vulnerable. Like Ivy, they often face sexual exploitation. It's common for girls to get married at the age of thirteen or fourteen. Often it's their best option. Often it's their only option. Once married, they become pregnant. They usually have child, after child, after child. Without an independent means of support, they are vulnerable to abuse by their husbands. In the best of circumstances, it is a hard life. In the worst, it is deadly. Christie wanted her students to have a better life, a better chance than Ivy.

After returning to Canada, Christie began raising money for the girls' tuition. She canvassed Edmonton-area Rotary clubs, schools, and individuals. They were all moved by her story. It took some time, but eventually Christie found sponsors for all twenty-two girls.

During her stay in Malawi, Christie had become close friends with another teacher who was volunteering at the school. Memory Chazeza was hardly more than a girl herself, but in her, Christie saw a common spirit. She saw honesty, integrity, and determination. In turn, Memory helped Christie through her term at the school. She explained the customs, she translated the language, and she interpreted the girls' behaviour. Before Christie left the country, she extracted a promise from Memory: "If I can find the money, you must help me see the girls go to school." Although Memory was still trying to find a way to go back to school herself, she agreed.

After Christie raised the money, it was Memory who travelled from village to village tracking down the former students. It was Memory who, not even knowing how to open a bank account, received the funds from Canada and arranged for the girls' schooling in Malawi. It was a massive undertaking. But eventually after completing their secondary school, five of the girls went on to attend university and the remaining seventeen graduated from technical school.

I met Memory Chazeza in 2006. She had travelled to Canada to speak at the annual Rotary District Conference, which was held that year in the town of Stony Plain. Memory was small. To me, she appeared almost childlike. She looked far younger than her actual years. I thought the crowds would overwhelm her; I thought she would be intimidated by a culture so different from her own. But I couldn't have been more wrong.

Memory is a fighter. She has lived a life that has taught her strength, adaptation, and resilience. When she stood at the mike in front of hundreds of Rotarians and their guests, she spoke with a big voice, a voice that compelled me and everyone else to listen.

"I fought hard for my education. Many people told me I couldn't do it," Memory said. "There were hardships, but I knew I just had to keep trying. What girls in Malawi need more than anything else is an education. They need to become independent, and they need an education for that."

Memory spoke with passion and conviction. She spoke about the women of her country. She spoke about their need for an education, their need for independence, their need to take control of their lives, their need to contribute to their communities. She spoke about her own journey, a journey of struggle and perseverance that has led her to this day. As an orphan herself, she has faced the same challenges as many of the women in her country. Her parents had died when she was a young girl, yet Memory had been able to complete a degree in theology with a major in education, and now she wanted to open her own girls' secondary school. It was still just a dream, but she was convinced that with help from Canada, she could make her dream a reality. Along with the rest of the audience, I was captivated by her words and her conviction. She seemed to be speaking to all of us, about our own personal struggles: "If you believe, you can make it happen." That was the message I left with that day.

The conference raised more than $17,000 for her school. It was a start. A school would cost far more to build, but it proved that people could be moved by Memory's dream and her passion. Soon plans took shape for the school. *Atsikana Pa Ulendo*, Girls on the Move, Secondary School was now a reality. Since the conference, Christie Johnson, Rotarians from both Western Canada and Malawi, and Memory and her husband Henry have worked tirelessly to make *Atsikana Pa Ulendo* (APU) a reality. Christie Johnson explains it this way: "Every so often you encounter someone with a dream so gripping and convincing, you resolve to help make it come true." Such is Memory's power to inspire and motivate change.

Since my first meeting with Memory, I have come to know her as an individual and a friend, a person driven by her convictions and her energy. She is passionate in her approach, and like many people with a vision, she is headstrong and expects from others what she is willing to give herself. But given the opportunity, she is able to accomplish the incredible.

This book recounts Memory's struggle to gain independence by going against the advice of her family and beyond the expectations of her community in the hopes of obtaining an education. But it is not just her story; it is the story of the changing role of women in Malawian society and the importance of education for girls in the developing world. It is a story of hope and courage in a time of poverty, famine, and hardship.

Abbreviations

ABC	African Bible College
ADMARC	Agricultural Development and Marketing Corporation
APU	*Atsikana Pa Ulendo*
ARV	antiretroviral drugs
CEAG	Canadians Educating African Girls
CGAP	Consultative Group to Assist the Poor
DPP	Democratic Progressive Party
EFA	Education for All
EHP	Essential Health Package
FITSE	Finance Trust for the Self-Employed
FPE	Free Primary Education
GABLE	Girls' Attainment in Basic Literacy and Education
GCM	Great Commission Ministry
GDP	gross domestic product
IMF	International Monetary Fund
JCE	Junior Certificate of Education
MCP	Malawi Congress Party
MDGs	Millennium Development Goals

MEJN	Malawi Economic Justice Network
MFI	microfinance institution
MGDS	Malawi Growth and Development Strategy
MIITEP	Malawi Integrated In-service Teacher Education Programme
MoEST	Ministry of Education, Science and Technology
MoH	Ministry of Health
MoIWD	Ministry of Irrigation and Water Development
MSCE	Malawi School Certificate of Education
NAC	Nyasaland African Congress
NFRA	National Food Reserve Agency
NGO	nongovernmental organization
SACMEQ	Southern and Eastern Africa Consortium for Monitoring Educational Quality
SAPs	structural adjustment programs
SCOM	Student Christian Organization of Malawi
SGR	strategic grain reserves
SIV	simian immunodeficiency virus
TBA	traditional birth attendant
TTCs	teacher training colleges
UDF	United Democratic Front
UNAIDS	Joint United Nations Programme on HIV/AIDS
UNESCO	United Nations Educational, Scientific and Cultural Organization
UNFPA	United Nations Population Fund (formerly the United Nations Fund for Population Activities)
UNICEF	United Nations Children's Fund (formerly the United Nations International Children's Emergency Fund)
USAID	United States Agency for International Development
WASH in Schools	Water, Sanitation, and Hygiene Education in Schools
WHO	World Health Organization

1

The Dream Becomes Reality

When you educate a girl,
you educate a nation.

—*Malawian saying*

MEMORY WALKED INTO THE COOL CLASSROOM, its walls painted white, its windows open to the breeze.[1] Five rows of shiny, dark brown desks faced the blackboard. The desks were so new that Memory could still smell a trace of varnish in the air. At the desks sat forty girls, half of the boarding school's eighty students. The girls proudly wore their school uniforms: dark green skirts, yellow button-up shirts, green ties, and matching jersey sweaters.

When the girls saw Memory, they stood up at their desks.

"Good morning, students," Memory said, pausing to take in all the faces.

The girls met Memory's eyes and responded in unison, "Good morning, Madam. We are fine, and how are you?"

Memory looked back at the earnest faces. They appeared full of hope, full of expectation. She had known the girls for a short time, but already she felt a deep sense of responsibility and protectiveness for each one.

Only a few months ago, the girls had been strangers, no different from the anonymous faces of the many thousands of Malawian teenage girls throughout the country. But Memory had met each of the girls during the student selection process several months earlier, and the girls were strangers no longer. They were her students and her responsibility.

Memory remembered meeting Maria. Of the 360 girls who came to write the entrance exam, Maria had been one of only 120 girls selected for oral interviews. When Memory asked her the question, "Why do you deserve a scholarship to learn at APU?" Maria had been unable to meet her eyes. Instead, she had begun to sob. Even after she wiped away her tears, Maria kept her head bowed and whispered, "I don't deserve to go to this school." Now Maria matched Memory's gaze with confidence and an open smile.

Solstina also met Memory's eyes. She didn't smile, but she stood straight and tall, full of hope and yearning for the future. Solstina's story resonated with Memory. In many ways, Solstina was a companion spirit. A girl, like herself, who had overcome great obstacles to get here and was willing to do whatever was necessary to get an education. Yes, Solstina would make it.

Then there was Efulida, bright little Efulida. Memory could see the hope in her eyes, a hope that had not been there at their first meeting. But there *had* been something about Efulida from the beginning. She had walked all the way from her home village to Kabuthu Primary School, where Memory had arranged for the girls to write their entrance exams, against her mother's wishes. There had been a spark, a desire to stay in school, a wish to improve her life.

Like many of the girls, Efulida had begun her journey to the school before the sun was up. It had taken her many hours to walk to the school to write the exam and many more to walk back home, an entire day of walking. She had done it again for the oral interview and again after her acceptance when she had had to convince her mother to come and meet Memory. That had not been easy.

Memory responded to the girls' greeting. "I am fine. Thank you. Sit down."

It was time to focus on the lesson, but Memory still found her thoughts returning to her first meetings with the girls.

Many of the girls told her they had been abused by their teachers at other schools or teased and harassed by the boys in their classes. Their stories were heartbreaking. "I wanted to go back to school, but each and every day, they said bad things about me just to discourage me from going on with my education," explained one girl. Another girl said, "I cannot go to school because where I come from there are not enough teachers, so I try to follow my step-uncle because he's close to the school. But the nieces and nephews of this uncle all the time they gossip about me and say all I want is food." All the girls were eager to receive a scholarship at APU. They were all eager to learn from Madam Mdyetseni, a *woman* and the headmistress of her own school.

Maria Nkhoma had nearly given up hope. She had been accepted at APU, but on the day she was supposed to bring her parents to the school, she came alone. Maria's mother was at home and unable to walk.

The day before the meeting, Maria's father had beaten her mother so severely that Maria had feared for her life. Maria, terrified, ran to a nearby relative's house for help. Her neighbours came and pulled her father away from her mother, but after the neighbours went back home, Maria's father turned his anger on Maria.

"Maria. Why have you done that? I wanted to keep beating your mother," he said. "From this day onwards, I will not be responsible for you."

When Maria told her story to Memory, she was frightened and confused.

"Now I don't have anyone to support me. My father has even stopped me from using his name. I really don't know what's going to happen to me, but I want to go to school."

Memory paused for a moment. "Go home, and ask your mother if you can come to school," she said. "Talk to your father for the last time. If he will not help you, come back to school, and we are going to see what we can do to help you."

Maria returned for the first day of school, but her father was still angry and still refused to support her. So Memory encouraged Maria to stay in school and keep using her father's name. She hoped Maria's father would eventually change his mind.

When the school opened, people were of the opinion, "Well, let's wait and see what happens." By the second term, the school was developing a good reputation in the area. People began talking about it in the surrounding villages and at the nearby trading centre, Nsaru. Parents wanted their girls to be selected for the school.

Parents felt their girls were safe at APU. The school didn't compromise on its rules. The students at APU followed the rules or faced the consequences. The girls were not allowed to go to the nearby trading centre, they were expected to treat each other with respect, and they were required to take their studies seriously. At other schools, exceptions are often made. When a girl breaks a rule, if she is particularly bright, if she is a teacher's favourite, if she comes from a well-to-do family, or if her father is a village chief, she may not be punished for an infraction. No such exceptions were made at APU.

Students and parents were also happy with the respect the teachers and other workers showed the girls. Parents came to the school and saw how their daughters were treated. They left satisfied that they could trust the workers not to make advances on the girls. In some cases, for the first time, the girls had teachers who were on their side, rooting for them. At other schools, teachers often said, "Education is for boys." But at APU, the teachers saw the girls' potential and encouraged them to succeed.

Families with girls at APU were also gaining status within their communities, and eventually Maria's father began contributing. He brought maize to the school, and when Maria needed soap and lotion, he paid for them.

Memory laughed to herself when she thought about her first meeting with Mr. Nkhoma. She had called a meeting with the parents, encouraging them to organize a parent teacher association (PTA). When the parents chose their representatives, Mr. Nkhoma was voted onto the committee. Memory watched to see what would happen. "But since they voted him to the committee, he has changed very much. He has come to support his daughter. He has come to reconcile with his daughter's mother." Maria's mother had gone back to live in her home village, but Mr. Nkhoma asked her to return to him, and now she is back home. "He is one of the people we trust. Whenever the school needs something, Mr. Nkhoma is always in the front helping."

Of course, it isn't just Maria's father who has changed. Maria has changed too. She has self-esteem. She has confidence. Now that her father supports her, she can concentrate on her education. And their relationship has changed too. In her father's eyes, Maria is no longer "just a girl."

Efulida came from a very different family. Her father had died in prison, and her mother had been left to care for seven children. As a subsistence farmer, her mother grew maize and groundnuts but was unable to provide for her children, so she began brewing beer as a way to subsidize her income. Eventually she became despondent under her strained circumstances. She began drinking and turned to prostitution. But even with this bit of extra income, the family was still poor. Efulida and her siblings were expected to quit school so they could work in the garden. Their mother also wanted them to take on piecework as a means to help support the family. Yet somehow Efulida had the strength to go against her mother's wishes and apply at APU.

Now that Efulida was a student at APU, she lived at the school. But she went home for the holidays. At home, her mother kept her busy working: doing piecework and labouring in the garden. With all her domestic responsibilities, Efulida was unable to study, but Memory's worries went beyond Efulida's inability to review her schoolwork during her trips home. Memory worried that Efulida would be pressured to go to bed with her mother's clients—just as her sister had been. Efulida's sister had become pregnant and now lived a miserable life taking on piecework, existing hand-to-mouth, barely able to feed herself and her child. Memory had faith that Efulida could do better, much better— if she received an education. So Memory encouraged her to stay at the school during vacations. Memory encouraged her to stay for two reasons: she hoped that Efulida would escape her sister's fate, but she also wanted her to make a contribution to the school.

Although they receive scholarships, the students of APU are required to contribute to the school. Memory strongly believes that all the girls must contribute in some way. Otherwise, they will take their education for granted. They will develop a sense of entitlement, and even worse, they will not appreciate their own abilities. Memory often reminds the girls, "You have got hands. You have got legs. You can do something for yourself."

A family must contribute the amount of maize and beans that their daughter would eat if she were living at home: sixty-seven kilograms of maize and five kilograms of beans each term. Henry puts it this way: "We're simply asking them to bring the *nsima* and beans they'd be eating at home. We feel sure that if they were to be alive at the end of the year, they would find something to eat." The same thing holds true for the school uniform. "They wouldn't be walking naked in the village, so we're asking them to buy a garment by the end of two years. We are not asking something extraordinary. We are asking something within the reach of even the poorest person here."

Memory and Henry had both witnessed the results of foreign aid programs that come at no cost to the community. People don't value aid when it is given with no effort on their part.

Henry recounts his country's experience with borehole wells. At first the maintenance of borehole wells was left to the government, and people didn't really care when they broke a borehole. They'd go to the government office and ask a maintenance man to come and repair it. Or they'd go back to drinking muddy water. These days the government says, "We've brought you a bore hole, and you do the maintenance." They contract one local trader who is the middle man for selling bore hole spare parts, so whenever it breaks down, the community has to contribute money to buy parts needed to fix it. "Today over 80 per cent of the bore holes are operational, but before there used to be less than 30 per cent of bore holes operational just because the community didn't contribute anything," says Henry. "It didn't pain them when anything had to get fixed."

Memory agrees with Henry's assessment. At other foreign-sponsored schools, she had seen how girls became disrespectful of their parents. When foreign sponsors were providing for their every need, children began to perceive their sponsors as more deserving of their respect than their own guardians. Memory didn't want these girls disrespecting their families, so she determined that APU would be a community effort.

If the families refuse to contribute or can't manage because of poor crops, they are asked to help in the school's gardens. In some cases, the parents were reluctant or unable to help in this way, so Memory gave the girls chores around the school, so they could contribute to their schooling too. Memory hoped to encourage Efulida to help out in this way during the holidays.

At first Efulida wanted to go home for the school breaks, but that soon changed. She quickly realized that she didn't want to go back to her old life, even for a short time. Finally, she approached Memory and said, "I don't want to go home. I want to stay here." Memory was relieved.

"We were so happy. If she stays here, then little by little, she is going to forget what her mother does at home." Efulida still goes home to visit, but her visits are shorter now, and she is a changed person.

"Efulida was fond of stealing. Her friends had been complaining that whenever she is left in the room, things go missing." But when she was confronted, she denied taking her friends' possessions. She was often rude, and when asked to share a desk with a friend, she would refuse. But that has changed, too, because Efulida has changed. Memory says, "Of course, she's not all that perfect." But she no longer lies, and she no longer steals. "Because of her interactions in the school and the food she's been receiving, she's really changed."

When Memory looked at her students, she saw their open, expectant faces and thought of how far they had already come, yet how far they still had to go, as students and as a school. It was a journey they were making together: she and this first intake of students, this first group of girls.

The school had opened on time, as promised, but it had not been an easy journey for anyone involved with the project. Memory had arrived at the school with her little boy, Teloni, on January 15, 2008, just one day before the girls were due to begin arriving themselves. There was no point in Memory getting to the school any sooner. The classroom block was built, but the cement hadn't been poured on most of the floors in the hostel.

Teloni was only seven months old when he and Memory arrived at the school, so they slept in the only completed room in the hostel. Even there, the cement was still damp. Memory carried a mat into the room at night, and that's where they slept—Memory with her little baby boy tucked in tight beside her. Memory's cousin, Nancy, slept in the room with them. Nancy would watch Teloni while Memory was teaching, but even that didn't work out the way Memory had planned.

During the second week of classes, Nancy became sick with a fever. Memory had no choice but to teach with Teloni wrapped on her back, in the traditional way. Teloni usually slept, but while he was awake he'd often make Memory and the girls laugh. When Memory tried writing on the blackboard, Teloni kept reaching for the chalk until finally Memory gave it to him. He began writing on the back of her head—the school's youngest student.

The hostel wasn't finished until the second month of classes. There had been a shortage of cement in Malawi the previous year, and as a result, construction had slowed. Now that cement was available, the labourers were working well into the night, completing construction and putting the final touches on the buildings.

The month was a difficult one for Memory, but the girls, who were used to dirt floors and two meals a day, were thrilled. None of them had ever lived in a building like the hostel. It was clean, and even before their beds were built, they slept on thick foam mats, not the thin grass mats they were accustomed to at home. At the school they ate breakfast, lunch, and supper, as well as two teas every day. For breakfast they ate maize porridge. For lunch they might have eggs, vegetables, and *nsima*— Malawi's traditional staple made from maize flour and shaped into patties. For supper they usually "took" beans and *nsima*, but once a week, they had beef, something they almost never ate at home. Tea was a treat, too, because it came with milk and sometimes a scone. So even though the hostel wasn't complete and the beds were not yet built, the girls were well fed and well taken care of. Their biggest problem was getting to sleep at night.

"The girls were too excited to sleep. They were just so happy to be here," recalls Memory. It was also the first time that most of the girls had lived away from home, and many of them were learning a whole new way to live.

Only one week into classes, Memory had to enact a "mango ban." It was mango season in Malawi, and the girls were gorging themselves on the mangoes that grew near the school. Memory began to worry they might make themselves sick, but the real problem was the pits. The girls are accustomed to living in dirt-floored houses. In rural homes, it's common to simply throw fruit pits, called "pills," on the dirt floor where they are swept away the next day. The pills were being dropped throughout the dormitory and were beginning to attract insects—hence the mango ban.

There were less-pleasant problems too. Many of the girls were unaccustomed to using pit latrines. At home they might pee in the shower room, a tiny outdoor building used for bathing, or simply squat in the bushes outside. Some of the girls were eager to use the latrines, but others didn't want to change, and they needed to learn hygiene if they were to live at the school. Memory knew about village life, so she was prepared for these challenges.

Memory assigned each of the girls' dormitory rooms its own latrine. The girls from that room became responsible for whatever went wrong with their toilet. The girls' attitude changed immediately. They took ownership of their latrine. They kept their toilet clean, mopping it out and making sure they were the only ones to use it.

Soon after, Memory noticed the girls were going behind the latrines to collect leaves. Memory knew the girls couldn't afford to purchase toilet paper, but they were throwing away the scrap paper from their exercise books. Memory told the girls, "In each and every toilet, I need to see a bag with the papers that you've used in class. You can hang the bag up, and when you go to the toilet, use that paper." And that's what the girls did.

Of course, there were other problems too—growing pains that could not be fixed no matter how hard Memory tried. Sharron had come to APU for the first day of classes, but she had rebelled against the rules from the beginning: she wanted to go to the trading centre. She didn't want to speak English. She didn't like doing community service. Finally, she came to Memory and told her she was sick. She asked Memory for permission to go home. Memory said, "Yes." But once Sharron left, she didn't come back to the school.

There is no easy way to contact the girls. Rural families have no phones and no addresses, no more than the name of a small obscure village composed of a few huts. So Memory waited for Sharron to return, but she didn't.

Finally, Faye, a student who lived in the same area as Sharron, came to Memory. Faye had been home for the holidays. She had heard Sharron talking, spreading rumours about the school. "We are not learning at APU. We just do village service. It's not a good school," Sharron was saying. "They don't let us go to the trading centre," Sharron was saying. Faye's siblings had heard the talk and wondered why she was still in school. This bothered Faye;.

Faye was sure Sharron wouldn't be coming back. Sharron was looking for a place at the nearby day school, but the school wouldn't let her in because she was slandering APU. "We have never heard anything bad about that school," they said.

After speaking to Faye and still not hearing anything from Sharron or her parents, Memory gave her place to another girl who was waiting to get into APU. Then one day, Sharron showed up and asked to come back, but Memory had to say, "No. We have no place for you here." But the Sharrons were in the minority, and Memory knew she was making a difference in the girls' lives.

It wasn't only the students who were benefitting from APU. Just the other day, Henry had taken the site foreman aside after noticing the age of one of the women working at the construction site. "It isn't proper for you to recruit minors," he said.

"The girl is a single mother of three under-fives. She also looks after her grandmother," the foreman told Henry. Terminating her employment would have taken away her only source of income and jeopardized her welfare, as well as the welfare of her children and her grandmother. The girl was fortunate to have the work at APU. It was keeping her and her family alive. So although APU was far from complete, it was already making a difference in many people's lives, just as Memory had known it would.

Of course, there was still much to do. The school was in Phase One. Ultimately, the school would house 320 students: eighty in each of forms

Memory and Christie cut the ribbon at the official opening of Atsikana Pa Ulendo, *March 22, 2008.* [Photo courtesy of APU]

one, two, three, and four. Even though eighty students seemed like a lot right now, it would be nothing compared to the number of students who would learn at the school in four years when it reached its full capacity.

Eventually, *Atsikana Pa Ulendo* would be a big school known throughout Malawi for its quality of education and innovative ideology—at least that was the plan. Within a few short years, APU would have four hostels, four classroom blocks, and a large multipurpose cafeteria. It would also have teachers' housing, a must since Memory wanted to attract the best teachers Malawi had to offer. So far, the teachers had been tolerant of the situation, but the first month had been difficult for them too.

The teachers had spent the first four weeks sleeping on the floor of one of the classrooms, and although they had all found accommodation at the nearby trading centre, it wasn't good housing. Nsaru was a poor community, and the only housing available was old and small—probably full of rats and other vermin—not at all like the residences that would eventually house the teachers of APU.

There would be vegetable gardens and a fishpond to feed the school, and eventually...well...who knew? Memory and Henry hoped to build a clinic that would serve not only the school but the surrounding community as well. They also planned to supply vocational training for the girls after they graduated. These were all big plans, but Memory knew she had to focus on the challenges of the moment, and there were many.

There were the usual boarding school conflicts: quarrels, rumours, and disputes—girls calling other girls ugly or stupid. But Memory was determined to enforce the principle of respecting themselves and others. She wanted the girls to learn to treat each other with kindness and love. "You should always think good things about other people," Memory would say to her students. "If you want something good to happen to you, you should think your friend also wants something good to happen to her."

Memory's teaching was already paying off. The belittling and quarrelling of the first weeks were tapering off. The girls were seeing each other as sisters instead of rivals. Maness had come to Memory just the other day. "To me," she said, "I've really learned very much from you. Whenever I'm wrong, you were not happy with me. Whenever I've done something good, you were always happy with me. You never favour anyone, and I want to learn from your example because we tend to love those people who we know we can get something from. When I go back home, I try my best that I should be able to love everyone." Maness and many of the other girls had changed for the better.

Efulida's attitude had also changed. Now she relied upon herself and her own abilities instead of going out with boyfriends to acquire money, clothing, and other personal items. Now she saw that hard work would pay off in the long run.

Memory found it amusing to see how quickly the girls forgot their old ways. Now that they kept the latrines clean and their rooms tidy, they didn't want to remember their behaviour during the first term. They valued themselves more now, and they wanted their lives to stay that way.

Education was the solution to so much. Memory believed that now more than ever. In Malawi there is a saying, "When you educate a girl, you educate a nation." If a woman is educated, she will want her children to be educated. She will see the value.

Memory was well aware that uneducated women were not respected in their communities. She knew this from experience: "Husbands feel like they are the leaders, the decision-makers." In Memory's experience, "most of the women, wives who are abused, are the ones who are not educated because husbands look down upon them." *Education empowers women*. In Memory's mind, it was as simple as that. When she looked back on her life, she saw it proven time and time again.

Solstina

NIGHTTIME COMES QUICKLY this close to the equator, and my flashlight barely flickers in the darkness.[1] At night, rural Malawi is truly black, nothing like the nightly twilight that crowds my home back in Canada.

I carefully pick my way through the piles of broken bricks and unfinished foundation between the teachers' residence and the classroom block. The girls are in their evening study session. I find my way to Solstina's classroom and approach her at her desk. I ask Solstina if she would mind coming outside to speak with me.

We sit on the school's cement step in the dark. There is just enough light seeping from the classroom windows for me to see her face. It is a face filled with a deep and abiding sadness, but there is a quiet patience in her eyes. Solstina is a determined young woman.

Even before tonight, Solstina stood out from the other girls. She was eager to learn and eager to try new things: whether it was my goofy writing exercises or the self-defense moves I taught the girls during their physical education classes. Solstina's calm attentiveness made an impression.

Solstina is one of the older students at the school. She repeated standard eight three times before moving on to secondary school at *Atsikana Pa Ulendo*. She didn't need to repeat the standard, but it was that or drop out of school all together.

After completing standard eight the first time, Solstina passed her exams and was accepted into a community secondary school. But her father didn't want to pay the tuition. Solstina decided to take standard eight a second time. She was convinced if her father saw how hard she worked, he would let her go to secondary school.

Solstina completed standard eight a second time, but again her father refused to pay. This time her uncle stepped in and tried to find her a cheaper school. Her father again refused to pay. He had taken a second wife and said, "The money that I have now, it should pay for that woman who I have married."

So Solstina went back to standard eight.

Solstina completed standard eight for the third time. This time, her two younger brothers were in the class with her, and they passed when she did. Solstina's father paid for her two brothers to go to secondary school, but not Solstina.

Solstina asked her father, "Why have you done that?"

He became very angry and shouted, "You can do what you want. I have paid for my children."

Solstina didn't know what to do. Out of desperation, she started standard eight a fourth time.

One day a few weeks later, when Solstina's mother was not at home, her father called several of Solstina's classmates to his house. Then he called Solstina into the room, "You girls don't chat with this girl, and you boys don't chat with this girl. This is not a good girl. She doesn't do good things here in my house."

Solstina was shocked. She cried out, "What have I done?" But her father wouldn't answer.

Soon after, Solstina began seeing a boy. It wasn't long before they were married.

Later that year, Solstina became pregnant, but her husband didn't treat her well. He would lock her in their house while he was away. Sometimes she would stay locked up all day.

When it came time for her to have her baby, she asked her husband if she could go to her mother's house. He agreed.

Solstina delivered a baby boy. She named him Peter.

After Peter was born, Solstina put off going back to live with her husband. "I will go another day," she would say, "I will go another day." Finally she outright refused.

Her uncle found Solstina work, and she took her baby boy to live with him. But she found she couldn't work. She was dispirited and sad. She stayed at home with her auntie, looking after Peter and helping with the chores. Finally, one day, she received a letter from her father: "There is a secondary school here. You need to go write the entrance exam."

Solstina's uncle found a bicycle, and Solstina travelled back to her village.

After she arrived home, Solstina's friends from the village were cruel to her. They laughed and said, "You don't know. Your father, he has done nothing for you by telling you to write the entrance exam."

Even though they were going to take the exam themselves, they didn't want Solstina to walk with them. And Solstina thought, "It's only God who is worrying about me now."

Solstina walked to *Atsikana Pa Ulendo* with her friends, but after the exam, they left without her. Solstina says, "That was my first time to come here. My home is far, and the sun was about to set." But Solstina is quick to add, "God is wonderful. I saw some girl. She is my friend that girl. She started going, and she came back to take something and she said, 'Ahh. Then let's go.' She took me and she led me to her home."

Solstina walked home the next day.

Solstina's mother was relieved to see her. She asked, "How were the exams?"

Solstina responded, "Hmm. Anyway, I just don't know if I will pass."

"Ahh. Your friends are saying that the exams are very simple."

"That means according to their thinking, but according to me, ahh no. I don't know."

Solstina was the only one of her group to be accepted into *Atsikana Pa Ulendo*. "Most of them, they have married now," says Solstina. "And me, I'm here."

Before I finish Solstina's story, there is something else I'd like you to know. When the women of Malawi speak English, their voices sing. It's as though something magical transforms their voices. There is a lilt and a rhythm that makes their voices sound like song. Solstina has one of these voices, and when she says, "Ahh no," it is like a sigh. As I type her words, I can hear her voice. It makes me want to weep.

It must be difficult for Solstina to talk about her little boy. Nearly everyone has reproached her for leaving him with his grandmother. They will say, "Why have you left this baby? Do you want him to die?"

Solstina responds by saying, "If he is to die, it means God has already said he will die, but if God has a reason for him, if God says he will grow up, it means he will grow. Nobody can stop him."

At this point in her story Solstina stops and asks, "Is it the fourteenth today?"

"Yes. I think so," I say.

"Now on the seventeenth, he will be two years old. And the girls they ask me, 'How do you manage? According to me, I cannot manage.' And I say, 'Mmm.'"

I ask Solstina what she would like to do after she finishes school. She says, "I want to do what Madam Mdyetseni has done."

Madam Mdyetseni is, of course, Memory Chazeza, and I am again reminded of the example she has set for these girls. I believe that with many more years of struggle, Solstina's future will be bright. We have Memory Chazeza to thank for that.

When the seventeenth comes, I think about Solstina and her little boy, Peter. I wonder what the future holds. Solstina is still many years from self-sufficiency. She is now studying in a good secondary school, but if she is to earn a living wage and support herself independently, she will need to go on to post-secondary school. She will face many more years of separation from her little boy—many more years of struggle.

2
The Warm Heart of Africa

It felt like coming to an old home to see Nyasa again and dash in the rollers of its delicious waters—I was quite exhilarated by the roar of the inland sea.

—David Livingstone, during his 1866 expedition[1]

MEMORY GREW UP IN KARONGA.[2] The small northern town sits on the edge of Lake Malawi close to the Tanzanian border. Karonga began as an early outpost of the British African Lakes Company and a stronghold for the infamous Swahili-Arab slave trader, Mlozi. There was constant friction between the two operations until the commissioner of the British protectorate, Harry Johnston, decided to purge the land of slavers once and for all.

After ridding the southern portion of Lake Malawi of its Yao slaving chiefs in 1895, Johnston travelled north to conclude his mission. He staged an attack on Mlozi's stockade, captured the trader, and handed him over to the local Nkonde chiefs for trial. Mlozi was summarily convicted and hanged from Karonga's landmark baobab tree that stands to this day.[3]

Today, Malawi is a quiet country. It is often referred to as "the Warm Heart of Africa," but it was not always so peaceful. The nineteenth century was a time of tragedy and change for Malawi. Colonialism and the trade in black slaves were occurring across Africa. Upheaval, displacement, and death raged throughout the continent.

While the West African slave trade dwindled in the early part of the nineteenth century, the trade continued to grow and flourish on the east coast.[4] The area around Lake Malawi was part of a commercial network controlled by Swahili-Arab traders. The traders were a mismatched group consisting of Africans of mixed Arab and African descent and the *ruga-ruga*, a collection of African mercenaries from the continent's interior. There were also white Arabs, like Mlozi, and, although the slave trade had been outlawed in Portuguese-controlled Mozambique, a Portuguese component was still involved in the coastal trade as well.[5] Many of this motley group became wealthy beyond their wildest imagining off the African men, women, and children upon whom they preyed.

During the nineteenth century, the land west and south of the lake was home to several tribes of Bantu origin: the Chewa, who live primarily in the central and southern parts of the country and whose dialect,

Chichewa, is now one of the country's official languages; the Nyanja, known as the people of the lake; the Tumbuka, who live in the mountainous northern part of the country; the Ngoni, who arrived in Malawi as a group of ruthless warriors from South Africa; the Ngonde, who live in the area around Karonga;[6] and the Yao, named after a treeless hill located in northwest Mozambique—the place of origin for the tribe.[7] There are others, too, for Malawi is populated by a diverse collection of people, united by geographical location and similar in their African culture but distinctive for their unique histories and tribal outlook.

The Yao were the last major tribe to arrive in Malawi in the nineteenth century. Because of their proximity to the slave-trading ports along the Mozambique coast, the Swahili-Arabs often used the Yao as middlemen. The Yao migrated to Malawi as part of the trade and introduced Islam to the country as a result.[8] In the latter part of the nineteenth century, they were feared and hated for the slave raids they conducted throughout a large portion of East Africa, including Malawi.

Estimates vary on the number of slaves taken from their East African homelands, but one estimate for the years from 1830 to 1873 was 6,480,000, while another estimate puts it at well over twenty-one million.[9] To put this death toll into perspective, an estimated six million Jews died during the years of the Nazi Holocaust. Decades later, in 1994, 800,000 Rwandans died violently during that country's genocide.[10] Unless we have friends or relatives who died as a part of these massacres, we probably only have a vague idea that these events caused immense hardship and sorrow for vast numbers of individuals. We can only imagine the death, displacement, and cultural upheaval that took place during the years of the African slave trade.

Another estimate is given by a contemporary of the time. Colonel Rigby, the mid-nineteenth-century British consul for Zanzibar, the slave-trading hub of the East African slave trade, estimated that nineteen thousand slaves from the Lake Malawi region entered and exited the ports of Zanzibar each year.[11] None of these numbers can possibly portray the personal suffering, hardship, and death caused by the trade, but they give us a glimpse of a catastrophe that had the scope and magnitude of a large-scale genocide.

The tragedy was not limited to the Africans who were transported to the Arab harems and clove farms of the east and the sugar plantations of Brazil, Cuba, and the East Indies.[12] The commercialization of slavery brought the breakup of families and communities throughout the continent, and disease, hunger, and starvation were soon to follow. Many societies lost vast numbers of their populations to warfare, abuse, and epidemics. Smallpox, cholera, sleeping sickness, and dysentery raged throughout the devastated communities.[13] Based upon his observations in the Shire Valley, Scottish missionary and explorer Dr. David Livingstone believed that 90 per cent of the Africans who were stolen from their homes died before they ever reached their destination.[14] During his trip through the area east of the Shire River, James Stewart, a Scottish theological student, made this observation:

> [It is] a lonely land of barbarism, of game and wild beasts, of timid and harried but not unkindly men, harassed by never-ending slave raids and intertribal wars...We passed through many villages burnt and deserted, just as their unhappy occupants had left them when they fled for life— that is those of them who were not speared or shot or captured. We saw in these villages heaps of ashes of charred poles in circles like the shape of the huts, broken pottery, a good many bones, but no bodies—the hyenas had attended to that.[15]

It was a land and a people raped and brutalized beyond imagining.

Slaves were abundant throughout this time, and the value of human life was cheap. In a stark quantification of the price for human flesh, Dr. Robert Laws, head of the Free Church of Scotland Mission in Malawi from 1875 to 1881, recorded the amount of cloth paid for slaves:

A young girl at school, unmarried, was worth fifty-six yards of calico.
A young woman with an unweaned baby was bartered for thirty-two
yards while the child was bought for four yards of calico.
A strong young wife without children was worth twenty-four yards.
A strong young man having good teeth was worth forty yards.
An old man, not very strong, was worth four yards.
A toothless old man fetched only two yards.[16]

To put these colloquial measurements into a modern perspective,
one can imagine the cost of a Malawian *chitenje*, a yard of colourful cloth
available at markets throughout the country. A *chitenje* is a multipurpose piece of fabric that can be tied across the body to carry babies or
wrapped around the waist as a second skirt. I've seen them used as a
shawl or, at times, as a turban. A *chitenje* might sell for between 250 and
300 Malawian kwacha (K). Three hundred kwacha is equivalent to US$2.
The life of a young woman without children was therefore worth approximately US$48—the cost of a dinner for two at an inexpensive restaurant.
A man, presumably a hard worker, was worth more, about US$80, while
a young girl fetched the equivalent to US$112, the highest price of all; it
isn't difficult to imagine why.

It was into this land of fear and upheaval that Dr. David Livingstone
travelled on his second trip to the continent in 1859. With the British
government funding his expedition, the Scottish missionary's goal was
to find a navigable route up the Zambezi River. Instead, he found himself
sailing up the Shire River, tramping the delta wetlands and standing on
the shores of Lake Malawi.[17]

When Livingstone saw the vast inland sea, he asked his Yao guides
its name. They called it *nyassa*, the Yao word for lake. Later, the region
was to become the Nyasaland Districts Protectorate, but for now
it was a lawless place where the native population sold their neighbours into slavery, huddled behind stockade walls, or lived as groups of
displaced fugitives. But it wasn't only a land of desperation and cruelty;

Livingstone also saw a land of beauty. It was a land where herds of hippo-potami "swarm[ed] very much at their ease in the creeks and lagoons,"[18] amenable elephants walked the lake's shores, and fish were in such abundance that the fishermen who trolled the lake were unafraid of the sated crocodiles that basked along the sandy shores.[19] But upon his return to Britain, Livingstone's primary objective was not to speak of the continent's beauty but to educate his countrymen about "the misery entailed by the slave-trade."[20]

Britain had abolished the transoceanic trafficking of slaves in 1807. The abolition of slavery itself took longer, but throughout most of the British Empire, slavery was a thing of the past by the time Livingston made his first journey to the African continent. In fact, the West African slave trade was slowing down, replaced by the trade in other lucrative commodities such as palm oil and ivory.[21] This was not the case in East Africa.

Livingstone was angered by the actions of the Arabs and the Portuguese in East Africa, but his censure didn't end there. He also condemned the practices of the Africans who aided them, and he never missed an opportunity to speak strongly about his objections. He wrote of one village's reaction to his fury: "The people are usually much startled when I explain that the number of slaves we see dead on the road have been killed partly by those who sold them; for I tell them that if they sell their fellows, they are like the man who holds the victim while the Arab performs the murder."[22] Livingstone didn't save his condemnation for those directly involved in the trade; he accused his own people of hypocrisy. In a letter to his son, Livingstone wrote, "Though the majority perhaps are on the side of freedom, large numbers of Englishmen are not slaveholders only because the law forbids the practice."[23] And Livingstone's actions were not limited to rhetoric.

David Livingstone was a man of action with a fiery temper and a willingness to stand by his convictions. In 1861, during the Zambezi expedition, while in the highlands near the Shire River, he famously freed eighty-four slaves from their captors. It was Livingstone's passionate hatred of the trade in flesh that galvanized his compatriots back home. In one famous 1857 address, Livingstone spoke to the Senate House at Cambridge University. He knew he couldn't accomplish his goals on his own and appealed to fellow missionaries to follow in his footsteps to the "Dark Continent": "I go back to Africa to try to make an open path for commerce and Christianity. Do you carry on the work, which I have begun? I leave it with you."[24]

By 1873, Livingstone had been back in Africa and searching for the Nile's source for seven years. His health had been failing for some time, and he was camped at the Zambian village of Chitambo trying to recover from his illness. On the morning of May 1, his servants went into his tent. They discovered Livingstone kneeling by his bed. He was dead.[25] At the age of sixty, Livingstone had fallen prey to malaria, the same disease that had killed his wife a decade earlier. Two years after his death, the first expedition of Scottish missionaries landed on Lake Malawi's warm shores.[26] They brought with them a strong Christian tradition that spread throughout the country and has lasted to this day.

Today Karonga is home to farmers, fishers, and craftspeople. Chickens peck in the dirt, and children sell dried fish in the streets. Outside the city, farmers raise goats and grow rice, beans, cassava, and maize. Although the town houses some government offices, it is a small community, far removed from the bustle of Blantyre in the south, named for Livingstone's Scottish birthplace, and the embassies and government ministries of Lilongwe in the central part of the country. But Karonga has a vast resource that these larger centres lack: Lake Malawi.

Lake Malawi holds an abundance of fish and other wildlife. Fishers harvest the large catfish, *kampango*, and sell it fresh or smoke the fillets and ship them to the larger cities. *Chambo* is sold in markets and eaten with chips; "*chambo* and chips" is a popular dish. It's said, "You haven't been to Malawi if you haven't eaten the *chambo* and chips." *Chambo* is still cheap in some places, but its numbers are diminishing, and the Malawian government is working hard to put a conservation plan in place that will sustain its stocks over the long term. But even with its recent problems of pollution, habitat loss, and overfishing, Lake Malawi still contains more freshwater species than are found in all of Europe and North America combined.

The cichlids of Lake Malawi are one of the great biological wonders of the world. Their diversity within the lake is astounding. No one knows how many cichlid species are native to Lake Malawi, but estimates range from five hundred to one thousand species. In 1984, the United Nations Educational, Scientific and Cultural Organization (UNESCO) named Lake Malawi National Park a World Heritage Site, saying, "Its importance for the study of evolution is comparable to that of the finches of the Galapagos Islands."[27]

Although Malawi is a landlocked country, one-fifth of its surface is water and most of that water is in Lake Malawi. Lake Malawi is a vast inland sea that feeds the people and brings tourists from all over the world. In all of Africa, only Lake Victoria and Lake Tanganyika are larger. The Rift Valley spans Malawi's eastern border, and Lake Malawi occupies most of the valley floor and occupies one-fifth of the country's total area.

The Great Rift Valley is a series of rifts and faults that scar the eastern half of the African continent. The Rift Valley that holds the waters of Lake Malawi is part of this system, so Lake Malawi is long and comparatively narrow. From its northern to its southern tip, the lake stretches 586 kilometres, with a maximum width of just 129 kilometres. In the north, there are fewer beaches. Rocks and high cliffs mark the lake's shorelines. Viewed from the shore, the water often reaches as far as the eye can see, its dark blue waters meeting a pale blue sky. Where the lake narrows, one can look east into the distance and see the smoky mountains of Mozambique rising from the far shore.

Running north to south, Malawi imitates the shape of its lake. Encompassing 58,459 square kilometres,[28] the country's land mass is long and narrow—just like the lake. Malawi's land mass is about the same as

A young boy plays in one of the many canoes used to harvest rice along the shores of Lake Malawi, 2009.

Nova Scotia. Excluding the lake, eleven Malawis would fit comfortably into Alberta. The country is bordered in the north by Tanzania, in the east and south by Mozambique, and to the west by Zambia. Although it covers a small area, with over seventeen million people,[29] Malawi has a dense population, much of it living near the lake.

Although it lacks the vast sandy beaches that are a magnet for tourists further south, Lake Malawi is easily accessible in Karonga. Rice paddies run parallel to the lake's rough waters, and clusters of dugout canoes hug the shore. On the beaches, women scrub their brightly coloured clothing, and children splash and play in the warm waters of the lake's shallows.

⌘ Memory's father, Duncan Chazeza, worked as an assistant accountant at the Ministry of Agriculture in Karonga, so Memory grew up close to Lake Malawi's sandy shores. Duncan's job paid poorly, and the family was kept on the edge of poverty. But even so, Memory loved her years in Karonga.

Memory's mother grew maize and pumpkins in the garden, but there was never enough food, so Memory was sent to buy maize at the Agricultural Development and Marketing Corporation (ADMARC) market. When she got older, her mother made fritters for Memory to sell, and Memory would sit for hours by the side of the road waiting for customers. In this way, Memory and her mother were able to help support the family.

In Karonga, there were five children: Stephano, Memory, Lucy, Danny, and Bodwin. Memory was the oldest girl, so she was expected to help around the house and care for the younger children.

Leaving beans boiling over the fire, Memory's mother would entrust Memory to look after the household. While their mother was away, Memory and Lucy, along with their friends, built houses from stones and broken bricks. They mixed dirt and water to mold plates, bowls, and dolls, and then let them dry and harden in the hot sun. Memory was always the leader in these games, always the boss. If her friends didn't do what she wanted, she would say, "Okay I'm going home." They would relent and comply. Memory would be the mother and send the dolls off to school. If there were many children, the games became more complex. "Let's pretend your child has died," they might say. This time Memory wasn't the mother. It wasn't fun being the mother when your child is dead. They broke the head of one of the dolls and formed a procession to go to the graveyard to bury the baby. The mother would have to cry and cry and cry. The children's games mimicked the lives of the people of Malawi.

From a young age, Memory was strong-willed and determined, so she usually got what she wanted, but Memory's younger sister, Lucy, was a very different little girl. She was quiet and gentle. She couldn't say "no" to Memory's demands. When Memory asked her to do something, she did as she was told.

Memory loved playing in the lake, but she couldn't swim, so her mother didn't like her going near the water. Memory knew if she went to the lake, her mother would be angry. But she went anyway.

Whenever she could sneak away, Memory would take Lucy and run down the path to the lake. Lucy remembered, "She would always force me to go so she wouldn't be alone when our parents started shouting. She wanted us to be disciplined together. She was very clever." Lucy did what her older sister wanted, and the two of them would stay at the lakeshore for hours: Memory splashing in the water and Lucy sitting in the warm, baking sand.

If her mother confronted her, Memory would say, "I just went there to get some sand for cleaning pots." But Memory's eyes would be red and her hair filled with sand. "And because of that, I wanted Lucy to swim; then all of us would be in trouble," Memory explained matter-of-factly. "It's not that I was teaching her how to swim. I didn't know how to swim myself."

On one of their trips, Memory said, "Lucy, you must swim." So Lucy got into the water and splashed around. But Lucy was small, and the current in Lake Malawi is strong. Before she realized what had happened, the water became deep and she couldn't reach the surface. She tried to paddle with her arms, but her mouth filled with water and she lost consciousness. The next thing Lucy remembered, she was vomiting into the sand. Luckily, there were people swimming and washing clothes at the lake that day. When they saw Lucy was in trouble, they pulled her from the water.

Not long after this incident, one of Memory's friends *did* drown in the lake. Memory remembers: "It was the same place we used to swim. People were washing, doing their laundry, doing their dishes. I understand he wasn't going very far, but there was a hole in the water that he didn't know about, so he just went there, and he died." Even the death of her friend didn't stop Memory. After a few weeks, she was back to "swimming" in the lake. Memory loved the warm waters of Lake Malawi, but she also has many happy memories of life in Karonga.

One of the biggest yearly events of Memory's childhood occurred every May 14. On that date, the town celebrated Kamuzu Day: President Banda's birthday. During the time of Banda's rule, Kamuzu Day was a joyous event with celebrations throughout the country. People sang and danced, and many of the larger cities held demonstrations of military bands and parades.

In Karonga, there was singing and dancing in the open field near Memory's house. Later in the afternoon, the older children played football, while Memory and her friends went to the lake.

Memory saved her money all year, one kwacha at a time. When the day came, she pooled her money with her friends. They bought beef, eggs, and rice—they even bought cookies. After the dancing, they took their feast to the beach where they ate and swam for the rest of the afternoon. Even though many people didn't approved of Banda's methods or his policies, Kamuzu Day was a countrywide holiday of celebration that marked the accomplishments of the nation.

Hastings Kamuzu Banda was born to Chewa parents sometime between 1898 and 1906. He grew up in poverty, but he was educated at the Church of Scotland's Livingstonia Mission School in Kasungu, where he developed an early passion for learning. During the time of the First World War, he began walking to South Africa, where he planned to continue his education. He made it as far as Zimbabwe, where he worked at a hospital until his uncle paid his way to Johannesburg.[30]

In South Africa, Banda worked as an interpreter in the gold mines, but he must have been a personable young man because a group of black American missionaries helped him get to America so he could continue his education. Eventually, he received a medical degree from the Meharry Medical College in Nashville, Tennessee.[31]

Banda travelled the world, eventually settling into a medical practice in London, but he didn't forget his homeland. In 1946, he paid ten pounds for a lifetime membership in the Nyasaland African Congress (NAC), an organization formed in 1944 to give black Malawians a voice in the country. He also offered to pay for an organizing secretary, for one year, should the NAC choose to appoint one.

The NAC's power grew, but its membership was young, and many of its members felt it needed mature leadership if it was ever going to lead the country to independence. Now practising medicine in Ghana, Kamuzu Banda was the most educated Malawian the country had produced yet. The NAC extended Banda an invitation to lead the party, and in 1958, Banda returned home to a hero's welcome.[32]

In 1960, the party's name was changed to Malawi Congress Party (MCP). Malawi (at that time still called Nyasaland) became self-governing in 1963, with Banda as its first prime minister. Nyasaland became fully independent on July 6, 1964, officially changing its name to Malawi.[33]

Problems between Banda and his cabinet surfaced quickly. The problems were complex. Banda was a relative newcomer, and by the time of independence he had already created a rift between himself and many of his ministers. In the long run, this probably contributed to his iron-fisted style of governance.

In 1966, Banda passed an act of parliament that made Malawi a single-party state, with the MCP as the country's ruling party. To reinforce his political power, Banda instituted several oppressive organizations. The Malawi Young Pioneers, the Secret Service, and the Censorship Board all helped ensure Banda's continuing authority.[34] In 1971, the parliament passed the law that made Dr. Hastings Kamuzu Banda the "Life President of the Republic," thus sealing the fate of the country for the next thirty-three years.

As a dictator, Banda was relatively moderate—if somewhat eccentric. He was nothing like the bloodthirsty Adi Amin, the dictator of Uganda from 1971 to 1979, who was responsible for somewhere in the range of 300,000 deaths.[35] He didn't demonstrate the kind of grand-scale poor judgment that has marked Robert Mugabe's three-decade rule of Zimbabwe. He did, however, rule with a blind willfulness that threatened Malawi's progress toward democracy. Banda's dictatorship was marked by repression, censorship, and human rights violations.

Hastings Kamuzu Banda.
[Photo courtesy of the National
Archives of Malawi]

In response to increasing pressure from all sides, Banda agreed to hold a national referendum to decide whether Malawi should stay with a one-party state or move to a multiparty system of government. Even with enormous barriers placed in the way of the prodemocracy movement, Banda lost the referendum, winning only 36.5 per cent of the votes. From there, he fought an impossible battle.

At somewhere around ninety-five years of age, Banda still clung to power, and when parliamentary and presidential elections were held in May 1994, he insisted on running as the leader of the MCP. He lost with 33.45 per cent of the votes. Bakili Muluzi was elected as the new president of Malawi.

Banda spent the next few years in relative obscurity. After being acquitted of charges relating to the murder of several rival politicians, on January 4, 1996, Banda issued an apology to the people of Malawi: "I offer my sincere apologies. I also appeal for a spirit of reconciliation and forgiveness amongst us all."[36]

Although some criticized Banda as self-serving and insincere, the people of Malawi are now willing to overlook Banda's transgressions. They prefer to remember him fondly as the father of independence. Dr. Hastings Kamuzu Banda died of complications due to pneumonia on November 5, 1997, in South Africa. After his death, his body was returned to his homeland, and Dr. Kamuzu Hastings Banda was given a state funeral.

After Banda's death, his successor, President Bakili Muluzi, abandoned the tradition of Kamuzu Day, but with the passing years, Banda's image has taken on the patina of nostalgia. He is now seen as more of a benign patriarch than a repressive dictator—remembered more for his Homburg hats and three-piece suits than his authoritarian laws and autocratic rule. In recent years, past President Bingu wa Mutharika, who governed from May 2004 until his death in April 2012, reinstated the holiday, and although it lacks much of its former pomp, a new generation of children celebrates the country's first president on Kamuzu Day every May 14.[37]

Lucita

LUCITA IS A QUIET GIRL.[1] When I met her in 2008, she was withdrawn and reticent. She appeared sad, and as it turned out, she was. She felt responsible for causing problems for her uncle, so she was having difficulty concentrating on school. When I met with her the following year, she seemed like a different girl. She was still quiet, but now she seemed self-assured and cheerful. She was no longer dwelling on her family's problems, and, consequently, she was performing much better in school. She was more comfortable around me, too, and when we talked she was forthcoming and eager to share her story.

Lucita is one of six children: four girls and two boys. Of all her family, Lucita is the only one to go to secondary school. One of her sisters was accepted into Lilongwe Secondary Girls' School, but after the first term, she dropped out when her father refused to pay school fees. Later, she got married.

Lucita's youngest sister, Catherine, is severely disabled. As an infant, she contracted neonatal tetanus, a condition that is often fatal. In Catherine's case, she is unable to speak, suffers from brain damage, and has difficulty walking.

Lucita's mother, Enet, returned to her home village several years before Lucita's acceptance into APU because, in Lucita's words, "My father would like to go to another place and enjoy other women." Since leaving her husband, Enet has struggled to survive.

After returning home, Enet did not remarry immediately, but after two years she met a man who she thought would help support her. Lucita recalls speaking to her mother: "I was not happy with that man, and I was trying to advise my mother not to get married, but I know she was not listening to me because I was young. She said, 'If there is no one to build a house for me, where are we going to sleep?'"

"I said, 'Okay.'"

Lucita told me that marrying her stepfather hadn't helped her mother. "According to my mother, there is nothing he is doing. Even to buy soap or lotion, she goes to some other place to work, and they give her money or maize."

Despite Enet's expectations, Lucita's stepfather didn't build the house where they now live. It was Lucita's brother who came forward and built the small, two-room, mud house for his mother. "I can just say he's like a husband. It's his responsibility to do everything that needs to be done for the family. But him, he maybe just goes there to chat and goes to sleep at his village and stays there for two weeks and then comes back. It's my mother who does everything for the family."

Lucita's mother was having difficulty providing for her children, so Lucita went to live with her uncle. She was living with her uncle when she heard about APU. Lucita explained: "I told my uncle about the school, but he said, 'I am busy. I can't take you to Nsaru because it's a long distance.'"

"I said, 'Okay, just find a bicycle. I'll manage. I'll go there with my friends.'"

Lucita's friends, Chifundo and Rejoice, also wanted to apply at APU, so the three set out together. They wrote their entrance exams at Kabuthu Primary School near Nsaru and returned home later that same day. The three girls discovered that they all had passed. They travelled together to Nsaru for a second time—this time to attend oral interviews.

Lucita had no money to buy food along the way and had not eaten all day. She was hungry. When they arrived at Nsaru, Chifundo said, "I have a relative at the trading centre. Let's go there and eat." Afterwards they walked to the school.

When they arrived, there were already girls waiting for their interviews. Memory said to them, "You are too many. I can't manage all of you. Some of you can come again tomorrow."

Lucita said, "But Madame, for me, I cannot manage to come tomorrow."

Memory responded, "No. You must come tomorrow."

The girls arrived home after dark. Lucita remembers being tired, so she slept. The next morning, the three girls set out again. All three sat for oral interviews. Lucita and Rejoice passed, but Chifundo did not. Lucita began school at APU the following January.

Yet Lucita's worries were not over. Each girl is required to contribute maize to the school and pay for other small expenses. After the first term, Lucita spent the break with her uncle. When she was ready to go back to school, she asked her uncle to take maize to the school, so she could pay her contribution.

"The maize is not yet dried," he explained.

"Okay, I will tell Madame," said Lucita.

But her uncle's wife interrupted, "No, if you allow this girl to take everything, it means, you and me, we will separate, and this family will end."

Lucita is a sensitive girl, and this worried her. She thought, "Should I make them to separate?"

She told her uncle, "It's okay. I will go back and live with my mother."

Lucita's mother was unable to support her and would not be able to help her with school. When Lucita told her mother the troubles with her uncle, she said, "You should not stop school because of that. I will go there and explain everything to Madame Memory."

After speaking to her mother, Lucita went back to her uncle and explained the situation to him. He said to Lucita, "I cannot say you should stop school because I know this world now. It needs women who are educated. It's our luck that you have gone to secondary school."

Despite his words, Lucita was not at peace. "Even though I can go to school," she thought, "I don't have anything."

Her uncle did his best to help out, but he didn't want to anger his wife any further. Instead of buying Lucita the exercise books she required, he visited one of Lucita's primary school teachers and asked him to help out. The teacher supplied Lucita with exercise books and pens for school.

The situation Lucita faced at home worried her. She felt like she was a burden to her uncle. "I was not happy. Even when a teacher was teaching me here, I was not getting anything because I was just thinking about my problem."

Memory noticed Lucita's mood and sat down with her to talk. Lucita recounted her problems and said, "Even though I'm learning here, it is nothing I am getting. I am just thinking about home."

Memory began paying Lucita to fetch the water for her home. At that time, the water for the teachers' residences had to be hauled from a nearby well. Lucita used the money she earned to buy her own exercise books and to pay for other incidentals.

Lucita's older brother also began helping her. He came with K2,000, so Lucita could pay for her uniform. He has continued to help Lucita with her expenses. "If I want my brother to come here and pay for things, I must tell Madame, and she will ring a phone to him." With the knowledge that she can overcome her difficulties with the help of others, Lucita has learned not to worry as much about her problems. Even so, she continues to face challenges.

After not seeing her father for three years, Lucita was able to travel to the Kasungu District to visit him during a holiday. Her brother also lives in that area, and he was able to pay for her transport. Lucita told me about the visit: "He treated me properly, but his wife would not allow me to bring maize to pay school fees."

On a more recent school holiday, Lucita decided not to visit Kasungu. It was only a two-week break, and she didn't want "to panic" her brother by asking for transport money.

On her way to her mother's house, she met with her other brother, and they stood chatting. Her stepfather must have seen her because by the time she reached home, he was gone. When she reached her mother's house she asked, "Where is my father?"

"He is going to his home village. He said that because you come here, it means you want to collect everything we have harvested."

"Ah, no. I don't come here to collect your things," Lucita said.

Later, Lucita told me, "I am feeling sorry. Because of me, it makes them to stop their love."

When she confided her worries to her brother, he said, "You should not be worried about that." The last time I asked Lucita about her mother, she told me that her stepfather had left her mother for good.

Lucita hopes that one day she will be able to help her mother and her little sister. "My mother, her life is not going well. Sometimes she is staying because she is still alive, but her life is not going properly."

Enet's troubles are compounded by the need to take care of her disabled daughter. "She's seven years," says Lucita. "She has not started school. She is just staying with our mother. When my mother goes somewhere, she just leaves that girl with her friends. It's really hard for her to stay with her friends because she doesn't know how to speak. When she's feeling hungry, she cannot tell anyone. Maybe she just starts crying."

Only a few days before, we had visited Lucita's village. Her mother was at a funeral, but Catherine had been left at the village, where we found her. "There is no one who can care for her," said Lucita.

It's a sad situation, and it's made more poignant because I've met Catherine. Her mother looks after her the best she can. The village looks after her the best it can, but she does not receive the care she should receive.

Lucita says of her mother and sister, "Sometimes they sleep with hunger. Just imagine that sister. She cannot know there is no food."

3
Education for All

Not only is education positively associated with better agricultural productivity, higher incomes, lower fertility rates and improved nutrition and health, it is also a pre-requisite for attaining these outcomes.

—*Anne Conroy et al.*, Poverty, AIDS and Hunger[1]

IN 1985, Memory began her schooling at St. Mary's Primary School in Karonga.[2] St. Mary's is an all-girls school for standards one to eight. The Catholic Church built the school, and in its early days, Roman Catholic missionaries ran the school. In Memory's time, nuns taught most of the classes, and the children went to mass every week. In those days it was a newer school, so it didn't face the same problems with infrastructure that it experiences today. As a child, Memory thought it was "a beautiful school."

I visited St. Mary's with Memory and Henry in 2009. With 1,780 students, it was bursting at the seams. The head teacher, Mr. Mughogho, was eager to explain the school's challenges. "Because of a shortage of classrooms," the classes are combined. In some cases there are as many as 160 children learning together in one room. "[The standard fives] are learning outside because we don't have [enough] classrooms." That's in the dry season. During the rainy season, he tells the students, "When you see there is no rain in the afternoon, you come." Sometimes the higher levels will use the classrooms after the standard ones and twos have left for the day. "So we make those arrangements. Making sure they learn."[3]

It's a bit haphazard, but for now, it's the best the school can manage. St. Mary's has seen a surge in enrollment since it began its daily feeding program. The feeding program is run by Mary's Meals Malawi, a nongovernmental organization (NGO) that began feeding children porridge during the 2002 food crisis in Malawi. Mary's Meals now operates in primary schools and orphanages throughout the country, but it has expanded to other developing countries and now feeds over one million children worldwide.[4]

The feeding program is run out of a small outdoor kitchen. The building is tucked into a corner of the school grounds near the office and contains four, large, circular, metal stoves fuelled by a pile of firewood stacked from floor to ceiling nearby. Parents volunteer to come to the school and do the cooking. Every morning, the children line up with their

Children play football at St. Mary's Primary School, 2009.

plastic cups in hand. They each receive a scoop of maize and soy porridge mixed with sugar. It's an enormous incentive. "The children, they have got in mind that at least when they go there [to St. Mary's], they'll have something to eat," says Mr. Mughogho.

For now, the school's biggest problem is infrastructure. There are several new classroom blocks that have been funded through the efforts of Sister Phiri and Father Chinula, as well as the generosity of the European Union (EU), but when I spoke to Mr. Mughogho there was no money coming in from the government for capital projects. The school is on its own in that respect.

Memory took me to see her old classrooms, which are still in use. They are clean, but they are showing their age. The walls are stained, and the rooms are dark. There is no electrical lighting. A dim filtered light penetrates the open pattern in the cinderblock windows—that is all. The cement walls and floors are bare. There are no desks, no books, no posters lining the walls—none of the learning tools we associate with North American classrooms. The wall of one class block shows a wide crack spreading up between the bricks. The foundation is beginning to sag in the middle, and the entire structure looks like it's weakening. It is the sort of building that would have been condemned long ago back home. But here, it keeps the rain off the students, so it is in daily use.

I'm not surprised when Mr. Mughogho politely says, "I hope one day you will come and assist this school."

I knew the request was coming, but it still hurt. "I'm sorry, but I'm helping another school," I reply. The best I can offer is a promise to try to get the word out. But St. Mary's Primary isn't the only primary school that lacks funding.

Malawi was one of the first African countries to abolish primary school fees.[5] School fees had always been subsidized by the government, the church, and other organizations, but to the poor, they were still prohibitive. The Banda Government began by eliminating fees for standard one in 1991. But it was the election of Bakili Muluzi in 1994 that brought an end to all primary school fees, a necessary step to making primary school accessible to all children. This breakthrough heralded an era of increased enrollment and educational spending throughout the country.[6] But increased enrollment was not without its challenges.

Prior to 1994, school fees had amounted to about 11 per cent of the annual primary school expenditure. Eighty per cent of the total yields from the fees were used to cover the cost of instructional materials, primarily textbooks and exercise books. There were also other expenses for parents. These did not raise money for government expenditures but did supplement their children's education: exam fees, exercise books, and textbooks, when they were not available through the schools, as well as sports expenses and school uniforms. Parents and communities often took on the responsibilities of school construction and maintenance. One way and another, parents heavily subsidized their children's schooling. This system came to an abrupt end in the fall of 1994.[7]

Prior to the abolition of school fees, there were approximately 1.6 million primary school students in Malawi, but with the implementation of the new policy, this number leapt to over three million.[8] Although the Malawian government expected to take on more financial responsibilities for their children's education, as a developing country, it was ill prepared for this sudden, dramatic increase in its student population.

In response to the crisis, the government provided twenty thousand "secondary school leavers" with a two-and-a-half-week teacher training crash course. [9] The majority of the teachers hired during this frantic recruitment period possessed only a Junior Certificate of Education (JCE)—the exam taken at the end of form two (the equivalent of grade ten).[10] "It was crisis management," said Esme Kadzamira of the Centre for Educational Research and Training at the University of Malawi.[11]

Later training for the new teachers came through the Malawi Integrated In-service Teacher Education Programme (MIITEP). MIITEP was intended to begin almost immediately. Instead, mired in students and amateur teachers, MIITEP got off to a slow start. The "temporary" teachers of those early Free Primary Education (FPE) days waited until 1997 to begin their training.[12] Even then, MIITEP was intended to give teachers twenty-one months of practise teaching with supervision, but due to lack of resources, the supervision was "substandard, if indeed it took place at all." In subsequent years, efforts were made to improve the system, but once again, success was limited.[13] Esme Kadzamira has been critical of the government's premature move to free primary education. "The whole system failed," she says. "It takes more time for children to get literate because the quality [of teaching] has gone down."[14]

As part of its FPE initiative, the Malawian government enacted other progressive measures. They chose to allow students to enroll in standard one irrespective of their age or to re-enroll at the level at which they previously dropped out. They also began allowing the readmittance of pregnant girls into the primary school system. In addition, they stopped requiring students to wear school uniforms—an expense that had kept many students out of school in the past.[15]

The country's student-to-teacher ratio has gradually improved since the commencement of the FPE initiative, but that improvement varies throughout the country. To compensate, some schools were still demanding fees to pay their teachers' salaries. "We found some schools with 3,000 children and four teachers," said Kadzamira.[16] This was in no way the intention of FPE.

Teachers are deployed to schools on the basis of the school's needs, so, in theory, there should be no disparity between urban and rural schools. In practice, however, many teachers go to great lengths to avoid teaching outside the cities. Female teachers argue against rural deployment on the basis of marriage. Some women have even reportedly faked marriage certificates to initiate a transfer. Transfers are also made for medical reasons. Antiretroviral drugs (ARVs) are available to people with HIV, but treatment can be an issue in remote locations. Teachers often request a transfer to a school near a medical facility. Those transfers are usually granted. As a result, there tends to be an oversupply of teachers in the most desirable locations and an undersupply of teachers in the least desirable areas. On average, there are seventy-seven students per teacher in rural schools and forty-four students per teacher at urban locations. This is an improvement from the mid-1990s, but it's still far from ideal.

Resources are hard to come by in both urban and rural centres. Like St. Mary's Primary, government-funded schools don't always have enough desks, textbooks, or even classrooms. Classes are often over-crowded, and teachers lack proper housing, particularly in rural areas.

Even in the larger centres, teachers can be limited in their choice of accommodation, but there is little incentive for a teacher to live in a mud hut with a thatched roof and dirt floor. Because of the low rate of pay, teachers often live in more affordable, but heavily populated, suburban townships and must commute to their schools.[17] As a result, many teachers experience low morale and minimal job satisfaction.[18] Many of these problems existed before 1994, but the rapid increase in student enrollment put an impossible strain on an economically strapped country struggling toward democracy after the thirty-year rule of the Banda dictatorship.

The school system suffered from "access shock," and as a result, teachers' attitudes, training, and professionalism suffered as well. Although hard numbers are difficult to come by, there are reports that the Ministry of Education continues to be "overwhelmed with disciplinary cases" involving teachers. The issues involve sexual misconduct, alcohol abuse, fraud, and theft. One study reported that students believed their teachers were giving private tutorials as a way to supplement their income. However, in cases where money was not available, girls were expected to supply sexual favours instead. Another study found that "sexual harassment of girls...was commonplace, and in some cases, teachers had affairs with school girls, which led to pregnancy."[19] Girls often appear to possess unrealistic expectations: "If a young male teacher seduces the girl, she thinks that relationship will eventually end up in marriage."[20] This is almost never the case.

Teacher absenteeism is another challenge for the ministry. In a 2004 study, the three most common reasons for absenteeism given by teachers were personal sickness, funeral attendance, and the need to care for sick family members.[21] But it is well known that many teachers take on additional employment to subsidize their incomes. "Teacher absenteeism is high. Teachers go vending or get secondary employment. For example, few teachers go for marking exam papers nowadays. They say it's better to do other jobs," said one Ministry of Education official. "[Even] in urban areas, teachers are finding ways of getting out of the classroom, even during lesson time. Vending keeps things going."[22] In addition to engaging in the informal buying and selling of goods—commonly known as vending—many teachers farm. Producing their own food can be vital for teachers trying to support their families.

Teacher turnover is high at the primary and secondary levels. Every year, Malawi loses about four thousand primary teachers to retirement, death, resignation, and transfer to nonteaching posts. Keeping up with attrition levels has proven challenging. Following the initial recruitment of eighteen thousand new teachers in 1995, the government stopped recruiting. The backlog of untrained teachers kept the government busy. In 1996, the government began training the unqualified teachers with the newly minted MIITEP, a program that relied heavily on foreign donor funding. The ministry hired an additional four thousand teachers in 2000, but due to funding constraints and dissatisfaction with the results of MIITEP, hiring was again frozen. The ministry was having difficulty paying the wages of the teachers they already employed, and in any case, they needed to come up with a more satisfactory system for training teachers. A new system was implemented in 2004, but by then the primary and secondary school system was severely short-staffed.[23]

Even now, the ministry has difficulty keeping its teachers. Teaching is perceived as a low-status profession in Malawi, particularly at the primary and secondary levels. Teachers are barely paid a living wage, and yet they teach under less than ideal conditions. On my first trip to Malawi in 2007, I met the head teacher of a small rural primary school near Chimama. I sat across from his desk on a low wooden bench in a crowded narrow office. Papers and files covered every available horizontal surface. Stored in a tall shelf behind me were the school's textbooks, a motley collection of dog-eared, soft-cover publications ranging in topics from science to agriculture. The head teacher was polite and eager to answer questions, but when I asked him how much teachers earned in Malawi, he became hesitant. He seemed ashamed and took a few moments to answer.

At the time, teachers with a teaching degree were earning K17,000 (C$120) a month, while teachers who possessed their Malawi School Certificate of Education (MSCE) were earning K9,000 (C$65) a month. While the government's own lack of resources limits the amount it can pay its teachers, the International Monetary Fund (IMF) also stands in the way of teachers earning a living wage.

The IMF was established by the United Nations as a tool "to promote international trade, monetary co-operation and the stabilization of exchange rates."[24] Since its inception in 1945, it has often been accused of a less altruistic agenda, an agenda based on economic neoliberalism.

Economic neoliberalism requires international markets to function outside of government regulation. Neoliberalism can only function in a state of "pure" capitalism. In simplistic terms, it advances a system based on free markets, privatization, entrepreneurial freedoms, and free trade.[25]

The concept of economic neoliberalism has been around since at least the 1940s, and probably much longer. Early economic liberalism was based on the concept of market forces that governed outside of the factual production of goods and services. A modern approach to neoliberalism could be said to encompass "the desire to intensify and expand the market, by increasing the number, frequency, repeatability and formalization of transactions"[26]—in other words globalization. In its purest form, neoliberalism is committed to "the elimination of the public sphere, total liberation for corporations and skeletal social spending."[27] It signals a detachment from the individuals who produce goods and who are affected by globalization in any number of ways. In effect, the market structure becomes an ethic or ideology in and of itself.

While its roots lie in the early nineteenth century, neoliberalism gained mainstream popularity during the Ronald Reagan and Margaret Thatcher years—through the now well-known philosophy of Reaganomics. Thatcher's popular acronym TINA makes the point: There Is No Alternative.[28] While the ideology of separating the markets from the state may sound expedient, neoliberalism has been disastrous for the everyman, and woman, in every country where it has been embraced in the past few decades. Chile, Russia, and China have all seen the growth of an elite class living without regard for the poor. Instead of a separation between markets and state, neoliberalism has led to the corruption of the state, a distortion of the line that should separate Big Business and Big Government.[29] According to David Harvey, Distinguished Professor at CUNY Graduate Center PHD Program in Anthropology, while pure neoliberalism calls for market self-correction, the practice has been somewhat different, with the state investing in those institutions and infrastructures that support financial services—instead of services that support the common good such as education and health care. This is called "creating a good business climate." Harvey further claims that where there is a conflict between "a good business climate" and the good of the people, business wins out.[30] The Occupy Movement represents a concerted pushback from individuals and groups who are dissatisfied with this current status quo, but for some time now, world powers such as the United States and Canada have pressed this ideology upon governments of sovereign countries through large multilaterals such as the IMF and the World Bank.

In 1986, the IMF did just that by opening its Structural Adjustment Facility. A year later, it added the Enhanced Structural Adjustment Facility with the intention of providing concessional interest rate loans to poor countries. In 1990, Michel Camdessus, managing director of the IMF, openly stated, "Our primary objective is growth…It is toward growth that our programs and their conditionality are aimed." After the East Asian financial crisis of the late 1990s, the IMF changed the name of the Enhanced Structural Adjustment Facility to the Poverty Reduction and Growth Facility, with the goal of receiving more input on policy conditions from the governments receiving the loans.[31] Since then, some have claimed the death of structural adjustment. This might be so, but there is still a great deal of conditionality imposed upon developing countries by the IMF.

By attaching conditions to its loans, the IMF wields a great deal of power over developing countries. Its critics say these conditions "result in the loss of a state's authority to govern its own economy." There is a disturbing "shift in the regulation of national economies from state governments to a Washington-based financial institution in which most developing countries hold little [or no] voting power." For groups, individuals, and nations who oppose the IMF's focus on the liberalization of trade and investment, "deregulation and privatization of national-ized industries,"[32] the power the IMF wields over the future of developing nations is deeply troubling.

For the Malawian government to comply with its agreement with the IMF, it must limit its total spending on the salaries of its civil servants to 7.6 per cent of the gross domestic product (GDP). If the government were to exceed this wage ceiling, that would constitute grounds for "the IMF to suspend future loan disbursements." Since the IMF applies a "rating" to each country, such a setback would also affect the country's relationship with other donor groups and private creditors. So the Malawian government is acutely limited on the number of teachers it is able to employ and the wages it can pay those teachers. While teachers' salaries make up over 37 per cent of the wage bill, the Ministry of Education is not involved in the negotiations that set this target.[33] The current wage ceiling imposed by the IMF on Malawi makes it extremely difficult for the government to enact progressive policies in areas such as education and health care.

OXFAM International and other major organizations have also spoken out against the restrictions. "IMF policies present massive obstacles for poor countries trying to employ more teachers and health workers... While the IMF is right that countries should manage their economies carefully, its overly rigid stance is incompatible with achieving the Millennium Development Goals on health [and] education," said one spokesperson for OXFAM International.[34] The Center for Global Development also criticized the IMF's unyielding policies: "The IMF has not done enough to explore more expansionary, but still feasible, options for higher public spending."[35]

The IMF has come under increasing criticism over its policies, yet the problem remains: the priorities and world view of a relatively small group of individuals have an inordinate amount of power in governing the direction a sovereign country wishes to take. The imposition, by an outside power, of a series of restrictions that limits the political will and moral intentions of a presumably independent, democratic society, in a way that could potentially undermine its future, serves to underline Malawi's handicap as a developing country. Ultimately, the ideology of a foreign group of individuals is once again affecting the destiny of African countries, communities, and individuals—including the teachers, and ultimately the students, of one small East African nation.

While receiving minimal pay, Malawian teachers teach in undersupplied, overpopulated classrooms that lack the most basic of amenities. Because 84 per cent of Malawi's population resides in rural areas,[36] the majority of students attend rural schools. Culturally, there is a core perception that once an individual moves out of a village, he or she will never go back. Yet for the system to work, the majority of teachers must teach in rural schools. For a Malawian who has struggled to leave village life, there is little incentive to return.

The challenges of the teaching profession also affect recruitment. While training to become a secondary school teacher requires an MSCE, secondary school students with the best MSCE grades tend to avoid the teaching profession. Since employment prospects have worsened, more students are applying for teacher training, but in many cases, it is simply a stopgap measure until they can find university placement.[37]

Malawi recently signed on to two major international agreements affecting its efforts toward a national primary education program: Millennium Development Goals (MDGs) and Education for All (EFA). The MDGs are a series of targets initiated by the United Nations with the input of 170 heads of state and government, along with nearly every leading development institution. The MDGs are aimed at developing a "new global partnership to reduce extreme poverty." There are eight goals ranging from halving extreme poverty to providing universal primary education—all by 2015.[38] As part of its MDGs, the Ministry of Education is attempting to decrease the national pupil to teacher ratio to 60:1.[39] And, to a degree, it has been successful. According to UNESCO, the ratio of students per teacher peaked at 80.68 in 2009. By 2012, it had fallen to 74.09 (according the most recent available data).[40]

Malawi also endorsed the EFA initiative. The EFA was founded on the principle that "education is a fundamental human right." Its goals reflect this principle: to expand early childhood care and education, to ensure that all children have access to free, compulsory, primary education by 2015, to ensure equitable access to "appropriate learning and life-skills programmes," to improve adult literacy by 50 per cent by 2015, to eliminate gender disparity, and to improve the quality of education throughout the developing world.[41] These are mighty goals for a small, struggling democracy.

The one achievement of FPE has been to increase the number of students registered in school at the primary level. In that respect, the program qualifies as a success. In 1990, 58 per cent of primary-school-age children were in school. That number rose to 82 per cent by 2004 but had fallen to 75 per cent by 2007. As part of its MDGs, the government of Malawi hopes to increase enrollment to 100 per cent by 2015.[42]

Access to standard one is "nearly universal," and there is now near gender parity for the first four levels of schooling. Repetition of grades is still high,[43] as is drop out between standard eight and form one. But in recent years, Malawi's completion rate for primary school has soared. According to the World Bank, as of 2012, 74 per cent of children are now completing primary school. This number is a trifle misleading as it's calculated using the "total number of new entrants in the last grade of primary education." Nevertheless, it reflects a considerable improvement, up from 65 per cent in 2009 and still climbing.[44] Along with the positive increase in enrollment has come an increase in grade repetition. Twenty-two per cent of students repeated standard three in 2011, up from 19 per cent in 2000.[45]

While it's estimated that the country contains over seventeen million inhabitants, Malawi's population is growing by 3.3 per cent per year. Of that population, 46.9 per cent fall into the zero-to-fourteen-year-old demographic, making the country's median age sixteen years.[46] This demographic puts an enormous burden on the educational system. Combined with Malawi's high rate of repetition, the country's growing population is sure to compound the problem.

Despite an initial bounce back in enrollment—the number of children attending primary school dropped to 2.9 million after four months[47]— and pervasive inadequacies throughout the education system, Malawi has largely been lauded for its attempt to bring education to its poorest citizens. A recent report commissioned by the World Bank concluded, "the education reforms undertaken in 1994 have clearly been pro-poor... During the expansion in the education system, real unit costs at the primary and secondary levels increased, implying large increases in real public education expenditure."[48] However, the report said the following:

These measures can be strengthened by cutting back on informal fees and contributions that are widely prevalent in primary schools and by improving secondary school funding...The focus ought to now shift towards improving the quality of primary and secondary education. Key measures would be greater financing of teaching and learning materials, greater community involvement in school management, strengthening the curriculum, restructuring the examination system and improving teacher training.[49]

Since the report, the government of Malawi has tried hard to implement these and other changes, yet the results of its efforts have been mixed.

The Southern and Eastern Africa Consortium for Monitoring Educational Quality (SACMEQ) has done extensive monitoring and analysis of Malawi's educational system. In 2005, SACMEQ tabled its comparative report on the "overall levels of provision of resources to primary schools in Malawi and the achievement levels" of the country's standard six (grade six) students based upon extensive data collected in two separate studies: the first conducted in 1998 and the second in 2002.[50] The report showed a mixture of positive headway and negative regression within the primary school system.

The study showed minor improvements in areas such as teachers' housing[51] and toilet facilities,[52] as well as some classroom resources:

cupboard space, books, and teachers' chairs.[53] However, the report also showed a decline in the minimum level of mastery in students' reading skills. Countrywide in 1998, 19.4 per cent of standard six pupils reached a minimum level of mastery, while in 2002, only 8.6 per cent reached the same level, a considerable decline in skill.[54] After six years of primary schooling, 15 per cent of children are still functionally illiterate.[55] If Malawi's FPE program is to be successful, it must concentrate on quality as well as quantity.

Children are kept home from school for a variety of reasons. They are expected to help in the gardens during harvest. Girls, especially, must often care for younger siblings. During famine, children may lack the strength or desire to walk to school since walking consumes calories they can't replace by eating. Aside from the added hardship of food shortages, as they age, children are often encouraged to take on piecework to help support their families.

Linda is a typical nine-year-old girl living in a typical rural village. She walks ten kilometres every day to reach school. She must walk those same ten kilometres to return home in the afternoon. Linda finds the journey tiring, but she is fortunate that her family provides her with maize porridge before she leaves home in the morning; most children are not so lucky. Chilamba Primary School has no feeding program, so Linda must wait until she returns home before she can eat.[56] Linda has advantages over some of her classmates, yet her pursuit of education is still a daily struggle.

Malawi has two official languages: Chichewa and English, but the SACMEQ report found that between 1998 and 2002, the number of students speaking English in their homes had dramatically decreased from 69.1 per cent in 1998 to 40.8 per cent in 2002.[57] This is a worrisome trend.

Until recently, students began learning English in standard five. English comprehension upon entering secondary school is vital to a student's ultimate academic success. There are two compulsory national examinations during the four years of secondary schooling. The JCE is written at the end of form two (grade ten), and the MSCE is written at the end of form four (grade twelve). Both of these examinations determine the student's progress, and both are written in English. Students ending primary school without adequate English speaking and writing skills will find it nearly impossible to succeed in secondary school, thus limiting their options considerably. A lack of English skills could account in part for the pass rates on these national examinations. These rates have fluctuated widely over the past decade, but in 2011, the pass rate was 66 per cent for the JCE[58] and 55 per cent for the MSCE,[59] a considerable improvement from a decade before when only 51 per cent of students writing JCEs and 18 per cent of students writing MSCEs passed the examinations.[60]

As part of the new Education Act, primary schools will be expected to teach English as early as standard one. Luscious Kanyumba, former Education Minister, announced the change in policy: "English speaking has been a problem to our pupils even to those who completed secondary school education. It is the wish of government to see most of the pupils write and speak good English while at primary level."[61] It isn't difficult to imagine the eruption of polarized viewpoints. Beaton Galafa represents the Steering Committee for Education Students at Chancellor College in Zomba: "[Malawians] wrongly think development comes with the language of colonial masters," he said.[62]

At the time of this writing, it's too early to know how an earlier start in English instruction will affect the quality of education for students, but back in 2007, the lack of English proficiency in rural students was immediately apparent to Memory when she began the selection process for APU. This lack of preparation became a substantial challenge for the instructors and the first-year students at the new school. Diliya, one among APU's first intake of girls, recalls her experience. "It was very difficult for us because we had never spoken English before, and at first we were very angry." Although Diliya and her friends snuck away to speak Chichewa secretly, they soon realized that they were falling behind the other girls. After this initial rebellion, Diliya sought the help of her teachers and became empowered by her ability to speak English. "We had a party for those who knew how to speak English. I was in that group... In my heart from that time and also nowadays, I am very happy for using my English as the language of communication at school."[63] APU's policy of English immersion ultimately paid off. In 2009, 100 per cent of APU's first intake passed their JCEs—an unprecedented achievement.

The SACMEQ report concluded that while "considerable achievement [had been made] in terms of meeting quantitative targets, consequent deterioration in quality raises questions about the extent to which the needs of the poor are being met."[64] Instead, students were "marshaled into schools" that lacked the infrastructure, personnel, and resources required for the dramatic increase in numbers.[65] Quite unhelpfully, the report suggests "that it might have been wiser to delay Education for All (EFA) and ensure that the school conditions and teachers were of reasonably good quality for some of the pupils, and then expand slowly."[66] Although it may seem a wise observation in retrospect, it doesn't improve the situation for Malawi's current students or provide insight for the future. The results of the comparison show the outcome of an ambitious primary school mandate struggling to supply universal FPE but unable to maintain the funding, infrastructure, and staffing necessary for the country's growing population.

The report also pointed out a dramatic decrease in enrollment by students as they progressed through primary school, a decrease that is more pronounced among girls.[67] Since the 1994–1995 school year, nearly 800,000 children have entered standard one each year. Of the groups that should have reached standard eight since the abolition of school fees, none has surpassed an enrollment in the final level of more than 200,000 students.[68] Some may make up the numbers in later years after repeating one or more levels, but the success rate in primary school is nonetheless remarkably low. However, despite the discouraging percentages, due to increased enrollment, the absolute number of children completing primary school has increased, however modestly, since the implementation of FPE.[69]

The problem of student dropout is entirely consistent with the observations I've made during my trips to Malawi. I'm reminded of my time spent travelling to primary schools in the densely populated, rural area surrounding APU in 2008. Tacked to the walls of many of the head teachers' offices were large charts depicting the enrollment in the schools' classes. There was something intimately moving about the hand-drawn tables and neatly penned numbers that a computer-generated bar graph could not depict. I pictured a teacher painstakingly hunched over a cramped wooden desk, ruler in hand, labouriously measuring and drawing the charts. I took photographs of some of those charts. The results are replicated below—this is a small sampling of the rural schools in Malawi, but the numbers clearly support the larger studies.

Standard	1	2	3	4	5	6	7	8
Boys	98	64	72	24	39	33	15	8
Girls	136	74	71	38	38	31	10	9
Total	234	138	143	62	77	64	25	17

Standard	1	2	3	4	5	6	7	8
Boys	127	87	117	75	68	48	20	29
Girls	125	95	142	106	74	33	29	23
Total	252	182	259	181	142	81	49	52

Standard	1	2	3	4	5	6	7	8
Boys	106	59	79	75	45	39	44	50
Girls	135	133	123	69	62	59	40	33
Total	**241**	**192**	**202**	**144**	**107**	**98**	**84**	**83**

Tables show enrollment at three rural schools in Malawi. These are replications of hand-drawn tables that are often tacked to the walls of the head teachers' offices.

Countrywide, a similar picture emerges. The following table shows the primary school survival rates per one thousand students for the country during the 2005 school year, as supplied by the Ministry of Education.[70] It's a grim picture—one that hasn't improved much with access to FPE.

Standard	1	2	3	4	5	6	7	8	Graduate
Boys	1,000	701	617	477	386	299	222	191	191
Girls	1,000	664	589	449	364	278	216	160	153
Total	**1,000**	**682**	**602**	**462**	**375**	**288**	**219**	**180**	**172**

Indicates the primary school survival rates per one thousand students for the country during the 2005 school year, as supplied by the Ministry of Education. The total is an average of the numbers of boys and girls who graduate.

I came away from those primary schools with an entirely new appreciation for the accomplishments of the APU girls. Many of the girls were still struggling with their studies. Some were learning complex concepts and ideas in a language they barely understood. When I looked at their faces, I knew I was seeing a series of many miracles. It was a miracle that, against all the odds, they had made it to the end of standard eight.

It was a miracle that they had each overcome their own personal challenges: poverty, social customs, poor nutrition, family conflict, abuse, a lack of parents or parenting, and other struggles. It was a miracle that they had learned about APU, had travelled to the school to take the entry examinations, had been among the few to pass their exams, and had been accepted into the program after passing the oral selection. It was a miracle that they had overcome their fears and reservations during those first weeks at the school. And, finally, it was a miracle that they overcame ongoing problems of parental support, learning challenges, and English immersion. It was a miracle, in itself, that the school was here at all. To this day, I'm overwhelmed by the enormity of their accomplishments.

⌗ Throughout Africa, girls at schools that lack latrines look for privacy behind bushes and at the edge of schoolyards. Unfortunately, Malawi is not an exception. Many of the schools in Malawi lack adequate toilet facilities for their students.

Water, Sanitation and Hygiene Education in Schools (WASH in Schools) is an NGO that focuses on improving drinking water and sanitation facilities at schools throughout the developing world.[71] In Malawi, the organization is led by the Ministry of Education, Science and Technology (MOEST) and guided by the policies laid out by the Ministry of Irrigation and Water Development (MOIWD).

In 2008, WASH released a comprehensive analysis on the state of water, sanitation, and hygiene within 5,369 of the country's 5,460 primary schools.[72] Malawi's Education Act states that there should be "one latrine for every twenty-five students," but with the installation of urinal blocks for both boys and girls at many schools, this number has been relaxed to just one latrine for every sixty students where adequate urinal blocks exist. The report concluded that to meet this standard, the country required an additional "37,142 new improved latrines in 4,142 schools,"[73] and the MOEST admits that only 23 per cent of primary schools have sanitation of "acceptable quality and quantity."[74]

Women use standing water to wash clothes, 2007.

Although boys and girls both benefit from improved sanitation, the
role of insufficient toilets may play a significant role in girls dropping out
of school as they reach the age of puberty. Although there have been no
comprehensive studies linking the availability of latrines to the dropout
rate, there is much anecdotal evidence. In a recent article written by
Monalisa Nkhonjera, she sites the case of two girls, Limbile and Lushani,
who dropped out of primary school once they began to menstruate. With
only one latrine, which lacked a door, for all the girls, they were unable
to change their sanitary cloths when needed. At times, the girls were
able to use neighbouring gardens to change, but this wasn't possible
when people were nearby. Instead, they often chose to wear the same
clothes throughout the day. This led to embarrassing situations. The girls
were ashamed when they smelled badly or their blood leaked through
their clothing, and eventually they chose to stay away from school.
Fortunately, these two girls returned to school two years later after more
latrines with hand-washing facilities were installed at the school.[75]

Menstruation is often a complication for girls as they mature. In a recent study carried out in seven schools in and around Lilongwe, 95 per cent of the girls said that since they could not afford to buy disposable pads regularly, they used reusable menstrual cloths all or some of the time. The cloths are cut from old clothes, folded, and tied to a string that is looped around the waist. While most girls are able to use underwear to hold their pads in place, many rural students are unable to afford underpants. The pads often become soaked through or fall off.[76]

Traditional beliefs may also play a role in girls' fears. "If someone sees my blood in the toilet she can use witchcraft to poison me." Although they didn't like to admit it, the girls in the study believed that if someone found a used sanitary pad, they could use it to cause the girl to continuously menstruate, become sterile, or die.[77] As a result, girls did not want to wash their pads at school, even if the facilities were provided.

It's unlikely that all Malawian girls will be able to afford disposable sanitary pads any time soon. Meanwhile, well-meaning pad donation programs, such as the now defunct Sanitary Pads for Africa,[78] are unsustainable and put girls in a position of dependency. In its recent report on the subject, WaterAid concluded that girls required education and support along with a private area where they could wash and dry their pads without fear of bullying by male students.[79] The United Nations Children's Fund (UNICEF) also recommends "involving girls and the community in planning gender-suitable facilities, which gives a sense of ownership, leading to improved maintenance."[80]

The barriers to girls' education may, at times, seem almost insurmountable, but improvements are being made. The SACMEQ report concluded that the Ministry of Education had achieved "a good level of literacy and an equitable distribution of physical resources in primary schools." The report did concede that the school system showed weakness in terms of "teacher motivation, school organization and school climate,"[81] and it generated a detailed and comprehensive catalog of policy recommendations. Those recommendations ranged from consultation with the community to a review of existing policies, from investment in infrastructure to improved data collection.[82] Change comes slowly. The "ideal" is simply engulfed by the "reality of sheer numbers." Malawi still lacks the economic vitality to provide the resources necessary to deliver quality education to all its children.[83]

There are additional, less tangible, challenges brought about by FPE that the report fails to address. Since families no longer pay fees for their children's education, many have lost interest in the idea of education. They no longer feel the need to take an active role in their children's education or oversee their children's progress: "Pupils and parents interpret FPE to mean that they are free to decide when to attend school, resulting in high rates of absenteeism and erratic patterns of attendance."[84] This is a problem exacerbated by the lack of schooling of parents. If parents themselves are uneducated, it's difficult for them to see the value of education, and if that education appears to lack practical value, then it may be discounted as valueless.

Malawi must move forward, and despite its economic handicap, the country is in an encouraging position to do so. Since 1960, Malawi's per capita GDP has generally crept upward reaching US$355.40 in 2012.[85] While Malawi's four-year Growth and Development Strategy (MGDS) has set economic growth as its priority, the government seems to understand that economic growth will benefit the social sectors and that improved education will ultimately benefit the country's economy. A recent MGDS report states, "[Education]…is a catalyst for socio-economic development, industrial growth and an instrument for empowering the poor, the weak and the voiceless. Education enhances group solidarity, national consciousness and tolerance of diversity. It facilitates the development of a culture of peace that is conducive and critical for socio-economic, political and industrial development. Hence, education is critical and necessary for economic and industrial growth and development."[86] As a result, the Malawian government remains committed to education and the Ministry of Education, Science and Technology is moving forward with plans to, once again, improve the educational system.

The ministry's most recent policy plan focuses on the need to improve "quality and efficiency within the sub sectors, in particular in the Basic Education sub-sector." To this end, the ministry plans to reduce the rates of dropout and repetition, reduce the ratio between students and qualified teachers, better manage the allocation of teachers, increase classroom construction, allow the private sector a larger role in supplying education, and put more emphasis on in-service training and continuous professional development for all teachers.[87] It has scrapped the disastrous MIITEP teacher-training program and is moving toward a more conventional mode of training to be implemented along with teacher upgrading.[88] It has also implemented Complementary Basic Education, an accelerated learning program designed to help over-aged children who have had limited or no access to primary education move quickly to a standard six level of literacy and numeracy.[89] The Ministry of Education has in the past been criticized for "developing excellent policies that unfortunately score lowly on implementation."[90] It seems likely that the results of this new plan will be a combination of lofty goals and modest strides. There can be no quick fix for Malawi's primary school dilemma.

Shakira

SHAKIRA WAS THE ONLY MUSLIM to be accepted into APU with the first group of students.[1] She is the youngest of seven children: four boys and three girls. At the time we spoke, her oldest sister already had six children. Her brothers were in business together selling shoes, blankets, and other goods at various markets throughout the area. Shakira's parents are hard-working subsistence farmers, growing groundnuts and maize. They live in the village next to APU.

I visited Shakira while the girls were on a break. She took me to a small, but well-kept, yellow house with blue trim around the windows and doorframes. Although the house was constructed from dirt like the houses around it, the blue paint gave it a cozy—and somewhat European—appearance and set it above the houses around it.

Shakira invited me into a tidy sitting room packed tight with chairs, well over a dozen in total. It was difficult to move in the cramped space, but I presumed the chairs were necessary for regular extended family gatherings. At first I thought the house belonged to Shakira's parents, but I found out later

Shakira, with her sister and mother, 2008.

that it was, instead, her brother's home. Shakira's house is located on the other side of the narrow dirt road that winds its way through the village. It's a much poorer, smaller house, with a broken door and weathered appearance.

When I met her, Shakira wore a white, lace-trimmed hijab that closely framed her face. She doesn't wear the scarf when she goes to school, and the following week I walked past her in the schoolyard without recognizing her.

When we talked, Shakira said she was looking forward to going back to school. She had been studying during her holidays. And I learned later that she was a diligent student. One of her reasons for wanting to learn at APU was so that she would be living at a boarding school and able to study as much as she wanted. In the past, her chores had kept her busy, but APU allowed her to focus on her schoolwork.

Shakira's mother sat in on our chat. Through Grace, I asked her, "Are you happy that Shakira is attending APU?" She told me it was a good school.

We ended our meeting by taking pictures on the front verandah of her brother's house. In the photos, Shakira's face is dominated by an enormous smile. Her entire being appears suffused with happiness.

But the following year, Shakira's smile had darkened. When I asked the girls to write their stories, Shakira wrote about the death of her brother, Jafali. Because Shakira's parents are so poor, Jafali had been helping her out by paying for her school shoes and other expenses. He was also the one to offer her encouragement in school. "My sister, you are supposed to work hard because school is very important," he told her.

Jafali had died only a few weeks earlier, and Shakira had been devastated. "I was crying until I was sick. I didn't eat anything for one week, also I wasn't wearing shoes," wrote Shakira. Jafali had been in the hospital, but Shakira was ignorant of the cause of his death. It is a sad, but not uncommon, story—one that I've heard repeated on many occasions on my trips to Malawi.

4
You Should Work Hard in School

Our parents failed us

Is it not shameful to be illiterate

School is the answer.

—*Chikondano Matewere, excerpted from his poem,*
"School Is My Name"[1]

MEMORY'S PARENTS ENCOURAGED HER to work hard in school.[2] In that respect, she was fortunate.

Dorothy, Memory's mother, grew up with relatives who didn't believe in the importance of girls' education. Dorothy's parents had separated while she and her sister were very young. Her parents went their separate ways, and the sisters were left "without anyone taking care of them." Dorothy and her sister grew up with various relatives and limited schooling. The girls were left with little choice but to marry. Memory's mother didn't want the same fate for her children.

Dorothy struggled as a housewife, living in poverty her entire life. She wanted more for Memory. She wanted Memory to have choices. "You should work hard in school, Memory. You should rely upon yourself," she told her daughter. "Then you will be able to support yourself and even other people." She wanted Memory to be self-reliant, so she taught Memory that the way to gain independence was through hard work and perseverance. And, while not all her mother's advice made an impression on Memory, many of her words stuck.

Memory loved St. Mary's Primary from the first day of school. It was only a short walk from her home: down a dirt lane and along a little path that led through a field of towering elephant grass. Memory enjoyed playing games like *fulayi* (dodge ball) and *phada* (hopscotch). She also has happy memories of going to church with her class on Fridays: "Being brought up in that school, I was falling in love with the church." Memory's family was Presbyterian, but Memory found herself caught up in the pomp and ceremony of the Catholic Church, enchanted by the images of Mary, Joseph, and baby Jesus.

Other school memories are not so happy. When the children were late for school or when they misbehaved in class, they were given chores. Sometimes the little girls were sent to the sisters' houses to husk corn. As they got older, the girls worked in the fields. Memory remembers applying fertilizer in the rain: "When the fertilizer is wet on your hands, it's itchy. I really hated that." Memory didn't question the punishment at the time, but when she thinks back on it now, she sees it differently: "It's now that I see it wasn't fair making us work. Because you know, you make the punishment fit the age, and that was too much for six or seven years old." She adds, "We didn't go to the teachers' houses to work. It was only the sisters'. In those days, the fathers and sisters had more power."

⊟ It's common throughout Malawi to use chores as a form of punishment for transgressions of all kinds. It's the way children are shown boundaries and taught societal expectations. It's a part of the culture. Chores are also performed at school as part of the children's daily duties. Boys and girls sweep and mop the floors of their classrooms. They pick up garbage, and are responsible for the upkeep of their own classroom blocks. By being accountable for their classrooms, children learn the importance of having a strong work ethic.

At *Atsikana Pa Ulendo*, the girls maintain their hostels and assigned latrines. They are also given chores in response to serious offences such as theft or bullying. The girls are usually accepting of the punishments they receive for their transgressions. "We are never given punishment that is not right for our age," they told me. Assigning children chores as a form of punishment is culturally acceptable, and children expect it as a consequence of unacceptable action.

Occasionally, teachers and other figures of authority take advantage of children, and the chores become a form of exploitation. A United States Agency for International Development (USAID) report explains, "Teachers commonly send students on personal errands to fetch or carry items from their houses, to buy food or personal items at the market and to transport them home on the back of students' bicycles."[3] While helping out a teacher may seem harmless enough, it can set a dangerous standard within the system. Unmarried teachers and married teachers whose spouses are away from home might demand that students come to their houses to perform domestic duties. This practice is contrary to government guidelines but is not uncommon.[4] While chores performed after school or at a teacher's residence may, in some cases, show poor judgment, they don't necessarily denote abuse. However, these encounters do provide the opportunity for sexual advances and abuse.

A study done by UNICEF in 2004 found that "a number of girls entered into sexual relationships with teachers for money, became pregnant and subsequently left school."[5] But there were reports of this type of abuse long before UNICEF did their study. Ivy's story demonstrates that. And during my trips to Malawi, many of the girls I spoke to told similar stories.

In one of my interviews, Sala, a young woman living in Lilongwe, told me about Esnet, a schoolmate who had been in Sala's form two class. Esnet had been impregnated by the school's headmaster. "She is dead as of now," Sala told me in a voice that barely reached a whisper. "She was just foolish. She was coming from a good family. Everything was there. I don't know why it happened." After UNICEF released its report, the Malawian government "expanded legal protection of students subjected to exploitation,"[6] but the exploitation continues.

With teachers seen as figures of absolute authority, it isn't surprising that abuse occurs, but there is a less apparent dimension to the problem. Girls are often enticed into "love relationships,"[7] relationships they believe go beyond good grades, relationships they believe have a future. "If [a] young male teacher seduces the girl, she thinks that relationship will eventually end up in marriage."[8] To a poor village girl, and even her family, a teacher could easily be seen as a good marital catch, so there is logic to this thinking.

In his definitive report on school violence in Malawi, Patrick Burton states, "Schools, as a microcosm of society, reflect the traditions and values inherent in the society as a whole."[9] Burton found that abuse occurs primarily in the two environments where children should feel the safest: at school and in their own homes. He looked into the location of four common forms of abuse: forced sex, forced touching, oral sex, and bullying. "Forced penetrative and non-penetrative sex"—rape—occurs at home 57 per cent of the time and at school 17 per cent of the time. Oral sex shows a similar trend, with 54 per cent occurring at home and 25 per cent occurring at school. Forced touching and bullying, on the other hand, take place mostly at school, with 55 per cent of bullying occurring at school and 35 per cent at home, while 53 per cent of forced touching happens at school and 29 per cent at home.[10] It may be difficult to control the behaviour of people in their own homes, but in this respect, schools hold an advantage and an opportunity. Schools are a gateway to the lives of children who, without outside influence, might assume the social paradigms of their families and communities. Schools may hold the key to social change.

Many countries, including Malawi, struggle to make their schools safer for girls. Governments are beginning to recognize that gender-based violence has an array of consequences for schoolgirls. Besides the obvious—physical injury and pregnancy—girls often have difficulty concentrating and participating in class. They receive lower grades or lose interest in school and sometimes drop out entirely.[11]

The benefits of schooling are quantifiable—and significant. Compared to children with mothers who have no education, children with mothers who have at least five years of primary education are 40 per cent more likely to live beyond five years of age. Numerous studies have also connected secondary school with a significantly reduced fertility rate: 5.3 to 3.9 children per woman in one study. Of course, wages increase with years of schooling as well.[12] All of these results are quantifiable, but there are other less measurable, and perhaps more important, changes that result from educating girls.

With education, girls develop confidence in their abilities. Their parents and communities also begin to see what they are capable of, and they become role models for other girls. Educated women are more likely to ensure their children, and in particular their girl children, go to school.

A girl or woman who lacks self-esteem or doesn't understand her rights is a likely target of abuse. Confidence in one's own self-worth makes it easier for an individual to withstand and repel abuse. A good example is the experience of APU girl, Maria Nkhoma. It wasn't until *Atsikana Pa Ulendo* gained a respectable reputation within the community that Maria's father began to respect her and her mother. It may seem strange at first until we consider that gender-based violence is often a result of a power imbalance in the relationships between men and women.

Women who possess insufficient resources to pursue personal options, who are ignorant of their rights and freedoms, and who lack successful female role models can easily become victims. It was not so long ago that women in many developed countries struggled to participate as equal citizens within their democracies. While gender equality has improved in many countries, throughout the world women still fight for equal representation and reproductive rights. Women don't only suffer from gender-based violence in Africa, but it is a common problem throughout the continent. Like many world cultures, Malawi's traditions sometimes promote inequality between the sexes, breeding conflict and violence.

Within Malawi's patrilineal tribal groups, men purchase their wives by paying *lobola* to the girl's parents. This is not so different from the matrilineal groups, except for the expectation. Within the patrilineal system, the *lobola* "signifies that the woman surrenders her rights to ownership of property and children and in turn empowers the man as the sole owner and distributor of property."[13] In this system, a woman moves to her husband's village, where she is at the mercy of her in-laws, and in particular her mother-in-law. In this situation, women are often mistreated or treated as "slaves." They are not encouraged to receive support from their relatives and often stay in abusive relationships because they do not want to be separated from their children. Some begrudgingly say, "We envy our friends from the centre and the south," meaning their tribal sisters born to the matrilineal system of marriage.[14]

On the surface, the matrilineal system appears to favour the wife, and for most women, it is preferable to the patrilineal system. The husband moves to the wife's village, and so it's easier for the woman to challenge her husband's decisions. If a marriage breaks up, the woman is left with her house and her children. This sounds relatively egalitarian, but, in practice, women within the matrilineal system hold little power. It is really the woman's uncle who holds the majority of power. After the uncle, power is deferred to her brother, then to the husband, and finally to the woman herself. These social structures lead women into relationships where they are vulnerable to abuse.

Gender-based violence or *nkhanza* comes in many forms. "Educational beating" is generally considered an acceptable form of conflict resolution within a marriage. As the "oil of a marriage," women often accept educational beatings. Many women regard them in an almost positive light: "He beats me so I could learn and not do it the next time again."[15] This acceptance of physical violence on the part of the abused establishes a relationship in which the husband is clearly the superior, and the wife is equally the inferior party. In one study, half the women admitted to having been abused by their partners, but only 4 per cent of those abused reported that abuse to police. They didn't report the abuse because they didn't think the abuse was serious or illegal.[16] In this way, the male/female power structure is passed from generation to generation, becoming endemic within a society.

Within this context, women lack self-respect and dignity. During a study of *nkhanza* throughout Malawi, men were questioned on their attitude toward a woman's ability to control resources within a household setting. "No matter how old they get, women's intelligence is not at the same level as that of men. They have low thinking capacity," said one respondent. Another explained, "A woman cannot slaughter a chicken while you are away—one can even throw away the cooked chicken in anger." Another man said, "Women are like trailers while the man is the truck driver, so we have to control the resources."[17] These comments clearly illustrate an imbalance of power between men and women. This imbalance has wide-ranging consequences for girls and women.

A piece in the *Malawi Voice* tells the story of a thirty-six-year-old man assaulting his twenty-four-year-old wife for failing to cook relish for his *nsima*. "The man...is said to have instructed his wife to follow him to his shop in order for her to collect relish for lunch. The husband reported back home during lunch time only to find out that his wife had just cooked *nsima* without relish." Police arrested the man, and he pleaded guilty to the offence of assault occasioning actual bodily harm.[18] This is a progressive step in a country where, until recently, disciplining a wife for failing to perform her "duties" was seen as acceptable.

Not all Malawian men are abusers. Joke van Kampen is the program director of *Story Workshop*, an MBC Radio 1 program that champions the growing movement against gender-based violence: "Violence is not culture. It is an individual man raising his fist against the helpless. It is one man following another in exploiting vulnerable groups like women and girls. It must be exposed." The Malawian Constitution also stands against gender violence: "Discrimination in any form is prohibited. All persons are guaranteed equal and effective protection against discrimination on the ground of sex."[19] While these are mighty assertions, they cannot resonate until people hear them. As long as women and girls don't know they have the right to "equal and effective protection," they will be unable to assert that right. As long as men don't recognize their responsibility to treat women with respect and consideration, they will not do so. That's why education is so important.

Adam Ferenando recently took part in the Protection of Women and Children's Rights, Inheritance and Domestic Violence Project. Catholic Relief Services and the Chikwawa Catholic Commission sponsored the Project for Justice and Peace. It is meant to reduce domestic violence and property grabbing within the participating communities.

Prior to the program, Adam, along with many of his fellow parishioners, believed that he was a god of the household, and that it was his wife's sole duty to perform the household chores. In the five years of marriage to his wife, Lonely, he had never raised a hand to help out at home. Now, if she is carrying the baby, he will carry her hoe back from the garden. While she is drawing water, he will lend a hand with food preparation: small steps some might say, but vital for change.

Nkhate, headwoman of Adam and Lonely's village, sees a fundamental change within her community. "Most men now allow their wives to leave the field earlier to draw water and [perform] other chores. The people now have knowledge about gender and human rights. There is a change in attitude and increased communication and openness between couples," says the headwoman. "Before the program, if a woman was beaten, the man would say, 'She was rude to me' but now, he will tell the truth and say that the wife came from the fields and was too tired to have sex." Some might question this progress, but Nkhate reports that violence is down and the program has created an "environment of openness." Here, too, education is key.[20]

Worldwide, individuals, organizations, and governments are recognizing the importance of education, especially girls' education. Sakena Yacoobi runs the Afghan Institution of Learning. She believes that education is a vital component of social change: "Education is the key issue for overcoming poverty, for overcoming war." Sakena also recognizes that many people feel threatened when confronted with change that challenges the status quo. "People are afraid of educating women—they are afraid that then the women will ask questions, will speak up...That's why I believe in education."[21]

The United Nations Population Fund (UNFPA) promotes girls' education through its various initiatives. Within their directive, the UNFPA states, "Investing in young people, especially adolescent girls, is one of the smartest investments a country can make. As parents, teachers and leaders of the next generation, they can help break the cycle of poverty, strengthen the social fabric and create a sustainable future."[22]

Memory has seen the change education can bring to a girl's life. When she conducts oral interviews, Memory often asks, "What do you want to do with your life?" Sometimes the girls will answer, "I want to become a preschool teacher." Or they might say, "I want to be a hospital attendant." These seem like very good jobs to the girls, but as they progress they become more ambitious.

At the end of form one, they might say, "I want to be a primary teacher." By the end of form three they may decide, "I want to be a nurse." But by

Girls study at APU, 2008.

form four they may "want to be a doctor." They seem to envision their worlds expanding as education broadens their opportunities and expectations.

⚎ Memory saw school as an opportunity to play with her friends. "I was there to play, not for school." When it came time for exams, Memory's class of standard ones lined up. The teacher called them forward one by one and tested them each orally. "I remember myself running away from the line and going to play because my friends were done the exams. So I put playing as the first priority," says Memory with a mischievous grin.

When Memory's mother discovered she hadn't passed standard one, she confronted Memory: "Why have you failed?"

Memory was honest. "They called me, and I refused."

"Why would you refuse to attend exams?"

With the bold honesty of a child, Memory replied, "Because I was playing."

Memory admits she didn't understand the importance of the exams, but she had to repeat standard one anyway. "It pained me that those young ones were with me in the same class. Then I said, 'Why can't I move forward to the next class?'"

But her teacher was firm. "Because you didn't write the exams. If you were to attend all the exams, you'd have gone forward."

Memory thought, "Well, I was not sick. I was healthy. Everything was fine, but I chose to play."

Memory learned a difficult but important lesson, and after that, she started applying herself. She still loved playing with her friends, but she never missed another exam, and she never repeated another grade of school.

School became easier for Memory after that. By the time she reached standard three, she began reading Chichewa—but not yet English.

Memory's family lived hand to mouth. Her mother grew cassava and beans in the nearby communal garden, but some weeks, they had no money for *nsima* flour or rice. To help supplement their income, Memory's mother made fritters. Fritters are a deep-fried donut without the hole. They're sweet, greasy, and tasty. More often on weekends, but sometimes during the week, Memory took her mother's fritters to the market to sell.

At the market, Memory sat on the cool cement step of the covered shelter that stood on the perimeter of the market. In the centre of the small square, makeshift stalls were pressed tightly into rows, leaving little room for people to pass. The stalls opened into small open areas crowded with bags of beans and other vendors. Women would sit on the packed, dry earth surrounded by baskets of potatoes, bags of beans—white, red, and black—and piles of small wrinkled onions. The women called out, selling their wares. *Chitenjes* would be piled high under an awning of scavenged wood, a blend of infinite colours and patterns—pumpkin orange, lemon yellow, sky blue. Strung by cord from awning to awning, shirts and sandals bounced and swung. Men sometimes stepped between the stalls carrying cardboard boxes heaped with small spotted bananas or oranges, some still hard and green. The market would be alive with the sounds of haggling and laughter.

Memory sat for hours waiting for customers, a plastic bowl of fritters balanced on her lap and a few sheets of newspaper for wrapping laid out on the cement beside her. While she sat, she thought, "If only I knew how to read." By this time, Memory was in standard three and just beginning to learn Chichewa, but the newspapers were written in English. She would look at the paper and pick out the few words she knew. That was how, little by little, she taught herself to read English. "That was fun for me because I was not left alone. I was accompanied by reading. I enjoyed that."

That was also the year Memory began working extra hard in school. "I remember in standard three, I started a competition in life that I should work hard in school, and I started studying, getting prepared for exams."

It was also the year her parents said, "Memory, if you place in the top five in your class, we will buy you a school bag."

Memory wanted a school bag for her books. Some of the other kids had school bags, miniature briefcases with blue and red or black and white checkered patterns, but Memory had been carrying her things in a plain, blue plastic, shopping bag. Sometimes the bag tore and her exercise books fell to the ground. Memory wanted a book bag. With a book bag she would look like "she came from a rich family." Memory was stubbornly determined and willfully tenacious. Once she decided she wanted the book bag, she focused her intention on placing in the top five of her class.

Memory worked hard, and eventually her parents presented her with the coveted book bag, where she proudly placed her pencils and exercise books for her next trip to school.

Memory's commitment to education began early with supportive parents, and in that she was fortunate. It was a commitment that she would carry with her through darker times when she no longer had parents to rely on, when her family accused her of laziness, doubted her ability to be independent, and insisted she should get married.

⊞ Malawi is one of the poorest countries in the world. With 76 per cent of the population living on well under two dollars a day, and in many cases less than a dollar a day, school is a luxury.[23] Education takes children out of the home where they may be needed to help with siblings, work in the garden, and tend to chores. Although uniforms are no longer mandatory, some children do not have clothes that are appropriate for school. These days, public schools generally provide textbooks, but even exercise books cost money that may not be available to some students. These may seem like minor expenses, but for a family barely able to feed its children, they often become prohibitive. Of course, once a child reaches secondary school, school fees become more than most families can afford.

For standard one, most often, girls are free to go to school, and this is true of the first few grade levels. But once they reach standard four, girls become responsible for many household chores. If the mother goes to a funeral or is working in the garden, a young girl may be expected to stay home and look after her younger siblings. She may also be expected to collect water and firewood, sweep and mop the house, and cook meals. Even if a girl does go to school, she is expected to come home after school and help with housework and gardening. Although boys are also expected to contribute, they are rarely expected to perform the same range of duties. They are usually free to play with their friends or study if they choose. This leads to increased gender disparity in the schools.

There are other barriers to education. Schools are often located a long distance from home, so roughly 24 per cent of children are afraid of walking to school. Many children fear being attacked. Others worry about bullies or the possibility of rape. Children also fear attacks by witchcraft, dogs, and the *gulu wamkulu*—performers of the Big Dance.[24] Some of these fears may be unfounded, but the majority of these probably reflect personal experience or the experiences of family and friends.

Many girls have recounted their worries to me. Most try to walk in groups or have an older brother escort them on their trips to and from school. But I have only spoken to girls attending APU, and they are not travelling back and forth from home except for holidays. For them it's much less of an issue. Nevertheless, they've told some harrowing stories.

Dogs present a serious threat in Malawi. Malawian dogs are kept as guard dogs. In my experience, they are vicious and unpredictable. I have not met a Malawian who is not fearful of dogs, and their fears are valid. Genezia told me about running from a dog, tripping, and breaking her leg. Tiyese wrote about a similar experience: "I started running, and when that dog saw me, it started chasing me. It ran very fast like a hare that is running from hunters. I tried my best to run fast; unfortunately I was tired so I couldn't run any more, and that dog found me when I fell down like a bag of maize from a bicycle. It bit me and left its poisonous saliva on my body."[25]

Children's fears are not limited to dog attacks. Walking to school can mean a child must begin walking before it is light outside, and this can make the possibility of being attacked an even greater concern. A recent study illustrates the problem: Researchers accompanied three primary school students from their home on their four-kilometre walk to school. The girls were between thirteen and sixteen years old and none of them owned shoes. "The route was a narrow footpath which wound its way through farmland and bush from their school...to their homes in a small isolated settlement." The researchers reported that along the way they crossed five streams, two lacking bridges. They also passed two grave-yards, where the girls were afraid of encountering witches and hyenas, and they cut through numerous farmers' fields, where, during cultiva-tion season, they were frightened of being chased off or harassed. The girls were understandably reluctant to make the journey if one or more of their friends were not making the trip on a given day and were likely to miss school as a result.[26]

In 1992, Malawi's primary school completion rate stood at 24 per cent for girls and 37 per cent for boys.[27] Those numbers have improved in recent years, and Malawi has reached gender parity within the primary school system. By 2010, 68 per cent of girls and 65 per cent of boys were completing standard eight.[28] But this is not the case in secondary school. One of the major obstacles facing girls' education is a fundamental cultural paradigm: girl children are not seen as financial contributors to their families.

There is a belief that if parents provide schooling for a male child, they can expect him to help once he gains employment. This same belief is not held for girl children. Parents assume their girl children will get married, have children of their own, and stop working. So if there are enough funds for one child to continue going to school, it will be the boy that is chosen to stay in school in the hopes that he will one day provide financial support to his parents and younger siblings. This is a deep-seated belief with which Memory and many other girls have struggled.

If a girl does not acquire some form of post-secondary education, she is left with few options. A girl who does not continue her education will almost certainly get married at a young age, have children, and become financially dependent upon her husband. Traditional Malawian culture and a restricted job market make marriage virtually inevitable.

From a young age, girls are taught traditional roles. As a young girl, Memory cooked "*nsima*," just like her mother, by stirring mud in a dirt pot. She raised her baked mud dolls, and she even helped her friends "bury" their dead "doll children." Later, she learned to cook *nsima* using real flour in the traditional fashion. In Malawi, it's said, "A woman who cannot make good *nsima* will not be able to keep her husband happy." Traditional skills for a traditional society. But Malawi is changing.

Malawi's dense population is making land scarce. Except for animals confined to a few small wildlife parks, the large game is gone, vanished from the land. When Memory's grandfather settled in the Kasungu area in the 1973, he counted only eight huts in the area, but the bush was alive with animals: elephants, leopards, and antelope.[29] Nowadays, except along the lake, Malawi is home to nothing much larger than mice. Even along the lake, while I hear there are crocodiles and other wildlife, I've seen only baboons and monkeys.

In Mr. Kapwayi's time, the harvests were plentiful, and there was no need for fertilizer. "Now," he says, "we fertilize and the harvest is not good."[30] Reduced soil productivity and decreased land allotments make subsistence farming an impractical way of life for many families. Drought and climate change have worsened the situation, and crops are no longer a certainty, yet hunger, poverty, and disease are commonplace. People are moving from their traditional villages into the cities in record numbers. Family groups and interconnected communities have been dispersed by urbanization and splintered by the AIDS epidemic.

Centuries of colonialism, and more recently globalization, have pushed and pulled at traditional values, cultural structures, and family dynamics, making them disconnected and often irrelevant to life in the modern world. All these factors make a traditional way of life uncertain and unappealing for vast numbers of people. Malawi is in a time of transition, and the health and welfare of the country's women is of vital importance if the country is to increase its standard of living, grow its economy, and improve its human rights record.

I was outraged when I heard about the experience of one of the girls at *Atsikana Pa Ulendo*. Matilda was fifteen years old, at the time, and a form one student at the school, a soft-spoken, gentle soul. She is sweet, if a bit naive in her sweetness. Matilda was instantly likable.

Before Matilda came to APU, her uncle had taken her in. He was the one who suggested she apply at APU, and he was helping her out with basic needs and school supplies. While staying at her uncle's home during a school holiday, Matilda met a man. The man came to see her several times throughout the holiday, bringing her small gifts: lotion, a Fanta,

Over 80 per cent of the population lives a rural lifestyle.

a few kwacha so she could buy her own soap, and other trinkets that
wouldn't appeal to most North American girls. Matilda was flattered. She
was also happy to have a few possessions that belonged to her alone.

When the break was over, Matilda returned to school, but within a
few days, her "boyfriend" showed up. He insisted that Matilda come with
him, and intimidated, she went. The police were called, and Matilda was
returned within a few days. There appeared to be no harm done.

Matilda didn't understand the connotations of the relationship. As a
result of his gift giving, her boyfriend had certain expectations, presumably of a sexual nature. He complained to the police and to Matilda's uncle.
He claimed he had spent money on gifts but received nothing in return.
The boyfriend demanded reimbursement for his expenses. Matilda's uncle
could hardly afford the expense, but to avoid bad blood, he compensated
the boyfriend. The boyfriend caused so much trouble for Matilda's uncle

that her uncle was forced to return to his home village. His wife, already unhappy that her husband was spending the family's resources on his niece, demanded that he stop supporting her. Unhappily, he agreed.

Matilda was devastated by the trouble she had caused her family, and her schoolwork suffered. It took her many months to refocus on her studies.

I recount this incident because it demonstrates the complexities of social relationships in Malawi. To my Western mind, Matilda's situation appeared to be a clear case of an older man manipulating a younger woman—a girl. If not criminal, it was at least morally reprehensible. I was outraged that Matilda's boyfriend would try to "purchase" her for the price of a few cheap trinkets. I was even more outraged that her uncle would feel the need to compensate the man for gifts he had freely given. But in a country where people are connected by a complex web of family, community, and societal ties, I realized he had no choice. If he had refused to pay the man, he might have faced physical threat. Matilda's uncle would have been condemned and criticized by the man's family and community. Her uncle had to compensate the man or risk causing long-term consequences for himself and his family.

It seemed unreasonable for Matilda's aunt to react to her husband's generosity with pettiness and jealousy, but her attitude is a common one. Since hearing Matilda's story, I've heard dozens of similar ones. In a country where poverty takes on a meaning I can't easily comprehend, there is little room for generosity to an outsider, not when that outsider is seen as a possible competitor and potential drain on the family resources. More often than not, instead of acting as allies, women end up playing the roles of hostile rivals.

Matilda is not the first girl to be drawn into a situation for which she was emotionally ill prepared, but Malawian attitudes are changing, if slowly. Children learn about human rights in school, and there is a gradual move toward educating girls on the importance of remaining in school. The Malawian Constitution guarantees equal rights for women, but societal change can take decades if not generations.

Matilda's disappearance may have gone unquestioned if she wasn't studying at APU. Young girls sometimes disappear once they reach a certain age. While containing uniquely Malawian touches, large formal weddings—weddings with all the pomp seen at a traditional Western Christian ceremony—are popular throughout the country. But sometimes a woman is attracted to a man she knows her parents will not approve of, so she simply disappears. This was the case for one of Memory's relatives, Inez.

After reaching puberty, Inez met a man who was passing through her village. He was selling dry fish from house to house and appeared successful. One night, Inez left with the man; they were married, in the traditional way, by living together.

Inez's parents didn't try to look for her. They accepted her disappearance, assuming she had found a man from a nearby village. Usually word would be sent back to the parents in these cases, but not always.

Inez and her new husband settled in Nkhotakota, where she eventually gave birth to a son. But this is not a happy story. Inez's husband changed his business several times, sometimes selling fish, sometimes selling used clothes at the markets. He was often away from home for long periods, leaving Inez to fend for herself. One day he didn't come home.

After nine years of marriage and with a small son in tow, Inez returned to her village. She was welcomed back, and she resumed village life. She never saw her husband again, but soon after her return, the police visited her. They were looking for her husband, and that was the last Inez heard of him.

Later, Inez remarried as a second wife. She has been married ever since and has several children from her second husband. Some thirty years later there is still an expectation in most village families, both spoken or unspoken, that a girl will find a man and marry at a young age.

As girls reach puberty, sexual harassment by men and boys can become a problem. It's such a common occurrence that parents may be reluctant to send their girls to school. Many girls are kept home for fear they will be raped or assaulted on the way to or from school.

In early 2008, *News from Africa* reported a marked increase in sexual defilement, rape, and murder meted out against women and young girls in the Lilongwe area. Charles Banda reported that six-year-old Sylvia Madondetsa was found dead near the Lilongwe River on a sunny Sunday in September 2007. She had been brutally gang-raped, tortured, and strangled to death. But hers was just one in a series of violent crimes against women and girls that have female activists lobbying the government for harsher sentences for the perpetrators of sex crimes.[31]

In early 2012, on the streets of Lilongwe and Blantyre, female vendors wearing trousers were attacked, stripped, and beaten. President Bingu wa Mutharika was accused of precipitating the attacks by criticizing women for wearing pants and miniskirts. Women took to the streets protesting the attacks. They wore trousers and miniskirts. Some wore their messages on their T-shirts: "Real men don't harass women," and "Vendor: Today, I bought from you, tomorrow, you undress me?"[32]

Later, President Mutharika denied that he had "ordered street children and vendors to attack women." He stated, "Every woman and girl has the right to dress the way they wish."[33] Vice-President Joyce Banda blamed the attacks, in part, on Malawi's economic troubles: "There is so much suffering that people have decided to vent their frustrations on each other."[34]

During President Kamuzu Banda's thirty-year rule, women were not allowed to wear pants or miniskirts, but his "indecency in dress" laws were repealed after he was deposed. Still, most women still wear skirts and dresses, but pants are a growing trend. It could be that some men feel threatened by a change in cultural norms. The attacks could be linked to the recent loss of traditional family supports and structure or the sudden displacement of large groups of people in Malawi's rapid move toward urbanization. Whatever the cause of this systemic disrespect for women's rights, it is likely to be a long and hard battle before we see true equality for women.

Agness

GIRLS WHO RECEIVE AN EDUCATION do go on to find employment, get jobs, and help out their families.[1] Agness owns and operates her own playschool. She has run the school since shortly after graduating with a diploma in tailoring. She worked as a tailor for several years until getting married. Before getting married, Agness's fiancé took the unusual step and was tested for HIV and AIDS. Agness and her husband have one planned child, a little girl—a miniature Agness with all the spunk and gregariousness that helped her mother endure years of hardship. Agness's story is a blend of tragedy, determination, and good fortune.

Agness bubbles and pops with life. Her voice is like carillon bells at Christmas, sweet and beautiful. She often interrupts herself with a burst of giggles that wrinkles her nose and come from deep within her soul. She'll drop her head and cover her face, and then, not quite sure of herself, she'll look up with a smile that dances from her eyes and twinkles throughout her face. Under her ebony skin, she must be blushing. Her laughter is absolutely genuine and hopelessly infectious. It's impossible not to love her. I loved Agness from the moment we met.

Agness's family is Jehovah Witness. Because of their faith, Agness's parents fled Malawi in 1970 after years of persecution by the Banda Government. The persecution began after the Witnesses refused to join Banda's Malawi Congress Party. Beginning in 1964, Witnesses were systematically beaten, tortured, and detained. Banda declared the group to be "an unlawful society." Their homes and Kingdom Halls were burned, and they were routinely driven from their villages. Often meted out by the MCP's Youth League, the oppression lasted throughout Banda's reign. Witnesses fled to neighbouring countries: east and south to Mozambique and later west to Zambia where they were often unwelcome but sometimes allowed to stay.[2]

Agness's family settled in Mwanza, Zambia. Agness was born twelve years later. When Agness was just five, shortly after her brother's birth, Agness's father died, so Agness's mother took Agness and her brother to live with her parents.

Several years later, Agness's grandfather became ill. His stomach began expanding. While his condition was never diagnosed, he knew he was dying. Before he died, he wanted to take his family back to Malawi. In 1995, Agness emigrated to Kasungu, Malawi, with her mother, brother, grandparents, and two uncles. Her grandfather died a few months later.

Now living in Malawi, the family struggled for survival. Banda no longer ruled the country, but Agness's family owned nothing. They were a family of subsistence farmers with no land to farm. Two years later, Agness's uncle said, "I cannot manage to stay in Malawi." He left with his wife to move back to Zambia, but a year later he returned. "I've found another place," he said. "I've come to get you and take you back to Zambia."

By then, Agness had nearly finished standard eight. She would be taking her Primary School Leaving Certificate Exam in just a couple of months, so she asked if she could stay in Malawi long enough to complete the tests. Agness's mother, a quiet woman who has always been supportive of her daughter, decided to wait with Agness. The two would follow the rest of the family in a few months.

Agness had just completed her exams when she heard of a small Canadian-sponsored girls' school opening nearby. The school was looking for form one students to start secondary school on full scholarship the following January. It was a once-in-a-lifetime opportunity, so Agness wrote the entrance exam and was accepted into the school. That school was the short-lived CEAG project.

When Agness wasn't at school, she lived with her mother in Kasungu. Their house had consisted of two rooms, but after the roof caved in, they were left with only one. Because the rest of the family had gone back to Zambia, there was no one to help repair the house. Agness says, "It was like I was the father of the house. I remember the day I put the grass and the plastic on the roof. The whirlwind took the grass and left holes in the roof. It was at night. I cried." Agness bubbles with laughter remembering her long-ago self. I picture her crying next to her mother in that tiny, dark, cold room with the wind blowing through the open roof. "My mother said, 'It's okay. It's not raining.'" But Agness still cried.

The next morning, Agness went back up on the roof with rocks and thick tree branches to hold down the grass. "But when I was putting on the trees, I worried that maybe they would be heavy, and this house is going to fall." It was a hard life for Agness and her mother, and CEAG likely saved them both.

Agness completed form one and form two at CEAG and later form three and form four at Phwezi. After two years of tailoring at the polytechnic and the help of a microcredit loan, Agness went into business with some friends. It was a bumpy journey that you'll read more about later.

Agness has never earned a lot by North American standards, but she has come a long way from huddling in the only dry corner of a small room with a leaky roof. Once she began earning her own money, Agness put what she had aside to pay off her loan, but the rest she used to build her mother a house, a small, dirt, thatch-roofed house, but a house with strong walls and a roof that doesn't leak.

Although now married, Agness is an independent, self-reliant woman with a husband who respects her and a little girl who did not come into the world as the result of an "accident."

As she finishes telling me her story, Agness becomes serious: "I don't think I'll go back to those years. I don't think I'll be the same. I struggled enough."

5

I Should Be Buried

The world favours those
who have money.

—*Memory Chazeza-Mdyetseni*[1]

WHEN MEMORY WAS EIGHT, she moved with her family to Mzuzu.[2]
After living her entire life in Karonga, Memory thought she was leaving
for the big city.

Mzuzu is the third-largest city in Malawi. It's located in the northern
part of the Viphya Highlands, higher in altitude than Karonga, but while
Karonga is hot and humid, Mzuzu is far more temperate, humid but
mild. The climate makes the area ideal for farming tea, coffee, and rubber.
Today the city is well known for its university, but Memory's family
moved to the city before the university opened its doors.

Mzuzu has a population of about 140,000, but it has grown steadily in recent years, so it would have been much smaller when Memory lived there as a child.[3] Because of its accelerated growth, the city has a disorderly appearance, like a sprouting village with a random assortment of low-rise buildings and bumpy roads that twist and turn haphazardly. There is beauty here too. Mzuzu sits on the edge of Viphya Forest, Africa's largest man-made forest, and the city boasts enormous cedars and pines. The Lunyangwa River also sweeps through the city, its basin a broad swath of green amidst the dust and grime.

Memory began standard four at Lunyangwa Girls' School, and she was committed to her education. Both her parents had high expectations for their eldest daughter, and Memory had no intention of letting them down. "I was very much into school. I really wanted to learn."

Memory can still recite many of the poems she learned in standard four:

Look at Mr. Spider going up the wall.
Big black spider crawl, crawl, crawl,
Be careful Mr. Spider don't you fall.
Big black spider crawl, crawl, crawl.

As they recited the poem, the students would point at the big spider that lived in the corner of the classroom.

Life was different living in Mzuzu. There were no more trips to the lake, and Memory had outgrown her mud dolls. She no longer cooked "mud" *nsima*. Now she prepared real *nsima*, with real *nsima* flour. Memory missed swimming in the lake, but Mzuzu had other "city" entertainment to offer.

As the largest city in the northern part of the country, Mzuzu has a big-city stadium, enormous to Memory's young eyes. The stadium was host to all sorts of events: football matches, dancing demonstrations, and military parades. On the weekends, Memory took Lucy to the stadium, where they sat on the wooden benches and watched Malawi's football teams play their games and the marching bands practise their drills. Because there was a military base outside the city, in the days leading up to Kamuzu Day, the military troops practised their drills at the stadium. Memory and Lucy would watch the men arrive in their trucks and follow them into the stadium. The two girls would sit on the stands and watch the practice. Memory loved seeing the men move in unison. Their movements and their uniforms intrigued her.

Memory no longer sold her mother's fritters at the market; now she sold eggs by the side of the road. Memory's father still worked for the Ministry of Agriculture, and through the ministry, he was able to purchase eggs at a reduced rate. Memory sold these eggs to make extra money for her family.

As she grew older, her parents gave Memory more responsibility. When there was profit from the egg sales, she handed it over to her parents, but she remained in charge of the capital so she could continue to purchase eggs and the business would thrive.

Memory was still attending primary school, and she was expected to take care of her brothers and sisters. Her mother was often out of the house attending meetings and choir practice. Dorothy belonged to the Women's Guild, and she was an active singer in the church choir. While her mother was gone, Memory prepared lunch for her brothers and sisters and helped keep the house clean and orderly. But Memory was still a child, and her age made the role of caregiver a challenge. She was stubborn, but so were her brothers, Stephano and Danny. When they disagreed over something, their quarrels turned into fistfights. "I was always the loser, but I couldn't give up," says Memory.

Memory's relationship with her father was also changing. Since the move to Mzuzu, they spent more time together, often talking about the importance of education. Memory wanted to be an air hostess when she grew up, but her father said, "No, Memory. I want you to be a doctor or a teacher." So while Memory was still young, she was already thinking about long-term goals.

Not long after moving to Mzuzu, Memory's father was transferred to a different department within the ministry. Because the family was living in government housing, they were expected to move to another area of the city. The new house was on the other side of the Lunyangwa River and much further from Memory's school than their last home. While Memory's siblings didn't mind moving to different schools, Memory wanted to remain at her girls-only school. She decided to stay at Lunyangwa Girls' School and make the long walk to and from home. The walk took her across the Lunyangwa causeway.

The Lunyangwa River has a broad riverbed. In the dry season, the watercourse narrows, and the riverbed fills with tall reeds and grasses. But in the rainy season, water fills the banks of the river, and for a time, even the causeway floods, filling the river's wide tract with water snakes and other wildlife.

The causeway was narrow but passable most of the year, but in the dark, it was a long crossing fraught with danger. Memory was afraid to cross the river before other people were out and about in the morning. Dawn doesn't come to Malawi until six o'clock, and by that time, Memory was already supposed to be at school. Classes didn't begin until seven-thirty, but all the children were expected to sweep and tidy the classrooms and gather for assembly before heading to their classrooms. Because of the walk from her new home, Memory was often late for school.

While corporal punishment in schools is deemed unlawful under Article 19 of the Malawian Constitution and also as part of the Teachers' Code of Conduct,[4] the wording is somewhat ambiguous and it is still practised. Recently, the Malawian government recommended that the Education Act be revised so corporal punishment is explicitly prohibited,[5] but it was still widely practised while Memory was in school.

In a survey taken in the Machinga district by USAID for the Safe Schools Program, 71 per cent of students explained they had experienced

< *The Lunyangwa River causeway, 2009.*

beatings and 69 per cent said they had experienced whippings.[6] It is a little difficult to interpret the findings because the percentage is a combination of beatings and whippings that took place at both home and school—corporal punishment is still a lawfully accepted practice of child-rearing.[7] However, 61 per cent of the students surveyed reported a male teacher perpetrating the most recent whipping. Seventeen per cent of the whippings had been perpetrated by a female teacher and 10 per cent by a head teacher.[8] Very few of the students who reported being whipped by a teacher reported the incident to a parent, PTA member, or other authority figure, suggesting either cultural acceptance of the practice or shame on the part of the student.[9] Despite these numbers, three-quarters of the teachers surveyed as part of the same study believed that corporal punishment was not necessary to discipline students.[10]

For her tardiness, Memory was forced to lie facedown on the cold cement in front of the entire class. Using a long, thick stick, Memory's teacher beat her legs and back until they were black and blue. "It was embarrassing," admits Memory. "Thank goodness it was only girls in the class, but these were male teachers, so it was still embarrassing. After that, I used to cry and cry."

The beatings didn't break Memory's spirit. They only made her work harder. "This made me work hard in class, so that I could one day leave that school." But there was worse to come.

While Memory was in standard six, her mother became seriously ill. Memory would arrive home from school and find her mother asleep in bed. "I'm not feeling well," she would say. On these days, Memory would prepare the meals for her brothers and sisters.

Sometimes her mother said, "I went to the market, but I almost fell down." Dorothy's stomach became distended: big and painful.

Thinking she was pregnant, Dorothy went to the hospital. But the doctors told her she wasn't pregnant, neither could they supply a diagnosis. Still in pain, she returned home from the hospital. At home, Dorothy grew more ill. Eventually, she visited another hospital in the hopes that they could help her, but they were unable to offer an explanation of her symptoms.

Memory hoped her mother would get better but watched her health gradually worsen. Sometimes Memory curled up next to her mother in bed and cried, but her mother always insisted, "I'll get well soon."

Memory wanted to believe her. It scared Memory to imagine her mother dying. "It was a battle within me. It affected my school because I was just thinking about her."

"I'm not going to school," Memory would say.

Her mother reassured her, "Go to school. You'll find me when you come home."

Dorothy had always taken care of her family, but there was no one to take care of Dorothy. Memory wanted to help, but she was still young, and there were many things she could not do. "She would fail to bathe, and I couldn't bathe her. It was horrible to see her struggling." Again, Dorothy was admitted to the hospital, and Inez travelled from Kasungu to look after her.

Memory often went to the hospital to visit. During one of these visits, Dorothy told Memory and Inez about a dream. She had dreamt she was in a new car dressed in her Women's Guild outfit. She was alone in the car. The women from her Women's Guild were outside surrounding the car, and she couldn't get out. In Dorothy's mind, the dream foretold her death.

Along with her stomach, Dorothy's legs began to swell, and she often cried out in pain. Before she died, she developed a cough and couldn't speak. Finally, coughing was no longer enough to remove the mucous from her lungs, and she died, drowning in fluids.

Memory's father took Dorothy's body back to Kasungu so she could be buried near her home village, and Memory knew her mother was never coming home. "Even though I knew she was dead, and she was in the coffin, I thought maybe I should just be buried with her."

When I asked Memory about the medical care her mother received, she replied, "I would say the world favours those who have money."

꙰ There are hospitals and clinics throughout Malawi, some public and some private, but the care people receive in public facilities is often substandard. There are a multitude of reasons for this.

The Malawian government is unable to pay its civil servants enough to be globally competitive. One of the primary reasons Malawi, and countries like it, lack qualified medical staff, particularly doctors, is the lack of competitive wages for health care professionals. Once they have completed their education, doctors often choose to go elsewhere.

Malawi's medical brain drain is a relatively recent occurrence. As reported by the World Bank, "The exodus of health workers out of [Malawi's] civil service started in early 2000 and was precipitated largely by the erosion of salaries, although there are other systemic under-lying causes such as poor working conditions, and lack of drugs and medical supplies to work with."[11] Salary is certainly not the only driving force behind the unprecedented emigration of Malawi's professionals, but it plays a prominent role. The majority of economists believe that the decrease in salaries due to structural adjustment has led to emigra-tion primarily among the mid- to high-income groups of skilled workers, which includes nurses and doctors.[12] Individuals with a higher income are better able to afford the expense of relocation.

Worldwide, Malawi's per capita percentage of post-secondary gradu-ates is one of the lowest. In 1998, only 0.4 per cent of the population aged twenty to sixty-four held a degree or diploma of any sort.[13]

The Ministry of Health (MOH) believes the lack of health care workers within the public system is in a "critical" state. Countrywide, only 36 per cent of nursing positions are filled, while the vacancy rate for doctors is nearly 100 per cent. The MOH recently reported that within a country of over thirteen million inhabitants, there are only 156 doctors working in the public sector.[14] That's the equivalent of one doctor for every eighty-four thousand people.

In its Essential Health Package (EHP), the government of Malawi defined a level of minimum care. According to the EHP, essential health services cost C$18 per person, but the MOH recently estimated that only 9.2 per cent of the country's health care facilities met the staffing guidelines required to comply with these recommendations. The EHP's staffing goals have since been revised downward.[15]

The equation changes if an individual is able to access private health care. Private clinics exist throughout the country. These clinics are well staffed and well stocked. But the majority of Malawians live in poverty, and accessing private health care is not an option.

In an attempt to combat the lack of public sector doctors, the MOH has increased wages for many of its public sector health care employees. Senior physicians' salaries recently increased from C$266 to C$1,753, while a mid-level nurse's monthly salary has increased from C$118 to C$208.[16] These salaries are not competitive with those in developed countries, but it's a start.

Malawi's national newspaper, *The Daily Times*, reported that nearly one hundred of the country's nurses have emigrated to "greener pastures" every year. The paper also claims the lack of properly trained personnel has led to deaths throughout the country. Dorothy Ngoma of the Nurses Association of Malawi confirmed the report: "It's true unskilled people are doing the job which they are not competent with guardians and hospital cleaners are attending to patients and doing jobs supposed to be done by a nurse."[17] Due to their historically strong connection, many Malawians choose to immigrate to the United Kingdom. "We lost the majority of registered nurses at their prime. In a country with one thousand registered nurses, we lost about six hundred of them," said Ngoma.[18]

Despite the challenges, headway is being made. With the help of funding from the Department for International Development of the United Kingdom, Malawi was able to implement a six-year initiative,[19] and through a combination of modestly improved salaries and expanded educational opportunities, the country appears to be turning the tide on the loss of health care professionals. In 2001, the country's worst year, it lost 111 registered nurses to emigration. That's the equivalent of two years of Malawi's nursing graduates. In the first half of 2008, this number fell to six, and Malawi's nursing schools increased their intake by 50 per cent.[20]

In 2009, Dr. Khumbo Kalua, a lecturer and researcher for the University of Malawi's College of Medicine and a senior eye specialist in Blantyre, reported that the brain drain of Malawi's doctors was over: "I can now confidently report that there are more doctors in Malawi at the moment, thanks to College of Medicine, University of Malawi who have now started producing large numbers of locally trained Malawian doctors. Most of these doctors are now remaining in Malawi."[21] Can Malawi maintain the success of the last few years? This remains to be seen. For now it must focus on a new problem: internal brain drain. As the country retains its health care workers, many of those professionals choose to work for private and NGO-run clinics. Dr. Kalua believes this problem will sort itself out. "These doctors are serving fellow Malawians...and very soon the mission and private hospitals will become flooded and the overflow will extend to the Government hospitals."[22]

The majority of reports decry the country's brain drain as a "workforce crisis" or as the "looting" of doctors and nurses by developed countries. However, in their paper, "An Economic Perspective on Malawi's medical 'Brain Drain,'" Richard Record and Abdu Mohiddin argue, "There are potential gains in managing medical migration to produce outcomes that are beneficial to individuals, households and the country."[23]

A survey of Malawian households in 2005 showed that 9.5 per cent of income came from "other current transfers," a number that rose to 14.2 per cent in female-headed households, suggesting that remittance payments could be having a significant impact upon the country's economy. Record and Mohiddin believe that migration will continue to be an economic factor for the country. Rather than discouraging emigration, they prescribe a fee structure in which students in certain fields pay a fee for their education that is written off during the time they spend working in their home country or paid off with their overseas earnings.[24]

While this strategy might have some merit, it's likely that the majority of Malawians would prefer to use their skills to help fellow Malawians, and it seems only right that they earn a wage commensurate with their skill while doing so.

Record and Mohiddin also see merit in a two-tiered approach to training. They suggest offering an "advanced training program" and a "basic training program" to potential medical professionals. With advanced training, the medical professional would be qualified to work overseas; with basic training, they would not. This strategy is already working in Malawi through its clinical officer training program. Clinical officers are given different training than doctors but take on many responsibilities traditionally reserved for physicians. But we are still a long way from the humanitarian ideal stated by the World Health Organization (WHO) over six decades ago: "The enjoyment of the highest attainable standard of health is one of the fundamental rights of every human being."[25]

Memory's parents did not receive the treatment or diagnosis they would have received if they had lived in almost any developed country. Superior treatment may or may not have had an effect on their physical outcomes, but much of the medical treatment and testing that we assume our loved ones should receive was lacking.

I continue to be surprised when I speak to Malawians about the deaths of their relatives and loved ones. I take the knowledge of "why" an individual dies for granted. I accept this knowledge as a right. So it seems outrageous to me when a girl says, "I don't know how my brother died."

Without expensive tests, diagnoses can be haphazard. Both her parents' deaths were mysterious; there were no definitive diagnoses. Sometimes Memory connects the death of her mother with that of her father. "I sometimes ask myself if my mother had AIDS because at that time, it was not fully known. After my mother died, my father stayed with us three, if not four, years. Most of the time husbands and their wives who are suffering from HIV/AIDS, they die a few years between each other." Memory, and hundreds of thousands of other Malawian orphans, will never know the cause of their parents' deaths.

꒦ After Dorothy's death, Inez stayed on to help care for the children. Grace was little more than a baby and needed constant care. Memory also took on more responsibility. She became serious about her education and about taking care of her siblings. Playing with her friends was no longer a priority. With the death of her mother, she took on the task of cooking for her family. She took maize to the maize mill. She washed the laundry for her father, her brothers, and little Grace. Stephano helped out sometimes, but Memory took on the burden of responsibility.

As Memory's father grew to depend on his eldest daughter, the bond between father and daughter grew too. They would sit and together they would plan the way forward for their family. They discussed the importance of Memory's education and the importance of working hard in school. Memory's father also discouraged her from having boyfriends. "In Malawi having a boyfriend means having sex. My father was very much discouraging me from having boyfriends."

Her father's advice stuck. Memory's days were occupied with responsibilities at home and at school. "I did not have time to go around and socialize with boys and other friends."

Memory joined the Katawa Gospel Choir, and at around the same time, she began raising chickens. Memory had sold eggs before, but now she sold eggs from her family's chickens, and she was in charge of the business: selling the eggs and broiler chickens, as well as collecting and managing the money.

Memory's father did more than encourage Memory's education; he actively supported it. Although the family had very little disposable income, when it came time for Memory to take the national exams at the end of standard eight, her father paid for extra tutoring.

While waiting to learn the results of her exam, Memory went to Viphya Private School in Mzuzu. Memory hoped to go to a girls' school, but without government support, her father couldn't afford that. So when she learned she had been accepted into Lilongwe Girls' Secondary School, Memory was thrilled.

Lilongwe Girls' is a national school; students come from all over Malawi to attend. Since she was attending a national school, the government subsidized Memory's education. Fortunately, it was further subsidized by GABLE, Girls' Attainment in Basic Literacy and Education, a fund set up to help girls receive their secondary education.

When the day came for her to leave Mzuzu, Memory was "halfway happy and halfway scared." It was her first time away from home, and she would be travelling to Lilongwe by herself. Lilongwe is a long way from Mzuzu: 280 kilometres.

Located in the central region, Lilongwe is the capital city of Malawi. It has been the capital of the country since Kamuzu Banda moved the capital from Zomba at the beginning of his presidency. The city has been growing ever since.

Memory was born in Lilongwe, but her parents moved north when she was still small, so she didn't remember the city. "I really wanted my dad to escort me." But when she asked him to come, he responded, "No, you can travel by yourself. Everything will be fine. Lilongwe is a big city, but you'll make it."

He couldn't go with her, but because it was her first trip, Memory's father paid for a coach. Coaches cost more than mini-buses, but they are also more reliable. So, at the age of fifteen, Memory set off for the big city.

After travelling most of the day, she arrived in Lilongwe at four o'clock. Even in the capital city, the darkness descends like a velvet curtain—at six o'clock sharp—on the streets and the people of the city. There are no streetlights in most areas of the capital, and the night is lit only by fire.

I'm reminded of an experience during my first visit to Malawi. I was staying at Memory and Henry's house in Lilongwe. The city is divided into numbered areas, each having its own demographic. Memory and

Henry lived in one of the poorer districts: Area 25. Christie and I had gone shopping. We left the downtown area while it was still light, and even as we drove through Area 25, there was still light in the sky. We didn't realize it right away, but we had taken the wrong minibus. It was a bus that didn't stop at Kababwa School near Memory and Henry's house. By the time Christie turned to me and said that she thought we were on the wrong bus, the streets were unfamiliar. We got off the bus immediately, the driver waving his hand in the general direction of the school. Christie thought she recognized the area, so I put my trust in her and followed. When we exited the bus, the streets were still lit with a glimmer of daylight, but almost immediately that glimmer disappeared. We walked through the darkness, a darkness so complete that our only guides were the sporadic open fires along the roadway. Small groups of people sat and conversed around these fires, looking up as we passed. Between fires, our way descended into darkness. At some point in our journey, I became agonizingly aware of the colour of my skin. Men and women would step from the darkness, and I would not see them until they were next to me. Yet my skin must have appeared like a beacon in the dark to those around me. I felt exposed and vulnerable.

Memory was arriving in the city just two hours before dark, and she didn't know how to find the school. At the bus depot, she asked several people, "Where is Lilongwe Girls' School?"

"It's not very far," they answered.

Fortunately, outside the depot, Memory met another student, and they set off for their new school together.

Moving into Lilongwe Girls' Secondary School marked another change in Memory's life. At her new school there were new hardships and new challenges.

The hostels at Lilongwe Girls' were named after African rivers. Memory's was called the Nile. Each room in the Nile Hostel housed twelve girls, six on one side of the room and six on the other, with a row of wardrobes dividing the room in two. There was little privacy.

The senior girls looked for reasons to intimidate the form one girls. Walking in the school corridors, seniors would tell the younger girls to "sit down" while they passed. In the evenings, the senior girls made the new girls sit on the cold cement floor while they sat on their beds in their rooms. It's the kind of power dynamic that often exists in boarding schools.

The showers and toilets were located in one large room. Many of the showers lacked curtains, but most of the girls didn't care. Most of them didn't close the curtains anyway. One day, on her way to the toilet, Memory passed a senior girl showering in one of the stalls. She didn't think anything about it, but the senior girl saw Memory's intrusion as an excuse to make trouble.

The senior girl went to her friends and said, "Memory saw me while I was bathing." They decided to "sit down with her."

"Why did you go while this one was bathing?"

Memory responded, "I didn't know she was bathing. I was going to the toilet."

"You have to give us the picture of what you saw," they insisted.

Memory refused to draw a picture of the girl, and the senior girls backed off—for a little while. Memory sometimes gave way to the seniors' silly demands, but she was not easily intimidated: "We're all students. We've all paid to come to this place. Why should someone tell me what to do?"

In spite of these challenges, Memory made friends quickly, but she lacked the support of close friends. For awhile she hung out with Hendrina, then Doris, and later Gertrude, but her girlfriends always seemed to have different priorities. They were more interested in boys than in school. Memory knew her friends weren't always going home for the holidays, but they were going somewhere. With men came problems, and Memory didn't want to lose sight of her goals. At the same time, she remembered her father's words: "If you walk with a prostitute, you will end up being a prostitute. When you walk with someone who is wise, you will also be wise."

Eventually, Memory met Annie. Memory and Annie became study partners. Annie was kind and smart. Like Memory, she was serious about her education, and she was good at mathematics. Memory struggled with math, and Annie was able to help her. The two went to church together on Sundays, and Annie shared her extra food with Memory. Having Annie as a friend made the transition to boarding school easier for her, but there was still more sadness and tragedy to come in Memory's life.

⌗ The transition from primary to secondary school is a difficult time for many girls. After primary school, the percentage of girls enrolled in school plunges. Most girls never have the opportunity to go to secondary school.

There are many hidden challenges in secondary education for girls. Once a girl reaches puberty, she must contend with monthly menstruation. This can be a challenge for some girls in primary school, but it becomes an even greater problem in secondary.

If you were to show a rural girl a sanitary pad, she probably wouldn't know what it was. If a girl has the money, she will buy "cotton" to put in her panties during her monthly cycle, but many girls can't afford panties, much less cotton to put inside. Some girls will use rags, but rags are not very effective. Instead, many girls will spend several days out of every month at home "sitting on a rag." UNICEF estimates that throughout Africa, one in ten girls misses school during monthly menstruation, or they drop out of school altogether due to lack of sanitation.[26] Florence Kanyike, the Uganda coordinator for the Forum of Women Educationalists, bluntly describes the problem: "[Girls] miss three or four days of school. They find themselves lagging behind and because they don't perform well, their interest fails. They start to think, 'What are we doing here?'"[27]

Traditional expectations and practices play an important role in a girl's development and her ability to attend school. In the past, after a girl began menstruating, she would undergo an initiation rite. The final portion of the initiation involved seclusion for the girl. Traditionally, on the last night of the seclusion, if the girl was not married, a professional *fisi*, an older man designated to "open the womb" of the girl, came to the girl during the night to perform sexual intercourse. Today this part of the girls' initiation rite is not widely practised, and during my conversations with Malawian women, no one admitted to participating in this ceremony. Instead, girls are now given herbal medicine to "act like a husband and protect her from danger until she is married."[28] It's likely the ceremony is only perpetuated in remote areas.

Malawi's Human Rights Commission is still concerned about the practice. The commission claims, "Girls are threatened with the occurrence of a misfortune to solicit their consent."[29] While the initiation is a violation of the girl's human rights, perhaps the more immediate problem is the chance of unwanted pregnancy or sexually transmitted disease (STD) infection. In a country where nearly 15 per cent of the population is infected with the HIV/AIDS virus, even one sexual encounter of this sort is dangerous. This rite, along with the practice of early marriage and polygyny, has been blamed in part for the high rate of HIV infection among young women. In southern Africa, the rate of infection is three to six times higher for women between the ages of fifteen and twenty-four than for the same age group of men.[30] Early marriage and pregnancy, HIV infection, and lack of privacy all decrease girls' ability to attend secondary school.

While these challenges decrease a girl's likelihood of going to secondary school, a major barrier to those girls who are determined to pursue their education can be a lack of parental support. It's important to be clear: many Malawian parents *are* supportive of their daughters' education, but many are not.

Solstina isn't the only girl I've met whose father could have afforded to send her to secondary school but chose not to. Tawina's father owns a small grocery store in a trading centre near the school. He is not wealthy, but by rural standards, he is well off. Yet he refused to pay Tawina's secondary school fees. Tawina's older sister had completed secondary school, but had gotten married shortly afterwards. Tawina's father didn't want to "waste" his money on another girl's schooling. But she was determined, and Memory recognized that determination and accepted her into APU.

According to Ester Msowoya, the coordinator of the Forum for African Women Educators in Malawi, "When a girl reaches standard eight, we haven't helped that girl. We want the girl to complete the education cycle to finish high school. Once the girl has reached form four, she can get a job. At standard eight, she will just get married."[31]

The completion rate for children in primary school has improved dramatically over the last decade, but the attendance and completion rates for secondary school remain abysmal. A mere 11 per cent of girls and 20 per cent of boys complete secondary school.[32]

Malawi's birth rate stands at 5.7 children per family,[33] but educated girls wait to get married and start their families. In a country with a high population and a small land mass, it's vital that parents reduce the size of their families. Fifty-six per cent of adolescents who lack education begin bearing children in their teens, compared to 20 per cent of adolescents with secondary education or higher. Of course, the health risk to both mother and child is also reduced when mothers wait to have their babies. Other risk factors apply to women who lack secondary education.[34]

In 2010, 53 per cent of women with secondary education used some form of birth control compared to 40 per cent of women with little or no education. Level of education also had a significant impact on whether or not a mother had a health professional present at her last delivery: 89 per cent of women with secondary education compared to only 63 per cent of women with no education. And the trend continues. Eighty-four per cent of children aged twelve to twenty-three months, with mothers who had completed secondary education, received a full course of vaccinations, but 75 per cent of children with mothers who lacked education received the same vaccinations.[35] Girls with a secondary school education have more earning potential, and they raise smaller, healthier families.[36]

A paper written by Xanthe Scharff, founder and executive director of the Advancement of Girls' Education Scholarship Fund, suggested a three-pronged approach to encouraging and supporting secondary education for girls in Malawi:

1. *Joint review and retooling of the current bursary system.*
2. *Promotion and partnership with donors to provide scholarships to disadvantaged girls.*
3. *Implementation of a gender-responsive initiative to improve schooling for secondary school girls.*[37]

These all seem like reasonable actions, but I would suggest a fourth action is necessary to improve the lot of girls in Malawi: the country's cultural paradigm must alter. Paradoxically, that change can only come from education.

It's Memory's belief that if parents are encouraged to keep their girls in school, they will gradually come to realize the importance of education. This has certainly been the case for the parents of the APU girls. While many parents were supportive of their girls from the beginning, many were not. Maria, Solstina, and Lucita's fathers were not supportive of their daughters' schooling, not if it required a monetary investment. Yet they were proven wrong. As more girls finish secondary education and set examples within their communities, more parents will look at their daughters and see their value. The girls of CEAG and APU are trailblazers within their communities, but it could take many more years for the majority of parents to see the value of educating their girls. In the meantime, secondary education is elusive for many Malawian girls.

Grace

GRACE WAS A BABY WHEN HER MOTHER DIED, and she was still very young when her father passed away just over a year later.[1] With her older brothers and sisters, she moved from Mzuzu to her grandparents' village near Kasungu, where she attended her father's funeral and remained, for a time, with her grandparents. But she didn't stay there for long. Grace spent her young life moving from house to house and family to family. Although she asked about her parents, it seemed to her that the answers she received were conflicting and confusing. It wasn't until she was a teenager that she finally accepted the death of her mother and father.

I've spoken to Grace many times over the years. I've seen her grow from an insecure, anxious, and confused girl into a confident, self-assured, and intelligent young woman. I believe I saw my own younger half-sister, Patricia, somewhere in Grace. I wasn't raised with Patricia. While I experienced relative stability and security living with grandparents who loved and cared for me, Patricia spent her childhood moving from house to house and home to home. Like Grace, she has searched for a family identity and struggled to make the

Grace, 2008.

best of a life that got off to a rough start. Maybe this is why I felt a strong maternal protectiveness toward Grace.

When I first met her, Grace was living in Area 25 with Memory and Henry. It was the year Teloni was born, my first trip to Malawi. Grace had recently moved from Area 15, where she'd been living with her aunt and uncle in a house filled with cousins and distant relatives. It was good for Grace to move in with Memory and Henry, but it was another upheaval, another monumental change in a life filled with monumental changes.

On that first trip, I asked Grace if she knew her family's story. She told me about going to school in Mulanje. During that visit, Grace was fourteen years old, and she still spoke in a rushed, stuttering voice: "When I was in Mulange, I was a child. When I was in standard two, I had a friend, a girl. She asked me a lot of questions. She asked me, 'Where are your parents?' When I said, 'I don't know where are my parents,' she said, 'You are lying. I'll go to your house and see.' From that time she said, 'Grace let's go to your home.' So I said, 'Let's go.'"

Grace and the girl walked to Grace's house where Grace lived with her sister, Lucy, and her cousin, Dixon. When they got there, Lucy was not home, but Dixon was. They sat in the sitting room. Dixon said, "Who is this one?"

Grace said, "This one is my friend. She wants to know where my parents live."

Dixon asked Grace, "What did you tell your friends?"

"This one was asking me where was my parents, and I answered, 'I don't know.' She said, 'You are lying.'"

Dixon looked worried. "Grace's parents are at Kasungu."

And Grace's friend said, "Grace, I'm going."

"Okay, we'll meet tomorrow."

After this conversation, Grace began wondering. My parents are in Kasungu, but I come from Kasungu. Why didn't I see them? Later, she asked Lucy, "Are my parents in Kasungu?" But Lucy didn't answer.

Before moving to Mulanje, Grace had lived with her grandparents and other family members in their village near Kasungu. It had been a fractured life for Grace. She would be living with her grandparents when an aunt would go to her grandmother and say, "I dreamt about her father and her father is telling me that I should look after this child."

Her stay might last for a week or two before another family might come and offer to take Grace in. But, again, before long, the aunt would come back and say, "I dreamt about her mother and her mother says I should keep the child. So give me the child."

Grace was always living with family, but she never had a place of her own. After two years in Mulanje, Grace moved back to the village to resume this nomadic life, but she didn't stay there for long.

Memory explains the situation this way: "The village was not a good environment for Grace because she was not encouraged to go to school. Many of the children of her agement would drop out and some were just staying at home."

Memory was visiting her aunt in Area 15 when Esther asked her, "Where is Grace?"

Memory responded, "She's in the village."

Esther felt sorry for Grace, so she said to Memory, "If you bring Grace here, we'll look after her."

In Malawi, the terms "aunt" and "uncle" do not always denote a familial connection. Memory's Aunt Esther and Uncle James had been family friends of Memory's parents. Calling them "aunt" and "uncle" was a sign of respect, not of blood relation.

So Grace moved to Lilongwe to stay with her aunt and uncle. They lived in Area 15, a middle-class area of the city with large walled yards near the city's centre. Grace's uncle worked for an NGO, so he made a decent wage, but the family lived in poverty. Within the walls of the three-bedroom home lived a collection of sons and daughters, grandchildren, and cousins. Depending upon the need, the number fluctuates, but it is always over twenty. They are all there because they have nowhere else to go. Esther and James are kindhearted and giving and would never turn away a relative in need. The home has city conveniences: a TV in the sitting room, a fridge and running water in the kitchen, but at night, the bedrooms are full, as is the sitting room, while the older boys sleep in an outbuilding. With James's wage there is rarely enough food to go around. It isn't the image of a middle-class North American household.

Even in Lilongwe, Grace moved around. For a time, she stayed with cousins in Area 25. Then she moved back to Area 15. By this time, Memory was enrolled in the African Bible College (ABC) and was able to visit Grace on weekends. Esther and James were kind and loving, but Grace didn't get along with her cousins so well. With competition for resources often comes rivalry.

When I first spoke to Grace, I asked her what it was like to live in so many houses with so many people. She recounted this story: "At Area 15 I would go to school with their children, but when I'm back home, when I want to start the readings, my cousin shouted at me: 'You, Grace, don't read. You have many things to work.' I asked them, 'Can you give me the work so I can do this thing?' They told me, 'Have you forgotten that your uncle told us that you can't do work because you are still young.' Then I ask them, 'What can I do?

I'm wasting my time here.' And one of them said, 'Grace, shut up your mouth. Why are you talking like that?'"

Many people who have grown up in large families will recognize this sort of bullying. It's the kind of dynamic that comes about when family members want to ensure their place in the family's hierarchy. As the youngest in a large extended family, I recognize this hurtful prodding from my own experiences. Yet I was the cherished child of my grandparents, and no matter what else happened, I never doubted they would be there for me. It was a different situation for Grace.

Grace's aunt tried to make Grace feel like a part of the family. One day, Grace asked her about her mother. Not wanting to upset Grace, her aunt replied, "No, your mom, she is still alive." Then she said, "Okay, you should call me your mommy." But this made Grace even unhappier, and she began to cry. "No, I know you're my aunt."

Memory thought Grace might do better in a boarding school where she could concentrate on her studies. Memory found a school in Mchingi. That's where Grace spent the next two years, coming home to Area 15 for weekends and holidays.

At the boarding school, Grace's friends often talked about their families. Sometimes they brought photo albums with family pictures. "Grace," they would say, "show us your parents. Show us the pictures that you have." But Grace had no pictures, so these demands made her uncomfortable. She did not know what to say to her friends.

On weekends, Grace would see Memory at Area 15, and one time Memory took Grace to visit their grandparents in the village. Grace remembers that trip: "They were surprised to see me because I had been there when I was very little and now was very big. I went to the borehole with my friends, and there were many people taking water from there. A woman asked, 'Who is this one?' And other people who know me said, 'That is Grace. She came from Lilongwe.' And other people said, 'Oh, I remember that little girl, but now she is big. When her parents died, she was very young. Her mother died when Grace was an infant.'"

Once again, Grace was confused. It seemed like no one would tell her the truth. Memory and Grace took a minibus back to Lilongwe. As they were driving, Grace looked out the window at a car with a family inside. This prompted Grace to ask Memory, "Where are our parents?"

Memory responded, "We have no parents. Our parents are dead."

Grace couldn't believe it. She started crying: "What! My parents are dead?"

"Your mother died when you were still an infant. Your dad died when I was in form one at Lilongwe Girls' School. He died because he was sick for so long in the hospital. Then he died."

Grace said, "I have to see their pictures because I can't even point to the picture of my dad."

But Memory said, "I can't even remember what they were like. Their pictures are gone."

This was difficult for Grace to accept, and for a long time she couldn't.

Recently, Grace reflected on her feelings from those years: "I used to say my parents were out of this country. I had nothing to tell my friends. I used to think they would come next year. They will come next year. When I saw my friends with their parents, I used to cry to myself."

After their trip to the village, Memory went back to ABC and Grace went back to boarding school. But Grace wasn't doing well in school. Instead of going to class, she said she was sick and stayed in her room. Memory went to the school and spoke to the teachers. "If you have a home, take her there and stay with her, but she can't stay in a boarding school because in a boarding school she doesn't concentrate on her education. Weekends she's well. Monday through Friday, she's sick."

It wasn't long before Memory was able to do just that. Once she and Henry married, Memory was able to offer a home to Grace. It was the beginning of Grace's new life.

After her graduation from APU in 2011, I spoke to Grace. I asked her how she felt about the difficulties she had faced and her ability to overcome those obstacles. This time she didn't rush her words. Her voice was calm and deliberate: "Once I go to college, I don't want to think anymore about the troubles that have been passing through my life. I just want to be somewhere that I can change everything that has been happening in my life. It should be a dream. I don't want to pass through troubles anymore, and I'm ready to work hard. If I can actually do something good in my life, I won't need to rely on anybody else. I will try my best to forget and to make my dreams true. I don't want to be the same as I was in past years."

6

What It Means To Be an Orphan

Orphan child return to your home
　　your father is calling you…
Orphan child return to your home,
　　it is foolish to delay
Return, return, return, return
　　to your home…

—Excerpt from a popular Tonga funeral song[1]

AFTER COMPLETING THE FIRST TERM of form one, Memory travelled home to Mzuzu to visit her family.² Memory already knew her father was ill, but once she saw him, she realized he was dying.

Before Memory left for Lilongwe, her father had been in a car accident and sustained internal injuries. He had spent time in the hospital but was released when the doctors decided they could do nothing to help him. There, his condition worsened. He was wasted and thin. Just as her mother had tried to encourage her as she lay dying, her father tried to do the same. He insisted, "I'll get well. I'll get well." But Memory knew better. Duncan Chazeza slept most of the time, but when he was awake, he and Memory would talk like they had in happier times, and he would encourage Memory in her studies.

Their time together was short—even before her break was over, her father returned to the hospital. This time with what the doctors thought was malaria. They soon changed his diagnosis to tuberculosis (TB), but they really didn't know. Memory wonders to this day if he died from AIDS, but as with her mother, she will never know for certain.

Memory feared for her father, but she also feared for herself and her family. Her family was poor, and Memory wondered what awaited her brothers and sisters if her father died. She also wondered who would pay for her education.

Having lived in the northern part of Malawi for their entire lives, Memory and her siblings weren't close to their extended family. On her mother's side, there was only one aunt, and she was a third wife, abused by her husband. On her father's side of the family, there were plenty of relatives but none that Memory knew or trusted. She had only been to her father's village once: for her mother's funeral.

After she returned to school, Memory wrote to her father, but someone else wrote back, sending her banal pleasantries. Being isolated from her family made the situation more difficult for Memory. She knew her father was going to die, but that didn't make his death any easier.

Memory had been back in class for only a few weeks when her cousin Dixon came to the school. "We should go to Kasungu and visit our father," he said.

Memory was confused. "We should go home, but my father is in Mzuzu." Dixon replied, "No, he's moved. He's in Kasungu." And then he was quiet.

Memory suspected that Dixon was keeping something from her, but together they travelled to Kasungu by minibus. Just before they reached the village, Dixon told Memory that her father was dead. Tragically, when Memory and Dixon arrived at the village, it was late afternoon, and they had missed the funeral.

Memory's father left words for her: "You should be courageous. You're the only one who can take care of your brothers and sisters." Despite the confidence he had in his daughter, Memory was still young. Now that the funeral was over, there was nothing for her to do but go back to school.

Memory's home in Mzuzu was emptied of the family's possessions, and a meeting was called in the village. The children would be split up among the family.

Throughout much of Malawian society, "uncles" have a position of responsibility. The Chewa is a matrilineal tribe. While roles are changing, it is the mother's family, and uncles in particular, who are primarily responsible for the well-being of a family's children.

Danny went to stay with an uncle. Jeffrey was a teacher, but he lived in a remote area of Kasungu. Bodwin went to live with another uncle, Jackson. Jackson was a clinic officer, and he lived in a remote part of Mchinji called Namatete. Stephano and Grace, the oldest and the youngest, went to stay in the village with their grandparents. That left Lucy and Memory.

Their Uncle John, from Area 18 in Lilongwe, stepped forward when he heard that Memory's father had passed away. Memory's parents had helped him out many years before when he was young and first moved to Lilongwe. They had found him a job and assisted him until he was able to provide for himself. Memory's uncle was now a successful businessman, selling cars and travelling back and forth from South Africa. He remembered those early days before he became a success, so he travelled to Memory's home village to speak with her grandfather. "I'm going to take care of Memory and Lucy. I'll pay for each and everything, for her food and everything," he said. But Memory knew none of this. She was at Lilongwe Girls' School.

Before her uncle stepped forward, Memory endured a difficult period in her life, a period of uncertainty. She wondered who would feed her, who would clothe her. She didn't know that while she was attending classes, her fate and the fates of her brothers and sisters were being decided in the village. "My hostel was upstairs, and I still remember two windows. I would go and look out the windows and think about throwing myself down so I should die."

Memory had no close friends at school. She had roommates and study friends and walking-to-class friends, but no one she could talk to about deeply personal issues. Even so her schoolmates rallied around her. It seemed to Memory that every time she became despondent, standing by the upstairs window, one of her school friends would walk by and say, "Oh Memory, why don't we do something?" Sometimes her friends asked her to come to a meeting of the Student Christian Organization of Malawi (SCOM). SCOM brands itself as "an indigenous interdenominational [Christian] organization committed to the evangelization, discipleship and training of students."[3]

One day, Memory was particularly despondent. She was sitting, once again, at the window when a form four girl, Patricia, came to see her. That same day, Lilongwe Technical College was hosting a SCOM conference. "Come with us, Memory," Patricia said. That day represented a turning point in Memory's life.

To Memory, the preacher at the conference was speaking directly to her. "If you're in trouble, try God. Try to believe that God can help." And he read from Psalms (68:5): "A father of the fatherless is God in his holy habitation."

These words spoke to Memory and her situation. She thought, "Let me just believe that. I need someone who can be a father. I will try to believe that God is going to help my situation and things are going to be better." Not long after, her Uncle John came to the school.

It was a Saturday. Memory's uncle went to the office first so he could explain the situation to the administration. Then he went to find Memory. "I'm your uncle. From today, I'll take care of you. I'll be your guardian, and I'll do everything for you." He left Memory with groceries, the suitcase her father had promised her before he died, and a lot to think about.

To Memory, the appearance of her uncle, a man she had never met, seemed like a miracle, a divine intervention. Here was the solution to her fears and anxieties. She looked forward to the next Saturday when he would take her to see her new home.

Memory's uncle was prepared to provide for all of Memory's needs, but his wife was cold from the beginning. When Memory went back to school she was not at peace. "I was very much scared with the aunt because even if my uncle is excited to take care of me, it is normally a woman who is in control in the house. I was worried about my welfare."

Lucy was not staying with her uncle yet, and Memory didn't know where her other siblings were living. The more she thought about her own problems, the more she wondered what her brothers and sisters were experiencing. "I didn't know how they were being treated, and I worried about Grace. She was just a little girl." Memory found these thoughts circling in her head, and again she thought about throwing herself from the window.

Memory became so sick that she couldn't attend classes. Instead, she hid in her room during the day—sleeping. Finally, the matron took her to the hospital, where the doctors ran tests, but they couldn't find anything wrong with her. Because Memory was sweating and her heart was racing, the doctors thought she might be developing a heart problem. They prescribed phenobarbital and sent her back to school.

Memory returned to class, but her condition worsened. The phenobarbital made her symptoms worse. Her thoughts were out of control. She went back to hiding in her room, but when her friends came to the hostel after classes, they made noise, and Memory could barely stand it. She was taken back to the hospital.

This time the doctors thought Memory might be pregnant. Once they confirmed she wasn't, they thought she might have tuberculosis. They took her off the phenobarbital, and that improved her condition, but it seemed that no one considered her situation. Memory was a young girl with an uncertain future who was mourning the loss of her father, her last parent.

Dixon came to visit and spoke to Memory about what she was experiencing. "What if they give me a one-week break? Maybe I should go home," Memory suggested. So Dixon asked the doctors to write to the school and recommend that Memory go home for a week of rest. They agreed.

Memory went to her uncle's house. She had a great deal of time to herself because both her aunt and uncle worked during the day. Memory had time to think, but instead of getting stuck on her problems, she spent her time looking for solutions.

Memory remembered listening to the preacher. She thought about his words and how they had made her feel: as if she were not alone, as if her life had a purpose. She remembered how each time she thought of killing herself, a friend appeared to stop her. Her parents were gone now, but Memory knew her uncle would provide for her. It occurred to her that her uncle had come to see her the week after she heard the preacher speak—the week after she became a new believer. "God does exist to me," she reasoned. "I tried him and somebody came who has more than my parents could provide. If God wants it, one way or another I'm going to die, but I'm alive. God is going to see me through all these problems. I need to trust that God is going to help me." These thoughts were a turning point for Memory. Recalling the sequence of events allowed

Memory to reason through her situation. She would go back to school, and she would survive.

The girls at Memory's school were sympathetic to her circumstances: "People were really touched to see that I had lost my father and that my mother had already died." Memory made some new friends, and with their support and her new outlook, Memory's spirits lifted. It was around this time that Memory became friends with Cattriss.

Cattriss was tall, beautiful, and bright, and the two found they had a lot in common. They were in the same classroom, and they were both active members of SCOM. They soon realized they both came from poor families, so their struggles were often similar. They became prayer partners and close friends. Having Cattriss as a close friend and confidante made school easier for Memory, and she found her spirits returning. She enjoyed learning once again, and it seemed as though her life might have a purpose after all.

While school was becoming easier, living with her aunt and uncle was not. By now Lucy was staying with Memory at their uncle's home in Area 18, so they were able to encourage each another and alleviate some of the stress caused by family dynamics. Most of the time, the girls were away at school anyway, and when they were home, the house was at peace if their uncle was there. "If he saw something my aunt was doing to us, he would say something." But if he was away on business, they were at the mercy of their aunt's bitterness and anger.

Memory and Lucy's aunt wasn't physically violent, but Memory describes her behaviour as "psychological torture." As with most Malawian city homes, their house was surrounded by a high brick wall and protected from the world by a solid sliding metal gate. When the girls were at home, their aunt wouldn't let them leave the enclosure; they were trapped.

When there were visitors—and visitors came to the house nearly every day—instead of introducing the two girls by their names, their aunt introduced them as "orphans." But she introduced her own children by their names, so Memory and Lucy wondered, "Why is she using that name of orphan?"

Keeping Memory and Lucy in the sitting room with the visitors, their aunt would say, "We keep orphans here. You should give them advice." Her words implied an accusation, and the visitors would shout and laugh: "You should be good girls. Look at what your aunt is helping you with. You need to be respectful." None of this advice was said with love; rather, it seemed to be said for the purpose of belittling the girls and putting them in their place.

While Memory and Lucy struggled to get by in Lilongwe, their siblings were also finding their new lives difficult. Danny was living in a remote village with his Uncle Jeffrey and his wife. "My uncle and his wife, I've never heard anything bad about them," Memory told me. But Danny must have been struggling in his own way because he was only in form two when he began drinking and smoking. In Malawi, smoking is a sign of bad behaviour and delinquency. Around this time, Danny also became disrespectful toward his aunt and uncle. Finally, his uncle would no longer support him.

Bodwin's situation was similar to Memory and Lucy's. Like Danny, he was living in a remote area, and his uncle was away at work most of the time. "When my aunt cooked good meals like beef, Bodwin was told to go into the garden and get greens to eat. One day my uncle saw that. He was very angry and chased away his wife. That was a good thing." Like many wives, when asked to take in their husband's relatives, she worried that Bodwin would use up their meager resources, resources she hoped to preserve for herself and her children. She might have hoped that by abusing him, Bodwin would turn mean and want to leave. If that was her intent, she failed.

After the wife was gone, Bodwin was treated better, but his uncle didn't want to pay for Bodwin's secondary education. Rather, his uncle wanted him to keep repeating standard eight because his marks were not good enough for him to be selected for a national secondary school. Bodwin was quiet, a respectful boy, and would not have complained.

Stephano, the eldest, was struggling too. He was staying in the village with Grace. He watched while his family's possessions—plates, pots, chairs, beds—were passed around to various relatives. He noticed that one of his relatives, one who was not helping to care for the children, applied for government money to care for the orphans. Stephano became frustrated. If he tried to talk to someone about the money or his family's possessions, they stopped him. He was labelled "troublesome."

Growing up amidst uncertainty and rejection and feeling as though a great injustice was going on around him, Stephano became angry and sad. He dropped out of secondary school and began drinking.

When I heard Stephano's story, I thought, "If I were in his position, I would be hurt and angry too." His despondency seemed understandable, so I put the question to Memory: Was Stephano acting reasonably?

"This is the stuff that he's been brought up with, and he doesn't have a voice to convince everyone that these things belong to him. At the same time, it wasn't reasonable because he was a mature person. He was supposed to think this would not take him anywhere. After all, these things will come to an end, but if he continues his education he will become a changed person. He did not think on those lines."

Initially, Grace was staying with Stephano and her grandparents in the village. But because of her age, she moved from family to family and village to village—never living in one place for more than a few months. Finally, she settled with her cousin Dixon in Mulanje, where she started primary school. Dixon was also looking after his sister, Lydia, a little girl the same age as Grace.

Grace was unhappy living with Dixon. She felt he favoured his sister, so she spent less and less time at home. She went to friends' houses after school, and she ate her meals with the neighbours. That was too much for Dixon. He became upset with her behaviour and sent Grace back to the village. She had lived in Mulanje for fewer than three years.

There is a popular Chewa proverb that goes like this:

Mwana wa mnzako ndi wako jemwe
Ukuchenjera manga udzadya naye.

Your friend's child is your own child
If you are flexible (or fast) with your hands
You will benefit from him/her.[4]

In this proverb, "flexible (or fast) with your hands" means to be
generous. The Chewa and other tribes of Malawi have a strong tradition
of helping to raise their relatives' and communities' children in times of
hardship. There is a web of familial relationships, bonds, and obligations
that serve as a tight social safety net for orphans and other unfortunates.
Despite some of the stories I have told and will tell within the pages of
this book, Malawian kinship bonds are far stronger than anything I've
observed or experienced in North America. Of course, this net is vitally
important in a country with minimal government resources, but it's
often not enough.

Life expectancy has improved dramatically over the last decade: rising
from less than forty years in 2004[5] to nearly sixty in 2014.[6] But there are
still many opportunities for death in Malawi: tuberculosis, malaria, lower
respiratory infections, and perinatal complications top the list. Many
children never even make it to adulthood. These illnesses and many
others have been at work in Malawi and other countries for millennia,
but the most recent harbinger of death is HIV/AIDS.

The AIDS virus originated on the African continent and has been
gradually making its way into households and communities for decades,
slowly picking up momentum. In 1985, Malawi reported its first AIDS
case. Unfortunately, this was during the Banda Government's reign.

Banda was a man with strong, puritanical values, and he was reluctant to recognize the problem. Few Malawians were properly diagnosed,
and there was little public education on prevention until he ceded power
in 1994.[7] By then, HIV/AIDS had become a full-blown outbreak of apoca-
lyptic proportions.

For reasons that are probably now self-evident—lack of proper diagnosis and treatment for most struck by the disease—statistics for the number of yearly deaths due to AIDS vary widely. According to the Joint United Nations Programme on HIV/AIDS (UNAIDS), sixty-eight thousand died from the epidemic in 2007. That number had fallen to forty-six thousand in 2012,[8] but to this day, AIDS remains the leading cause of death for adult Malawians.

HIV/AIDS primarily strikes young adults: the most productive, the most sexually active, the parents of the country. According to UNAIDS—in 2012—there were 770,000 AIDS orphans in Malawi.[9] Within a country of only seventeen million people, caring for this many orphaned children is an enormous burden. Grandparents and other relatives are sometimes able to take in orphaned children, but as Stephen Lewis pointed out during the 2005 Massey Lectures: "When the grandmothers die, there's no one coming up behind, and so you have the phenomenon of what we call 'child-headed households,' or 'sibling families,' where the oldest child is the head of the household, looking after his or her siblings."[10] There is no doubt that Memory's siblings suffered a great deal as a result of their parents' deaths, but when one considers the larger context—the poverty, the sickness, the family tragedy—the solidarity with which Memory's extended family rallied around Dorothy and Duncan's children is remarkable, taking them into households that could barely support their own. They may have suffered at the hands of jealous spouses or lacked the support they would have received from their own parents, but they were never cast aside.

Wiseman Chijere Chirwa writes about the "social rupture" that occurs when the existing system of care is burdened beyond its capacity to cope: "When the nuclear family becomes incapable of providing care...the responsibility is increasingly assumed by the extended family through the 'economy of affection.'" Chirwa goes on to discuss the expanding ripple pattern of support systems within the extended family, the community, the state, and, finally, the international community that is in turn regulated by "legal instruments and human rights standards governing the

A young boy sells sugar cane by the side of the road, 2007.

care of children. Social rupture occurs when HIV/AIDS attacks weaken and destroy the inner circle, and the effects spread outwards until they affect society at large."[11] This is the tragedy that has come to Malawi and much of Africa.

The majority of Malawian orphans find themselves living with extended family or living in NGO-run orphanages. Orphans living in orphanages often have access to more food, better sleeping conditions, more schooling, cleaner water, and superior sanitation than children living in foster homes with extended family. Since the government of Malawi largely stays out of the running of orphanages, the reason for the superior conditions is found in the rules guiding the formation of orphanages run by NGOs, faith-based charities, and foreign donor countries. In some cases, the standards for the orphanages exceed the living conditions in the surrounding communities.

This might sound idyllic, but there is a downside. The number of orphanage placements falls far short of the demand, and only the neediest are taken into orphanage care. The government is unable to contribute much more than coordination services, and Malawian orphans who have no family with whom they can live are often dependent upon resources coming from outside the country.[12]

While there are reports of foster children sleeping with livestock, waking early to perform chores, and consuming inadequate nutrition, such conditions don't necessarily denote abuse. The majority of Malawians live in extreme poverty; children do sleep with livestock, they do wake early to perform chores, and the majority of the population does lack adequate nutrition, so these conditions are not unusual and not restricted to orphans.

While there is purposeful cruelty within many foster homes, much of the lack of care comes from limited resources. We come back to the "social rupture" that Chirwa describes in his study. Resources were limited in the country before the HIV/AIDS epidemic; the epidemic has strained those resources further.

In Lilongwe, Esther and James took in both Lucy and Grace at different times while they were teenagers, and Memory has also spent time living at their home, yet their house was already filled to overflowing with relatives. Esther and James are not related to Lucy and Grace. They are old friends of Memory's parents who felt a responsibility to the children. Memory and her siblings refer to James and Esther as uncle and aunt out of respect and love.

James works for an NGO and, while he doesn't make a good wage by North American standards, he makes enough to support himself, his wife, and family. But James doesn't earn enough to support the twenty-plus dependents—children, grandchildren, nieces, and nephews—living in his house at any given time. James and Esther are generous people, so they opened their home to Memory and her siblings. There were many times when members of the household went hungry, not out of neglect but simply because there was not enough for everyone.

I was deeply moved by a story Grace wrote about living with her aunt and uncle. She recalled the coconut biscuits her uncle brought home with him from work. The coconut biscuits I've purchased while in Malawi come in small packages and sell for around eighty kwacha. They're inexpensive and tasty. Her uncle would often share his biscuits with the children.

For a time, her aunt and uncle experienced financial difficulties, and James stopped bringing home coconut biscuits. Grace missed the biscuits, so when her uncle brought a package of coconut biscuits and gave her one she was happy. But when he told her she couldn't have a second, she began to cry.

"Why are you crying?" her aunt asked her.

"I want coconut."

"Grace, why are you behaving like a rich person? I told you already that I haven't any money," her uncle said.

Her aunt added, "Your parents have never left money for you to buy coconut biscuits. You should be thankful for what you are receiving from us."

Grace told me she no longer likes coconut biscuits because she felt like she had disappointed her aunt and uncle.[13]

Malawians have a strong tradition of supporting each other in times of need. Children are the responsibility of the community, not just the parents. Sometimes an entire village will pitch in to care for orphaned children. There is a strong sense of communalism and a deep regard for extended family that is not always found in the typical nuclear family living in North America.

That is the case in a small village in the Dedza district, where the community is working together to care for a number of orphans. Village headman, Kamwala, says, "It has now become a norm for families around the village to take in orphans. It does not matter whether they are related to them or not. I adopted three children to set an example." The initiative includes volunteers who help care for the children. Georgina Kagwa is one of the volunteers. "We hold village meetings to ensure that all orphans are treated well," she says.[14] Not all orphans are so fortunate. Many find they have no choice but to turn to begging, and in some cases prostitution, to survive.

Using the term "prostitution" might be misleading, so I will clarify. Prostitution may conjure up the image of hookers clad in leather mini-skirts and black stilettos walking the seedy streets of a large North American city. Here I'm using the term to define the act of exchanging sex for goods or money. In this sense, prostitution can be seen on a continuum. At one end of the continuum are the single women who occasionally sleep with men in exchange for meals, trinkets, and a temporary boost of self-esteem, in the middle are the women who are taken care of by out-of-town "boyfriends," and at the other end are the bar women and freelance prostitutes for whom prostitution is a way of life and their primary source of income.

It isn't my purpose to delve into the profession of prostitution but rather to point out the lack of choice and opportunity that many Malawian girls and women face. It is an especially great tragedy that, in many cases, girls are so powerless and desperate that they must sell their bodies for a meal or become a second wife because they simply have no other option.

Fortunately, Memory never became so desperate that she had to contend with these kinds of choices, and despite her aunt's unsympathetic attitude toward the girls, Memory and Lucy were both grateful for their uncle's support. When Memory and Lucy were at home, they did everything they could to help around the house. They helped with the cooking; they swept and mopped the floors; they washed the laundry. With time, their aunt's attitude toward them changed, and once Memory's uncle became ill, her relationship with her aunt changed dramatically.

Memory was beginning form four when her uncle's health began deteriorating. On a weekend visit home, Memory was surprised when her aunt welcomed her warmly: "Memory, how are you?" Later that evening, her aunt said, "I think we should be having prayers at night before we go to bed."

In the past, her aunt had mocked her for praying and singing Christian songs, so Memory asked her, "Why do you want to pray?"

She replied, "Your uncle is sick."

Memory's uncle didn't appear ill. He was still going to work every day, but at night he wasn't sleeping well, and sometimes he fainted.

Memory couldn't stay long at her uncle's house that time. She returned to school but came back home for the next school holiday. By then, her uncle's condition had worsened. His fainting became a regular occurrence. He fainted when he was in bed, when he was walking, and sometimes while he was driving.

It's difficult for Memory to recall the details of her uncle's sickness. She was still going to school, and she wasn't privy to all that happened in the household. But whenever they could, she and Lucy went home to help with their uncle's care. By this time, John was no longer able to work, so when they could, the girls stayed with their uncle while their aunt was at work. They cooked him porridge and prepared the water for his bath. John and his wife employed a young houseboy, Peter, and he was able to help too.

Memory's uncle went to see the doctors at the hospital, but Memory has no knowledge of their diagnoses. As time went on, John began to suffer from dementia. He would walk outside naked. Peter would rush after him, wrap him in a sheet, and gently walk him back into the house, all the while speaking kindly and offering encouragement.

It wasn't long before John couldn't move from his bed. He could no longer eat solid food, and Memory fed him juice and other liquids. Soon he developed bedsores, and Memory was dismayed to see that her aunt was not always changing the bed linens when they were soiled. He was moved to the hospital.

For a long time Memory had hoped that her uncle's health would improve, but it was apparent that he was dying. Memory and Lucy prepared food for their aunt to take to the hospital, and their aunt came to rely upon them. She also began showing them love. Although Memory knew the source of this love lay in her aunt's need for their support, Memory is not one to hold grudges, and she accepted her aunt's affection with gratitude.

Memory's uncle died shortly after she completed form four. Memory had loved her uncle and would miss him, but she was also worried because she no longer had anyone to pay for her education. Before he became sick, he had said, "I will take you to school once you are finished form four. I will pay for your courses." Now, Memory realized, that would never happen. But in spite of John's death, one positive experience occurred during form four: Memory met Audrey.

In Malawi, when someone dies, family and friends gather for their funeral and internment. A second ceremony might take place a year or even more after the initial funeral. The interval gives the family time to put money aside for a headstone. At this second gathering, the headstone is revealed to the deceased person's family and close friends.

Memory had just finished writing her MSCEs when she was called home to her village to take part in the unveiling of her parents' headstones. Memory had not seen her brothers and sisters, except for Lucy, for four years. It was a difficult visit for Memory. Bodwin looked at her as if she were a stranger. Stephano was the oldest, so they recognized one another, but they had lost the closeness they once had. Grace had been very young the last time the two had seen each other, so she had no recollection of her sister. She acted shy, running away and peeking around the corner to look at Memory. It was a disappointing reunion and served as a reminder of the time when they had all lived together as a family. There was little time for the siblings to become reacquainted. Memory was only in the village for a short time before she felt compelled to return to Lilongwe to help care for her uncle. But, during her stay, she needed to take care of family business in Kasungu. To travel to Kasungu, Memory took a minibus.

Minibuses are chaotic and crowded. Passengers get on and other passengers shuffle over to create space. People are squeezed in thigh-to-thigh, and when it seems like no one else can fit, the driver will stop for more passengers standing by the roadside. The conductor will jump out and beckon the men and women inside. This was particularly true before the minibus industry became regulated. Buses were so crowded that children were pushed in through the windows to allow for more passengers—usually to the groans and grumblings of the other commuters.

On this particular bus ride, Memory saw a white woman sitting in front of her. She noticed that the woman's purse had fallen to the floor of the bus. She leaned forward and tapped the woman on the shoulder. "Excuse me. You dropped your purse."

The woman turned, and seeing her purse, said, "Oh, thank you so much. All my things are in that purse. I don't know what I would have done if I'd lost it." Then she said, "My name is Audrey. Who are you?"

"My name is Memory."

"Are you from this area?" the woman asked.

"Yes, only I've just come to stay. I live in Lilongwe with my uncle."

"Do you go to school?"

"I just sat for my MSCE exams."

"Your English is different from the people in this area," said Audrey. And she began to tell Memory about the Canadian-funded school located near Memory's home village where she was volunteering. She explained the problems they were encountering, and said, "You know what? Do you mind coming to help us?"

"How am I going to help? I've just finished form four. I don't have any experience."

Audrey replied, "You've gone to girls' secondary school. We don't know how to run a girls' secondary school, so it would be a privilege if we could have you to help us do this."

Memory couldn't commit to helping just then, but she said to Audrey, "Okay, but I won't be staying here. I'm going back to Lilongwe to my uncle. He is seriously sick in the hospital, and he promised to send me for a course, so I don't see myself staying here."

Memory and Audrey exchanged addresses and left each other in town, but later, after returning to the village, Memory visited Audrey at the school's volunteer house, where they chatted about the school and Memory's plans for the future. Soon Memory returned to Lilongwe, but it was not long before Memory's uncle passed away.

Now that her uncle was dead, there was no one to pay for her post-secondary education. Although her relationship with her aunt had improved, Memory was not at ease in her company. She couldn't stay with her aunt, so she weighed her options. Jobs were scarce and paid poorly, but she didn't want to get married. She wasn't ready to give up on her education.

She recalled a church sermon from a few months before. As Memory sat in the pew listening to his words, the pastor had spoken about the importance of loving one another and helping each another. He had spoken about the orphans living at an orphanage in Mchingi. He had explained that the orphanage didn't just need money; it needed volunteers to help bathe the children and cook their meals.

Memory had been moved by the pastor's words, and she had thought, "Even me, I need to do that. I don't have money. I don't have clothes to give those kids, but I have hands. I can cook for the kids. I can clean the place." For Memory, it was a pledge, a promise, that once she had finished school, she would offer her free services to people. She was still a student then, and her uncle needed her, but when the time was right, she would fulfill her promise. That pledge would decide Memory's future.

After her uncle passed away, Memory began thinking about Audrey's offer and her promise to God. "I think I should stay in the village with my grandparents. I think I should go home and help Audrey."

Chifundo

ON THE NIGHT OF MAY 6, 1990, Chifundo's mother waited in fear for her child to be born.[1] As her contractions grew in strength, she listened to the bombing and gunfire outside the small rural hospital. She was listening to the last gasp of nearby Mozambique's sixteen-year civil war spilling into her peaceful homeland of Malawi. While her head ached from the blasts and her bed rattled with each shockwave, it was small consolation for Chifundo's young mother that Mozambique was a country nearing peace.

The umbilical cord was hardly cut and the afterbirth barely pulled from her body when Chifundo's mother fled into the night with her newborn daughter. "She should be Chifundo," whispered her mother into the darkness. In Chichewa, *chifundo* means "mercy."

Chifundo is the second-born of five children. She came to *Atsikana Pa Ulendo* in 2008 as part of the first intake of girls. By that time, her older brother had already dropped out of school due to lack of funds, so Chifundo knows that without APU, she would be out of school and married, perhaps with children of her own.

Chifundo and her siblings live with her grandparents, subsistence farmers who barely grow enough maize and beans to feed themselves, much less their many grandchildren. It's a common tale throughout Malawi. Orphaned children raised by a much older generation.

Chifundo's father died in 2004 after being ambushed by a group of men. He had just been paid for his job, and the men who jumped him must have known he had money. Instead of taking his money and leaving him be, they beat him to death—and took his money. His family was left to fend for itself. Just three years later, Chifundo lost her mother.

I asked Chifundo how her mother died, and she quite frankly replied, "It's another one who killed her through magic."

"Why do you think your mother was a target?" I asked.

"They are jealous. That's why they do those things. They put medicine in her way, and she walked too fast, and she just stepped in the medicine. After that, she had a headache, and then she died three days later."

Now Chifundo wants to get a job so she can help her family. She wants to be a policewoman.

It's difficult to believe, but even though she is orphaned and desperately poor, many people wish her ill. "And now they just do bad things to me because I'm in school, and they are not going to school."

People tell her: "You should just marry. You are just wasting your time." Or they say, "Ahh. You are pregnant."

But Chifundo remains strong. She says, "But it's not true, and me, I just leave them."

I have tried to understand the "village" attitude toward education. My observations have led me to believe that the problem with many foreign aid projects, especially those directed toward Africans, has been an attitude of "we know best." So I do my best to understand, in the hope that I can transfer whatever insight I gain to the reader.

Malawian culture demands that everyone works together toward a common goal: survival. Family helps family. Grandparents raise grandchildren and the majority survive through a sense of common purpose. Perhaps when an individual moves beyond these basic objectives by seeking to become educated it is seen as a betrayal, an act of disloyalty to the community.

Chifundo doesn't appear daunted by any of the rumours and abuse. "They are uneducated, and they have stopped school. They think I just come here to play instead of learning. They know if I finish school I can work, and I can help my relatives."

Like Maria and Solstina, Chifundo is not easily discouraged. At her core, she is strong and determined.

7
Life in the Village

Culture is like an umbrella
under which some people like
to hide from rain, and also to
shade themselves from the sun.
But sometimes you need to fold it.

—*Dr. Mampela Ramphela*[1]

KAPWAYI VILLAGE IS SMALL AND POOR.[2] It sits by the side of a dusty road, a collection of mud houses thatched with elephant grass. A few chickens peck at the ground in hopes of finding stray kernels of maize, and dogs lie in the sun, scratching at fleas and growling at flies. The ground is dry and packed from decades of traffic, but the slightest breeze stirs up clouds of dust. Today a borehole well stands in the centre of the village, but this was not the case when Memory returned to live with her grandparents in 1998.

Audrey was ecstatic to see Memory: "Oh, Memory, I'm so glad that you came back." Memory was expected to work at home, so she could only help at the school once or twice a week. But Audrey got to work teaching Memory how to teach, and in return Memory taught Audrey about the Malawian educational system. Because Audrey had been unable to locate a form one curriculum, Memory explained the course requirements. She also helped Audrey prepare for class and marked the students' papers for subjects like English and Chichewa.

Audrey tried to repay Memory by offering her essentials like soap and lotion, but Memory remembered her promise to God. "By that time, I had no money, but I really wanted to do something for free. I felt compelled." She also says, "I was happy to do it, and I learned a lot from Audrey." From there, she started a new life in the village.

Memory had always worked hard. Her mother had taught her to carry water, clean the house, work in the garden, and cook *nsima*, but city work is not village work. Village work is back-breaking labour.

Living with her grandparents, Memory was expected to do her share of the chores. She would rise early: usually around five o'clock. They didn't eat breakfast, so Memory's first task would be to fill the large storage bucket in the kitchen with water. It took six smaller pails to fill the large pail—six trips to the water dugout. The task of fetching water took Memory nearly two hours. By the time she was finished, the roosters had finished their crowing, the sun was bright in the sky, and the men and her grandmother were already at the garden. Memory would take her hoe and follow.

A portion of the garden would be assigned to each person. That person was free to go when they had completed hoeing and weeding their section. Memory usually finished her portion by noon. Then she prepared to cook lunch. Before walking home, she collected greens for a relish: pumpkin or bean greens or whatever greens were in season. Then she collected firewood from the stands of trees and shrubs that speckle the savannah landscape. Finally, carrying her hoe, the greens, and the firewood, Memory returned home, where she would start a fire and prepare lunch, cooking *nsima* and relish prepared with the greens she had collected that morning. After lunch, she often spent the afternoon pounding maize.

To pound maize, the women of Malawi place dried corn kernels in a large wooden mortar. The pestle they use to grind the kernels is nearly five feet tall. To pound the maize, a woman stands with her feet braced widely apart, grasps the pestle with both hands, lifts it high above her head, and, using gravity and strength, plunges it into the centre of the mortar. It takes fifteen to twenty minutes to liberate a cup or two of kernels from their husks. Then she must do it all again. Once this punishing task had been performed several times, Memory would spread the corn out in a broad, shallow basket and hand-pick the husks from the corn so it was ready to soak in water. By the time she had put the maize aside to soak, the water she had collected that morning would be depleted, and she would go to fetch more water, this time to heat for the men's baths. By now it would be getting dark and time for Memory to prepare supper: *nsima*, relish, and beans. Once supper was prepared and eaten, there was only enough time for Memory to prepare her own bath before she crawled into bed, exhausted. The next day, she would carry out a similar routine. "There is really no time when you can just sit in the village. All the time you are occupied with work," says Memory of rural life.

Each day was not exactly the same. Sometimes Memory carried maize to the maize mill. The mill was a thirty-minute walk from home, and while Memory knew how to carry a pail the traditional way—on her

Ground maize dries in the sun, 2008.

head—she was unaccustomed to the extreme weight of the water and the distance she needed to walk. She often went with other villagers who walked quickly while Memory struggled to keep up, fearful of stopping along the way. But the weight of the bucket made her neck ache. "That pain, it was crying inside me."

While village women are accustomed to the hard work and long days, it ages their bodies. When Memory went to see her friends, they would say, "Oh Memory, you've changed."

Memory was fortunate to have met Audrey before she went to stay with her grandparents. Helping Audrey gave Memory a task on which she could focus, and more importantly, it gave her hope for the future.

While she was helping Audrey, Memory was able to read books, practise her English, and learn new skills. But there was a trade-off. Memory's grandparents thought Memory was going to the school so she could avoid her chores. They said to her, "If you go there, we cannot give you food." Memory didn't eat at the school. On the days she helped out, she had no breakfast and no lunch. She ate only one meal: supper.

For Memory, the rewards outweighed the sacrifices. By working at the school, she was able to keep her dream of returning to school alive. Without Audrey, she could not have stayed in the village with any hope of attaining a post-secondary education. Audrey says, "Memory has drive and determination. She has no idea what giving up means. Nothing is going to bombard her. She just keeps going."

Memory had learned to "just keep going." Even before her uncle's death, Memory's aunt, Loveness, was ill. Memory had noticed changes in her aunt while her uncle was still alive. Loveness had suffered from shingles, but she recovered and was still able to work.

After some time in the village, Memory learned that her aunt was in the hospital. She travelled to Lilongwe to visit. Loveness was now frail and sickly. As with Memory's Uncle John, she had suffered a series of illnesses: shingles, TB, headaches. The headaches affected her eyes. They would turn up into her head, and she couldn't see.

Loveness's relatives told Memory that her aunt wanted to see her. "She's been mentioning you, and she really wants to meet with you."

When Memory arrived at the hospital, her aunt was no longer coherent. Memory explained, "She couldn't recognize me. She was talking about her past." It seemed to Memory that she was narrating her life, but her aunt's words were baffling and incoherent. Her aunt talked on, and Memory knew she was nearing the end of her life.

The following morning, Loveness died.

Memory returned to her village and her volunteer work at the girls' school.

While Audrey was able to learn how to cook *nsima* and handwash clothes like a true Malawian, she was unable to find a Malawian curriculum. She and Larry, the other Canadian volunteer teacher, went to Lilongwe to visit the Ministry of Education, but the ministry didn't have a copy of the curriculum because they were in the middle of devising a new one. So Audrey and Larry had to make one up. They needed students too.

When Audrey was asked to volunteer teach for CEAG, she had little knowledge of what she was facing. When she arrived in Malawi in June 1998, she thought she would be teaching almost immediately, but that was not the case. The school was still under construction. The foundation had been laid, but the bricks were still being fired when Audrey and Larry arrived at the school. Until recently, primary and secondary school began in January. CEAG wouldn't be ready to open its doors until January of the following year.

Audrey and Larry busied themselves, learning the customs and meeting the people. They watched the workers and learned to make bricks: finding the best soil (an old termite mound), mixing the dirt with dried grass and water, forming mud bricks in a mold, and drying them in the sun. Later, they fired the bricks and built the school's teachers' house. It was a motley structure, but it kept the rain off their heads and the sun off their backs. It lasted until the school closed two and a half years later.

For the first intake, Audrey enlisted the help of Jerry from World Vision. She rode on the back of Jerry's motorbike while he took her around to the outlying feeder schools, where she spoke to the girls completing standard eight. Everyone was invited to apply, and there were seventy-five hopeful applicants wanting to fill fourteen places. To pick the girls who would study at CEAG, Audrey and Larry created a standardized entrance exam. From there, the top fourteen girls were chosen: Basimati, Agness, Chidothi, Eunice, Bernice, Ferig, Saliza, Asane, Daborra, and several others.

The girls who came to study at the school were the poorest of the poor. Asane lived with her grandmother, but her grandmother was ill. The house was small and showing the effects of time and neglect: the mud walls eroding and the roof lacking thatch. Audrey remembers Asane well. "When I met Asane, she wouldn't raise her eyes. She felt like nothing. Out of all the girls, I think she had the most trouble learning—who knows why? The girl probably hadn't eaten well for many years of her life, but she kept trying."

World Vision saved Asane from her plight; they chose to sponsor her. The girls' education and most other needs were paid for, but until the school got running the way it was intended, the girls were expected to bring their own food. Asane would not have been able to do that. "World Vision was her saving grace," Audrey explained.

Audrey and Larry were Canadian teachers, so they knew how to teach. But nothing could have prepared them for the unexpected challenges they faced at the school. "The first day of school. I didn't know much," says Audrey. "I took a schedule from here and put it in place there. It had two eighty-minute blocks, an hour for lunch, and two eighty-minute blocks in the afternoon. That's how I started the school. That first day at lunchtime, an hour went by, and there were no girls. An hour and a half went by. Then I heard them all skipping down the road—just as happy as can be. All they had to say was '*nsima*,' and I realized they all had to cook *nsima*, which means starting a fire. It takes forty-five minutes just to cook the *nsima* itself. I changed the schedule so they would have an hour and a half for lunch."

Audrey and Larry soon learned they had to make many concessions around the realities of the girls' lives. Audrey remembers: "They would have to go after school to get their wood, and they would be gone for hours searching for wood. They were trying to be schoolgirls and do their homework by daylight and get their wood by daylight too. The girls actually asked me one day, 'Can we *not* do homework today? We need to find wood.' They were gone three or four hours just to find enough wood to cook their *nsima*."

Audrey and Larry tried to learn all they could about Malawian rural life, so they carried their own water. They grew their own maize, and they tried to pound it. "I couldn't pound maize," says Audrey. "My muscles were strong from carrying water and washing clothes, but I simply couldn't do it."

In the early days of CEAG, Memory could not help out very often, but Audrey depended on Memory and her insight into Malawian culture. Memory helped in ways that might have seemed insignificant to an outsider, but her contribution was invaluable.

Before the girls' dorms were completed, they lived in rented accommodation in the nearby trading centre—a less than ideal situation. Audrey would ask the girls if they had enough to eat, but "I could never get a straight answer." There were other considerations too. "Too protect them I had to know what was going on because these were young girls away from home. Some of the girls started hanging around with boys, and there's no way they would tell me, but Memory dug it up." One girl was dating a boy. But with Memory's help, Audrey was able to talk to the girl and put a stop to the relationship. "Of course, teenage girls anywhere will try to cover up something they know is wrong, but with Memory there, we knew what was going on, and we could deal with it as it came up." Not until many years later did Audrey learn that after she left, men had approached some of the girls, many married, with offers of gifts and promises of money. The gifts would have come with the implicit understanding that they were in exchange for services rendered.

Audrey is a kind woman, genuine in her actions. After her return to Canada in 1999, she was dismayed to learn of the girls' experiences. "I just about fell to the ground when I found out. Here we were wanting to protect these children and honour them—but now to know the deceit and dishonesty of others..." Audrey pauses. "We went to another school to play net ball. Well, of course, all the local boys showed up at the game, and I tell you, if I had had a shotgun with me...that's how protective I was. When I was there, I thought we were just dealing with girls choosing to go out and date."

There were problems from the start. The villagers had mixed feelings about the girls, and for a time they were referred to as the "Canadian Whores." In far off Canada, nearly ten thousand kilometres away, the decision to billet the girls at the nearby trading centre must have seemed like a harmless plan, a way to get the school up and running a year earlier than would otherwise have been possible. But the situation was not harmless. The girls were away from their families, and Audrey's ability to protect them was hampered by an enormous cultural and communication gap.

The trading centres of Malawi are not safe places for unmonitored, unchaperoned girls. As the name suggests, trading centres are primarily places of trade. They lack the familial connections and reciprocal responsibilities that exist in villages. They are filled primarily with hard-working business people and their customers, but they are also places where young men go to drink and socialize—bustling centres where transient vendors come on market days to sell their wares and young and old come from the surrounding areas to mingle, purchase goods, grind their maize, and charge their cell phones. Most trading centres have at least one pub, but these are not the quaint pubs one might imagine from a trip to the English countryside. Rural pubs in Malawi are not always polite places. Some are little more than low-ceilinged, one-room shacks, with dirt floors and no electricity—redolent with the aroma of *chimbuku*: home brew. I walked through one of these establishments while I was staying at Memory's home village in 2007. It included two empty rooms, dusty with piles of rubble in the corners. There was a third room at the back. This one was only partially constructed and open to the elements. These pubs supply alcohol on the cheap, and they can attract a rough crowd. In a country with little disposable income, for most, drinking can only be done at the expense of food, clothing, and education. It isn't taboo, but it isn't respectable either.

While families may live in trading centres, they are places of commerce, attracting a variety of people and allowing for situations that are potentially dangerous for young women. This was the case for the girls of CEAG.

The girls had been given a unique opportunity. They all came from poor families, and they were being given a free education. The majority, if not all, of the girls would not have gone on to secondary school had it not been for CEAG. They would have had no other option but to marry and continue in the role passed down from their mothers: the hard rural life of childbirth, poverty, and relentless physical labour. Secondary school gave the girls the opportunity to break out of that cycle. It gave them choices.

At first, I had trouble understanding why some of the girls would consider putting this new-found opportunity in jeopardy for the sake of a man, in some cases a married man. But rural girls often lack role models. Education can seem like an abstraction. Even when education is given to them, girls who have only experienced village expectations have difficulty imagining a different outcome. The girls were also young: teenagers. We all make poorly considered decisions as teenagers, and it can be flattering to catch the eye of a man, especially an older one. The third reason is more complicated. Christie Johnson explains it this way:

> I can't even glimpse how a human being becomes the way they are, growing up in the kind of poverty that those girls were coming from. It's a culture of desperate need, so you do what you need to do. These girls, they didn't have a vision of what staying in school and not becoming the second wife of a man was like.
>
> They're walking to school every day, and they're being mocked because they're going to the white school, and they're being told they're too proud. I'm just imagining, but maybe they've got a man who is coming on to them and saying, "Here come be my second wife." What is she going to do? As soon as a girl is sleeping with somebody they can be called a wife. Memory will talk about a girl who has never been through a marriage ceremony. She'll say, "She's gotten married."

In the village, if a girl were to become pregnant, the boyfriend or husband would be expected to support her as a wife. If he didn't, the girl's family would be very angry. In an interconnected culture like that of Malawi, there would be serious repercussions for a man if he didn't take care of his "wife." Young women often think their lives will be easier if they become a first or even second wife. They believe that once they have children, they will be cherished.

Marriage is important within the Malawian culture. Christie adds: "There is so much buildup culturally about marriage, and the wedding songs and celebrations are part of a folk tradition." Even when no "official" wedding has taken place, marriage is a part of growing up and becoming a woman.

It can be easy for a girl who has lived her entire life in desperate poverty to be dazzled by "things." Christie explains:

If there is a flashy, well-dressed man giving a girl things, and she has never in her life had a new hand mirror or comb or toothbrush. But now she's being given the first brand-new thing she's ever had, and she's also being given sex and maybe love, why not?

The mindset of a girl who is impressed by a ten-cent mirror is difficult to fathom, but one must consider the situation from that girl's perspective. She can get an education—but she may lack the personal experience to comprehend its potential—or a man can support her. She might believe that becoming a second wife or a girlfriend means she'll have security.

Audrey did her best to protect the girls from danger, but she lacked the language skills and the cultural experience to fully grasp the girls' situations. Audrey relied on Memory to help her deal with some of the struggles the girls were facing: this girl dating that boy or more mundane concerns. "I could never get a straight answer from the girls if they had enough to eat. Memory was able to tell us: 'No, they don't have enough food.' And when some of the girls started hanging out with boys, there's no way they would tell me, but Memory was able to find that out. There were men in the village who were starting to offer them money for services, and I had no idea." Because the girls were living in the trading centre, it was difficult to pin down a precise timeline for these events, and Audrey admits she didn't learn about some of the dangers they faced

In 2008, Audrey and Memory were reunited during Memory's Canadian speaking tour.

until years later when she met Christie in Canada. "Here we wanted to protect them, but people saw it as an opportunity. At least with Memory there, we knew some of what was going on, and we could deal with things as they came up." One of the CEAG girls who was dating a boy did become pregnant and had to drop out of school, but in that case Audrey said, "That was okay for Winnie. It was sad to see her go, but at least she got married to this boy." Winnie was a tall, lanky girl who always had a carefree smile. Audrey had realized early on that Winnie probably wouldn't stick it out, but Audrey said, "I was just so glad to meet her and give her the experience of being in that school because that probably changed her life in some way." Another girl, Bernice, began spending time with boys, too, but with Memory's help, Audrey was able to put a stop to the dating before it went too far.

Audrey faced many challenges, but she also experienced many happy times with the girls. "I wanted the girls to have a theme song. I thought we would sing the national anthem in the morning, and then we would sing this theme song, but I didn't realize how big the language barrier was until we tried to write the song."

Using a stub of white chalk, Audrey wrote a list of words that she thought would inspire the girls on the blackboard: possibility, education, honesty, respect, learning, hope, and future. "I thought the girls had some idea how to use these words, so I sent them away, and their homework was to come up with a song that we could use. Well Saliza, she put all the words together. She strung them together. She didn't make sentences or anything like that. She just used all the words that I had written on the board, and she made them into a song. It was the funniest song I had ever heard, but it became our theme song: 'Young Women We.' We sang it every morning, and it's beautiful, but if you really look at it, it's a string of words made into a beautiful song. [The melody] was made by the girls: Saliza, and I think Eunice and Margaret helped her. We didn't change a thing after the girls came up with it."

"Young Women We" was not only the theme song for the girls of CEAG, but later, when Memory and Christie founded APU, they decided it should be the theme song for another generation of girls:

Young women we
Young women we
Young women we
Young women we

Making our lives better
Young women we
Young women we
Young women we
Young women we

Making our lives better
Education is the hope for tomorrow's future
Endless possibilities and honesty
Respect yourself
Respect others
Respect property

Somebody knows
Somebody knows
Somebody knows the power of learning
Hallelujah
Somebody, somebody knows
Somebody knows
Somebody, somebody
Somebody knows the power of learning
Hallelujah
Somebody, somebody knows

We'll be ready
We'll be ready
We'll be ready to fix our future
We'll be ready
We'll be ready
We'll be ready to live our lives.

I've heard the APU girls sing "Young Women We" during their morning assembly. They sing it with conviction and enthusiasm, and with their gift for harmonization, they are able to make this funny little song ring across the land. It is truly inspiring, and I am always moved by its performance.

Audrey wanted to give the girls the tools they required to take charge of their lives after they left school, but Audrey and Larry weren't the only

Canadian volunteers at the school. Young men and women came and went, and when they left, they would often give their things to the girls: leftover shampoo, clothes purchased for the trip, and other odds and ends that either the volunteers wanted the girls to have or couldn't fit into their luggage.

Gift giving may appear innocent, but in this case, it created problems of dependency and rivalry among the girls. "It's not necessarily a healthy thing to always have stuff given and not have to earn it," Audrey told me.

Audrey came up with a creative solution. One day in class, she said, "Okay girls. We have nothing, but we have a lot."

The girls were puzzled.

"What do we have at our disposal that we could use to make something that would cost us nothing?"

The girls responded, "Nothing."

But Audrey pushed on. "What do we have?"

They began listing all the things they had at their disposal: mud, clay, sacks, and strings, maize, and grass.

And Audrey said, "All these things cost nothing. This is what we have at our disposal to start a business. It's your job to go home and figure out what you can make with these things. If you can make something out of grass and mud, someone will buy it."

The girls were not convinced. "Nobody's going to buy mud."

"Of course no one is going to buy mud, but what can we make the mud into?"

The next day, the girls came to class with their ideas. They made beads out of mud and strung them together on strings pulled from maize sacks.

According to Audrey, they were sorry-looking beads, but she had an idea.

"You know, I have to go to Lilongwe once a month, and there are foreigners there who will buy these necklaces to take home."

The girls had all seen the vendors in Lilongwe, but they were men, and they sold wooden carvings and canvas paintings.

Audrey said, "You have to create your own market."

Audrey worked with the girls. The fine motor skills required to make beads weren't developed in the girls, but together with Audrey, they made beautiful beads and fired them at night while they cooked their *nsima*.

Then Audrey asked them what they were worth. And they said, "Five kwacha."

"No," said Audrey. "Let's try seventy or eighty kwacha."

Audrey took the necklaces with her the next time she went to Lilongwe. "I knew a bunch of the ex-pats there, and I sold them to the ex-pats. Then I brought the cash back."

When she returned from Lilongwe, she gave the girls their money, but Audrey wanted to give the girls a goal. "Before I go back to Canada, I'm going to have an auction, so you can buy the outfits you like, but you must have money. I won't give them to you."

Audrey gave them each a balloon to store their money in. That way they couldn't access it without tearing the balloon. They had to wait for the auction. Later, Audrey said, "It was the funniest thing to see all my outfits walk away." Before she returned home, Audrey used the money she made from the auction to take the girls to the game park in nearby Kasungu.

Memory was happy to help Audrey whenever she could, but she still kept dreaming about furthering her education. Completing secondary school was an accomplishment in itself, but without post-secondary education, employment opportunities, especially for a woman, are limited. Although she felt pressure to do so, Memory was not ready to get married.

Rita Adams, the school's Canadian director, would be visiting the school for its grand opening. Audrey knew about Memory's dream of going back to school. She hoped that if Rita heard Memory's story, she might be willing to raise the funds to help her out. Audrey wanted to recognize Memory's role in the school, so she gave Memory a prominent part in the ceremonies. She made her a "flower girl," thus ensuring that Rita would notice her.

After the celebration, Rita wanted to meet Memory. She was thankful for Memory's help at the school, so she called Memory over, and the two of them sat and talked for a long time. "Memory," she said, "If you want to go back to school, that won't be a problem. I think you should be looking for a school. I will make sure we pay for your tuition."

Memory was excited. The door had been opened, and she was ready to pursue her dream.

Memory wasn't making money teaching at the school, so around this time she took a job enumerating for the upcoming election.

The 1999 election saw Dr. Bakili Muluzi's bid for a second term in power. His government had been responsible for free primary education, and he insisted that it was his government that represented democracy in Malawi:

[Muluzi] had to downplay the problems for which many blamed the UDF [United Democratic Front], including extremely difficult economic conditions, a drastic 37% devaluation of the kwacha in August 1998, widespread corruption, and deteriorating security. Meanwhile, the fortunes of the two main opposition parties seemed to be in decline in the months preceding the elections. The MCP [Malawi Congress Party] sought to present itself as a new and reformed political party, radically different from the dictatorial clique that ruled the country for three decades. While painting the UDF as corrupt and fiscally irresponsible, the MCP campaigned on a platform of free-market economics and fiscal austerity.

Muluzi's campaign sought to characterize the MCP as intent on bringing the country back to despotic rule while the opposition countered that the UDF leadership [had] enriched itself at the expense of the starving and unemployed masses. They also blamed the UDF government for the collapse of the agricultural infrastructure and accused it of corruption, and undemocratic and divisive politics.

The 1999 electoral campaign was marred by many reports of violence and intimidation. In addition to anti-UDF violence in the north, Chakuamba and his supporters were attacked in areas of UDF support. The result was a campaign that reflected more heat than light on the issues.[3]

Despite friction among party supporters throughout the campaign, the election was relatively peaceful, and ultimately Muluzi was re-elected with 2,442,685 votes, while his closest contender, Chakuamba, came in a close second with 2,106,790.[4]

By the time the election was over, and Muluzi was sworn in as president on June 21, 1999, Audrey had returned to Canada. A string of Canadian volunteers followed. Matthew and Raylene were the first. Later, there were others: Mike, Nadina, Alicia, Holly, Evan, and finally Christie. Throughout, Memory was the one constant in the girls' lives.

Memory set out to ensure that the girls stayed on task and continued their education. She knew the difficulties; she struggled against becoming discouraged herself. She wanted to go to university, but there was no one to encourage or support her. Quite the opposite. The people of her village saw her as an educated person, someone who had completed her education, someone who should get married.

Memory struggled to convince the people of the village that she should continue her schooling, but she also tried to fit in: going to the maize mill, carrying water, working in the garden. Audrey had encouraged Memory, but Audrey was gone. Memory still volunteered at the school, and Memory still had the hope that "one day it would happen."

Although Memory met with opposition in her village—and her experience is common—village attitudes are slowly changing. I spoke with the chief of Lucita's village, Moses Nyama. He told me this:

When one is educated her future is predictable. In our village, we relied on farming, but now soils are not responding to our crops. We need fertilizer and having all these things is becoming very hard. People are increasing in number, but the land is not increasing. If one is educated, at least her future is predictable.

Moses explained that he did not allow any child to stay at home when school was in session. He told me that he was sitting down with the parents in the village and explaining to them the importance of school. "More especially when we are running out of land for farming. The only solution is to send children to school."

As the realities of the modern world move through the country-side, traditional beliefs surrounding education are beginning to change. Memory's own persistence and her position as a role model for other girls is helping to lead this change.

Traditional beliefs can be harmful in other ways. I've spoken to many girls who have grown up in villages, and all of them fear witchcraft. There are few statistics available on the practice of witchcraft, and the perpetration of witchcraft violence in Malawi, but these are both chronic problems that haunt otherwise close-knit rural communities and pit neighbour against neighbour, family member against family member. Many people worry that these practices may be increasing with the modernization of the country. They worry that practitioners of magic are corrupting the young by exploiting their innocence and secretly teaching them their trade. The trade in human body parts used in the production of magic potions is a thriving industry in many African countries, including Malawi. And while there may be genuine cause for concern about the practice of spell casting and other supernatural activities, witches and wizards are often made the scapegoats for tragedy within a community. These problems must be addressed if Malawi is to modernize and take its place among the developed nations of the world.

Witches and wizards, known as *mfiti* in Chichewa, are believed to possess supernatural powers of invisibility. They can fly through the air and cover enormous distances within a matter of minutes. *Mfiti* can also turn themselves into animals such as cats, hyenas, rats, and owls.[5] People complain of bad dreams as the result of their spells or potions, and believe that sickness or death is caused by their black magic.[6] It is widely believed that witchdoctors, now called traditional healers, are the only ones with the power to stop the *mfiti*.

Traditional healers are the accepted purveyors of traditional medicine. They will put a spell on a home to protect it from harmful witchcraft. They dispense medicine to cure disease. They sell charms to protect individuals from danger, or to help women attract husbands. Traditional healers are the intermediaries between the living and the dead. They are the herbalists and the diviners, the traditional surgeons and midwifes for their communities. But some healers are unscrupulous and liable to use their powers to make a profit at the expense of others.[7]

Some witchdoctors hire themselves out for large sums of money to sniff out witches,[8] and they are sometimes involved in cases of witchcraft violence and ritual murder.[9] Reputable healers believe that instead of focusing on the healing aspects of the traditional arts, many of the younger healers are responsible for a more acquisitive approach to their profession. While other healers condemn this practice, witch sniffing is conducted in many communities and leads to fear and suspicion among their populations.

During the 1970s, Catholic priest J.W.M. van Breugel spent time studying the traditional beliefs and practices in rural communities southeast of Lilongwe. In an informal survey, van Breugel found that out of 451 cases of death, relatives and neighbours believed 296 were the result of *ufiti*, or witchcraft.[10] Although most cases of death were attributed to "people in his village" or "his enemies," where possible, van Breugel recorded the relationship between the suspected murderer and his victim. A pattern of suspicion and mistrust arises that shows uncles suspected of killing their sister's children, fathers accused of killing their own children, and brothers blamed for killing their brothers.[11]

In recent years, it's the elderly, women, and young children who are most often accused of practicing witchcraft. Sixty-three-year-old Gladys Kasito is still recovering from the injuries she suffered when her neighbours attacked her and destroyed her house in an act of vigilante justice. They accused her of pushing a small boy out of her witchcraft plane after he refused to bewitch his sisters. Gladys lost her front teeth during the beating, and she now walks with a pronounced limp. She spends her days in a ramshackle hut where her kitchen once stood. She no longer wants to live.[12]

In 1998, the National Conference on Witchcraft Violence declared: "Poverty and illiteracy, particularly among women, are a major contributory factor to the superstition and false accusations which lead to witchcraft violence. The eradication of poverty and illiteracy and the achievement of gender equality, are central to all strategies for ending this scourge."[13] The conference was convened as a result of increased witchcraft violence throughout Malawi, and in particular within the northern province. But change is slow in coming, and despite the recommendations made as a result of the conference, witchcraft violence persists throughout the country.

Credo Mutwa, a traditional healer, spoke at the conference. He addressed a group of traditional healers, traditional leaders, government officials, community members, and survivors of witchcraft violence.[14] Mutwa is himself a survivor of attacks. In 1987, he was nearly burned alive. Mutwa spoke of the need for people to understand their heritage and use their traditions wisely. "[In the past] witches were never killed, but exiled. Most of the people killed today are killed because of suspicion. People are killed because they are ugly, old, or have been caught sleepwalking… I stand here insisting that the burning of women as witches must stop. I don't care who is doing it, for what reason. We have to stop the carnage, stop the holocaust. The burning of people in Africa is a taboo."[15]

Attempts to address the problems of witchcraft and witchcraft violence through education and reform have met with limited success. Unfortunately, the Witchcraft Act of Malawi is a throwback to the days of colonialism. The legislation was enacted in 1911, with the best of intentions by the British, while Malawi was still a protectorate. The British governing body was concerned with "dangerous practices such as trial by ordeal, the use of charms and witchcraft itself."[16] But the act fails to acknowledge the existence of witchcraft, a fundamental belief held by the majority of Malawians.[17]

Under the heading "Pretending Witchcraft," the act states the following:

Any person who by his statements or actions represents himself to be a wizard or witch or as having or exercising the power of witchcraft shall be liable to a fine of $50 and to imprisonment for ten years.[18]

Many Malawians now believe that this outdated legislation is counterproductive. A law that doesn't admit to the existence of a practice can hardly be expected to regulate it. Many also claim that the country's lack of appropriate legislation against the practice of witchcraft leads to the kind of vigilante justice that crippled Gladys Kasito. Justice Kamwambe of Malawi's High Court believes, "The law does not reconsider [the] existence of witchcraft. Therefore it cannot provide for a law against it; it only provides against proclaiming by word or actions [of] its existence."[19] Chief Law Reform officer Chizaso Nyirongo agrees. Nyirongo and many others believe Malawi needs laws that clearly criminalize the practice of witchcraft.[20] Not everyone agrees.

Many others see a correlation between the witch hunts of modern-day Africa and the European and North American witch hunts that took place during the sixteenth and seventeenth centuries. With the move to criminalize witchcraft in many African countries, such as Cameroon and South Africa, comes the fear that Africa will mirror the mistakes of the past, mistakes that cost thousands of alleged witches throughout Europe and North America their lives.[21]

Gerrie ter Haar, professor of religion, human rights, and social change at the Institute of Social Studies in the Hague, believes that the influence of Islamic and Christian fundamentalist movements have led to the "demonization of the spirit world." Ter Haar and other researchers see this as contributing to the increase in witchcraft violence in Africa. They believe African traditional beliefs have evolved as a result of continued exposure to Western and Middle Eastern religions, changing a characteristically neutral concept to one steeped in fear and evil.[22]

Support for some sort of resolution to the social, legal, and personal problems caused by witchcraft violence has increased, as more innocents become victims. The Human Rights Consultative Committee, an NGO working to protect and promote human rights in Malawi, is lobbying for a "normative legal position" on witchcraft.[23]

The Civil Liberties Committee—Malawi's first human rights organization—is also asking the government to enact legislation that will protect witchcraft suspects.[24] Emmie Chanika, executive director, says that people are using the country's widespread traditional belief in *ufiti* as an excuse to persecute innocent people by accusing them of witchcraft. Once accused, people are often ostracized within their own communities, and in some cases they are the victims of mob violence.[25]

A study, done in 2004, of the female prisoners in Zomba, Chichiri, and Maula prisons showed that 43 per cent of murder cases were witchcraft-related.[26]

Maureen Bwanali is one of the inmates serving a sentence for murder. Maureen was arrested and convicted, along with her aunt and brother, for the murder of her brother's two children. Prior to the killings, Maureen was believed dead. Funeral arrangements had been made, and she was prepared for burial. After two days, she revived. After her resurrection, Maureen claimed supernatural powers and, consequently, her family believed her assertion that the children were witches. For two days, Maureen inserted pieces of reeds into the children's anuses to exorcise them from evil while her aunt and the children's parents looked on. The children died from their injuries.[27]

It's difficult to pinpoint Maureen's motivation for the killings, but it's likely that she suffered severe trauma from her own "death and resurrection." Perhaps she feared persecution as a witch herself and wanted to redirect suspicion. It could be that after her own traumatic experience, she suffered a psychotic breakdown. In an interview conducted during her incarceration, Maureen appeared confused. She wondered why her family didn't stop her from killing the children.[28] It appears that many instances of witchcraft violence are the result of lack of knowledge about the nature of disease and illness.

HIV/AIDS, diabetes, senility, birth defects, and other conditions have been blamed on witchcraft. In many areas of Africa, men infected with the HIV/AIDS virus believe that sex with a virgin is their only hope of a cure. This belief has resulted in the rape of young girls and even infants. Governments have fought back with various public education strategies. In Malawi, the government has erected large roadside signs reading, "AIDS is real...It is not witchcraft."[29] But superstitions about the spread and cure of AIDS persist, and a few signs aren't enough to change that—not yet.

Albinos can also be the victims of superstition, particularly in neighbouring Tanzania. Albino Tanzanians live in fear and often must go into hiding. Although albinism is rare, there are approximately seventeen thousand black Africans whose hair is red or white and who lack natural skin pigmentation. Their appearance is quite striking among their peers, and they are seen as "ghosts" within their communities and hunted for their skins and body parts. Their white skin and other body parts are used in black magic and as a component of various potions to heal disease and sickness.[30] In Malawi, albinos are less of a target, but even so, officials have confiscated their skins from criminals, and their communities marginalize them.[31]

The trade in body parts, and in particular genitalia, for the purpose of witchcraft is another matter. Recently, a Blantyre man asked his wife if he could have a portion of her private parts. The man wanted to use his wife's genitalia to make charms that he could then sell and become rich. The woman refused, but during the night woke to find her husband cutting off her vulva. And this is not an isolated event. "It's everybody's guess that this is not small business. It involves a cross section of people," says police spokesman, Willie Mwaluka.[32]

The national conference where Credo Mutwa spoke recommended substantial legislative reform. Conference stakeholders wanted to see legislation that would separate "those who are engaged in harmful practices...from those who are falsely accused; so that those who make false accusations can be brought to book." The conference also wanted legislation that would bring about "a clear paradigm shift from the current act which operates from a premise that denies the belief in witchcraft," since that paradigm ultimately leads to accusations of witchcraft "being dealt with outside the criminal justice system." Conference delegates also felt it was necessary to "introduce structures to deal with certain witchcraft-related complaints by means of conciliation and mediation, thereby attempting to resolve underlying tensions." As a result of the confusion between legitimate healing practitioners and destructive charlatans, legislation is necessary "to control the practice of traditional healing, which should be accompanied by a Code of Conduct to ensure that the practice of traditional medicine is separated from sinister practices."[33] So far, these reforms have not taken place.

Education is also a viable solution. Increasing literacy and educating the public about the symptoms and transmission of diseases will help to take some of the mystery out of death and illness. Give people the information they need to put sickness into an accessible context, a context that allows them to reason out frightening situations, and they are less likely to blame their neighbours for their troubles.

Jealousy and petty rivalry are part of human nature. They exist in all cultures in all continents throughout the world. It's unfortunate that so many innocents have become the scapegoats of their communities, but using witchcraft as an excuse to cause harm to others is just that, an excuse. Through education, people become more tolerant of another's thoughts and ideas, their differences, and their infirmities. Education promotes understanding, corrects misinformation, and dispels prejudice.

Florence

THE BELIEF IN BLACK MAGIC is still very much alive throughout most of Malawi—particularly in the rural areas. Many of the girls at APU talk openly of their belief in magic and the harm it can cause.

Chifundo wrote about her mother's death in this way:

We called her Monicah. She died from a disease. [Magicians] killed her because some people chose her to be a chief and some other people did not agree...They took medicine and put it on the way. She had a journey to go somewhere, and she stepped on that medicine and started getting a headache...Then she passed away.[1]

Even when people are taken to a hospital or clinic for treatment, the diagnosis may be vague or inconclusive, and relatives can be left to wonder at the cause of their loved one's illness or cause of death. Black magic is often blamed. These beliefs can sometimes cause mistrust and fear among families.

Florence, an elderly relative of Memory, was found wandering around in a neighbour's yard in the dark. The yard was surrounded by a tall grass fence, and the neighbour couldn't understand what Florence was doing there in the middle of the night. They escorted her home, but the next morning, Florence's mouth was drooping on one side. She had difficulty speaking, and she couldn't walk. She admitted that she couldn't remember how she had gotten into the neighbour's yard.

The family's home, where Florence had been found, was protected with magic medicine. The family believed that if a wizard were to fly to the roof of the house, the medicine would make them fall down, and they would become paralyzed.

The people in the village said, "She is a witch."

Families often place protective magic around their homes to ward off evil. APU student, Mirriam, recalls the time her parents warned her to stop stealing mangoes from a neighbour's garden: "My parents advised me that in gardens, [people] put medicine there, and as a result, I could be trapped in the garden for the rest of my life."[2]

Florence could no longer care for herself. She was "smelling badly," and since people believed she was a witch, no one wanted to care for her. People said, "She is the one who has been giving us diseases in this village."

When Memory found her, Florence was lying in her own feces, unable to walk outside to relieve herself. Because she couldn't carry Florence on her own, Memory asked a neighbour to help her. "Please come and help me to pull her to the toilet," she pleaded. The woman reluctantly agreed, and together they dragged Florence to the latrine. But the woman helping Memory tugged on Florence as if she were "a log." She clearly had no sympathy for Florence's suffering.

Florence had children living in Mbonara, and after a few weeks, they came to take her home with them. "As of now, she is not fully healed," explained Memory.[3]

8
Canadians Educating African Girls

It is true that it would be
much easier for girls to protect
themselves if they just had the
opportunity to go to school. If a
girl is confident, it's easier for
her to say no to sex.

—Sellina[1]

DURING ITS SECOND YEAR OF OPERATION—2000—CEAG lacked qualified teachers, so the Canadian Board was looking for a volunteer.[2] Christie's father, Larry, happened to hear about the position and passed the information on to his daughter.

When Christie received the email from her dad, it seemed like the perfect fit: a small school in Malawi needed an experienced, qualified teacher. Christie wanted to go. She was working at the Bamfield Research Centre on Vancouver Island, but she had started her teaching career at the Nellie McClung Girls' Junior High School in Edmonton. She knew how to teach girls in a segregated learning environment. She had also spent time in Africa, travelling through Kenya and Tanzania, and wanted to go back. "I felt as though I'd missed something important. I'd climbed Mount Kilimanjaro and seen the animals, but I felt as though I had no connection with the people, and there's no better way of connecting with people than teaching," says Christie, and then she laughs. "Dad thought I would just pass it along, but a few days later when I saw him, I told him I was going to Malawi."

Based on her teaching qualifications, Rita hired Christie to take over as head teacher of the school. Christie was eager to go, but there was much she didn't know about the school and what awaited her there. Evan, Rita's son, and his girlfriend, Holly, were running the school: Evan as the school coordinator and Holly as the head teacher. Neither were qualified teachers. Neither had teaching experience. Christie soon learned that they did not recognize her role as head teacher.

By August 2000, the first group of girls had moved up to form two, and they no longer lived at the trading centre. The two classes, fewer than thirty girls altogether, lived in two, small, cement-floored hostels. The teachers still lived in the building Audrey and Larry had helped build when they first came to Malawi, and the site was guarded at night by a watchman. In that respect, the situation had improved since Audrey's time.

In July 2000, when Christie landed at the Kamuzu International Airport, she was jetlagged and ill from the long trip, but after collecting her luggage, she found Mark, one of the volunteer teachers, and Calvin, the project manager, waiting for her. They loaded Christie's bags into Mark's truck and drove several hours until they reached Kasungu, where the three stopped at a pub for dinner. After they were finished their meal, the men dropped Christie off at a guesthouse and told her they would be back to pick her up in the morning. They were going to the Gab Pub.

Christie spent her first night in Malawi alone and frightened. She was in a strange country where she knew no one, and she hadn't had the opportunity to exchange her money for kwacha, so she was penniless.

Christie was relieved when Calvin came to pick her up late the next morning. Mark was not with him. The two drove the bumpy, dusty roads the rest of the way to the school together. When Christie arrived, the girls were on a school break, and all the teachers were gone. Christie was told that Memory and Holly were at the teacher-training centre in Kasungu. She explored the school on her own.

There were two brick classroom blocks and two, small, square, cement-floored hostels where the girls slept. There was also a garden and a chicken coop. There was a small, grass-roofed kitchen, but someone had been using the grass to start fires, so the roof was patchy, and it leaked. The volunteer house that Audrey and Larry had built during their stay still stood. Mark, Calvin, and Evan slept in the dirt-floored house, and in addition to their bedrooms, there was a small curtained-off area with a cement floor and drain for bathing. The kitchen leaked, so the rest of the volunteer house was taken up with stacked bags of maize and other supplies. Because the house was used for storage, it was plagued by rats. When the sun went down at six o'clock, they began scratching and crawling on anyone who slept in the volunteer house. The rats were so loud that Mark couldn't sleep without earplugs. Fortunately, the office was in a separate building. It was small, but there were no rats. That's where Holly and Christie slept.

Christie set to work tidying her sleeping area. She put up her mosquito net. She found fabric that had been donated for sewing. The girls weren't learning to sew, so Christie used the fabric to make curtains.

Christie also wanted to make the office look more like an office. There were boxes of books stored on the office floor, but cement sweats during the day, so the books were damp. Christie found some lumber lying in the grass near the school and used it for book shelving. She found the original plan for CEAG and tacked it to the wall. She also found a small table and chair and placed them in the office. By the time Holly returned a few days later, Christie had settled in, and the "office" looked like a real office.

Although Christie had been told the girls were on holiday for another week, the same day she arrived at the school, the form two girls began arriving too: Agness, Saliza, and a few others. Christie asked Calvin why the girls were returning so soon. "They are here for Holiday School."

"Who is teaching them?" asked Christie.

"Evan, but he's not back yet."

Christie didn't know what to teach the girls, but she took them to a classroom and tried to get to know them. She had brought pencil cases with her, so she gave each of the girls one of those. They were excited to have pencil cases, so that helped Christie break the ice. She began working with the girls on their math, and the first days passed.

Five days later, Evan arrived. "I got stuck at the lake. I didn't have money, so I had to borrow some," he said, but he didn't seem concerned.

Christie was upset. The girls needed a teacher, and Christie was a new volunteer. She didn't know where to get food or how to cook it. For Christie, it was not a joke: "My relationship with Evan was on the wrong foot from day one."

Christie had quit her job to come to Malawi to volunteer teach and to take over as head teacher at the school, but she soon discovered that no one had told Holly that she would be head teacher. Holly still believed she was head teacher of the school. It was not the ideal situation for a young teacher far from home, but Christie decided she would embrace her new role. She was a qualified teacher, and that's what the girls needed.

Christie was the only qualified teacher at the school. But Mark and Memory—being native Malawian—knew the Malawian curriculum, so Mark continued to teach geography and agriculture, and Memory continued to teach Bible knowledge. Holly maintained her role teaching theatre arts and Evan continued teaching math. Christie began teaching science and English. After a few days, she realized that, in most cases, the school was not covering the Malawian curriculum, so she went to Memory for advice.

The form two girls were due to write their JCEs in a few short months. It would take a lot of effort on the part of the teachers and the students if they were to pass. On Memory's advice, Christie made changes to the class schedule. Since the school had books, she devised a lending library for the girls so they could practise their reading. And on a trip to Mzuzu, she purchased ten lanterns so the girls would be able to study in the evenings.

When Christie arrived at the school, Memory had been volunteering there for nearly two years. She had stuck it out in the hope that Rita would fulfill her promise. She didn't know any other way to make it to post-secondary school. She had worked at various part-time ventures to make a little money and help her grandparents, but it wasn't enough to pay for school, and the volunteering came at great personal cost.

By living in the village and waiting for her education instead of marrying, she was defying tradition. Many people saw her as "getting above herself." Her grandfather had warned her that there was a rumour in the village that some men were planning to rape her to "put her in her place." Memory was terrified. There was no way for her to know where the threat came from. In a community of aunts and uncles, second and third cousins, everyone talked. The area was a patchwork of trading centres and village communities. The warning had been filtered through many people and could have come from a nearby village or closer to home. Memory was afraid to walk to the latrine at night, so she would wait out the discomfort until it was light outside. It wasn't more than a ten-minute walk from the school to her grandparents' home, but if she needed to walk home at night, she would ask Mark to walk with her. The threat of rape was a constant in her life throughout those years. A frightening reality.

There were challenges at the school too. Holly and Memory had gotten along well at first. They were both Christian—that was important to Memory—and they had the girls to look after. Memory began to trust Holly and see her as a close friend. She thought Holly saw her the same way.

One day, she saw that Holly was getting together with the other volunteers to go into town, so she asked her, "Holly, where are you going?"

"We're going to a party in town, but the party is only for the whites."

It wasn't that Memory wanted to go to the party, but she was surprised that she wasn't invited—especially when she found out that Calvin, a native Malawian, was going. The party wasn't just for the "whites." It was incidents like this that made Memory wonder if her friendship with Holly was reciprocated.

When Christie came to the school, Memory wasn't sure what to expect. She knew Christie came with teaching experience, but she was cautious in her judgment at first. She had become close with most of the volunteers, but then they would go back to Canada. Amidst their tearful goodbyes, they would promise to stay in touch, but Memory never heard from them again. When Christie arrived, she had set to cleaning and organizing the office, and Memory saw this as progress, but it took time for her to decide what kind of a person Christie was.

It didn't take long before Christie felt the tension at the school. The Malawians were at odds with the Canadians, and Evan and Holly were at odds with each other. Everyone had a different story, and everyone wanted Christie to be on their side—everyone except Memory. Memory was quiet and reserved. Because Memory stayed out of the bickering, Christie went to her for advice.

Not long after her arrival, Christie asked Memory to come for a walk so the two of them could talk in private. They sat down by the well in the shade of an acacia tree.

"Memory," Christie asked, "what is going on here?"

Memory didn't open up to Christie on that first talk, but she did explain some of her frustration. She explained that she was volunteering at the school because Rita had told her she would help her get her education, but nothing had come from that promise. They also spoke about Memory's life, and Christie got the sense that Memory might be someone she could trust. Toward the end of their conversation, Christie said, "Let's go to Mzuzu University. At least we can learn about the universities in Malawi, and we can talk to them." The following weekend, Memory and Christie took an overnight bus to Mzuzu.

Public transportation in Malawi has improved a great deal in recent years, but this story took place before passenger capacity was monitored and limits were enforced. Memory and Christie caught the bus at the depot in Kasungu. Along with dozens of passengers, they were pressed into a single bus. They were fortunate to be able to sit together rather than stand with the rest. The bus was loaded with people and luggage far beyond its capacity. Bags were piled to the roof. People stood in the aisle. Women with babies on their backs were wedged together so tightly that when the babies peed, it ran down their mothers' legs. There was nothing they could do but stand and wait for the journey to be over. They travelled for six hours along the twisting, winding roads that led through the mountains around Mzuzu. Amidst the stench of human sweat, urine, and feces, the overheated bus tipped from side to side, and the people jostled and bumped into one another. Christie watched as one woman fainted. There was nothing she could do to help.

It was still dark when they arrived in Mzuzu. They had to wait in the bus depot until morning. "I felt like a white target," says Christie. "I remember hiding under a blanket and lying on Memory's lap." It was the first time Christie needed Memory to protect her.

In some ways, the trip was a failure. Memory learned she would not be accepted into the university unless she upgraded her English, but it marked a significant change in Memory's relationship with Christie.

It demonstrated to Memory that Christie was a person who didn't just talk about helping. She helped. It was the beginning of a trusting relationship.

It would take time for Christie to win the girls' trust too. They were excited to meet her, but they were also a little standoffish. Although the girls had been learning English, there was still a communication barrier, and Christie found herself communicating through charades at first. Despite her struggles to communicate, Christie quickly realized that many of the older girls were rebellious and challenging. The girls didn't challenge the teachers' authority openly, but they didn't show the level of respect necessary to establish a successful learning environment.

The girls addressed all the Canadian teachers by their first names, and Christie knew this was not common practice in Malawi. It was considered disrespectful to address a teacher without using Madame, Miss, or Mister. The girls *did* know better, and they addressed Memory as Miss Chazeza.

Memory was not only Malawian; she was also a member of the nearby community. She had a great deal of insight into how the school and its students were perceived. As Christie and Memory became close, she confided information to Christie that she had not expressed to the other volunteers, and she gave Christie valuable insight into Malawian culture.

For their first year, the girls had been boarded in the nearby trading centre. This was a choice that Malawian administrators would probably not have made. As mentioned previously, trading centres are transient in nature. They are often home to single males—families, too, but those families are not tightly connected. As well, trading centres usually have pubs and other gathering spots, and they can become quite rowdy at night. During my stay at Memory's village, I was often woken by drunken shouts issuing from a ramshackle pub in the nearby trading centre. A trading centre is not a good place for a group of girls to live on their own.

It's likely that CEAG chose to board the girls at the trading centre because of internal and external pressures. The hostels were not complete, but the first classroom block was. Both donors and the Malawian community would have been impatient for the school to open its doors. As well-meaning as it was, this decision had alarming consequences.

In the school's first year, Calvin caught and expelled three girls from the school for inappropriate behaviour. The details of this "inappropriate behaviour" are unknown, but it's likely they involved sexual encounters in which the girls received money or food from their "boyfriends." Later on, many of these problems were remedied when the girls were moved to the hostels and a night watchman was hired to protect them, but it was a poor start for the school, and it probably led to some of the attitude problems inherent in the older group of girls.

Within the context of day-to-day life, education can appear an abstraction. Many girls raised in rural villages have no role models other than their mothers and aunts, so they have no way of truly understanding the impact that education can have on their lives. At APU, I've begun to see how valuable Memory's own story and modelling is for the girls. They look at her and see that there is another way, another choice. Many of the APU girls want to be teachers "just like Madame Mdyetseni." One of the APU girls writes, "I want to work very hard with my education so that in the future, I should have a better future and my own school like APU."[3] The girls recognize that education can lift them out of poverty and give them independence. The CEAG girls lacked an educated female Malawian role model.

For Christie, the communication barrier made it difficult to define the atmosphere in the classroom, but she knew the form two girls were mocking her—not openly, but enough that their attitude made the classroom tense and uncomfortable, a disquieting place to teach.

Christie began to understand the significance of these seemingly insignificant events around her, and, like Audrey before her, she came to rely upon Memory for guidance. Christie finally confronted the leaders of the group. She pointed out their sullen, catty behaviour and said, "This is what you're doing. Whether or not you know you're doing it, you must stop." She hoped by addressing the problem, she might shame them into a better attitude, but suddenly it seemed troubles were all around.

The school was coming apart—quickly. Because they had not been paid for at least two months, the carpenters had stopped construction on the school. Piles of lumber sat rotting in the tall grass. Isaac, the boy who worked in the kitchen, complained that he wasn't getting paid and that the project manager was treating him badly—yelling at him and insulting him. He refused to work. Another Malawian, a teacher who had experience teaching at Kamuzu Academy and who had taught at CEAG for two terms, said he had never been paid. He eventually quit, but he kept coming back to the school, asking for his money.

Christie began to get to know Memory and Mark. Because they were Malawian and understood the school system better than anyone else, Christie went to them for advice on curriculum and scheduling, but more importantly they were her connection to the girls. They understood the girls' lives, circumstances, behaviour. They especially knew when the girls were taking advantage of the Canadians.

Many of the Canadian volunteers had given the girls gifts: small things like shampoo or food. Holly had given one of the girls a teddy bear. It was innocent, and the volunteers had meant well, but the gifts caused competition among the girls. The girls began asking Christie for small things like toothpaste and underwear. Christie wasn't always sure how to respond, but she became aware that the gift giving was causing tension throughout the school.

By the time Christie came to volunteer at the school, the problems with CEAG had become nearly insurmountable. There were serious flaws in the administration of the school. There were ongoing questions surrounding missing funds, the lack of qualifications among the teachers, a curriculum that did not conform to Malawian standards, conflicts among many of the volunteers, and the disturbing absence of administrators and volunteers from the school for unspecified periods of time.

On top of it all, the school was running out of money. At times, Christie had to use her own savings to feed the girls. While the school had been founded to help Malawian girls gain independence by receiving their education, it simply was not viable. Without the money to make changes, Christie wondered what hope there was for the school and the girls. It seemed to her that the girls were in an unhealthy situation.

Memory and Mark had already written reports outlining their concerns about the school, but they had begun to wonder if their words were finding their way to the CEAG board. Christie stayed up late one night writing about her observations and concerns. The next day, Mark and Calvin would be going into town, so before they left in the morning, she gave her report to Mark and asked him to fax it to her father. Mark and Calvin were friends, but Christie trusted Mark. Once they were gone, Christie walked to the nearest phone and called her father: "Fax my report to every individual board member. Don't just send it to Rita."

The two men left to go to the World Vision office, where there was a fax machine. Calvin was usually the one to send faxes, but Mark tried to send Christie's fax himself. Calvin discovered him in the act of sending the fax. "But to Calvin's credit, he allowed Mark to send the fax," explained Christie. "He could have taken it, but he didn't."

When the two returned, Calvin confronted Christie, and they discussed the situation for a long time. "I had to be honest about what was going on at the school," said Christie. "I told him, you disappear for days and when you come back, you've clearly been drinking. You are not well. Money has gone missing. People are not getting paid, and they are coming to me." Calvin was not happy about being confronted, but Christie had witnessed the situation. He couldn't deny his actions.

It wasn't long before the school received a response from the Canadian Board. The board wanted Memory, Mark, and Christie to stay until the end of the year. They asked the rest of the volunteers to return to Canada, and they fired Calvin. I asked Christie about the board's reaction: "This must have been what you'd hoped for."

I was surprised when she replied, "I didn't want to stay. I was angry with the whole thing. The girls were behaving so badly, and I hadn't formed strong ties with them yet. I'd had a few good lessons, but I still wasn't connecting with them." Christie had been jaded by all the conflict and was ready to go home. The situation was simply intolerable.

Despite the frustration of the past weeks, Christie respected Memory and Mark, so when Mark asked her to sit and talk with him, she agreed.

They went to the Gab Pub in Kasungu. They sipped their beer in the small, dingy room and discussed the school's problems. Mark had suffered too. Calvin had been his friend, had been the one to suggest he come and teach at the school. But Mark cared for the girls' well-being, so when the situation deteriorated, he had taken Christie and Memory's side.

Mark leaned forward and said, "Look. These girls...we are their only hope."

In Christie's words, "Mark was a good guy." He felt for the girls, and being Malawian himself, he knew what they were up against. Christie knew he was sincere, and reluctantly she agreed to stay.

There were many tears from the girls when Holly left—Ferig was especially unhappy—but Evan simply disappeared into the African landscape. Calvin accused Memory of using witchcraft to turn Mark against him, but otherwise he left quietly as well.

Once everyone else was gone, teaching became easier for Memory, Christie, and Mark. The three got along well. They respected each other's skills and ideas. They were united and worked as a team. Over the next few months, they did everything in their power to give the girls a stable learning environment, but they were left with many challenges.

It was around this time that two of the senior girls, Basimati and Ferig, were caught pretending to smoke a cigarette. The cigarette was old and dried out, but the intent was there, and cigarette smoking was against the rules. Christie and Memory spoke to the two girls, and they were sent home for two days as a result. The other form two girls were angry on behalf of Basimati and Ferig and decided they would go on a hunger strike.

There was also tension between the form ones and form twos. The form two girls felt they were older, more experienced, and therefore superior to the form one girls. This generated hostility that became unbearable for the younger girls.

Memory and Christie were in the office when they noticed the form one girls leaving the hostels en masse with their tiny bundles of possessions. Memory went to stop them. "What are you doing?" she asked.

Estel was their spokesperson. "We are being treated like dogs by the form two girls. Worse than dogs. We refuse to sleep with the form two girls." Their plan was to sleep in the classroom.

"Everything was just a mess," remembers Christie.

Through these difficulties Christie, Memory, and Mark kept teaching. The form two girls were told they were out of line, and the form one girls went back to sleeping in the hostels. But the form two girls decided they needed to make a point.

The form two girls refused to cook, and they refused to eat. They came to class, but while they were "on strike," they would put their heads down on their desks. They wouldn't respond to questions, and they wouldn't look at their teachers. This went on for the better part of three days. Memory and Christie pretended not to mind. "Oh well," they said, "You're the only ones suffering. We are eating. We are having a great time. In fact, it's easier when you're behaving like this because we can go through the material faster." But Christie says now, "Oh, those were long, long days."

Eventually, the girls became too hungry to continue their strike. They began eating again. Ferig and Basimati returned to school. The form twos stopped belittling the form ones and began treating the teachers with more respect. They had been outbluffed.

Once it became clear that Christie wasn't a pushover, the girls tried other strategies. They sent her notes: "I want to be your best friend." Christie was determined to ignore them.

Some of the girls had become favourites of the volunteers. Agness was one of those. Jackie, a young girl from Ontario, was popular with all the girls, but she and Agness had developed a special relationship. She had given Agness her clothes and even bought her gifts: sanitary napkins, curlers, and vitamins. Agness knew she could get things from Jackie, and so she began asking, "Can I have this?" and "Can I have that?" It had become an imbalanced relationship, and it caused jealousy among the other girls. The same sort of relationship had developed between Ferig and Holly. The girls weren't learning independence. They were learning to manipulate and to beg.

Christie was uncomfortable with the girls' behaviour, but she wasn't sure if she was doing any better than the other volunteers. She was fortunate in her relationship with Memory. When she was unsure, Christie was able to ask her, "Memory, is this okay?" Christie says now, "I was prepared to give them things, but I didn't know what was right."

Christie had many profound experiences, but one in particular helped her see the "giving" for what it was. She was at the school when one of the girls' parents came to see her. The mother held out her hands, palm up, and said, "Don't teach us to do this."

Christie now talks about that experience. "Of all the lessons I've learned in Malawi, that's the one I get. I *really* get it. Memory and Henry and I, we want to safeguard the APU girls from that. These are lovely girls, and if you go and see their homes…*Oh My God*. All you have to do is open your pocket, and with a hundred dollars you could fix their floor or stop their roof from leaking. But you would be teaching them to beg. If you want to get involved in another culture, there is some learning that has to be done."

Gordon Poultney, founder of the Simon Poultney Foundation (SPF) (a small NGO based in Zambia), has seen the problems caused by throwing money at a problem. Living in Zimbabwe at the time it gained its independence in 1980, he watched as wave after wave of foreign aid entered the country. NGOs came with tractors. They gave the tractors to the

Memory and Christie pose with several CEAG girls, 2007.

farmers, showed them how to use them, and left, but there was no plan in place to keep the machines running, no spare parts. Gordon laughs, as he says, "They say, there's no word for maintenance in any African language." The tractors were used until they stopped working and then they remained in the fields. Maybe they are there still. "[The people of this region] are used to building a house, living in it, and when it falls down because the ants have eaten it, they'll just build another one," says Gordon.

Gordon told me another story. Shortly before he left Zimbabwe in 1987, he took an eight-day canoe trip down the Zambezi. As he travelled down the river, on the Zambian side, he noticed a row of at least a dozen windmills. He asked the guide about the purpose of the windmills. "That's some project," said the guide. "The NGO put these windmills in the middle of nowhere. The idea was to pump water out of the river to grow vegetables, but once the people made enough money to last the rest of the year, they said, 'We've got enough money.' So the whole project collapsed."

It isn't uncommon for African aid projects to collapse or go awry. In fact, it happens far too frequently. Well-intentioned foreigners see the suffering of Malawi's poor, and they want to help. Sometimes they have the wealth or connections that lead them to believe they are the ones who should found the next NGO or start the next initiative.

Perhaps the most famous case lies in pop star Madonna's messy undertakings in that country. In 2006, soon after adopting a young Malawian boy, Madonna founded the charity Raising Malawi to "bring an end to the extreme poverty and hardship endured by Malawi's 1.4 million orphans and vulnerable children once and for all."[4] In 2009, the celebrity travelled to Malawi where she planted a moringa tree on land donated by the Malawian government and promised to build a $15 million school, Raising Malawi Academy for Girls, on the site just outside the capital city. The school was to be designed by New York architect Markus Dochantschi and would house nearly five hundred students. Initial plans for the school were truly spectacular, with sketches of the proposed school appearing in *Architectural Digest*. The artist's depictions showed a sprawling campus with modern rippling roofs and covered open-air walkways.[5]

Madonna claimed she wanted to give opportunities to underprivileged girls. "I realized how much they deserve to be educated and so for me the best thing I could do was to build a school, a unique school that will create future female leaders, scientists, lawyers, doctors, and if this school is successful it will be used as a model to replicate in other countries," she said.[6]

But the school was not successful. Two years later, and without a single brick laid, the elite academy was scrapped due to "alleged mismanagement of funds."[7] John Bisika, Malawi's national secretary for education, science and technology, called it a "mockery of the government."[8]

Soon a new plan was put into place. Raising Malawi wished to return the land originally intended for the Raising Malawi Academy for Girls. The old Raising Malawi board had been sacked,[9] and the charity now intended to follow a "community-based approach." They would "provide the opportunity for many more girls to receive a quality education."[10]

The new plan involved partnering with buildOn, an existing NGO, to "construct ten new schools in the district of Kasungu."[11] But it didn't take long before Madonna's plan received harsh criticism from government and other Malawian officials. Undule Mwakasungula, executive director of the Centre for Human Rights and Rehabilitation, accused Madonna of "playing games with Malawians,"[12] and Lindiwe Chide, a spokesperson for Malawi's Ministry of Education, said, "We now feel like this is all about propping up her global image and not in our interest."[13]

I've no doubt that Madonna and the vast majority of grassroots NGO founders have nothing but the best of intentions for the country and its people when they drill wells or fund orphanages or build schools, but there needs to be more to an aid organization than good intentions. There must be integrity, cooperation, vision, collaboration, under-standing, knowledge, and a willingness to invest the time it takes to appreciate the complexities of a foreign culture.

Gordon Poultney displays both hope and cynicism as we talk about grassroots NGOs. He's met many people who decide to set up their own organization because they want to be the person who "saves the world." They'll raise some money and make contact with someone they think is a good local leader. Then they'll decide to construct a couple of houses, but they only have a month, so they'll leave the project in someone else's hands. This is invariably a disastrous formula. Gordon bluntly states, "Unfortunately, in my experience the majority of charitable ventures in this area just don't make it." Gordon believes that if a group or an indi-vidual wishes to start an aid initiative, they've got "to spend the time to learn the community's priorities and then be prepared to spend quality time there. Or find an existing organization and partner with them."

As I speak to Gordon, I can see that, like me, he is torn over this issue, and he soon concedes, "The only way things are going to change, in Africa in particular, is through small organizations working at the grassroots level." And then he adds, "But whatever you do, it's got to be sustainable, or it's got to create sustainability."

Sadly, since my conversation with Gordon, SPF has had to discontinue its initiatives in Zambia. It's sad because the organization had many qualities that could have ensured its success. Gordon possesses knowledge of the Zambian culture and its people, and the organization had strong connections to Canada, building up a powerful support structure over the years. SPF's decision to withdraw from the country further demonstrates the difficulty of sustaining an overseas NGO whose funding originates on a separate continent.

Companion of the Order of Canada and former UN special envoy for HIV/AIDS, Stephen Lewis, advocates for a staunch brand of global humanitarianism: "You feel positively delinquent if you can be self-indulgent when all around you, people are moving heaven and earth to survive."[14] And this is the reason for the founding of NGOs: people do want to help.

In her book, *Give a Little*, Wendy Smith, a twenty-year veteran of the nonprofit sector, suggests people become "enlightened donors," and she sets out a series of criteria for giving:

1. *The organization creates substantial change in the lives of the recipients.*
2. *The organization creates long-term, demonstrated, positive outcomes that are measurable.*
3. *The organization generates high returns.*
4. *The organization builds self-sufficiency.*[15]

Smith uses the example of providing goats to families in India as a project that creates substantial change. A goat "improves the family's physical and economic health by providing milk...to consume and to sell. More income allows families to send children to school."[16] For an impoverished Indian family, a goat is more than just a goat.

APU has demonstrated long-term positive outcomes through the success of its students. Some of the successes of the project, such as improved self-esteem, are difficult to measure, but others are easily measurable by evaluating the girls' success on their MSCEs, their acceptance into post-secondary programs, and their employability.

A well-conceived, successfully implemented NGO will exhibit all of these characteristics and others as well. I would add to Smith's list the necessity for local consultation and involvement. It is not enough to "want to help." That help must come in a form that gives voice to the community's needs, empowers the population, and involves input from the local population. Otherwise, a project sets up an unbalanced relationship between the donor and the recipient, demonstrates a distasteful kind of neocolonialism, and is almost certainly doomed to failure.

⊟ As Christie learned about the culture and developed confidence, she began to enact rules that she thought would benefit the girls and their learning. They began calling her Mrs. Johnson, which some would say in a mocking tone. Mesi continued mocking long after the other girls had stopped. Christie talked to her after class.

"I don't like how you said that."

"I was only teasing," Mesi responded.

"No, that's not teasing. Your teasing feels like mocking to me."

So she said, "Okay. No more smiling. I'm not going to make any more jokes."

But over time, the girls' attitude improved, even Mesi's.

Because Christie was a science teacher in Canada, her fondest memories are of the science classes she taught the girls. One day, she taught them about the food web. As the girls walked into class, she handed them a paper cutout. She had placed folded tape on the back so the girls could stick the cutouts on their foreheads. Selina's was a fish, and it was so big it covered her eyes, but she was proud of it and didn't want to take it off. She wore it the entire day. To teach the girls about buoyancy, Christie blew up a balloon and the girls tried to push the balloon down into a bucket of water. The balloon didn't want to go. Each time a girl pushed it down, it popped back up, and the girls giggled. To illustrate bacteria growth, Christie had brought agar with her from Canada. The girls swabbed the insides of their cheeks to see what would grow in the petri dishes. They loved the experiment.

There were sad times too. Christie and the CEAG girls often saw a young girl, Ivy, picking termites with her two brothers in a nearby field. The children would pluck the termites from the ground, snap off their legs, and stuff the insects into their pockets. The termites were taken home and later eaten.

Not much is known about Ivy. I've tried to learn more about her since I heard her story, but despite enquiries, I was unable to learn anything apart from what Christie and Memory had already told me. For me, this reflects the silent anonymity of her fate.

Ivy didn't come from Memory's village, nor was she related to any of the CEAG girls. She was simply small and tragic, with an enormous, pregnant belly; thin, young limbs; and a gaunt, defeated expression. The girls had heard that she had been impregnated by a teacher and expelled from school, but no one seemed to know much more about her.

Some months after Christie first noticed her sitting in the field searching for termites, Ivy died in childbirth. Christie recalls hearing her death cries as they were carried across the plains. "It was unholy." That night, Christie went to check on the girls in their hostels. "They had their *chitenjes* over their heads, and they were just sitting, waiting it out."

According to UNICEF, there are 810 maternal deaths for every 100,000 births in Malawi. That number jumps to 1,100 when adjusted for error and underreporting. The lifetime risk of death during delivery for a Malawian woman is 1:18. To put the number into perspective, Canada records seven maternal deaths for every 100,000 births, or a lifetime risk of dying in childbirth of 1:1,100.[17] It's still dangerous to give birth in Malawi.

According to UNICEF, a girl who gives birth before she reaches the age of fifteen is five times more likely to die in childbirth than a woman in her twenties.[18] As this statistic suggests, a young girl is far more likely than a mature woman, with a fully developed body, to suffer from complications during pregnancy and delivery.

In adolescent girls, the pelvis is less mature and the birth canal is narrower.[19] This alone can lead to numerous complications. Obstructed or prolonged labour, hemorrhaging, and fistula can all result from delivering a child from a small immature body. Sepsis, or infection, can result from prolonged labour and delivery. Other complications, such as eclampsia, are also more common throughout pregnancy in young mothers.[20]

Young mothers who survive their pregnancy are often left with traumatic injuries. An obstetric fistula is an opening between the vagina and the rectum or urethra that allows urine or feces (in some cases both) to flow from the vagina.[21] A fistula results from "extended pressure of the child's head against the soft tissue in the mother's pelvis. The tissue eventually dies from the lack of blood supply."[22] UNFPA reproductive health officer, Dorothy Lazaro, says, "We have come across girls as young as thirteen giving birth, and this age group usually risks developing fistula."[23]

Apart from physical difficulties—incontinence and sometimes infection—caused by obstetric fistulas, women can face years of shame and ostracism, by both their families and their communities.[24] As a result of their incontinence, they smell badly and often leak feces and urine as they try to go about their daily chores. Two thousand pregnancies result in obstetric fistulas every year in Malawi. It is a condition for which the country's health care system is ill equipped.

In 2007, Stella Kawelama developed a fistula trying to deliver her first child at the age of nineteen. Soon after, "[my husband] chased me out of the matrimonial home, and I had no choice but to join my grandmother."

In 2008, Stella attended a "Fistula Week" at Zomba General Hospital. The event was sponsored by UNFPA and brought together two specialists and eleven clinical officers. The one-week clinic became two, during which time forty-five women received treatment. Stella's operation was a success. "I can't wait to get back home," she said upon her release.[25]

A new clinic, opened in 2012, has given women renewed hope for improving their lives. At the opening of a fistula care centre in Bwaila District Hospital, the first of its kind in the country, President Joyce Banda said, "It is sad to see such women often alienated from their families and community to the extent that they find it difficult to return to their homes even after being assisted. I wish to appeal for an end to stigma and discrimination against women with fistula."[26]

The experiences of the women of Malawi are often unimaginable and sometimes bizarre. On one occasion, Memory told me about her cousin, Luwiza. Luwiza married young, at the age of thirteen, and soon became pregnant. When it came time for her to give birth, she was unable to deliver the child. The baby had to be cut into pieces so it could be removed from her body. Later, there was no money to hire a car to take mother and child to the funeral, so she bundled her baby in a basket. Carrying the basket in her arms, Luwiza caught a minibus to go to the cemetery, all the while pretending nothing was amiss.

Once married, there is a great deal of pressure on women to have children soon afterwards. "Women from the village, when they are not educated, the only thing that can keep their marriage is the children," says Memory. After a miscarriage, a woman will try for another baby as soon as possible. Soon after Luwiza's first pregnancy, she became pregnant again. She was able to deliver the second child successfully.

Very few rural women go to a clinic or hospital to deliver, but within many villages there are women who help with deliveries. Now known as traditional birth attendants (TBAs), these women will attend pregnant women for a small fee, likely goods or services in kind. Their skills are usually passed from one woman to another. In general, an elderly TBA will teach her skills to a younger relative or someone she trusts.

For a time, TBAs were banned in Malawi, and they were forced to work in secrecy. The ban went into effect in 2007 because it was thought that TBAs were "unable to identify obstetric emergency cases early enough."[27] But the sad truth is that Malawi lacks sufficient medical facilities, doctors, and nurses to effectively support all the country's pregnant women, so the ban was lifted in 2010.

"We need to train traditional birth attendants in safer delivery methods," said President Mutharika when he lifted the ban. And many, although not all, TBAs do attend a two-week training session. Dorothy Ngoma, executive director of the National Organization of Nurses and Midwives in Malawi, believes the country needs to establish a two-year midwife training program that would improve the care women receive during their deliveries, as well as the support they require pre- and postnatal.[28]

Despite exceptions such as Ivy, it is far more unlikely that a girl who is pursuing secondary education will become pregnant than a girl of the same age who is not attending school.[29] According to South African Health Minister Barbara Hogan, "If young girls are not in school, they are more vulnerable. It's not just a health issue; it is about the status of young women and girls."[30]

In a traditional village setting, girls can be quite naive about the reproductive process. Christie once told me, "The girls who haven't had sex, they wouldn't even know what parts to put in where. Most children have seen their mom and dad having sex night after night. But they don't necessarily know [what's happening]." Christie recalled teaching biology at the CEAG school: "I had a book of the female body, and it showed the baby growing inside the mother. All the girls, they couldn't believe what they were seeing." If girls are going to make informed decisions about sex, it's vitally important that they understand their own bodies. During secondary school, girls learn about reproductive health and become informed about their bodies.

Memory's sister, Lucy, taught at APU for several years before moving back to Lilongwe to pursue other opportunities. Lucy was an exceptional teacher and when I visited the school, it was evident that she was able to connect in a meaningful way with the girls. "Teaching gave me the platform to communicate and meet the girls' needs," she said.

While Lucy was pregnant with her first child, Wanga, she was teaching biology at the school. The form four students were learning about reproduction, and Lucy was able to use her own body as an example: pointing to the baby and explaining the birthing process. Lucy remembers, "The girls were laughing." And she felt like she was connecting with them and having an impact on their lives. If girls are to make informed choices about reproduction and birth control, they need to feel comfortable with their bodies. Reproduction is only frightening if it's a mystery.

Audrey

WHEN I LEARNED that Audrey was living in the Greater Edmonton area, I phoned her and asked if she'd meet with me.[1] Audrey had spent an entire year in Malawi, and I wanted to get her perspective on the country. I wondered why she had never gone back.

Audrey and I met in a small tea shop on the north side of Edmonton. We drank herbal infusions, and Audrey explained why she'd chosen to come back to Canada. "A woman cannot have true independence there because they are always a victim of the culture," she said. Then she related the following story.

Audrey would often go with Calvin to Kasungu by minibus to do business for the school. On one such trip, they spent the day in town and were getting ready to catch another bus back to the village. Before leaving Kasungu, they stopped at a hotel to pick up a cold drink for the trip home. An election was coming up, and while they were getting their Fantas, a local politician began talking to Calvin. He knew about the school, and he knew Audrey and Calvin were connected to it. "My driver and I are having a cold drink here, but we'll be done in a few minutes. Then we'll drive you back to the school. I'd like to give you some money for the girls' education." The few minutes turned into an hour and then two. It was now late in the afternoon, and there were no more buses until the next day. Audrey and Calvin had no money for a hotel room. They were forced to wait for their ride. They had nowhere else to go.

Calvin is Malawian, so he knows the customs, and he's a large, intimidating man. Audrey hoped she could trust his judgment. After several hours of drinking, the politician was drunk. Finally, he said, "All right. We are going now." They all piled into his car.

The politician passed out in the front seat, but instead of driving in the direction of the school, the driver drove the opposite way. It was dark by now, and the driver took them through a maze of criss-crossed, rural, dirt roads. Eventually, they came to a clearing filled with people, their silhouettes lit by fire and their shadows shifting in the dim light. Audrey was frightened. "What is going on here?" she thought.

The driver woke up the politician, and they all got out of the car. The crowd was gathered around a small stage. The politician stepped up onto the stage and began throwing handfuls of money at the crowd. He spoke loudly in Chichewa. Audrey asked Calvin, "What is he saying?"

But Calvin would only say, "Don't worry about it."

After a half an hour or so, they all got back in the car, the politician passed out again, and the driver kept driving. They came to another clearing with more people. The politician again got up on stage and began speaking and throwing money. At one point during his speech he pointed toward Audrey, and the people cheered. Audrey turned to Calvin and asked him what was going on.

Calvin said, "He just told them that you are going to buy them a well." Audrey was both terrified and livid.

The politician got back in the car, and they drove to his house outside Kasungu. When the car stopped, he said to Audrey, "You stay at my house tonight." Audrey refused to leave the car. Instead, she waited in the dark, frightened. Eventually, the politician came back out of his house. "Okay, my driver will take you home," he said. He took Audrey's hand in his and stroked it with his fingers. "It was a pleasure to meet you. I'll see you again soon." The driver didn't drive them home. He drove them into Kasungu, and they were forced to stay at a hotel after all so they could catch a minibus back to the village the next day.

The following week, the politician sent Audrey a note saying, "I'm going to meet the President. Pack your bag and come with my driver. You will accompany me."

Audrey wrote back, "Thank you very much for the invitation. Unfortunately, I have plans. I hope you and your wife have a wonderful time with the President." And she gave it to the driver, but she knew this was a problem that would not go away, and she was frightened.

Audrey didn't see the politician again until the next time she was in Kasungu. While she was at the supermarket, he showed up with several men. The men forced her into a back room, and he began yelling at her, "What's wrong with you? Why didn't you come with me, you stupid woman?"

Audrey had no recourse. She was simply fortunate that they eventually let her go, but she feared for her life. "I was allowed to live because they decided that I should. My saving grace was that the election hadn't happened yet."

There were many things about Malawi that Audrey grew to love, but it was her helplessness in the face of this situation and others that made her decide she could never stay.

9
A Trip to the Lake

Home to many hundreds of fish
species, nearly all endemic,
[Lake Malawi's] importance
for the study of evolution is
comparable to that of the finches
of the Galapagos Islands.

—UNESCO[1]

BEFORE SHE LEFT FOR MALAWI, Holly had asked her mother to fund-raise through her church.[2] The money was to be used for the girls to go to the lake. Even though it was less than a half-day's drive away, it was the first time that most of the girls would see more water than they could "carry in a bucket." It would be a great adventure.

Holly had returned to Canada, but the trip had already been arranged. CEAG was partnering with a nearby primary school. The date had been set, and the money had been paid. The headmaster of the primary school had arranged for transportation.

On the morning of the trip, the girls woke up early. They boiled eggs. They packed flour and cooking pots so they could make *nsima* at the lake. They all went into class to play games and wait for the truck to arrive. Every twenty minutes or so, a vehicle would drive by on the road, and all the girls would race to the window. When the vehicle didn't stop at the school, the girls would walk glumly back to their desks—disappointed. The truck never did come that day, but shortly before dark, a boy rode up to the school on a bicycle. He handed Memory a note. The note said the truck would come tomorrow. The girls ate hard-boiled eggs for dinner that evening.

The next morning, the sun rose again over the African savannah. The cooking supplies were repacked, the girls boiled fresh eggs, and the waiting began again. The girls waited. It was nine o'clock. Then it was ten. Then it was eleven and then twelve. The girls were crazy with excitement, but no truck came.

The same thing happened the following day, and the day after that, and the day after that. No more notes were delivered to the school, and Memory and Christie thought the trip had been called off. Then, one day, a truck pulled up in front of the school. It was a big truck, but it was already filled to capacity with primary school children and teachers—mostly teachers. The girls gathered their things. They packed the boiled eggs—saved from an earlier day—and squeezed into the back of the truck. Memory rode in the back with the girls, but the girls thought

Christie should ride in the front. Christie was already spitting mad when she hiked up her skirt and climbed into the cab with four men. It was a tight squeeze. The only place she could put her feet was on either side of the gearshift, and throughout the drive her butt got hotter and hotter. There was a broken seal under her seat, so it felt to Christie like she was sitting on the engine. By the time they reached Lilongwe, her skin had blistered and she was bleeding through her skirt.

The driver parked the truck, and without telling anyone where they were going, all the men got out. An hour went by and then another. The women and children sat in the hot sun waiting for the men to return. Most of the girls had never been to Lilongwe, and they wanted to explore, but Memory and Christie had to say no because they didn't know when the men would return. The girls didn't have anything to drink, but they took out their hard-boiled eggs to eat. In the days they had spent waiting for the truck, the eggs had turned bad, but the girls didn't want to complain, so they choked them down. When the men finally returned, Christie learned they had been checking their tobacco stocks, and they had all eaten. They brought back pop and snacks for their own children, and it dawned on Christie that the teachers' children were the only students they had brought with them.

When they finally reached Salima, it was dark, so they had to wait until the following morning to see the lake. Arrangements had been made for them to stay at Salima Secondary School and sleep in the science classroom.

Other than Memory and Christie, all but one of the teachers was male. They had brought one female teacher along to cook and care for the children. The woman cooked *nsima* while the men talked around the fire. Christie could hear them speaking in loud voices: "That is a lazy woman."

After they had eaten, one of the men came to see Memory and Christie. "I'm sorry," he said. "We need to leave first thing in the morning, so we won't be able to see the lake. The driver is demanding more money if we stay." They added, "We don't have enough money to pay him."

Christie was outraged, but she tried not to show it. "There's no way that waiting another couple hours should cost more money."

But there was no point in arguing. If she wanted the girls to see the lake, this was the price. She angrily paid the bribe.

It had been a terrible day for both Memory and Christie, but for the sake of the girls, they kept their cool. While the air buzzed with mosquitoes, Christie laid out her sleeping bag, and Memory and the girls laid out their *chitenjes* on the hard cement floor of the science room.

In the morning, they woke up covered in mosquito bites, but the girls didn't care. They were at the lake. With the last of her money, Christie bought fresh fish, and the girls ate freshly cooked fish, for the first time in their lives.

The water seemed to go on forever. From the broad, sandy beach, the girls couldn't see far-off Mozambique. All they saw were the rolling waves and endless sky. It was a cloudless day—it nearly always is in Malawi—and the sun was warm on their faces. The girls were wearing their shirts and skirts. They had no bathing suits, but they took off their shoes and ran through the sand. Ferig, always the bravest, ran right in. Once the other girls saw her do this, they tried it too. The girls who had bras took off their shirts and plunged into the water. The rest dived in with all their clothes on. None of them could swim, but Christie had taught them about buoyancy, and now she taught them how to float.

Memory had borrowed a bathing suit for this trip, but she felt very uncomfortable. She had never worn a bathing suit before, so it was a whole new awkward experience. But she loved the water, and joined the girls in their play.

Christie had put herself through university by teaching swimming and lifeguarding, so she watched the girls closely. As she stood back, a tourist came by to tell her they had just seen a crocodile in the area, so Christie was hyperalert, but she wasn't about to call the girls in. They deserved to have this experience.

Ferig plowed into the water head first, thrashing her arms and legs. Estel had found a mango and ate it in the water. Memory and the girls skipped and laughed. They ran and held hands, splashing and singing songs. They had turned into little girls. It was the happiest Christie had ever seen them. It was the first time she'd seen some of them laugh. It was the first time she had seen Selina smile. They stayed until late in the afternoon and all went back to the school exhausted. For the girls, the trip was a huge success.

The women who were once the CEAG girls still talk about the trip. The rotten egg incident is legendary. Selina says, "To this day, I can't eat eggs." And teasing Christie, she giggles, "Not after those eggs you fed us."

They were back at school for not much more than a week when the girls asked Memory and Christie if they could have a couple of days off school to go to a funeral. Christie asked them, "Who has died?"

"It is Mr. Phiri from the field trip." And the girls described one of the teachers who had gone to the lake with them.

"We just saw him. What did he die from?" Christie asked.

"He died from AIDS."

"Does he have a wife?" Christie asked, thinking she, too, would be infected.

"His third wife just died," she was told.

"Well, what did she die from?"

"She died of AIDS."

Christie began to wonder. "What happened to the second wife?"

"She died of AIDS," the girls replied.

"And what about the first wife?"

"She died of AIDS too."

Christie was astonished. After the death of the first wife, the second and third wives would know they were marrying someone infected with the HIV/AIDS virus. So she asked the question that was suddenly on her mind. "Would any of you marry someone you knew had AIDS?"

Basimati put up her hand. "Yes," she said. "At least I could eat until I died."

On my trips to Malawi, I have not met a Malawian who has not had his or her life altered by the HIV/AIDS epidemic. Mothers and fathers leave behind children, while neighbours and friends leave behind spouses to carry on without them. Often, as in the case of Memory's aunt and uncle, and perhaps her parents, the diagnosis of AIDS is not a certainty but rather a conjecture based on the accumulation of familiar symptoms: headaches, fever, weight loss, a slow wasting away, and, finally, death. Memory can never be sure what killed her uncle and later her aunt. She can't even be sure what killed her mother and father. It could have been HIV/AIDS, and in the cases of her aunt and uncle, it almost certainly was, but as with so many of her fellow Malawians, she will never know for sure.

The HIV/AIDS epidemic has devastated sub-Saharan Africa. It rode in slyly and cut down entire communities. It left children orphaned and mothers widowed—entire communities decimated. One tragedy among many is this: In the early days of the pandemic it went largely unnoticed. What were more deaths among so many on a continent where life was already perilous?

It's possible that cross-species transmission of the precursor to the HIV virus could have taken place sporadically over the centuries, but according to Jacques Pepin, a Canadian doctor and author of *The Origins of AIDS*, it was the combination of urbanization, enforced vaccination programs, and the colonial construction boom that turned it into an epidemic.[3]

Simian immunodeficiency virus (SIV) is carried by chimpanzees and was likely transmitted to humans—and transformed into HIV—through the butchering or consumption of bush meat. Chimpanzees are difficult to hunt: they are extremely mobile and usually inhabit isolated areas of the forest. However, colonialism led to the widespread use of firearms and the construction of roads that led into previously uninhabited areas.

These conditions prompted an increase in the killing and butchering of these primates.

Pepin traces ground zero of the epidemic to the construction of the Congo-Océan Railway. Construction began in 1921 and continued until its completion in 1934. An initial 127,250 native African men were conscripted to work on the line. They were housed in torturous conditions—fifty to sixty men slept in a room. They were poorly fed and forced to work long hours six days a week. Not surprisingly, epidemics broke out in the work camps and many died as a consequence. The resulting scandal back in the French homeland led to improved conditions. One of the improvements was to allow a limited number of women into the camps. The men, having been taken from their wives, families, and communities, became the impetus for a thriving sex trade: "Prostitutes were noted to collect 'their fees on paydays amidst long palavers.'"[4]

Once the disease was established on the continent, it's likely that overly ambitious and strictly enforced vaccination, diagnostic, and treatment programs amplified its transmission. Throughout the first half of the twentieth century, the French colonies put into practice a number of aggressive tropical disease control programs. Sometimes humanitarian, but as often self-serving—after all, a diminished workforce was not conducive to colonial objectives—these programs targeted sleeping sickness, leprosy, yaws, as well as various STDs. I will supply one historic example, but keep in mind, there are many others.

In 1929, the Croix-Rouge du Congo set up first one and then another STD clinic in Léopoldville (now Kinshasa) in what is now the Democratic Republic of Congo (DRC). Léopoldville was a quickly expanding urban centre and provided free care for men and women suffering from STDs. However, the majority of clients entering the clinic were free women: unmarried women with an independent source of income. Free women were required by law to come into the clinic for screening on a monthly basis—adding up to thirty-two thousand visits in a peak year for approximately 3,500 women.[5]

Ninety-seven per cent of patients with "syphilis" were treated repeatedly with drugs administered intravenously or intramuscularly. Unfortunately, for these patients, the majority of these cases were probably cases of yaws, a non-STD with a similar bacterium. A similar scenario prevailed for the treatment of gonorrhea.

During the 1930s and 1940s, the clinics issued fifty thousand injections a year. In the 1950s, this number increased to around one hundred thousand injections a year. A report written by Dr. Paul Beheyt in 1953 sheds light on the treatment of patients:

> At the Dispensaire Antivénéien de la Croix-Rouge in Léopoldville, on average three hundred injections are administered each day. The large number of patients and the small quantity of syringes available to the nursing staff preclude sterilization by autoclave after each use. Used syringes are simply rinsed, first with water, then with alcohol and ether, and are ready for a new patient.[6]

The earliest confirmed case of HIV infection comes from a sample taken in the DRC (likely Léopoldville) in 1959 and discovered miraculously some twenty-six years later.[7] Once HIV gained its foothold in Central Africa, it was free to spread throughout the world. An isolated, but instructive, anecdote comes to us from Norway and demonstrates how easily the virus could have travelled from continent to continent. In 1976, a Norwegian family died (a father, mother, and their nine-year-old daughter), all in that same year. Their sera was tested twelve years after their deaths and found to be HIV-positive. The girl had been born in 1967, implying that her mother was HIV-positive at the time. The father had been a sailor who had visited a number of African ports in the early 1960s. He probably contracted the disease from prostitutes in Nigeria or Cameroon, where he spent time in 1961 and 1962.[8] The AIDS epidemic is indeed a collection of tragedies both global and personal.

Although the National AIDS Control Programme claims that the HIV/AIDS epidemic entered Malawi in 1982, there is evidence to suggest that it infiltrated the country much earlier. During the late 1970s, Sister Ursula worked as a nurse at Mua Hospital—a Catholic hospital located in the Dedza District of Central Malawi. Sister Ursula remembers a patient she cared for in 1978:

> *The man could have been an AIDS patient. He wouldn't recover from TB treatment. We tried everything, but finally, he died. Other missionary sisters who were also working here in hospitals and in primary health care, and who have been here for over thirty years and thus have seen many AIDS patients, also claim to have come across similar cases.*[9]

The first validated case occurred in February 1985 at the Queen Elizabeth Central Hospital in Blantyre. Since then, hundreds of thousands have died.

Stephen Lewis was the UN Secretary-General's special envoy for HIV/AIDS in Africa from 2001 to 2006. During that time, he encountered death, disease, and suffering on a grand scale. Since then, he has been a tireless advocate for HIV prevention and treatment: "The ongoing plight of Africa forces me to perpetual rage. It's all so unnecessary, so crazy that hundreds of millions of people should be thus abandoned."[10] He condemns the international community for its slow and often inadequate efforts to assist African countries in stemming the spread of the virus, and reserves particularly stern criticism for Canada's Conservative government under Stephen Harper. When an NDP motion to allow the production of low-cost, generic ARVs for use in developing countries was voted down by the Conservative majority in 2012, Lewis explained, "When a government prioritizes the balance sheets of drug corporations over the lives of children, they have lost the authority to govern."[11]

Lewis is unrepentant in his condemnation. He will accept no objection, reminding developed countries of the chaos caused by colonialism, sudden national independence, conflicting Cold War influences, and the structural adjustment programs (SAPs) of the IMF and World Bank: "SAPs were Reaganomics gone berserk. It is my contention that for almost twenty years, those rigid fundamentalist policies did extraordinary damage to African economies from which they have yet to recover." It's Lewis's belief that the SAPs insistence on user fees for health and education services lies at the heart of many countries' inability to respond effectively to the HIV/AIDS crisis.[12] "They weren't being allowed to hire more staff and pay better salaries, because it would breach the macroeconomic straitjacket,"[13] Lewis explains.

Attaching conditions, meant to improve Africa's governance, to large loans and other forms of foreign aid may seem like a prudent strategy, but it is a case of developed countries imposing their own paradigms, and often their own arrogance, on the desperate. Ultimately, it became a case of trying to hammer a square peg into a round hole: it simply didn't fit.

Thankfully, the HIV/AIDS epidemic has slowly reversed its course throughout most of sub-Saharan Africa—including Malawi. In 2001, an estimated sixty-eight thousand Malawians died from the outbreak. By 2012, that number had decreased to forty-six thousand. It's still a lot of deaths, especially for a country of only seventeen million people. Compare that to Canada, with a population of approximately thirty-four million. In each of those years, we have documented fewer than five hundred AIDS-related deaths in this country.[14]

In the 2010 United Nations report, *Global Report: UNAIDS Report on the Global AIDS Epidemic*, UNAIDS Executive Director Michel Sidibé states, "We have halted and begun to reverse the epidemic. Fewer people are becoming infected with HIV and fewer people are dying from AIDS."[15] This is the general consensus among international agencies. Yet, while the rate of infection is dwindling, the epidemic has left an indelible mark on Malawi and other African countries. It may take decades, if not generations, to erase the damage the HIV/AIDS epidemic has done to the country and its people. Nearly an entire generation has been wiped out, leaving behind a generation of orphans.[16] With grandparents left to raise grandchildren and sisters left to raise brothers, it is a country still in mourning.

Many of the girls at *Atsikana Pa Ulendo* have lost a close relative to the epidemic, but I know this because of my conversations with Memory. The girls will tell me about distant relatives or neighbours who have died from AIDS, but when we discuss close relatives, they speak differently. They say, "She stepped on some medicine. Then she became sick and died." Or they might say, "He was sick for a long time, and then he died." I can't be sure if they do not know the details of their mother or father's death, or if they are simply uncomfortable sharing them.

Memory explains the effects of the HIV/AIDS epidemic on her country: "Instead of going forward, we are going backward. There's no development when people are sick." According to the WHO, "the evidence is stark: disease breeds instability in poor countries."[17]

Malawi depends on labour-intense subsistence agriculture. Agriculture accounts for more than a third of Malawi's GDP, 90 per cent of the country's export income—with the majority of that income coming from tobacco crops.[18] Families throughout rural Malawi—and many in urban Malawi as well—maintain gardens for personal consumption. If a family has access to enough land and labour, they often choose to grow tobacco as a cash crop. Subsistence agriculture relies upon a healthy, vital population.

On my first trip to Malawi in 2007, I met with Memory's grandfather and grandmother. They grow maize, groundnuts, and tobacco (or *fodia*)—as well as small quantities of other staples such as tomatoes and beans. Working daily in their gardens, the two are able to grow and harvest enough food to sustain themselves throughout the year. That year they hoped to earn 15,000 kwacha (C$93) from the sale of tobacco. A large portion of this "spending money" goes to purchase fertilizer for the next year's crops.

Memory's grandparents are well off when compared to many rural families. They have their health. They have their land. They have their community. But 2007 was a year of good harvests. It's easy to imagine what would happen if one of Memory's grandparents became too ill to

Memory's grandfather speaks about his changing country, 2007.

work the garden, if the rains didn't come, or if they couldn't afford to purchase fertilizer. Rural life in Malawi exists with a narrow margin of error.

If a husband becomes seriously ill, his wife might need to till, plant, weed, and harvest without assistance. This is strenuous labour, especially when you consider that she would still need to pound maize, haul water, wash clothes, cook *nsima*, care for children, and complete all the other daily chores that are required in rural Malawi. In the case of serious illness, hospital bills compound these hardships. Except for the most basic of services, there are almost always user fees attached to medical care.

APU girl, Tiyamike, told me about a time when her parents were both ill. Her family's hardship began when her father fell from a tree and broke his leg. He sent a neighbour to ask one of his children to help take him home. Tiyamike took his bicycle so he could ride it home. "My father failed to peddle the bicycle. He tried his best until he reached home. When he reached home, he slept. From that time he felt very sick."

It wasn't long afterwards that Tiyamike was called from her work at the garden to go home and help her mother. "When we were still digging, Elice [my sister] came. When I asked her why she was crying, she said, 'Go home fast. Our mother is sick!' Because she was crying, I started crying too."

By the time she got home, Tiyamike's mother and father had both been taken to the hospital. "Me and my sisters finished digging alone while our parents were sick. Although we were going to school, we tried our best until we finished. When my parents were sick, I felt the earth was against me." While their parents were ill, Tiyamike and her siblings had to take on additional responsibilities, but Tiyamike's story had a happy ending: "After three months, my parents were fine, and they harvested the crops with us. We were happy and joyful to see them working with us."[19] One can only imagine the consequences if Tiyamike's parents had failed to recover or suffered a terminal illness. This is the fate of many Malawian children.

Lack of education, existing cultural norms, and an absence of opportunities have left most women economically dependent on men. This reinforces their social dependence and increases the likelihood of their contracting HIV. A disproportionately large number of women within the fifteen-to-nineteen-year age demographic are infected with HIV. Perhaps this is not surprising as one in five women in the adolescent age bracket say they were forced into their first sexual encounter, and young women are often pressed into marriage with an older man.[20] John Aberle-Gaffe of the US Centers for Disease Control believes, "When the poverty is this bad, you'll trade sex for food, sex for shelter, sex to not get beat up, sex to not get thrown out of the house."[21]

In 2008, the charity Theatre for a Change conducted a survey in five primary teacher training colleges (TTCs). Male teachers were questioned on their attitudes and knowledge about HIV risk and prevention. The findings were enlightening.

Of the 336 respondents, 77 per cent claimed they sometimes or always used condoms. Half of the respondents stated that condoms were against their religion, and over half had never heard of antiretroviral HIV treatment. The report concluded, "The findings of the survey indicate a high level of HIV-risk among pre-service teachers and a strong indication that this will be passed on to their future pupils."[22]

Malawi has taken many steps to curb the AIDS epidemic, mostly through educational programs. Travelling through Malawi, I saw large billboards intended to educate the public on the value of condom use: "Don't be fooled. AIDS is real. It is not witchcraft. Protect yourself. USE A CONDOM." I wondered at the efficacy of this approach, since the majority of Malawians, at least those who have not attended secondary school, have little or no written English-language skills. In fact, during the Family Health International study cited, billboards were the least-reported source of information on HIV/AIDS—the radio was the most-reported. Still, the country is making strides in education, and it is attempting to take away the stigma attached to the disease.

Voluntary counselling and testing for HIV/AIDS began in Malawi in 1992, but at first, access was extremely limited. Eventually, improvements were made to the system, and in 2000, same-day testing for HIV became available. In the early days, the system had its problems. Because of the associated stigma, most people were reluctant to get tested for the virus and resources were limited. Dr. Thafatatha, a district health officer for the Kasungu District Hospital, admitted, "It's difficult to meet the needs of the patients because we don't have sufficient staff, training or equipment. Patients have to wait several hours to get their HIV test results. Many leave and have to come back the next day; a few never return for their results."[23]

In 2004, then President Bakili Muluzi called for an end to the shame attached to HIV/AIDS. Three years previously, Muluzi's brother had died of the disease. "I am not ashamed myself to disclose that my beloved brother Dickson died of AIDS," he said, after initiating the county's first wide-scale HIV treatment program. The program "makes anti-retroviral drugs available to the public, offers a framework for the care for AIDS patients and orphans," but more importantly it has attempted to reduce the stigma of the disease by prohibiting discrimination against AIDS patients and encouraging the public to be tested for the disease. Muluzi publicly declared that he had gone for testing himself.[24] From 2004 to 2008, following the implementation of Muluzi's initiative, Malawi saw a 10 per cent decrease in AIDS-related deaths in the rural adult population.[25]

Two years later, President Muluzi's successor, President Bingu wa Mutharika, launched a week-long campaign devised to reach remote rural areas of the country, but a week was not nearly enough to reach even a fraction of the population. It was, however, a start. By 2008, 68 per cent of pregnant women were receiving HIV tests. That same year, the United Nations funded a project to distribute female condoms through beauty salons, and male condom use is gradually becoming an accepted practice throughout the country.[26]

ARVs do not cure the disease, but they can delay the onset of AIDS in people with the HIV virus. ARVs have been available to a small segment of the population since 2003. By 2008, 146,657 infected Malawians were receiving ARV therapy, and by 2010, that number had reached 245,000. Yet challenges abound. There is always a shortage of medical staff to administer the drugs and according to Mary Nata, a practising nurse, "Malnutrition is now endemic, meaning that even in cases where treatment is available, lack of food means the drugs are not as effective."[27]

During the 2005 Massey Lectures, Stephen Lewis recounted a visit to Malawi during which he spoke to a group of widows and grandmothers in a rural community hall:

The conversation was dominated...by pleas for food...Sure, I steered things into talk of treatment, even tried to raise the issue of condoms,

but every voice came back to food...The women constantly pointed at
their mouths and stomachs to make absolutely sure that I wouldn't miss
what agitated them most.[28]

During his speech, Lewis went on to state the increased difficulty of
treatment in cases where the patient lacks adequate food or good nutrition: "The body can't handle the drugs without food," he says.[29] This tale
demonstrates the disconnect that often arises when international good
intentions meet local reality. When their basic daily needs are not being
met, it is impossible for people to plan for the future, even when that
future could contain a dire consequence such as HIV/AIDS.

One of the benefits of education is the sense of empowerment it
gives women. For many girls, the idea of asking a partner to go for AIDS
testing can be mortifying. Christie spoke to both Agness and Eunice
about the importance of insisting their boyfriends get tested. When
Eunice insisted that her boyfriend, Owen, go for testing, he refused.
Eunice stood up to him and broke off their relationship. Her next
boyfriend, Charles, agreed to testing, and eventually the two married.

The prevalence of HIV/AIDS peaked in Malawi in 1998. Since then, the
country has seen a steady decline in infection rates. In 2010, the national
rate of infection was 10.6 per cent, with deaths from HIV-related complications at fifty-one thousand per year.[30] Compare this to the infection
rates of 2003. In that year, it was estimated 14.2 per cent of the population was infected with the HIV virus and eighty-four thousand people
died of the disease.[31] The message of condom use and other forms of
prevention has been promoted throughout the country for nearly two
decades. It has finally stuck.

The following lines are taken from a poem written by APU student
Angella Benjamin:

What is wrong that it takes so long
To realize our wrong

That it is not right
To have premarital sex and get pregnant
That make people stop school.

What is wrong that it takes so long
To realize our wrong
That it is not right
To fight against the gentleman called HIV/AIDS
That makes people die.[32]

Angella's words clearly reflect her frustration. They also allude to the personal nature of this epidemic. Even now that the epidemic has reached its apex, and the country is beginning to mend, "the gentleman called AIDS" is a frequent visitor.

However, when Basimati made her dramatic statement, "At least I could eat until I die," Malawi still had many hard times ahead, and the gentleman AIDS was more than a frequent visitor, he was a constant companion.

⚏ David Werner's classic, *Where There Is No Doctor*, has been in print for decades and has been used widely by NGOs throughout the developing world. It offers practical treatments for a variety of common ailments, as well as instructions for delivering babies, practising birth control, and administering vaccinations. It contains simplistic line drawings and easy-to-read text. Christie read the book from cover to cover and used it to treat the girls for a number of skin disorders and other ailments.

Selina had a worm come out of a bump on her neck. Other girls had open sores on their bodies. Asane's sores would open, drain, and dry, and then open, drain, and dry again. Christie finally gave her the antibiotics she had brought from Canada, and the sores cleared right up. But she didn't have enough for all the girls with this condition, and it wasn't a cure-all anyway.

Christie had encouraged Memory to read *Where There Is No Doctor*, and Memory read the entire book. When she read the section on breast cancer, the book said, "Every woman should learn how to examine her own breasts for possible signs of cancer."[33] Memory looked at the diagrams and followed the instructions. She discovered a lump.

"To me, it was big. I could feel it."

Memory didn't know if the lump was normal or not, so she went to her grandmother. But her grandmother said, "No, it is just a small thing. Does it pain?"

It didn't hurt, so she said to her grandmother, "No, it's fine."

Memory wasn't so sure. She went to Christie and Holly and asked the two women if they thought she should see a doctor.

Both Christie and Holly gave her the same advice. "You need to go to the hospital as soon as possible. You need to check on this."

The next time Holly went to Lilongwe, she said, "Memory, you should come with me. I'll take you to the hospital."

Lilongwe Central Hospital is one of the largest, most modern, public hospitals in Malawi, but it is overworked and understaffed. During the 1990s, Malawi lost many of its nurses and doctors to the HIV/AIDS epidemic. It has lost even more to hospitals in the United Kingdom.

The halls of the hospital were crowded. Women and children sat on wooden benches, lined up against the pale green walls, waiting their turn for treatment. Memory sat with Holly, waiting with the other young women for her chance to see the doctor. Finally, a nurse came to see them. She quickly examined each of the women. When she came to Memory, she said, "This one should be something." And Memory was taken in to see the doctor.

The doctor asked Memory to lie down on the bed in the examination room. He examined her breast and said, "Oh no. This is just a lump. But any time you are free, you should come, and we'll remove it."

Memory took the doctor's words seriously, but coming back to the hospital frightened her. Rightly or wrongly, many public hospitals have a reputation for carelessness. If they aren't sure how they have contracted

AIDS, people sometimes blame the doctors and nurses. Memory didn't know if these claims had any merit, but she was frightened of surgery. While she had been a student at Lilongwe Girls' School, Memory had spent a night at a public hospital.

Memory's friend, Chifundo, had been a prefect at the school. When a student got sick, it was the prefect's duty to escort the student to a clinic or hospital and take care of her while she was there. So when one of Memory's friends, Brightness, became ill, she offered to accompany her and Chifundo to the hospital.

Brightness was cared for in a small room with many patients. The narrow metal beds were squeezed in tightly, leaving little room to step between. The smell was nearly unbearable: cleaning chemicals mixed with the sweat and body odours of the patients and their guardians. Memory sat in the hallway, waiting for hours. By midnight she couldn't stay awake any longer. Along with Chifundo, she curled up on the hard linoleum under Brightness's bed and went to sleep.

When Memory told me this, I asked her, "Does the hospital depend upon relatives to care for the patients?"

"Oh, yes." Memory answered. "If a patient is sick, you take care of them. That means if Henry gets sick, I will be taking care of him in the hospital, and if I don't have anyone staying with Teloni and Trevor, Teloni, Trevor, and I will be looking after him." At Central Hospital, relatives live alongside patients. They build fires in the courtyard, cooking *nsima* and relish in the pots they've carried from home. They wash their clothes and bed linens with water from the hospital taps and hang them to dry from the hospital windows.

I wondered what would happen to patients who had no one to look after them.

"The nurses take care of them, but maybe when it's time for medication, they don't pay attention. Maybe they are overworked, but it is still pathetic. You don't even dare to get sick. Even if you are in a situation whereby your close relative is there, you suffer."

"When you knew you'd be going back to the hospital for surgery, you must have been scared."

"I was very much scared. Their washrooms...oh no. Dirty." Memory scrunched her nose in disgust.

"Don't they have someone cleaning?" I asked.

"They do, but imagine those flush toilets. Someone who is sick comes from a typical village. Do you expect him to know how to use the toilet? No. He doesn't. So as a result, these workers, I think they get tired. And those people who take care of their relatives may prefer just sitting without bathing." Memory would have to wait for her surgery, but in the meantime she had a school to help run.

It was now October, and Memory, Christie, and Mark needed to get to the serious business of preparing the girls for their JCEs. Since the exams are written in English, many students struggle to pass and many do not. The girls had not been learning the Malawian curriculum for much of the past year, and they were behind on their studies, but they were determined to pass the tests. Memory, Christie, and Mark spent many hours preparing the girls. Everything was riding on these exams. The form two girls didn't know how, or if they would have the opportunity, to go on to form three, but they did know that if they didn't pass their JCEs, it wouldn't be an option.

Now that the school was running more smoothly, and the girls were behaving better, Christie began to care for them in a way she hadn't before. She pushed herself and the girls to their limits so they could pass their exams. Even so, she knew that once the exams were finished, the girls' schooling would be over too. "In those last weeks, I remember the darkest feeling standing in front of those kids. I was still building a relationship. I was still taking care of them, but their hope for future schooling was gone. They knew it, and I knew it. It was a dark, dark time."

Ultimately, most of the form two girls passed. Ferig's determination paid off, and she passed the exams. Basimati passed, and so did Agness. Bernice failed and never completed school. But Chidothi failed and repeated the exam, passing the second time. Passing the JCEs gave the girls the confidence they needed in the years to come.

Christie, Mark, and Memory decided to celebrate the girls' accomplishments with a big feast. They didn't want the experience to end with a sense of "oh, poor us." They wanted the girls to leave with a sense that they still had more than anyone else, and that it was their right and their responsibility to share what they had. They wanted the girls to see the end of their schooling as a success rather than a defeat. The girls needed to leave school feeling empowered, not embittered.

With the help of Estel, Christie baked four cakes, and Memory made cabbage salads. There was rice, pails of rice, and beef and chicken. There were still lots of supplies left at the school, so the girls used glitter glue and construction paper to make place markers and candles. Candles were a part of the theme for the event, so Christie purchased a single candle for each girl. The girls also prepared skits and songs and poems to share with each other.

The big day came. Once the classroom was decorated and all the food was set out in the middle of the room, they ate their feast. The girls talked and giggled, and they all stuffed themselves. Later, the girls performed.

In Malawi, lighter-skinned children are usually favoured and the darker ones mocked, so Christie and Memory had tried to teach the girls to be proud of their colour, whatever it was. One of the younger girls, Tabitha, had nearly black skin. To this day, Christie remembers a portion of the poem she read that day: "My body, my body, my beautiful black body…" Cecilia went from person to person. She knelt down, held their hands, and sang a song. The song was in Chichewa. It was a song of farewell: "I will remember you forever…" And all the girls cried. As a group they sang "Young Women We," and then they went outside into the darkness.

The girls gathered in a circle, each holding an unlighted candle in front of them. Memory, Christie, and Mark began by lighting their candles. The candles' flames were meant to represent the light that education brings.

The three teachers passed the flame to the girls' candles and slowly, one-by-one, the flames spread until all the girls' faces were lit by the glow of the candlelight. The girls went from standing in the dark to standing in the light. Christie said to the girls: "Education is like a candle. Your light alone can only light up a small part of this world, but if you share your knowledge, you are powerful." That was the message of the ceremony: pass your knowledge on to others, and you will create light in the world. It's a strong message, and that ceremony is now repeated at APU at the end of every school year.

Chidothi

ONE OF MALAWI'S MOST WELL KNOWN TRADITIONS is the Big Dance
of the *Gule Wamkulu*.[1] The *Gule Wamkulu* is a *nyau*, or secret society, that
practises the Chewa's traditional animist religion, primarily through dance. The
Gule dress in colourful, elaborately adorned masks and costumes that represent animals, trees, and spirits. The dancers are called upon, and paid, to dance
for various celebrations: weddings, funerals, appointments, and initiations.

While a performance of the Big Dance is thrilling and a source of great
excitement for the community, the dancers can often be unpredictable.
Particularly during the time of harvest, the *Gule* will wear their costumes even
when they are not performing, and because they may embody evil or mischievous spirits, it's best to give the men a respectful distance.

Because of their unpredictable and sometimes violent natures, the *Gule
Wamkulu* are sometimes used by parents as a kind of boogieman to ensure the
good behaviour of their children. Cecilia, one of the APU students, recounts
a day when the chief of her village used the *Gule Wamkulu* to encourage the
children to go to school. "If I see children walking around without going to

Gule Wamkulu. *[Photo courtesy of MASK: Secrets and Revelations, February 13, 2011–January 22, 2012, Main Gallery, Michigan State University Museum; Rachael Zylstra]*

school," he announced, "I will tell other people to make the *Gule Wamkulu* beat those who refuse to go to school."[2]

Many years later, Cecilia admits the motivation worked: "I was frightened of the *Gule Wamkulu* because they wear masks and costumes and cover their face, including the whole body."[3] While most Malawians are cautious of the dancers, they take pride in their Big Dance.

By the time Chidothi came to CEAG to study in January 2000, she was living with her grandparents. Her mother had died of tuberculosis when she was only eleven, and her father had died of malaria shortly before she was accepted into the school. This is a common story that resonates with much of Malawi's population.

Many Malawian men drink beer in the evenings, but—as I've mentioned before—in a culture where every kwacha makes a difference, and famine and poverty are a part of daily life, drinking has negative connotations. In Malawian culture, drinking alcohol is a sign of weakness and poor character. It causes a great deal of suffering in many families.

While he was alive, Chidothi's father often went out in the evenings to drink beer. Chidothi loved her father, but he could be violent and unpredictable if he had been at the pub. When Chidothi was just ten years old, her father went out drinking. When he came home, he was belligerent. He bragged of talking about the *Gule Wamkulu* with his friends, insulting them and calling the dancers beggars.

Chidothi said, "My father, don't do that."

But he responded, "No, I do this." Then he went to bed.

In the morning he left, and the Big Dancers came. There were fifteen *Gule* outside the house and only Chidothi and her mother inside. The *Gule* began yelling and throwing stones—finally breaking down the door. They were on one side of the house, so Chidothi and her mother escaped through a window on the other side.

They ran through the bushes and the gardens; her mother left Chidothi far behind. "They were running to get me," says Chidothi. "I hid in the garden, and my mother climbed up a tree. I was just crying, crying, crying."

Chidothi laughs when she tells this story, but there's no doubt she was terrified at the time. I admire the resilience of many Malawian girls, but I recognize there are those who lack Chidothi's strength. Perhaps they are the ones I see in the villages looking worn out and dispirited. Life has gotten the better of them, and they lack hope for the future.

Chidothi related another story: "One day I went to see my friend. We were chatting and chatting, and around seven o'clock I went back to my house."

"Where were you?" her father asked when she came in the house.

"I was chatting with my friend."

"No, this is not the time to be coming back to the house. You have to be earlier than this time."

"Okay, next time I will try to do what you have told me," she said.

But he said, "No, you sleep outside the house today."

Chidothi wanted to say yes, but instead she said, "No, I will sleep with my grandparents."

"No, I will tell them not to let you in their house. If they let you in, I will beat them."

Chidothi's grandparents were afraid of being beaten by their son, so Chidothi walked to her friend Akive's house.

"My parents have chased me because I was late," she said.

But Chidothi's father followed her to her friend's house, and when he saw her going inside, he caught her, took her home, and beat her. "I said you should sleep here on the verandah," he said.

So she did.

Again, Chidothi laughs as she tells her story. She seems to hold no grudge, no animosity, toward her father. I find it difficult to share her laughter.

10
The CEAG Girls

If a woman is educated, her
children are going to be educated.
If a woman is educated, she has
got a voice because people respect
a woman who is educated.

—*Memory Chazeza-Mdyetseni*[1]

ON THE EVENING BEFORE the last day of school, Agness knocked on
Christie's office door.[2] When Christie opened the door, Agness came
in and sat down. Her expression was sombre. She said, "I only have my

mother, and we are so poor that I will be forced to get married. Please help me stay in school."

Christie didn't know what to say. She had no way to put Agness through school, but she felt like she needed to do something. She thought, "Maybe I can find the money to help a few of the girls through school." She said to Agness, "I just don't know, but I will try."

Christie wanted to help, but it seemed like an impossible task. She confided in Memory. "Where am I going to get the money?" Even if she found money in Canada, she needed someone in Malawi to organize the effort and look after the girls, so she said, "I'm willing to do this if you can help me, Memory."

"No, Christie. Remember, I was thinking of going back to school, and now this is another responsibility. I don't think I'm in a position to do this. Of course, I know it's a good thing, but I feel like I'm being torn. It's just very huge for me. Why don't you ask someone else?"

"I just trust you. I feel as if maybe we should work hand-in-hand helping these girls. If you do not do it, that's fine; I'll just go home."

Memory remembered the parents' voices: "What is going to happen next? What will happen to our daughters?" In her mind, she could see their faces—worried and anxious. The more she thought about it, the more Memory felt like she was killing the future of the girls. She felt like their blood would be on her hands. Finally, she said, "Okay, I'll do it."

Christie said, "I'll go back home, and I'll try to do what I can. Even if I can find a little money, maybe some of them can go back to school." Memory would need to find a private school willing to accept the girls.

Before she left for Canada, Christie and Memory gathered the parents together for one last meeting. Christie explained that she would try to find funding for at least some of the girls. She couldn't promise that she would find the money, but she could promise that she would try.

The parents were grateful. They thanked Christie and Memory and left the meeting with the knowledge that someone was looking out for their daughters. Not long after, Christie flew back to Canada.

A few weeks later, Rita came back to close down the CEAG school and explain to everyone involved why the project had failed. She called a meeting of all the beneficiaries: the parents, the community, and the chiefs. Representatives from World Vision also attended, along with the project manager, Calvin, and, of course, Memory.

At the assembly, Rita and Calvin stood up. Rita said, "The school has been experiencing financial difficulties." She explained that the Canadian Board had decided to close down the project. The parents were concerned about their children, but Christie had promised to try to raise money in Canada so that some of the girls could continue their education. They asked Rita about Christie's plan. Rita was quick to reply: "There is no way she'll be able to find the money for your girls."

Calvin agreed, "Where will she get the money?"

The meeting came to a close, but the parents stayed to talk among themselves. "Maybe Christie won't be able to find the money for our girls."

"We shouldn't have agreed with her idea."

Memory listened to their comments. She was disappointed and angry. "Today, you're agreeing with Christie's ideas. Tomorrow, you're not, simply because she is not here, so now you don't want to agree with her ideas. What is this one doing for your child's future? I think I'm going to tell Christie. I think she should stop what she is doing because you're not thankful." And Memory left the meeting.

The parents were moved by Memory's words and began to regret their own. They realized they'd done something wrong, and they followed Memory down the path to the village.

Memory was on her way home, but the group of parents caught up and stopped her. They lined up next to her. "Please, come back. We should discuss."

But Memory replied, "We should discuss what? I thought you already said that Christie is lying, that she cannot do anything for your children." Now that Memory was angry, she kept talking. "What has Rita promised you? Did she say she's bringing back this school? What did she say about your children's future? I think I cannot work with you parents. You are too easily taken up. I feel like you betrayed me."

Many of the parents apologized. "We're sorry. We shouldn't have done that."

Memory relented. She realized they had been manipulated, so she said, "I've forgiven you, but I'll just tell Christie the truth. She needs to know what is happening."

The parents were worried. "No, don't tell," they said.

"If I say I'm not going to tell, then I'm lying," said Memory. "I will tell, but maybe she won't stop what she has started. She needs to know the minds of you parents, that you're easily taken up."

In Canada, Christie was unsure how to proceed. It was a difficult time for her for a number of reasons. "I remember that Christmas being the most difficult in my life. I couldn't stand anyone giving me a Christmas gift. I remember going to my closet. I had five pairs of pants and ten tops. I thought, 'If I could sell them, I could get money for those girls to go to school.' I was a bit of a wreck."

She confided to her parents. Her father, Larry Johnson, was a long-time Rotarian. He suggested she come to a Rotary meeting so she could tell the club the girls' story. Christie remembers, "I didn't want this to be just a story. I didn't want people to hear this and rush back to work. It would all be forgotten." But as Christie says, "My dad's pretty persuasive."

Not long after their conversation, Christie found herself standing in front of the Edmonton West Club, showing slides from her trip and telling the stories of Ivy and Agness, Estel and Eunice.

While she was talking, she noticed that one table was chatting amongst themselves. As a teacher, Christie said, "I didn't take kindly to that." Silently seething, Christie began to wrap up her presentation, asking if anyone had questions.

A man from the offending table stood up. "How much would it cost to put one of the girls back into school for a year?"

Christie answered, "I don't know."

The man continued, "If you can find a way to move the money and make sure that every cent is spent on the girl, our table will support a girl for one year." The man sat down.

Within a few moments, a second table stood up, and then a third, and then a fourth—all pledging money for the girls' education. Christie could hardly believe what was happening.

In that moment, something moved inside Christie. "I realized that telling the story was exactly what I needed to do. I realized I had power and so did everyone I knew." She phoned Memory and told her that she had found all the money they needed to send the girls to school.

When she told Memory that she had found *all* the money they needed, Christie was not being entirely truthful. But now she had confidence that she could succeed. During the days, she taught her classes, but in the evenings, she went to Rotary clubs and schools, making presentations and telling people the girls' stories.

Before Memory could begin looking for a school for the girls, she needed to go for surgery. Holly and Christie had left the country, so Memory faced the prospect on her own.

Again she went to her grandmother, but her grandmother said, "It's just a minor thing. Forget about it."

But Memory thought, "This is serious. I should go to the hospital."

Memory told her relatives, "I'm going to the hospital."

Fortunately, for Memory, she still had friends. Theresa, Memory's friend from secondary school, was working in Kasungu. She offered to look after Memory while she was in the hospital. Theresa excused herself from work and travelled to Lilongwe with Memory.

Memory arrived at the hospital early in the morning. She waited in line with ten other people, each waiting for their own surgery. One by one they were called in. "I was very scared." Soon Memory's name was called.

Even though she was frightened, she recognized her good fortune. "For me, I was lucky. There were no problems. That's different from what other people have experienced, and to me I felt like maybe it's because

Holly and Christie helped me book this appointment, and maybe that's why it worked out. People are told, 'You should come for your operation on this day.' You go there and they give you another date and maybe it's two months or three months later."

A nurse told Memory to remove her clothes and put on white "robes." Memory lay on the bed waiting. At first, Memory was scared, but the nurses were chatting. "What do you want to do after school?" they asked her. Memory relaxed and went to sleep.

"When I came back, I was surprised. I was dizzy. I was lying on a plastic mattress in a room where twenty people were lying on different beds. I was naked except for a cotton blanket. They just cover you like that."

After awhile, Memory said to Theresa, "What if we go home today?"

"No, Memory. They're saying you shouldn't go home."

"I don't want to sleep here. It's smelling very bad for me. I need to go." Memory was determined to leave the hospital.

"If anything happens, don't come back," said the nurse. "And we do not have any pain medicine we can give you."

Memory went to Theresa's aunt's house to sleep. "Her aunt was a nurse. She had some pain relief pills, so she gave me some at night because it was very painful."

The next morning, Memory went to stay with her uncle in Chillinde. Her uncle was poor, but Memory was comfortable staying there. She went back to Central Hospital, a week later, to have her stitches removed.

When she arrived at the hospital, the nurse was cold and abrupt. "Where you are coming from, there's a small clinic," she said.

Memory went back to the hospital in Chillinde, where they removed her stitches. She was still in a lot of pain, so she stayed with her uncle for another week before going back to the village.

By the time she returned home, there were rumours in the village. "She was pregnant," some said. "She went to the hospital to abort." Memory showed her relatives her scar so they would believe her and know that she went to the hospital for surgery. Her grandmother believed her and many in her family believed her once they saw her wound, but that led to more gossip. "Do you think she is a normal person showing people her breasts?" they asked.

I asked Memory, "Why was there so much gossip? Was it because you were different than most girls your age?"

"Exactly. At my age, they expected me to get married, to have a husband, and to have kids. But to me, I said, 'No I can't do that.' I went to the village out of desperation after my uncle died, but I just wanted to change my destiny. I would not listen to them—no matter what they said."

Memory struggled against the local gossip throughout her stay at the village. After failing in her attempt to find a placement at Mzuzu University, Memory wanted to upgrade her scores, but because she couldn't go back to school immediately, she was worried about losing the knowledge she had, and it was hard for her to study on her own.

Morocco, a distant cousin through marriage, was in form four. He had formed a study group with his friends, Moffat and Jeffrey. Memory thought, "Whenever they are studying I should be there, so they can share their learning with me." Memory began attending their study group, but it didn't take long before the gossiping began: "Memory is going out with Moffat. She will get married to that one."

At other times, people said, "Oh, she will not get married because no one will come and propose to her."

Encouragement came from an unlikely source. Memory's grandmother had begun to respect Memory and to understand her convictions. She told Memory, "People are not happy when they see other people doing well. So it's better for you to just be determined with what you are doing. You are going to prove to them that whatever they're saying is lies." Her grandmother's words helped Memory and encouraged her to stick to her convictions.

It didn't take long for Memory to find a secondary school for the younger girls. The school was in Lilongwe. They would take the girls who were going into form two, but they did not teach past form two, so she needed to find a different school for the older girls.

Memory's grandmother pounds maize outside her home in the village, 2007.

Memory travelled north to Phwezi Private School, a large school near Mzuzu, not far from the small community of Rumphi. It teaches secondary school to boys and girls, but the sexes are segregated into separate dorms, classrooms, and teachers. Phwezi had a good reputation, so Memory wanted the girls to go there.

Once she was granted a meeting with the principal, Memory made her case. She explained the history of CEAG and her need to find a place for the fourteen form three girls. The principal chuckled, "All these students coming to this school, and you say someone is paying. Who is this one?"

"Christie Johnson. She is from Canada."

"And how are you going to communicate with this one? How will she get the money?"

Memory said everything she could think of to convince the man, and finally he said, "Okay. We'll see, but I still don't believe it."

By the time Memory returned home with the good news, many of the girls had scattered. She wrote letters, spoke to parents, and organized meetings. It was not so difficult to get the younger girls to their new school in Lilongwe because it was nearby, but getting the older girls all the way to Phwezi was another adventure.

Memory hired a minibus. For most of the girls, it was the first time they had travelled further than walking distance from home. Most of them had never been to town.

Memory had the bus stop in Kasungu so the girls could shop for their groceries: mostly soap and lotion. Memory took them into a small grocery store, but she found it hard to control them: "They'd buy soap and they'd forget something, so they'd take the soap and go back. Then the owners thought they hadn't paid." For these girls, this was a brand new experience.

Once they finished shopping, the girls piled back into the bus. From Kasungu, it was a nine-hour drive to Phwezi. The girls filled the bus. They were excited and anxious. Then they reached a checkpoint.

Checkpoints are found along all major roadways throughout Malawi. At a checkpoint, three or four police officers will inspect the vehicles as they go through. They will ask to see vehicle registration and the driver's license. Sometimes they will ask to see the luggage, and they might ask questions: "Where are you going?" or "What's in your bag?"

None of the girls had ever gone through a checkpoint, and they were afraid. The policeman asked, "Who's the owner of this bag?" But no one answered.

Memory became impatient. "Enough. You don't need to get scared. You just need to answer the question." There were some tense moments, but eventually the police waved them on. Already the girls were learning.

They arrived at the school late in the day, but the principal was not there. Memory spoke to the matron. "I have spoken to the principal. These girls have been accepted into this school. They are here to learn."

The matron was not impressed. "Where are the school fees? Where's the letter that they should come in?"

"I don't have the school fees. The money is coming from Canada, and I don't have a letter because I'm the one standing on their behalf." Memory had no money, and she looked to be the same age as the girls.

"I cannot welcome these girls into this school. You'll have to wait for the principal to come back. Maybe he'll approve, and if he doesn't, it's better you just wait and take your students back. We cannot give them rooms."

"When will he be back?" asked Memory.

"Maybe tomorrow, maybe in a few days."

Memory pleaded, "Where am I going to sleep with these girls? I don't have money. What I have is my transport back home." The matron was unmoved.

Memory went back to speak to the bus driver. "I need a few more minutes. Please. Wait for me."

"No," said the driver. "We can't wait for you."

Memory insisted, "It's just getting dark. How am I going to travel back home? I don't have a place to sleep. You just need to wait for me."

"If I have to wait for you, then let's just go."

"How can I leave these girls—a group of girls just standing with their bags? Please, just wait."

Memory went back to the school. She asked to speak to a teacher, but after explaining the situation, the teacher said, "No, I cannot accept this." Memory found a second teacher to talk to, but the answer was the same.

Memory spoke to a third teacher. She explained the situation and begged the teacher to allow the girls to stay until the principal arrived.

"Well, okay," the teacher said. "If the principal doesn't come, we're going to give them accommodation, but no food."

"Thank you," said Memory. She left the girls at the school.

But Memory wasn't going home until she knew the girls were safe. By then, the minibus had left, so Memory found another bus to take her to Mzuzu where she had family she could stay with for the night.

The next morning, Memory returned to Phwezi.

The girls had been fed, and the principal was back. Memory was told, "The school fees should come quickly; otherwise the girls will be sent back home."

"I assure you the money is coming."

That night, when she spoke to Christie on the phone, Memory said, "Make sure you send the money as fast as you can because if you don't, I think we're going to be in trouble."

Christie confirmed, "It will be there." But while she reassured Memory, she was facing her own challenges. The money had been pledged, but she was in a constant state of worry, not knowing if someone would back out. She also worried that the funds would be delayed, but the girls were fortunate to have such strong supporters, and they were fortunate to have Christie raising the funds. At the last minute, the sponsors pulled together and sent Christie the money.

Because it had taken time for Memory to find schools for the girls, and it had taken time for Christie to find sponsors, some of the girls had moved away from the Kasungu area. Now that their education was paid for, Memory was determined to find them all.

Before she went home, Memory wanted to find Estel. She knew that if she went home first, her grandparents would say, "You will lose your life." They thought she was travelling too much, and they were right. They would say, "What you've done is enough. You've helped a lot of girls find their way back to school, but you shouldn't insist on finding those girls that you have not found. It's too much." Because her grandparents were beginning to worry, Memory didn't tell them that she would be looking for Estel on her way back from Phwezi.

Memory had heard that Estel was living with an uncle near Mzimba. She had never been to Mzimba, but she took a minibus as far as she could. The bus dropped her off by the side of the road. It was already five o'clock, which didn't leave her much time. Darkness falls quickly in Malawi: at six o'clock.

Memory stopped at a small house by the side of the road. There were people outside, so she asked if they knew where Estel's family lived. She was given directions, and she went on her way.

When she reached Estel's house, she found it locked up and empty. She went next door to a neighbour's house. "Where is the owner of that house?" she asked.

"Oh, it's a long way," answered the woman. The explanation seemed easy, but this was a typical village. There were no cars, no bicycles, and it was too late in the day for Memory to begin the journey.

"You should come to our house and sleep," said the neighbour. Memory was reluctant. The village was remote and surrounded by bush. There was no electricity. Anything could happen to her. Her grandparents didn't even know she was there. "If I die here," she thought, "I don't know if my body can be taken back home." Despite her reservations, it didn't seem to Memory that she had any other option, so she accepted the invitation.

The house was small and cluttered—just a small sitting room and two tiny bedrooms. While the woman put the children to bed, the man used a lantern to guide Memory to the bedroom next to the outside door. There was a mat on the floor, and that was all. The man left with the lantern, closing the door behind him, but the door was made of rough wooden slats. It didn't close tightly, and there was no lock. Memory felt exposed and frightened.

She slept lightly that night, but in the morning the woman gave her water to wash her face and brush her teeth. Then Memory left to find Estel.

Memory travelled by truck, minibus, and truck again. When the driver dropped her off, Memory was able to find someone with a bicycle who would take her to the primary school near the house where Estel lived with her uncle. Memory asked for directions.

"You're just going to have to walk to get to the primary school where you are going to find Estel's uncle."

After travelling all day, Memory could hardly believe what she was hearing. "Is it far? How do I get there?" she said.

"We're going to give you two boys to escort you."

Memory set out walking along a worn dirt path with the two small boys. After her long day, she was tired. "Are we not there yet?" she asked the boys.

"No, not yet," said the boys.

Just as it was becoming dark, they arrived at Estel's house. Memory was greeted by a swarm of people: Estel, her uncles and auntie, and many children. They all wanted to know what Memory was doing there. "How did you manage to come this far?"

Memory explained, "Estel should go back to school. The tuition has already been paid."

"Okay. We're going to send Estel to school," said her uncle.

After they had eaten dinner and chatted, Memory got ready to go to bed. Estel approached her. "I don't think I'll make it to the school. My relatives said they are going to give me transport money, but I don't think they'll manage."

Instead of being annoyed, Memory said, "Thank you for telling me the truth." Memory paused and shook her head. "It was going to pain me more if I would hear you had not gone to school." Christie had sent Memory money for just such emergencies, so Memory gave Estel the transport money she needed.

The next morning, Memory said, "I'm happy that I've found you, but I have to go back home. My relatives don't know where I am. They think I'm still at Phwezi." Memory said her goodbyes and was on her way. She was anxious to get home.

Estel

ESTEL FASCINATED ME from the beginning.[1] She radiates self-assurance and projects a no-nonsense approach to life that I found immediately appealing. She has the voice of Lauren Bacall and is one of the most physically striking women I've met on my trips to her country. Her posture and carriage reflect a confidence and self-worth that is often lacking in Malawian women, and under that lovely surface, she vibrates with energy and drive. Hers is a purpose-driven life.

I met Estel for the first time in 2007. I was staying with Memory and Henry while they still lived in Area 25 of the capital city. She came to the back door. I heard her voice before she entered the sitting room. "Hello," she called in a husky voice. I heard the back door latch behind her, and she entered the house through the kitchen. With a face lacking makeup and dressed in second-hand clothing, she would have looked at home at a Hollywood movie premiere or the opening of an urban art gallery.

At the sight of Estel, Christie squealed in delight and the two hugged. After we exchanged greetings, Memory, Christie, Estel, and I sat down at the small round kitchen table to chat. Estel was full of news.

She had opened a nursery school, but it was not just any nursery school. She had set up a structured volunteer board, and there were plans to invest the money coming into the school to build an actual "bricks and mortar" school. It seemed like an elaborate plan, but Estel was full of strategies and ideas. She was teaching the mothers of the students how to sew. The women would learn valuable skills, and Estel wasn't charging the women for her services. When they began selling their wares, they would give Estel a portion of the profit. Estel seemed to have the drive to make all her initiatives, including the school, a success.

After awhile, Christie said, "So last time I was here, there was talk of a wedding."

Estel's laugh was like slow water running over a worn riverbed. Memory laughed too, "You tell her."

Estel had returned to Phwezi for upgrading. The school was near where her boyfriend, Malcom, lived. Estel was staying in the school's dormitory, but she and Malcom soon met to chat and discuss plans for their wedding. All should have been well, but shortly after she returned to the school, Estel began hearing rumours: "That guy is going out with a second girl." After she heard this, Estel sat and thought, "If it's true, I'll find out."

The day after they had sat together and talked about their wedding, Estel went to Malcom's house and knocked on the door. There was no answer.

People within the community knew about Estel and Malcom's engagement, and on the way to his house, Estel had met a friend. He had told Estel, "If you are going to Malcom's house, he is there. You will find him." So Estel knocked again, but there was still no answer.

Estel sensed something was wrong. She thought, "Maybe it should be that girl."

She walked up the hill to a neighbour's house. She chatted with the woman for the next couple hours. At the same time she was able to keep an eye on Malcom's house down below.

The afternoon passed slowly, but finally Estel saw Malcom walk out the back door of his house. He looked around and went back inside. A moment later, a girl emerged, leaving the house by the back door. Estel said to the neighbour, "You see, the woman is coming out of that house, and yet I knocked and he didn't open it for me."

Estel walked down the hill. "Hey, girl. You stop." The girl moved on, so Estel went up to the back door and knocked.

Malcom called out. "Yes?"

"It's me. Would you please open?"

Malcom came to the door. "You should use the door which you always use."

Estel didn't answer.

"Oh, oh what? What have I said?"

"What is happening between you and this girl?" asked Estel.

Malcom dropped his head and mumbled.

"No, it's okay, but you'll regret losing me," said Estel, and she walked away.

Now people knew something was amiss, and they said, "Let's go and beat that girl."

But Estel said, "No, we shouldn't do that."

Later that day, Malcom phoned Estel. "What are you doing coming to my house and accusing me of those things?" he yelled.

Estel replied, "I'm not the person to be shouting at." And she hung up the phone.

Later, they met at the market.

Once they were together, Malcom became defensive. "Your people are poor," he accused.

But he didn't receive the responses he expected. "Yes, I am poor. It means you and me, we can't make a family because somebody is poor and somebody is rich. It's okay. Keep on going with that girl."

After that day, Malcom became threatening. He demanded Estel see him, and when she refused, he sent his driver to confront her. But Estel was immovable. Her uncle called her every day to make sure she was okay. Estel kept reassuring him. "I'm not worried," she said.

Estel was at the school for another ten days. After that, she was glad to go home, but Malcom kept phoning. "Where are you? I want to talk to you."

Each time, Estel would respond the same way. "Well, talk."

"No, I want to meet you face-to-face."

"Why do you want to do that?" Estel would ask. "I'm nothing to you. It's over. When I say it's over, it's over."

Finally, after months of harassment, Malcom called Estel to tell her their relationship was over. Estel responded, "Don't you know it's already over?"

Estel was still hurting from the experience when we had our conversation around Memory's kitchen table. "I feel like each and every guy will be the same with me. I'm afraid," she confided.

Memory spoke up. "You just need to be strong."

Christie said, "It sounds like your family has been so supportive. Some girls would still choose that guy because they don't have a support system."

Then Memory added, "They would really want to go get married to someone who is rich despite all the negatives they see."

And that is the unfortunate truth. Most girls lack Estel's confidence and level of education. They would almost certainly forgive a man like Malcom and go through with the marriage only to experience a lifetime of misery in return.

11
Growing Up

Life is what you believe, really.
If you've made a choice that [you]
want to lead a life of change, you
can change regardless of wherever
you're coming from. No matter
you're coming from poverty, you
can change that.

—*Memory Chazeza-Mdyetseni*[1]

AFTER CEAG CLOSED, Memory continued living in the village where she was kept busy doing chores for her grandparents, but she was also responsible for organizing the CEAG girls' education.[2] She needed to coordinate tuition payments from Canada to both the school in Lilongwe and the school at Phwezi. She also needed to support the girls emotionally, and she felt responsible for all of them.

The form two girls soon reported problems at their school in Lilongwe. The teachers didn't always show up for class and some were being fired from their positions after only a short period of time. Word came back that one of the form two students at the school—not a CEAG girl—had been impregnated by the head teacher of the school. The head teacher was fired from his position, but it seemed to Memory that she should try to get all the girls into Phwezi.

The impregnated girl, Esnet, was beautiful and gregarious but an average student. She never did have the opportunity to reach her potential, however. After having an abortion, she developed an infection and died.

Further north, the form three girls were facing their own challenges. The teachers at Phwezi were much more dedicated to their jobs, but they were also strict. On school days, the students had to leave the hostels at 6:30 AM so they could make it to morning assembly by quarter to seven. If the students weren't out of the hostels in time, the teachers came in and "chased" them out. The students' days were busy with classes, reading, studying, and meals. They were in bed by 8:30 PM. "We were always busy," said Eunice, but she adds, "We just got used to it. When you get used to it, it's easy." It was much harder for the girls to "get used" to the attitudes of the other girls.

Phwezi is a private girls' school. The majority of the girls who attend it come from well-to-do families. Eunice explains, "We were afraid they were going to laugh at us because we were coming from the village and most of them live in town."

At first, the other girls laughed at the CEAG girls, and the CEAG girls became afraid to speak in public. "Whatever we said, they would laugh.

Some of them thought of us as useless people." The girls hung out together and tried to sit together whenever they could. It took several months before the Phwezi girls accepted the CEAG girls, but by the third term they had begun to fit in. Eunice says, "That's when they got used to us."

Despite these challenges, Phwezi was a good school. Lucy told me about her experience there: "The competition at Phwezi was very stiff, and every weekend we were writing exams. To my surprise, I found that I was always in the top ten or the top five, so it really encouraged me to work extra hard."

That year, Christie travelled from Canada, so she could discuss the girls' progress with Memory, and they could both meet with the parents. Once the happy reunion between Memory and Christie was over, they began discussing the girls' future.

A meeting had been arranged with the parents. They were proud of their girls and praised their accomplishments. They thanked Memory and Christie for all they had done, and it was a joyful occasion. But once the meeting was over, Memory began to question herself.

Memory wondered, "Well Memory, what is going to happen to you? You are working tirelessly for other people's education, and very soon the students will be in form four. They will have the same education as you. And what have you done?" She began to think about her own future and that of her brothers and sisters. Sometimes she wondered if the girls appreciated her help, and that made her feel angry, especially when she considered the time she had put in to helping them. It was like a job with no future and no wage.

Even her grandfather had criticized her for the work she was doing with the girls: "You cannot be working for free. There is nothing in this world for free, and you are expecting me to struggle to find soap for you. You look to me to find food for you. You must be hiding something." These words hurt.

One day, Memory said to Christie, "I think I've helped enough."

Christie said, almost pleading, "If you stop, who is going to help?"

"The girls are grown up. They can handle themselves," said Memory. "Now I need to think about my future. My brothers and my sisters need my help. I cannot just do it by helping these girls."

Christie said, "Memory, look at me. I'm just helping."

"Yes, but you have an education. You have things. That's why you're thinking of other people. As for me, I don't have anything." Memory felt that she was no closer to going to university than she had been before Rita made her promise three years before.

After a few moments, Christie responded, "Okay, I'll see if I can find the money for your tuition."

Memory had not spoken to Christie earlier because she didn't want to beg for money, and Christie had not thought about the situation from Memory's perspective. Christie says now, "I felt like there were so many times when I'd missed the point."

When Christie returned to Canada, she searched for a sponsor for Memory. At first, she wasn't able to find anyone, but gradually, through her contacts, she collected enough money for Memory to begin post-secondary studies.

In 2002, Memory began her bachelor of arts degree at the African Bible College (ABC) in Lilongwe. ABC offers "quality, university-level education with a Christian emphasis," with both theological and core curriculum courses.[3] Memory was busy with her studies and still worked with the CEAG girls. But she also found time to continue her volunteer work, primarily with two organizations: the Kasupe Ministry and the Youth Care Ministry.

Fletcher Padoko, a former student of ABC, founded the Kasupe Ministry to help "orphans, widows, caregivers and other vulnerable people in order to meet their spiritual, physical and social needs so that they can live productive lives in the society."[4] The ministry works in Southern Malawi in an area that was hit hard by the AIDS epidemic, so Memory helped when she had time off school and could manage the long trip to Balaka. There she worked with orphans and trained nursery school teachers, who were also working with the orphans. Memory remembers working with a young orphan girl named Martha. Martha had lost both of her parents at a young age. Memory remembers her as "one of the brightest girls I've ever met." Not long after they met, Martha became pregnant, dropped out of school, and got married.

Memory also recalls working with a family of five children. The eldest was fourteen and the youngest five years old. The parents were still alive, but they were separating, and the children had been left on their own. There was no food in their home. When Memory went to their house, the roof had leaked and the floor was wet. It was these children and others that Memory helped by providing food and comfort.

Memory also worked for the Youth Care Ministry in Lilongwe, a ministry founded to care for street kids and homeless mothers. The organization looked for housing for homeless mothers and provided them with basic needs, even teaching them how to prepare meals in their homes. The organization also worked with street kids. Memory would look for children living on the streets of Lilongwe and offer them a twice-a-week feeding program. The goal of the organization was to encourage the kids to get off the street and go back to school. In some cases, Memory was able to reunite the children with family members who were willing to care for them. Many of the kids had suffered a great deal of abuse, and some had committed crimes. Memory said, "I got scared with them, but at the same time these are kids that I feel sorry for." She wanted to transform them into better people, and often she saw positive change in the children she learned to care for.

Memory remembers three siblings: two boys and a girl who begged on the street together, looking for food for themselves and their mother. Their mother was in the hospital, dying of TB. They grew to love Memory. "Why don't you come with us and see our mother?" they would ask. Memory showed all of the kids love, and for years afterward, when Memory was in town, she'd hear children from her Youth Care Ministry days call out: "Auntie Memory. Auntie Memory." Memory would stop to chat, and they would tell her how much they missed her.

I asked Memory why she felt compelled to help other people. "I'm not very happy when I see people suffering—especially kids. I regard them as innocent. I don't like seeing them not being fed, not being clothed properly, not being educated because of someone who did not think. Their parents maybe they didn't know the result of what they were doing and now they have died. The problem is left with the kids. I wonder, 'Why them?' Maybe I can help."

Poverty is chronic in Malawi, as it is in other developing countries. It is on a scale that I have never experienced in Canada. I think of the children I've met, both in the villages and the cities. Hundreds of children with dry, patchy skin scarred from malnutrition, their hair lost to ringworm. I remember the man I saw in downtown Lilongwe, thin and hunched, walking the streets dressed only in scavenged plastic bags that he had pulled from the gutters and tied to his body. I recall the man I walked past in Nsaru, his ragged pant leg revealing skin oozing with open, weeping sores. I can never forget sitting across from a man in a minibus whose groin was swollen to the size of a basketball. I'm also reminded of the words of the APU girls. Maness spoke to me about her time before entering the school. "For me, life was really hard and seeing many people going through the same hardships in the village, I thought that's what life was meant to be like. Life meant almost nothing to me."

For many North Americans, poverty is an abstract. We feel as though we go through hard financial times, but for the vast majority of us, those hardships simply cannot compare to the daily brutality of chronic poverty. And in North America, there is always the possibility of lifting oneself out of economic misfortune. Even if we can only earn minimum wage, in most communities, we can find jobs if we are persistent and willing. Imagine if there was no hope for the future. Imagine if there was nothing we could do to change our situations. That is the plight of many Malawians, and in particular poor, uneducated, rural women.

According to World Bank statistics, in 2010, 88 per cent of the Malawian population lived on less than $2 per day, with 72 per cent of

Many Malawian children suffer from malnutrition, disease, or infection, but they are not defined by it. They are still kids, and they still love to play, 2007.

the population living on less than $1.25 per day. [5] Perhaps these numbers are difficult to grasp, but it should be clear that living on less than $1.25 or even $2 per day leaves the majority of the population existing from harvest to harvest and day to day. There is no money for investment in the future. There is barely enough to supply food for hungry mouths, much less luxuries like education or school uniforms.

While Memory worked on her degree at ABC, the CEAG girls laboured in their studies at Phwezi. They had completed form three together. When they began form four, Lucy joined them at Phwezi. It was the end of term, and the girls were preparing to write their MSCEs when the boys raided the girls' side of the campus.

During the senior group's first year at the school, the form four boys had raped some of the form one girls. Now that the form one boys were in form four, they wanted to do the same to their peers.

Although the boys struck in the dark of night, they made a lot of noise. The girls couldn't see them, but they could hear them coming. The boys were singing and shouting. First they vandalized the science laboratory and burned the maize in the storage shed.

The first girls to hear the commotion yelled to the other girls, "The boys are coming. Girls. Run!"

The girls ran to the teachers' houses, where they sat crying, "Why do these boys want to do such a thing? What have we done?"

The police were called. At first, there were not enough men to quell the riot. More police came. They were able to take enough of the boys into custody to stop the rioting. Many of the boys did not finish their exams that year.

Selina was in form three when the boys attacked the school. She remembers that night. "The boys started fighting. They came to our school and switched off the lights. They wanted to destroy the buildings and the offices."

The girls still had most of their exams left to write. Lucy remembers the hardship the incident caused. "They damaged the laboratory before we could use it for our practical exam. We had problems with the physical science exam. We used the laboratory, but we did not have enough materials. And the roof was damaged, so it was almost like we were outside." It was an unfortunate end to a significant time in the girls' lives. But the following year they graduated from Phwezi and that counted.

Now that the girls had completed secondary school, Christie felt sure she could find the funds to send them to post-secondary school. The girls who had not been selected by another institution were given the opportunity to study at Phwezi Technical College. Because it is a technical college, even the girls who didn't excel in their MSCEs were able to go. Estel went into welding and general fitting, while Agness, Asane, Saliza, and Sala pursued tailoring. Chidothi went into business. Basimati was accepted into the Natural Resource College. Selina, Mary, and Witness were accepted into Bunda College. Auralia was accepted into Chancellor's

College. Although all the girls succeeded, they each experienced their own challenges along the way.

In the first year, Christie wired the money for Auralia's tuition directly to the college. Somehow, Auralia's father, a teacher at a primary school in Kasungu, was able to convince the registrar's office to give him the money. He then loaned out the money, at a high rate of interest, to the teachers at his school. Christie was furious.

On Christie's next trip to Malawi, she and Memory were able to track down Auralia's father. They confronted him over his actions. Their encounter was tense, but he agreed to pay back the tuition, asking for two weeks to find the money. By calling in the loans, he was able to get most of the money back and return it to Christie.

By then, Auralia had missed her intake, but she was soon able to get accepted into the University of Mzuzu, where she was still studying when I met her in 2009. Auralia's degree had been slowed by university closures, but she told me, "I have a hard working spirit in me." Despite her many setbacks, she said, "When I went to CEAG, I thought I'd have a bright future, and that's what I have right now." Auralia graduated from university later that year and is now a fully qualified secondary school teacher with full-time employment.

For Christie, there was always much to do when she visited Malawi, especially now that Memory was going to school. She made one of these many trips after the girls' first year in post-secondary school. While she was there, she learned that Estel had been welding in the metal workshop wearing bare feet in sandals and without protective glasses or gloves. Estel's eyesight was being affected. Her eyes would water so badly while she was working in the workshop that, by the next day, they would barely open. When she met with Christie, she asked, "Is there any extra money for protective glasses for me?" Both Christie and Memory felt terrible when they realized the pain Estel must have been suffering for the past year. When speaking to the girls, Christie had repeated over and over that the money for their schooling was hard to come by, so "you better not waste any." Estel was not the sort of person to complain and had suffered in silence.

Although all of the girls were successful with their studies, their trials were not over. They needed to find jobs or establish businesses. In some cases, they went on to marry and have children, but every one of the girls is grateful for the education she has received, and each one appreciates the profound difference that education has made in her life.

Asane and Sala opened their own tailoring shops. Estel worked as a general fitter for Alliance One Tobacco Company for a time, but as mentioned previously, she later went on to open a successful nursery school in a rural village where she also trains local women in tailoring so they can become more self-sufficient. Selina now works for the Ministry of Agriculture as an agriculture advisor. She married Memory's cousin, Morocco. Witness also works for the Ministry of Agriculture as an accountant. Mary works for the Department of Irrigation. Another CEAG girl became a nun, another opened a restaurant in partnership with her sister-in-law, and others found work as seamstresses and secretaries.

Christie was able to arrange microcredit loans for the girls who wished to start their own businesses. Ferig, Mesi, Saliza, Agness, Eunice, and Memory (a common name in Malawi) decided to pool their loans and start a business together. The girls rented a house in Lilongwe. Agness used some of her money to purchase a sewing machine, but the majority of the business was in chickens. The girls would raise chickens and later sell them for a profit. At first, all went well. The chickens were growing, and it seemed like the girls were going to be successful in their venture. The girls' dreams of success didn't last long though. Before long, a number of the chickens disappeared: stolen in the night. Many of the remaining chickens became sick and died. Eunice tried setting up a small tuck shop in front of their house. She made money selling soap, lotion, bread, and other necessities, but the profits were slow to come. One by one, the partnership split apart, leaving Eunice and Agness to run the nursery school that I visited when I met with the girls in 2007.

Eunice stands in the doorway of the preschool she ran with Agness in Area 25, 2007.

To an outsider, the venture might appear to have been a failure, but in many important ways it was a success. All of the girls gained valuable experience that they were able to apply to their future careers and relationships, and even though they didn't make the money they had hoped for, they learned how to look after themselves and remained independent long after their peers had married and begun having children.

In 2011, experts at the fifteenth global microcredit summit called for the development financial institutions and world leaders to use microcredit as a means to end extreme poverty throughout the world. A statement released after the summit claimed, "The goal, when accomplished, will ensure the attainment of the Millennium Development Goal (MDG) target of halving absolute poverty."[6] It's likely the MDG in question will be met in any case, but the statement demonstrates the enthusiasm for microcredit by some proponents.

While microfinance can be a valuable tool for helping people out of poverty, it must be implemented in a way that empowers people rather than putting them in a position of indebtedness. One cannot assume that people who have never run their own businesses are natural entrepreneurs. They often require counselling on marketing and banking skills. They may require help with troubleshooting problems, both professional and personal, as they arise.

When handled in a fashion that meets the needs of the poor by taking into consideration the on-the-ground realities of dispensing loans to people living in extreme poverty, microcredit has the potential to be a blessing to many. But without an emphasis on the individual, microfinance can become a burden rather than a boon.

Some microfinance institutions (MFIs), as they are often called, charge exorbitant interest rates to their clients. Banco Compartamos, a Mexican MFI, received international criticism for charging, at times, over 100 per cent interest on its microcredit loans. Muhammad Yunus, 2006 recipient of the Nobel Peace Prize for developing microfinance in Bangladesh, said of the bank's practices, "Microcredit was created to fight the money lender, not to become the money lender."[7] While most MFIs do not charge anywhere near this level of interest, Yunus worries that the practice he pioneered has become corrupted to serve the investor rather than the people it is purported to serve.[8]

Microcredit is not an across-the-board solution by any means. Richard Rosenberg, senior advisor on policy issues and research at Consultative Group to Assist the Poor (CGAP), points out that "many low income people simply do not want a microloan, while others may want a loan but would be likely to have payment problems if they were given one."[9]

I'm reminded of a story told to me by Lucita. Lucita's mother, Enet, has lived in extreme poverty her entire life. Some time ago, Enet was offered a microloan of ten thousand kwacha from the government. Enet jumped at the opportunity to have extra money, but when her husband asked for the money, Enet handed it over. He kept the money, and Enet was left with no way to repay the loan. She was still repaying the loan years later. Lucita explains, "There was no profit from that money."

When I spoke to Lucita, her mother had recently been offered another loan. Lucita advised her mother, "You must not take this money." But she had no way of stopping her mother, and she was afraid her mother would accept, go further into debt, and end up in prison.

Smita Premchander, author of *Multiple Meanings of Money*, tells us that we must encourage microfinance programs that focus on "creating spaces for women to have a stronger collective voice, greater control over their own resources, improved access to external resources and leadership and representation that enables them to influence policy."[10] As is often the case, when a program becomes successful and, in this case, universally popular, some of its original intent and merit can become lost in the rush to duplicate the results or corrupted for the purpose of self-interest. For microcredit to continue to be a valid tool for helping to empower the poor in general, and women in particular, we must remember the principles on which it was based: sustainability, security, and empowerment.

⚎ During her second year at ABC, Memory went to visit her friend, Cattriss. Cattriss Mdyetseni had been Memory's friend when they both went to Lilongwe Girls' School. Cattriss had often talked about her brothers, Richard and Henry, and the rest of her family. And Memory had even met the boys while she was still in secondary school.

Now Cattriss lived in Blantyre, and she wanted Memory to stay with her over the Easter holidays. She phoned Memory: "Why don't you come visit? I will send you transport money?"

Memory decided to go.

Cattriss picked Memory up at the bus depot. When they got to her house, Memory was surprised to see Cattriss's brother, Henry. "Do you stay with your brother?" she asked.

"Yes, I'm sharing with my brother," Cattriss replied. Memory was dismayed.

Cattriss worked for a telephone company in customer care. She started work early in the morning and often worked late.

While she was staying with Cattriss, Memory visited Annie, another friend from Lilongwe Girls' School, during the day, but she made sure she returned to Cattriss's house before it got dark.

On one occasion, Cattriss was late coming home from work, but Henry was home. Memory had always felt shy around Henry, but there was no way to avoid him. Memory sat down for tea with Henry. They began chatting. Henry asked her questions about her schooling, but he already knew the answers. Henry had been asking his sister about Memory ever since the two had met while Memory was still going to Lilongwe Girls' School.

Before Memory left Blantyre, Henry asked, "Memory, what's your phone number? How can I reach you?"

After she got back to ABC, Henry called. "How was your trip?" he asked. After that, he kept phoning. He would ask her how she was doing at school or what her plans were for the future. One day, he phoned Memory and said, "I'd like to talk to you about something."

"Okay, what?" asked Memory.

"I'll talk to you later." And he quickly hung up the phone. Memory didn't know what to think.

The next time they spoke, Henry said, "Memory, I'd like to fall in love with you."

Other boys at ABC had also "proposed their love" to Memory. Memory weighed her options. "Who should I accept?" wondered Memory. "Who's serious?"

Memory had decided she would have a boyfriend, so boys would stop bothering her. She said, "I couldn't go to the cafeteria. I couldn't study in the library, I couldn't go to the chapel. I was tired of being followed."

Memory decided to accept Henry. Because he was in Blantyre, he wouldn't be able to disturb her while she was studying. "At least he's far away."

Memory's plan worked. When she told the other students at ABC that she had a boyfriend, all the unwanted attention stopped.

At first, Memory did not expect to have a serious relationship with Henry, but she began to appreciate his honesty and his openness. She also realized they shared many of the same values, and Henry respected and shared her dream of one day opening a school. There was no question that Henry was serious about their relationship.

Memory wondered if Henry would wait for her to finish her education. She was only in her second year, but Memory would not compromise her education for anyone. At the same time, she didn't want to face disappointment. Henry did wait for her though, and they married shortly after Memory graduated from ABC in 2006.

Basimati

BASIMATI FELT A SMALL KNOT OF FEAR clench her stomach.[1] She was
pregnant.

Everything had been going well. Basimati had a nice boyfriend, and she was
in her final year at the Natural Resources College. Once she completed her
diploma, she would qualify for a good job.

Getting pregnant meant no diploma, and no diploma meant no job. With
no job, Basimati had no hope of independence. "My future—it was bad."
She didn't want to join the thousands of Malawian women who spent their
lives forever dependent on their husbands. Basimati thought she knew her
boyfriend. He was a good man, but what if he didn't take her? How could she
support herself and her baby without even a diploma? If she went back home
with a baby but no husband, her family would be furious.

The weeks passed. Basimati felt her waist grow and her breasts swell. She
tried to cover her pregnancy, but it became more difficult every day. Her
grades were good, and her tuition was paid for. Basimati thought maybe, just
maybe, she could finish school before the baby came.

Soon the baby was kicking. Basimati rested her hand on the swell of her belly and felt a little bump push against her fingers. Sometimes she was so happy, she cried. Sometimes she cried out of fear. Fear of the future. Finally, she told her boyfriend.

At first, Roger was worried, but as they talked, he became more and more excited. He felt the baby's movements, and with them, his heart filled with happiness. He was a father. "Come to my parents' home when you are ready," he said in his soft calming voice, "They will take you in."

Basimati's belly grew and grew. The other students began to talk. Basimati remembers, "Some of the students, they were looking at me and laughing at me. Some of them were just telling me to go home." Basimati concentrated on her studies. She stayed in her room when she wasn't in class, too ashamed to go out. Still, she had a few good friends, friends who brought her extra food, friends who looked after her.

Basimati grew bigger every day. Her belly weighed her down. She had trouble climbing the stairs to get to class. She became out breath just walking between the dormitory and her classrooms. Sometimes Basimati fell asleep while her teachers were talking. She was tired all the time.

With one week left until exams, Basimati couldn't wait any longer. Her belly was huge. The baby didn't know how important her diploma was, and Basimati was sure it would come at any minute. She caught a minibus to Blantyre where she would meet Roger.

Like all minibuses in Malawi, this bus was cramped and dirty—crowded with people, bags, baskets, and chickens. Women sat with their babies on their backs. Children crowded on their parents' laps. The bus lurched and sped toward Blantyre, braking every few minutes to drop someone off or to pick up someone standing by the side of the road.

Basimati had no food and only enough money to get to Roger. She was dizzy and hot and hungry. Many hours later, tired and sick, Basimati reached Blantyre. Roger was happy to see her. The next morning, they caught another minibus. Mvumbwe village was still a minibus and a long, bumpy, bicycle ride away. Forty-five hours after leaving the college, Basimati arrived at her new home.

Basimati had never met Roger's parents. They owned a farm that they ran with the help of their children. Meeting Roger's family should have been a happy occasion, but Basimati was arriving in shame, asking for the charity of strangers. Roger had his natural resources diploma, but he didn't have a job yet. They would live on the farm until he got one.

A week later, Basimati went into labour. She needed to get to a clinic—fast. Roger's two sisters went with her. To reach the clinic, Basimati rode sidesaddle, balancing on a small, red, plastic-covered seat on the back of a bicycle. They took the same, long, dusty path that Basimati had come in on a week earlier. The bicycle swerved and bounced. Basimati felt every contraction and every bump.

When she arrived at the clinic, Basimati was taken in and examined. "We cannot keep you here," they said. "You must go to the district hospital. You are going to have twins."

Basimati laughs now, but it wasn't funny then, "I was afraid by that time," she says. Having twins in Malawi is no joke—it means hardship.

The clinic relented and kept Basimati. There was no time for her to get to the hospital. A half hour later, she gave birth to two healthy baby girls: Chisomo and Sharron.

Basimati and her babies stayed just one night at the clinic. The day after giving birth, Basimati was again riding on the back of a bicycle, this time with her babies.

The first months were hard for Basimati. She lived with Roger and the babies in a small dirt house. The house had two tiny rooms. There was no bed and no furniture—just a grass mat that covered the dirt floor. Neither room was big enough to stretch out in, so at night Basimati and Roger curled up on the floor with the babies in between them. "The babies, they were just crying and crying," says Basimati. Sometimes they cried all night. Boney and thin, her red blouse stained with milk and dirt, Basimati would sit on the floor of the little house, feeding one baby and then the other, while bits of soil sifted down from the ceiling.

As the daughter-in-law, Basimati was expected to do her share of the work for the family. She cooked two meals a day.

Basimati, Roger, and their twins, 2007.

Preparing meals in Malawi means cooking *nsima*, and cooking *nsima* is hard, physical work, especially when it's for an extended family. *Nsima* is a paste made from corn flour. It starts out as porridge and is gradually thickened till it can be formed into patties. Basimati stirred the porridge and pressed out the lumps until her arm was sore and her back ached. It took nearly three hours to cook every meal, every day. Basimati struggled to do what was expected of her, but she was always exhausted.

In Malawi, twins are not a blessing. They represent a disproportionate drain on the family. Many see twins as "bad luck." Roger's mother wanted to bring in a witch doctor. A witch doctor would perform a ritual so that no other twins would be born into the family. But Basimati didn't want a witch doctor anywhere near her babies, so with Roger's support, she said no to her mother-in-law. The witch doctor was never called. But Basimati's rebellion didn't make life on the farm any easier.

It seemed that a month didn't go by without the twins getting sick, but little by little they put on weight and they grew. They began sleeping through the night, and at eight months, they survived their first bout of malaria. Although they both have asthma, the twins continue to thrive and are now healthy, busy toddlers.

A few months after the twins were born, Basimati wrote her exams and received her diploma. Roger got a job as an agricultural outreach worker. They moved off the farm and now rent their own house. Basimati received a small loan last year and started her own business raising and selling chickens. She saw her first profits in September 2006 and hopes that once the twins are a little older, she can get a job as an agricultural outreach worker too.

Basimati is quick to let people know, "It's not very hard for me now because Roger is helping me a lot. Some people in Malawi, they do say caring for the baby is the work of the woman. So most of the people, when they are having twins, it's hard for them because they do take care of the children. They take care of the man. They take care of everything. So, as for me, Roger is helping me with everything—cooking, taking care of the babies—everything."

For Basimati, the struggle to raise a family is not over, but she now has hope for the future. And it seems likely that with parents like Basimati and Roger, Chisomo and Sharron will grow up to be two strong, determined women, just like their mother.

12

Quietly, Malawi Begins to Starve

I remember people dying—people literally dying because of starvation. People surviving on water, plain water and nothing else, and they started trying to eat some of the things that were not eatable...and some of them, they ended up eating poisonous things.

—Memory Chazeza-Mdyetseni[1]

THROUGHOUT THE FIRST DECADE of the new millennium, sub-Saharan Africa was plagued by drought and chronic food shortages.[2] By August 2001, worries of a coming food shortage had spread throughout the country. Spring harvests were low due to both drought and localized flooding. Maize production was down by 32 per cent from the previous year,[3] and other factors were making matters worse. The government of President Bakili Muluzi had been accused of corruption by the European Union and charged with economic mismanagement by USAID. Denmark, Britain, the United States, and the EU suspended aid to Malawi.[4] It turned out to be very bad timing for the country's people.

To make matters worse, USAID, the IMF, and even the Malawian government seemed reluctant to declare that a famine was even taking place, but Malawi's Catholic priests sounded the alarm early on: "What we are experiencing is a real human disaster, a famine—it is killing many people especially in the rural areas."[5] Despite the warning, it was not until the Malawi Economic Justice Network (MEJN) released a statement to the media on February 22, 2002, that the global community began to take notice. The MEJN called for government and donor action: "The government should acknowledge that there is hunger in Malawi: make the holding of maize a crime, subsidize the price of maize in Malawi: government and civil society should provide food supplies to vulnerable groups."[6] Yet help was slow in coming.

As the Malawian people suffered, recriminations spread from the lips of one official to another. President Muluzi wasn't going to take responsibility for the crisis: "The IMF is to blame for the biting food crisis... they insisted the government sell maize from its strategic reserve and requested that the government abandon its starter pack agricultural subsidy program."[7] The IMF denied the accusations: "We have no expertise in food security and we did not instruct the Malawi Government or the National Food Reserve Agency (NFRA) to dispose of the reserves."[8]

The government's decision to sell the strategic grain reserves (SGR) was on the advice of the IMF, but instead of suggesting they sell all of their stocks, the IMF had pressured the government to reduce their stocks from 165,000 metric tonnes (MT) to 60,000 MT.[9] Most of the grain was sold to the governments of Kenya and Mozambique, but people believed government officials and well-connected business people, aware of the coming crisis, bought grain early in the year and later profiteered from its sale as the price of maize soared.[10] Although the immediate causes of the Malawian famine were poor yields and drought conditions, the level of devastation brought about by the famine was caused in large part by a combination of meddling, corruption, incompetence, and poor decision making on the part of the government, intergovernmental organizations, the IMF, the World Bank, and various donor groups.

The common people were not ignorant of the government's ineptitude. Chrissy Phelani, an APU student, recalled the country's zeitgeist. "Bakili Muluzi was destroying the country. He should find some food for people to eat, but he just told lies: 'I will buy maize for you.' People were saying, 'Ahh, this guy is saying he will buy us food.' Many people were just complaining." No one believed he was serious with his promises.

Donor groups and the IMF had every right to be suspicious of President Muluzi's government. More outgoing than his predecessor, "President for Life" Hastings Banda, Muluzi became known for his frequent appearances at ribbon-cuttings and funerals. Yet much of his promise as a democratic, forward-thinking leader never came to pass. "When the administration took power in 1994 after thirty years of oppression, there was a lot of goodwill towards it," says political analyst Edge Kanongolo. "However the administration did not take the opportunities at the time to right the wrongs of the Banda administration."[11]

In one particularly unpopular move, Muluzi's MPs tried to pass an amendment to the Constitution that would eliminate presidential term limits. Although Muluzi denied that he was responsible for the proposed amendment, another bill quickly followed. This bill proposed a three-term limit, but after the ensuing public outcry, that bill, too, was scrapped.[12] Muluzi's grasping for power continued after his presidency ended. Four years after Bingu wa Mutharika replaced Bakili Muluzi in 2004, Muluzi was arrested, along with five party members and three army generals, on charges of plotting a coup.[13]

Controversy dogged Muluzi's presidency. Toward the end of his final term, many church leaders criticized him openly, accusing him of allowing corruption and wastefulness in his government.[14] It is for these reasons, as well as Muluzi's "we will rather remain poor" attitude, that Malawi received less aid from the international donor community in the years leading up to the famine.[15]

So Muluzi was responsible, in part, for the suffering of his people, but there were other factors at play. The drought of the 1991–1992 growing season, a decade earlier, brought about a harvest that produced less than half of the crop production of 2001, yet the outcome was not nearly so devastating to the majority of the population. The reasons for these perplexing results are complex.

The IMF has been criticized roundly for its insistence on privatization throughout the developing world. Up until the early 1990s, Malawi had a system in place that subsidized fertilizer and enforced stable pricing in the maize market. These policies were often criticized as inefficient, but they worked. As a requirement of doing business with the IMF and the World Bank, Malawi was forced to move toward economic liberalization: the reduction of fertilizer subsidies, the collapse of the Smallholder Agricultural Credit Association, and the privatization of ADMARC,[16] Malawi's agricultural marketing parastatal. In the past, ADMARC had managed the SGR, but the IMF, the EU, and other donors thought the reserves should be managed on a cost-recovery basis, and in 1999 the National Food Reserve Agency was born. To capitalize the quasi-independent agency and purchase its first grain stocks, the NFRA borrowed K600 million at a rate of 56 per cent. It was to service this debt that the NFRA sold its reserves in the spring of 2001.[17]

Later that year, the World Development Movement published a report that heavily criticized the IMF and the World Bank for their lack of foresight. The report said, "Rather than ensuring that social aims are achieved through accountable government, the IMF and the World Bank and other donors have pursued an agenda of austerity, deregulation and privatization. Not only have the outcomes been disastrous, but the agenda of good governance and accountability has been abused by donors."[18]

Malawi's problems are legion. The country's steadily increasing population, declining soil productivity, and limited, off-farm, income-generating opportunities have put Malawi's people at risk of starvation. Combine these factors with the imposition of economic liberalization policies, the HIV/AIDS epidemic, and an increased incidence of drought and flooding, and it isn't difficult to see why the country's food security came under threat in the spring of 2001.

The Famine Early Warning Systems Network knew of the shortfall in maize production from the beginning, but based on the Department of Agriculture's assurance that the production of cassava and potatoes was high, it insisted that food production would be more than adequate. Even a year later, it continued to insist, "Malawi has a national food surplus in 2001/2002."[19] It was wrong.

As early as August 2001, NGOs were reporting a rise in the price of maize. In November 2001, Save the Children called for government intervention.[20] There can be no doubt that aid workers at the grassroots level knew about the coming food shortage for months before Malawians began to suffer. The famine became "official" in February 2002. By then, people were already dying.

The previous summer, the NFRA had ordered 150,000 MT of maize from South Africa to replenish its reserves. Unfortunately, by the time exchange rates, delays in negotiation, and price increases were factored in, the total added up to only 134,000 MT. Still, this may have been enough had the maize been delivered on time. Instead, only 94,000 MT had arrived in Malawi by April 2002. By then, rural farmers were already consuming green maize, and the famine was nearly over.

Most of southern Africa suffered from the same food shortages as Malawi, so Malawi found itself competing for food with other desperate countries: Zambia and Zimbabwe. In addition, rainfall was heavy that season, and the relief effort was further hampered by washed-out roads, bridges, and railway tracks.[21] The Malawian people were on their own.

As always, the poor and the unfortunate suffered the most. With only enough food to last from one year to the next, subsistence farmers face hunger whenever there are crop shortages. There is not money to buy food, and when the food runs out, there is nowhere to go for more. Chrissy remembers the devastating effects of the famine. "Some people, they didn't know that year there would be famine, so they sold their crops. Unfortunately, the famine came and many people had swollen legs and were dying."

Many died from starvation. Many more died from malnutrition, food poisoning, and cholera. Others died from the complications of diseases like malaria and AIDS, diseases that may not have proved deadly if people were not already weakened by hunger. Locally, the famine was often referred to as "the swelling," because many people's faces and extremities swelled up from malnutrition shortly before they died. During the famine, deaths from cholera more than doubled.[22] People consumed maize cobs and stalks, banana roots, wild mushrooms, and other food that resulted in widespread food poisoning and other abdominal illnesses. These deaths were not factored into the final death toll. Desperate for food, many people consumed pumpkin leaves, which led to undersized pumpkins, and green maize, which led to a decrease in that year's harvest. Chrissy recalled, "Some people go to the forest. They dig to find roots and start pounding them like maize. They even go to the maize mill in order to have flour from those roots, but it was very hard." Fortunately, for the Malawian people, the 2002 harvest, while below average, was not a repeat of the previous year.

Four years later, Malawi's maize crop was even worse than it had been in 2001. The year 2005 would also be plagued with empty plates and hollow bellies. According to a report released by the Malawian Vulnerability Assessment Committee, 34 per cent of the population would be in crisis.[23]

In August 2005, the United Nations issued a "flash appeal" for support from countries worldwide to address the needs of the Malawian people. They called it a "smart appeal." They were hoping to elicit funds from the international community to help with the food shortage. It was estimated that "approximately 4.2 million people [would] not be able to meet their minimum food requirements." The second part of the appeal was intended to gain enough funds to help with seed and fertilizer subsidies. The UN was asking for a total of US$87.8 million from donor countries.[24]

On October 13, President Bingu wa Mutharika declared a national disaster. "A consensus has emerged that we have a serious food shortage affecting many people in Malawi and accordingly...I declare all districts in Malawi disaster areas with effect from today." He went on to say, "So far... the Government has distributed a total of 22,000 metric tones to about one million people from June to September this year."[25]

Government assistance and international aid programs were helping some people in some areas, but many more were in need of help. As in the 2001 famine, Malawi's poor had resorted to eating water lilies, poisonous roots, wild yams, termites, and other unconventional food sources.[26]

During times of crisis, some are affected more than others. During the famine, single mothers, orphans, and the disabled struggled for survival. Rural women were one of the groups who suffered the most. Few village women complete primary school, while some go no further than standard one or two. As a result, most have no more than a rudimentary knowledge of the written word and few, if any, possess marketable skills. According to the National Statistics Office, 65 per cent of Malawian women are illiterate.[27]

Rural mothers train their daughters for traditional roles. Girls are taught how to cook *nsima*, wash clothes, carry water, pound maize, and work in the garden: An arm moves in rhythmic circles twirling a wooden spoon to remove the lumps from the latest batch of *nsima*. Hands move with lightning speed scrubbing the dust and grime from shirts and *chitenjes*. A head remains perfectly level above a stately model's walk while carrying a crushing twenty-five-kilogram pail of water. Malawian women portray a proficient level of skill and expertise when performing the tasks for which they have been trained. However, many are ill equipped for anything but the most menial of work and nothing that is marketable on anything but the smallest scale. It's not that traditional skills are pointless—they are practical and useful in a traditional setting—but they ensure women's dependence on male support. Without a male wage earner, a woman's traditional skill set does not ensure her survival or the survival of her children.

On average, a Malawian woman will give birth to six children (more in rural settings). There are many reasons why a mother can end up raising those children on her own: death, mistreatment, and desertion are a few. Since the HIV/AIDS epidemic, many women have been left to raise their children alone. These women may receive an insignificant amount of money by taking on small, part-time jobs like working in gardens or washing laundry. But this piecework offers little income.

On one of my trips, I met an elderly woman sitting next to a pile of colourful bits of rag on the cement-covered ground of a small courtyard. Using a metal hook, she was pulling small scraps of cloth through rectangles of fabric cut from empty maize sacks. The result was small, multicoloured rugs that she sold at the local market. It took her many hours to produce one of these miniature works of art. I purchased one of these mats for 150 kwacha—about a dollar and a quarter at the time. As enterprising as some of these endeavours might be, they are not nearly enough to sustain one person, much less a family.

During times of scarcity, even survival through prostitution is not ensured. During a famine, more women are willing to engage in sexual activity for money. Prior to the famine, sex workers reportedly earned

A woman hooks small rugs using scraps of fabric and pieces of discarded maize bags, 2009.

K1,000 (less than ten dollars) for sex without a condom, or K200 for sex with a condom. However, due to the food crisis, more women were engaging in prostitution, and fewer men possessed the disposable income to pay for their services. Eventually, many women were willing to have sex for K100 (less than one dollar).

After a divorce or a husband's death, a woman will often look to her extended family for help. In good times, she may receive assistance, but that support quickly dries up when famine or some other crisis strikes. More often than not, children will quit school early to help in the family garden or perform a menial job for a few kwacha. This is one of the ongoing tragedies of this small country. Out of necessity, responsibility is equated with quitting school—not continuing.

Children also suffer during famine. According to Malawi's Health Ministry, one thousand acutely malnourished children were admitted to hospitals across the country in August 2005.[28] But in my experience, the majority of children suffer in silence.

Before Memory took her youngest sister into her home, Grace was living with her aunt and uncle. James and Esther were doing what they could for her, but they were looking after over twenty children: their own children, grandchildren, nieces and nephews. There was never enough food to go around. Grace would sit in a corner and wait until the other children had finished eating. If there was food left after they were done, she was permitted to eat. This sounds harsh, but when there is not enough food to go around, there is a necessary pecking order, and some suffer more than others.

As the 2005 famine put increased pressure on family resources, women—single and married—lined up to buy subsidized rations at local ADMARC markets. Because of the severe shortage, purchases were limited to one twenty-five-kilogram bag per family—an entirely inadequate quantity of food for most. Women walked great distances and sometimes waited for days to purchase one of these bags. Even so, the ADMARC market system was hopelessly inadequate for many of Malawi's poor. Many could not afford the subsidized price and others found themselves at the front of the line, after days of waiting, simply to be told there was no maize available.[29] There was simply not enough food to go around.

卍 While the suffering mounted, Memory began the final year of her teaching degree, but she heard about the famine on the radio and from her family in Kasungu. As a student at the college, Memory was sheltered from the famine, but she remembered the 2001 famine and the misery she and her village had experienced then. She worried about her family, but she didn't know how to help.

While at ABC, Memory had joined the youth group, Great Commission Ministry (GCM). As part of her work for GCM, Memory toured nearby villages, telling families about the love of God. She remembers visiting a village outside Lilongwe with her friend Ulemu.

When they arrived at the village, Memory called out: "*Odi. Odi.*" Two women sat chatting on the porch of a small hut. They looked up when they heard Memory's voice.

"*Muli Bwanji*," Memory said, greeting the women. She introduced Ulemu and herself and let the women know the purpose of their visit.

Memory asked one of the women, "Can we have a visit with you?"

"Well, let's go to my home," she said. The woman's name was Yankho.

They walked next door to a small, thatched, mud house. The door was open, and there were children lying on the dirt floor inside. The children's lips were chapped, and they looked sick. Their mother also appeared ill: tired and gaunt. Memory and Ulemu chatted with Yankho about the gospel, while the children listened intently, but Memory suspected they had no food. It was nearly noon, and no lunch was being prepared. There was no cooking, no fire. Finally, Memory asked the woman, "Are you sick? What about your children? Why are they just lying down?"

Yankho responded by explaining, "It's because of the famine. I don't have anything in the home to feed these kids. This is the second day without taking anything, and I cannot help it because I don't know where to go and get food."

Memory asked her, "Where is the father?"

The woman replied, "My husband passed away two years ago." So she didn't have a husband, but she had six children, no food, and no source of income.

Memory felt badly for the woman. She felt worse that she had no way to help her. She recalls, "I chatted with her about the gospel. But at the same time, I was thinking, we've fed her spiritually, but what about physically. That was the missing thing for this family. I did not have money. I did not have food. I felt sorry leaving them empty-handed because you could see these people were desperate."

Memory returned to school, but she couldn't forget Yankho and her family. Back at ABC, Memory watched other students throw away their food in the cafeteria, and she thought about the children she had seen, too weak to stand, "waiting for someone to help them."[30]

She spoke to her friends, Ulemu and Maria, thinking they might be able to come up with some way to help the victims of the famine. She knew it wasn't just the woman and her children from the nearby village who were suffering. The famine was causing suffering throughout most of Malawi, and her home region of Kasungu was one of the hardest hit areas.

Ulemu and Maria thought the students of the school might be willing to donate their food to the people of the surrounding villages, but Memory knew that not everyone felt the way she did. She knew student donations were not the solution. NGOs were bringing in aid for many of Malawi's poor, but that aid wasn't reaching Kasungu or the woman and her children in the nearby village. It wasn't reaching many of the people who needed it most. "I just sat down because I couldn't eat. I couldn't go to study. I couldn't do anything because my heart was on that family and the people in Kasungu who are also suffering the same."

Memory didn't know what she could do, but she wanted to share her thoughts and fears with her friend Christie. The next day, she left school early. She went downtown to the Internet cafe. There, she wrote an email to her friend.

⚎ There are many reasons for Malawi's ongoing food shortages. The government and government agencies have often been criticized for their mismanagement of funds and food stocks. In 2004, a commission presented their report to President Bingu wa Mutharika. The commission had been appointed by former President Bakili Muluzi to investigate alleged mismanagement of the country's grain reserves in 2002. The report accused Friday Jumbe of questionable decision making, corruption, and a lack of transparency during his tenure as general manager of ADMARC. It also raised questions about the unauthorized withdrawal of maize from the country's grain reserves and the still unaccounted for US$40 million from the sale of those reserves. Jumbe was also questioned about the financing he received to build a US$800,000 hotel for which his testimony was found to be "false, fraudulent and unsustainable."[31]

Even past President Muluzi was openly criticized in the report. Muluzi was censured for not taking disciplinary action against Jumbe during his period in office. In response to public outcry, Jumbe had been removed from his position as general manager of ADMARC and made Finance Minister within the Muluzi government.[32]

Of course, food insecurity is caused by more than administrative gaffes and shortfalls. Since the start of the HIV/AIDS crisis, Malawi has seen a large percentage of its workforce die, often leaving the very old to care for the very young. Of its current population, HIV infects 18 per cent of its most productive segment.[33] I have not visited Malawi without being aware of the death and sickness around me. While more fortunate orphans might crowd the homes of distant relatives, the truly wretched beg in the streets of the capital. They hold out their grubby hands. "Give me money," they say. It's their only English.

Death is far from uncommon. The signs of the dead are all around. Coffin shops open onto dusty streets, and the roads are often strewn with branches to mark the homes of the recently departed. During my last trip in 2009, Shakira, one of the girls at the school, lost her brother to an unknown malady. Shakira recounts, "I just heard that my brother was dead...He had been in the hospital, but I don't know how he died. Me, I was crying until I was sick."[34]

While the death of Malawi's workforce contributes to food insecurity, it's not the only cause. Malawi is one of the most densely populated countries in Africa. Subsistence farming is the primary industry, and farmers grow their hand-tilled crops on diminishing plots with declining soil fertility, making them increasingly dependent on fertilizers and donor countries. Yet fertilizers are at best a short-term remedy, and dependency upon foreign aid is certainly not a long-term solution.

According to a recent report, almost 2.6 million square kilometres of cropland in sub-Saharan Africa has shown a "consistent significant decline."[35] This decline is caused by a multitude of factors ranging from lack of fertilizer to poor agricultural practices. In a country where vast regions are now severely deforested, farmers often use postharvest stubble for fuel, while small plots of land are cultivated year after year. United States Department of Agriculture soil scientist Hari Eswaran explains that before the 1950s, African farmers routinely would leave less productive fields fallow for a generation. Then the population exploded, and now "every piece of land is taken up."[36]

In 2005, Wulf Killman, chairman of the UN food and agriculture organization's climate change group, delivered a chilling warning. He believes the chronic droughts that many South African countries have been experiencing over the past several years are part of a larger pattern: "Southern Africa is definitely becoming drier and everyone agrees that the climate there is changing. We would expect areas that are already prone to drought to become drier with climate change."[37] And weather patterns are becoming less predictable as well. Hydrologist Henrie Manford Njoloma is concerned with rainfall trends in sub-Saharan Africa. "Rainfall distribution is no longer uniform and predictable as it used to be in the past."[38]

Many scientists, activists, and humanitarians see a crisis on its way. Andrew Simms, spokesperson for the Working Group on Climate Change and Development says:

Africa is more exposed to the impacts of climate change than many other regions of the world. Climate change is happening, and it is affecting livelihoods that depend on the natural environment, which in Africa, means nearly everyone.[39]

Our planet's climate is changing, and developing countries will be hit the hardest by these changes. Njoloma explains, "Every year that food insecurity has been declared as a national problem in Malawi by the authorities, rainfall has been erratic causing droughts, dry spells besides flooding during critical grain filling stages."[40] If global weather patterns remain unpredictable, it could prove disastrous for Malawi's rural poor, causing food insecurity and spikes in maize and other essential commodity prices.

When world maize prices soar, like they did in August 2012,[41] it doesn't help subsistence farmers. They are not selling their crops, so they make no profit from the increase. Instead, should they need to purchase additional maize to supplement their own harvest, they pay an inflated price. The same goes for the Malawian government. During times of famine, when the government attempts to purchase maize to stave off starvation within the population, they often pay a premium. The point is this: Malawi's population continues to grow, but the land mass is finite. Soil nutrient content has been depleted, and even with adequate rainfall, crops are dependent on chemical fertilizers. The population, at large, can no longer rely upon subsistence agriculture as a dependable way of life.

Malawian agriculture will likely need to diversify in the future, and more importantly, the Malawian economy must diversify if it is to survive. The average Malawian has little control over which industries the government chooses to invest in, but education is key to solving the country's problems, at both an individual and a national level.

In his book, *The Bottom Billion*, Paul Collier points to secondary education as a key precondition to economic turnaround. He says, "Countries need a critical mass of educated people in order to work out and implement a reform strategy. The impetus for change must come from within the society—the heroes."[42] A country needs an educated population if it is to solve its problems.

Memory was aware of her family's vulnerability when she poured out her heart to Christie: "Christie, my family is dying, and I can't in good conscience not ask you. What can we do? I've never asked you for anything before, but now I'm asking for your help because I don't know what else to do." In her email, Memory wrote about the suffering she had seen around Lilongwe and her concern for the people of her village. She spoke of the distended bellies, chapped lips, and crying children.

Christie listened.

Attaching a plea for funds, Christie forwarded Memory's email to every person she knew. She requested that people forward the email to everyone they knew. She ended by saying, "There will be no tax receipt, so if you don't trust me, don't send money." But people did send money. Christie began receiving cheques from her friends, family, and past students, as well as Rotary clubs and individual Rotarians. The cheques came in ones and twos, but by the end of the effort, she had raised over C$28,000.

"I was really surprised by how she reacted and by how much money she fundraised," Memory later commented.

But raising the funds may have been the easy part. How does one person purchase food? Arrange for its delivery? Ensure it reaches the people in the most need? It was an immense undertaking.

One thing I've noticed about Memory is her ability to work out a problem one step at a time. Some people would be overwhelmed by the enormity of a task like running a famine relief effort, but Memory picks at a challenge from the edges. She prioritizes and plans, and little by little—*pang'ono pang'ono*—she reaches her goal. She never gives up.

Once Memory received the first installment of money from Christie, she returned to the family that started it all, but this time she took food. "I bought groceries. I went and gave it to them because I felt like this is the reason I started to do this program. For this family."

Memory and Ulemu couldn't carry the groceries by themselves, so they hired a car. The villagers ran out of their houses to see who was in their village. They thought Memory must be there to see someone important. They were shocked to learn that she was there to visit their poorest resident.

"Do you remember us? We came this other day. We thought about coming back and having a chat with you," they said.

Yankho was delighted to see them, but there had been no improvement in her situation. She and her children still lived day-to-day, gathering what they could. Memory and Ulemu went back to the car and retrieved the groceries. "They couldn't believe it, and the neighbour, she was so happy we did that for this lady."

After taking care of the woman and her children, Memory went back to her village in Kasungu to assess her people's needs. It occurred to her that even if she found maize for the people this year, they might starve the next. It was near planting time, so she decided the first order of business was to buy the best maize seed she could. Then she sat down with thirty-seven chiefs from the Kasungu District. "I felt like this is not for my village only, so I wanted them to know what was going on. I felt as if this doesn't belong to me."

Memory thought the chiefs were in a good position to help her choose the people who needed the aid most. She asked the chiefs for the names of the disabled, the single mothers, and the families caring for orphans. It would be the chiefs' responsibility to inform the people on the list that they should come to the seed distribution and later the maize distribution. The chiefs would also come to the distribution to make sure the recipients were who they said they were.

Fertilizer was another concern for Memory. That year, the government went against the advice of the World Bank and continued to offer fertilizer subsidies, a practice that would later be heralded as ending the country's dependence on foreign aid, but at the time was hugely controversial.[43] Memory realized that for people unable to purchase seed, fertilizer—even subsidized fertilizer—was too expensive. So along with seed, Memory purchased fifty bags of fertilizer. Memory gave each family who came to the seed distribution a small pail of fertilizer.

From the start, Memory recognized that she couldn't run a successful famine relief operation on her own. She needed help. So she enlisted the assistance of people she trusted: her grandfather; her cousin, Morocco; her brother, Danny; her friend, Maria; and several of the CEAG girls: Asane, Chiconde, and Benia. With their assistance, she was able to set up monitored distribution stations.

At the first distribution, Memory would hand out seed and fertilizer, but before she began, she stood in front of the gathering crowd and
spoke. Because some of her helpers had already been approached with
bribes, she warned the chiefs against corruption. "I will report to the
police whenever I find anyone practising corruption," she said. At this,
the people laughed and clapped their hands.

Carrying pails and makeshift containers, the villagers stood in line
awaiting their allotment of seeds and fertilizer. Later, they came to thank
Memory. Many women knelt down, saying, "Thank you so much. We
have rich people here, but they do not help the weak and poor like us."
Another woman said, "Now I have hope for next year because I will be
able to grow maize." Another woman cried with joy. "Memory you have
been an answer to me. I have prepared the land last month, but I did
not have the seeds to plant." That was the beginning of Memory's relief
effort. The next month would see the start of maize distribution.

Henry was in charge of purchasing the maize and transporting it
to the village, where it was being stored in the old CEAG school, which
was now nearly empty. Memory had made arrangements to use one of
the classrooms for storage so the maize could be locked up. She also
employed a watchman to guard the maize at night.

For awhile, the maize remained safe in the classroom. But, as Memory
learned later, a group of thieves was staying at the nearby trading centre. The
thieves were close enough that they were able to keep an eye on the school.
They waited and watched. One night, the watchman didn't go to work. "To
us he pretended that he had gone to work," Memory said, but he hadn't.

Early the next morning, a villager reported to Memory's grandfather
that CEAG had been broken into the night before. People from the village
gathered together and went in search of the maize. Some of the bags had
split open, leaving a trail of kernels on the ground. Memory laughs when
she tells me this part of the story. "So you see how they were caught
these people." Many of the bags were discovered hidden in gardens or
behind houses. Some had been buried in the ground. Out of twenty-five

bags, the people of Memory's village recovered seventeen. The others were never found and had probably been sold for quick cash.

Who had done this?

A few days after the break-in, Memory's brother, Danny, was spending the evening in a nearby pub. Danny had already been drinking with a friend for some time when his friend turned to him and said, "Okay, Dan. I know something about what happened to the maize of your sister. I will only disclose this when you give me some maize because I'm starving at my house." Danny went to Memory with his story.

"I'm willing to compensate him if he tells me the truth because I want to find out the truth." Memory promised him a pail of maize if he came forward with the names of the conspirators.

The man named five people from his village. "You know I was one of the people who was consulted that I should break into the house where you were keeping the maize, but it was me who discouraged them because the maize is helping the rest of us." He went on to explain, "They've been having meetings for one month before they broke into that house." And he told Memory where they were having the meetings. At this point, he hesitated: "The wife of that man who was holding the meetings is my relative from my village."

Memory went to the police with the names of the men, and the police arrested them. There was a hearing, where the police asked the culprits the names of the others involved in the theft, but the men refused to divulge the names, so the police kept them in custody until they finally came clean. There were a total of twenty men involved.

After they had all been arrested, Memory asked the police, "What is going to happen to my maize? This maize was meant for me to distribute to other people. Are these thieves going to pay me back?"

But the police said, "No, but we are going to keep them for some time, and if they do it again, they will remain prisoners."

Memory was devastated. "I felt like I had lost because the whole point of making those men go to the police was to make sure they bring back the maize." But Memory is not one to give up. "Well then I'm a loser, but how am I going to show these people that what these thieves did was not a good thing?"

The following day was a distribution day. Memory made a decision: "All the people coming from the same village as these people who were involved with stealing are not going to receive any maize."

People began arriving early the next day—long before sunrise. They waited in line until the sun rose over the savannah. They waited into the daylight hours in the scorching African heat while Memory organized the distribution and spoke to the police.

Memory gathered the people together and spoke to them. She told them about the theft and the arrest of the thieves. She also told them about her plan to punish the thieves' villages.

The people stood up. "Why don't you punish only the families of these people?"

Memory responded, "No. I should punish the whole village because through that you are going to be responsible not to keep things in your villages." Many people went home hungry that day.

"Oh, it was a hard one, but I had no option," says Memory.

When the men were released from police custody a month later, they went back to their villages, but their families chased them away. They were no longer welcome.

Trouble was not over for Memory and her family. Because of his involvement with the relief effort, Memory's grandfather became a target of violence.

One night, while it was raining hard, thieves broke down the door to Memory's grandfather and grandmother's house. The thieves' heads were covered, and they all carried big machetes, called pongo knives. Because of the heavy rain, her grandparents' cries for help went unheard. Memory's grandfather jumped out of bed and tried to defend himself with a rake, but he was cut deeply in his shoulder and back. As he bled out on the floor, he lost consciousness, and the thieves searched his home. When the men realized there was nothing to steal, they left. Memory's grandmother ran for help, and Danny dragged his grandfather out to the road, where he eventually flagged down a truck that took them to the hospital. Memory's grandfather recovered, but it had been a close call. After his wounds healed, he told Memory, "My suffering is not enough to stop helping these hundreds of people."

The famine lasted until harvesting began in April 2006.

Memory and Christie's "little" famine relief effort helped thousands of people that year and in the years to come. Many of the families who received seeds continue to grow improved crops. When we walked through the area the following year, Memory pointed out the crops descended from the seed she had purchased.

The relief effort also changed the attitudes of many people in the area. "Men were humbled because they did not expect a girl to come up with such a good program. I hope this will be a learning point since they regard women as people who are dull and always waiting for the ideas from men," said Memory, recounting the events of that year.

When Memory reached out to trusted friends and family, her cousin, Morocco, was there to help with the famine relief. Morocco lived through the early days of the famine before relief came to his village. He described seeing a starving woman sleeping on the road "in order to involve herself in a deliberate accident." The incident made his "eyes swim in tears," but he had no way of helping her.[44] The following is taken from a report he wrote to the Canadian donors:

> People are very grateful to the Canadian donors who responded positively to Memory's plea…Chief Wimbe said that the donation had come on time [and] that this is the first time for him to see such an impressive thing in his area. It has been the song of the people that Canadians are kind and understanding people. Canadians alongside with Malawians have proved Memory as a trusted person. People have been recommending her for her faithfulness. "Instead of only helping her relatives

and friends, she is including us who are not her relatives, that one is a merciful and kind person," say people whose villages are benefiting from the donation. Some people have been saying that if I were Memory, I would have got rich because part of the donation would remain in my pocket. Some inconveniences had been shunned by sending the money directly to Memory. If the donation were sent through the government, there would be a tremendous deduction by some of the top officials who would be responsible for it. Officials would not have just looked at the money but they would wish to benefit from it and this is obvious.... People are ardent that Memory should be a member of parliament. Memory has exposed her full love during a terrible situation like this. She is eligible to be a member of parliament because her faithfulness will always accompany her in trouble and happiness...

Wonderful news is that people who are not the beneficiaries and they are starving are very grateful over the donation and faithfulness of Memory. They express their gratitude just because some of their parents, friends and relatives are among the beneficiaries. Such people assist the police to ensure that security is maintained as the people are receiving maize. People complain some village headmen have been flocking to Memory to be enlightened why their villages were not included. They are always answered the donation is not enough for everyone. They return sympathetically, amazingly at last they say, "God bless Canadians for assisting our fellow Malawians."[45]

The relief effort lasted until the spring harvest. In all, Memory and Christie's efforts helped feed around five thousand people, but it did much more than that. It showed people what a woman could accomplish.

Christie Johnson believes it was the famine relief effort that gave Memory the skills to become a leader:

Memory has become a leader, but she didn't just become a leader. That famine in 2005 turned her into a leader. The famine relief turned her in the eyes of thousands of people, her own home community who always put her down, into a leader. That gave her the ability to make big decisions on behalf of lots of people. And that to me is a huge part of the story. It gave her the ability to dream of having her own girls' school. It takes guts to have a dream and to have the expectation that you can pull it off.

Memory has experienced great fortune and great loss, but she has had the support and encouragement of many people who have helped her realize her vision. Make no mistake, she is a determined individual, and it is through her resolve and strength of character that she has succeeded.

Henry

DURING THE 2005 FAMINE, there was very little maize in Malawi.[1] The maize shortage had left the country with depleted stocks, and the relief effort needed a lot of maize if it were to feed over three hundred people. Memory couldn't purchase and transport the maize herself. She needed a man she could trust, so she asked Henry for help. During the time of the famine, Henry made several trips to purchase maize and transport it back to Kasungu.

Because maize was impossible to purchase in Malawi, Henry travelled across the border to Tanzania. It turned out to be dangerous work.

Henry took a bus, leaving Lilongwe at eight in the evening. It took hours to travel to the northern tip of the country, and he slept along the way. With him, he carried a small bag containing K600,000—the money needed to purchase the maize in Tanzania. The bus arrived at Karonga at four in the morning. It was dark at the depot, and Henry had never been to Karonga. He planned to meet his friend, Jeremiah. Jeremiah had promised to help Henry get across the border. To find his house, he had told Henry to walk left from the bus depot, but while Henry had slept, the bus had made a U-turn. As Henry recalled, "The left had turned into right." Henry began walking out of town. Soon, there were no houses, and "I was getting lost in the bushes." He traced his steps back to the bus depot.

Henry decided not to wait for his friend. Instead, he took another bus to the border.

At the border stands a checkpoint. The border police asked Henry to open his bag: "You are carrying a lot of cash. You're not supposed to carry so much money outside of the country. Wait right here." Henry immediately knew he was in trouble. He was certain the men would take the money, and there would be no maize for the people of the village.

Henry ran into the darkness that surrounded the checkpoint. He waited there, in the shadows of a nearby house, until he saw a taxi heading back toward Karonga. He hailed the taxi and got in. On the way back to Karonga, the driver turned off the main road.

As he told his story, Henry explained the situation: "I didn't really know why he stopped there, but here I am running away from the police, and he stopped somewhere in the middle of the bush."

Henry asked the driver, "Why are we stopping here?" The man didn't answer. When Henry got out of the taxi, he could see they were near the Songwe River: the Songwe River marks the border between Malawi and Tanzania. Shapes moved above the water in the darkness, people walking through the waist-high water. They carried bags of flour above their heads. Instead of paying taxes at the checkpoint, they were crossing here, and the taxi was there to pick them up. "So there I was," Henry said. "If the police had found us, it would be double trouble. I've already been told I have too much cash and now here I'm found among smugglers. How would I say I'm not involved?" As he spoke, Henry chuckled at the memory of his own predicament.

Henry made it back to Karonga. He met with Jeremiah, who reassured him, "I've got a friend at the border. We just go together." With his friend's help, Henry was able to cross the border, purchase the maize, and return to Kasungu.

By the time Henry made his second trip, maize was even scarcer. It was being sold, but rationed, at government depots. Henry needed to find maize for three hundred people: three tonnes of maize. After his last experience, Henry realized that purchasing the maize in Tanzania was simply too risky. Usually an individual would need permission from the government to purchase and transport that volume of maize across the border. Government permission could easily take three months, and even that required a business license permitting the purchase. A business license could take years. They only had one option: Henry arranged to purchase the maize from an agent. It would cost more, but Henry could pick the maize up on the Malawian side of the border—in Mzuzu.

Driving a rented truck, Henry successfully purchased the maize from the agent. He had just left the outskirts of Mzuzu when the police stopped his truck. They confronted him, saying, "So you are carrying maize." Henry told them where he had bought the maize and showed them the sales receipt. The police were not convinced. "No, you can only buy maize from government depots." They took him to the police station.

At the station, he phoned Memory. "I'm at the police station." But there was nothing Memory could do.

In the meantime, the police brought in an expat who was in charge of distributing government maize. The expat said, "You can release this guy. He's not taking government maize." The man left, but the police didn't release Henry.

While he was waiting, Henry started up a conversation with a man who said he was from the Kasungu area. "You know, it's a question of money. If you part ways with K2,000, they will release you. Or you can wait here for two more days."

Henry thought, "Well, what choice do I have?"

He paid the K2,000 and was released immediately, along with a letter of clearance that he could show if the police stopped him again.

Relieved, Henry climbed back into the truck and continued his journey. He was getting close to Kasungu—not far from the small community of Mboma—when, around midnight, the truck got a flat tire. Henry was able to flag down a truck passing on the road. The driver agreed to transport Henry the rest of the way, but he said, "We can't take you into the cab. We don't know who you are. You might hijack our truck." The night was dark and rainy. By the time they reached Mboma, Henry was drenched.

After asking around, Henry found someone who could change the tire. "I was lucky to find this guy in a pub. He was still drinking at something like 3 AM." Henry asked how much he would charge. "K1,000."

They drove back to the truck, and the man fixed the tire. When he noticed the maize, he probably thought Henry had a lot of money. He tried to increase his price to K10,000. "It's a big job," he said.

Henry wasn't about to be taken advantage of. "I'm going to pay you K1,000," responded Henry, in a flat, even voice.

Each time Henry transported maize, he risked his life. Times of famine are dangerous. Crime rates are elevated, and tension is high throughout the country. Without Henry's willingness to take on this responsibility, there would have been no maize and no famine relief.

13
A Global Perspective

If you think you're too small to make a difference, you haven't spent a night with a mosquito.

—*African proverb*[1]

AFTER SUCCESSFULLY HELPING the CEAG girls, Memory began to wonder what her next step would be.[2] At ABC, Memory's major was theology, but for a minor she could go into education or communication. While she had planned to become a teacher, some of her friends had moved their minors to communications. Memory began to think she'd like to be a radio announcer.

One day, after giving a speech for her speech class at the college, Memory was approached by the director of the school. "Memory, have you applied for communications?" he asked.

Memory told him that she had not.

"You need to enroll in communications," he told her.

This gave Memory pause. She admits now, "I got carried away." The next time she spoke with Henry, she shared her experience, but Henry was unmoved. "No, Memory," he said. "We are going to have our own school. This is part of our vision."

After their conversation, Memory thought, "Henry is right. Somehow our dream will come to pass."

But how?

Memory had dreamed of having her own school for many years. Even during secondary school she had thought about beginning with a nursery school and gradually expanding it to include the primary and maybe even the secondary grades. She had even spoken to Lucy. "Lucy," she'd said, "don't you think we can start a school? We should start simple. We'll start with a nursery school."

When Memory spoke to Henry in the early days of their relationship, her dream hadn't changed, although it had evolved. Henry wanted to build a school too. He thought he could get a loan from work, so they could get the project off the ground. He believed they could build a school that could become a successful business and help the girls of their country get their education.

Memory hadn't spoken to Christie about her plan yet, but she knew they made a great team. They were both stubborn and tenacious, they both knew the importance of educating girls, and when they decided on a goal, they were both visionary in their approach. Memory decided to discuss the project with Christie.

Memory wrote Christie a letter. In the letter, she laid out her plan. She wanted to open a secondary school for poor, rural girls so they could realize their goals and their potential. She suggested they form a business partnership.

When Christie responded, she said, "The school can be built. I can fundraise." In Christie's mind, it should be a charitable organization.

"This is something that shouldn't be owned by you or me; it should be something for the community."

It took some time for Memory, Henry, and Christie to agree on a vision for the school, but they all wanted the same thing: they all wanted to help girls become educated. They decided to move forward with the vision. Henry said, "Let's not talk about something we can't do. Let's start talking seriously."

Almost immediately, Henry was able to procure land for the school. His family came from the area near Nsaru trading centre. Many of the local chiefs were thrilled at the prospect of having a girls' boarding school in the area. The *Atsikana Pa Ulendo* Secondary Girls' School project was granted twenty-two hectares of land on which to build a school.

I met Memory for the first time in 2006, when she came to Canada to speak at the Rotary District Conference, held that year in Stony Plain, Alberta. I had been asked by Elly Contraras, the district governor, to photograph the event. Elly had been essential in arranging Memory's trip to Canada and giving her the opportunity to promote building a girls' school to the Rotary clubs throughout the district.

The conference was a big event. Hundreds of Rotarians were gathered from throughout the region. The conference would feature a keynote speech by then Senator Roméo Dallaire, author of *Shake Hands with the Devil* and *They Fight Like Soldiers, They Die Like Children,* and a Canadian icon. It would also feature a speech by a young Malawian woman, Memory Chazeza.

I had heard Christie talk about her time in Malawi and her work raising funds for the CEAG girls, so I was eager to meet Memory and hear her speak. The first time I met Memory, though, was at the conference's wine tasting the night before she spoke. The Rotarians were excited for Memory to experience all things Canadian. So although Memory doesn't care for alcohol, she gave in gracefully. One taste was enough. I remember her wrinkling her nose, shaking her head, and firmly saying, "Oh, I don't like that."

Memory sits with Roméo Dallaire, 2006.

The following day, the crowd sat in hushed silence as Memory talked about her experiences growing up as an orphan and struggling to get her education in distant Malawi. She also spoke about her dream to open a girls' secondary school to help the girls of her country. Memory was dressed in an outfit she had sewn herself, a skirt and blouse made with a brilliant-patterned fabric like the designs I would see when I made my first trip the following year: black, red, and vibrant yellow. Memory was herself vibrant, resolve and commitment emanated from every word. "Life is really what you make it," she said in strong, determined tones. She clearly inspired the audience.

After her speech, people congratulated her and said, "You are like Mother Theresa."

The following day, Memory sat with Roméo Dallaire. The two ate lunch together and chatted. Later, Christie and Memory received Paul Harris awards for "exceptional service." Memory recalls, "I was treated like a celebrity."

Memory had brought hand-sewn dolls with her to sell. Agness and Eunice had helped her craft the dolls from scraps of fabric. They had sewn on button eyes and black yarn hair. The dolls were a hit. The proceeds from the sale of the dolls, as well as the conference's silent auction, went to start construction on the girls' school. In total, the event raised over C$17,000 for the future school.

Shortly after Memory returned to Malawi, she graduated from ABC. Then on August 26, 2006, she and Henry Mdyetseni were married. The ceremony took place at the Church of Central Africa Presbyterian Kaninga Church in Lilongwe. Later, they moved to a church hall for the reception.

There were so many weddings in Lilongwe that day that Memory and Henry weren't sure how many people would come to theirs, but the hall was packed. People were standing in the aisles.

The day after the wedding, Memory and Henry drove to Salima to spend a few days at the lake. After that, they moved into a small house in Area 25 in Lilongwe and continued to plan the school.

In Malawi, close family and friends usually attend the wedding ceremony, but the reception can be a raucous affair, with hundreds of people in attendance. During one of my trips to Malawi, Memory and Henry were away for the day at a wedding in Lilongwe. Another wedding had taken place that morning at the Catholic church in nearby Nsaru. The groom, Robson, was the brother of one of the APU girls, Alefa. Memory's sister, Grace, wanted to attend the reception. She was in charge of baby-sitting Teloni for the day, so she took Teloni; my daughter, Nastassja; and me to Nsaru, where we met up with Alefa. Alefa took us to meet her mother, and they ushered us into a house where some of the wedding guests were gathering. We were invited into an empty room, where we sat on a mat on the floor. They politely asked, "Would you like *nsima* or rice?" We asked for *nsima* since Nastassja hadn't tried it yet, but they brought us both. They also brought us bowls of goat meat and relish. Teloni sat for a long time on Grace's lap, contentedly sucking on a piece of goat. It was my first time to eat goat. It's a rich meat, sweet and strong in taste, laced with fat.

While we were eating, a man brought us bottles of Fanta and Coke, but for the most part, we were left on our own to enjoy the meal. As hard as we tried, we couldn't eat all our food, but that didn't seem to be the point. This was a celebration with plenty for all.

Henry's family lives near the school, so it wasn't a surprise that we met his mother on the way to the reception. Henry's mother is a school-teacher by profession. She is bold and strong-willed. The only word that effectively describes her character is "indomitable." She is the sort of person who could overcome almost any challenge. She is "tradition-ally" built and speaks in a resounding voice. She must make a formidable mother-in-law, but her heart is big—just as big as her personality.

We exchanged greetings and she insisted we come for a visit. We sat on a mat in the shade near a house while Henry's mother danced with a friend. They laughed and sang as they danced. It was just for fun, but still a striking performance, full of vocal ululations and butt wiggling—no one can butt wiggle like a Malawian.

Soon we said our goodbyes: "*Tsalani bwino!*" meaning "stay well" and walked down the road to Nsaru Secondary School. The school is in a large compound, just outside the trading centre, and the reception was being held in a large hall. The hall was meant to hold around six hundred people.

When we arrived, the hall was nearly empty, so we found seats close to the front. Once the bride and groom entered the hall, it quickly filled with people. Soon there was standing room only. Families lined the walls or poked their heads in at the doors. I can't be sure how many people were present, but it could have been close to a thousand. The bride and groom sat on chairs on the stage at the front of the hall with more people sitting behind them.

The music was loud, and when the MC spoke into the microphone, it sent feedback screeching through the speakers, filling the hall with squawks and crackles. Someone turned down the sound, but it seemed to magically increase in volume until feedback squealed once more throughout the room. The MC began calling out to the crowd, encouraging them to give money to the couple. He spoke in Chichewa, so I had to rely on Grace for the translation. A basket was held out to people so they could throw in their money. Groups of people danced up the centre aisle, lifting their money high in the air and throwing it dramatically into the basket, some lifted a kwacha bill into the air, threw it down, lifted another, threw it down, repeating the action several times to the cheers of the crowd and the encouragement of the MC. People clapped and ululated their voices, competing with the high-pitched, distorted music. The MC asked groups of people to contribute. He called on the groom's family and the bride's family, the groom's coworkers and the bride's friends. This went on for some time until Grace said it should be our turn. I'd been warned in advance and had my money ready. I'd also purchased a blanket at the trading centre that morning, so I'd have a gift to give too.

We pushed our way to the front of the hall amidst the jostling crowd. Dutifully, I lifted my money in the air and the crowd cheered. Then we made our way to the side of the stage where they were collecting gifts, but before we could return to our seats, a man ushered us up onto the stage so we could sit—as guests of honour—behind the bride and groom. It was one of those strange and unexpected experiences that was a bit overwhelming at the time, but that I can now recall and treasure.

Grace would have been happy to stay for hours, but Nastassja and I were tired. It had been a lot of Malawian culture for one day. So, after an hour on stage, we left the hall. Outside, we found Stephano waiting for us, ready to drive us back to the school in the wedding car.

꙳ Weddings and marriages are important aspects of Malawian culture. Girls grow up dreaming of becoming brides and having big weddings, and if they lack the opportunity to learn a trade or attend post-secondary school, they often marry sooner rather than later.

Attitudes may be changing, but it is still common for girls to marry when they reach puberty, sometimes as young as twelve or thirteen years of age. Boys tend to marry later than girls—usually by the time they are seventeen or so.[3] Once a girl marries, she will almost certainly leave school. She is expected to care for her husband and their home, and soon she will begin bearing children.

This is the setting for today's Malawian woman. Many of the country's women still depend upon a husband to provide for them: "Because marriage is good. I [know he can] take care of me and feed me....You get married because you expect the man to look after you"[4]—this is the expectation. Unfortunately, for vast numbers of Malawian women, the reality doesn't live up to that expectation.

Although some areas of the country, mostly in the extreme north and the extreme south, follow the patrilineal tradition, the majority of Malawi is traditionally matrilineal. In the past, the husband moved to his new wife's home village, where he would build a house and granary. In Malawi, he was also expected to "provide service," working his in-laws' land for a designated period of time. The man had no control over his children and within this system, girl children "were valued because they could make a strong lineage and develop a strong production and consumption unit." Within the setting of the wife's village, a husband's actions came under close scrutiny by his wife's relatives. If the husband decided to leave his wife, the house, granary, and children remained in her possession. If a husband decided to enter into a polygynous relationship, he was required to supply equally for both (or all) his wives. Francine van den Borne, author of *Trying to Survive in Times of Poverty and AIDS*, claims, "Given the workload involved in building houses and granaries, and working on the fields for in-laws, it seems unlikely that formal polygyny was very common in pre-colonial Malawi. Even if husbands married more than one wife, each wife was entitled to equal treatment."[5] So although polygyny was an acceptable practice, it was closely monitored within tightly knit community groupings.

Today most women have very different experiences with polygyny. Many of their stories follow a familiar pattern. A man will marry, and at first, all is well. After a few years, he decides to take a second and even a third wife. The wives become rivals within the relationship. They complain to their husband about each other's faults or demand favourable treatment. The husband often favours his most recent conquest and denies his first wife fair treatment. At this point in the relationship, the first wife often leaves, taking the children with her. She will probably go back to her home village, but she rarely has a means to support herself beyond taking on piecework and asking relatives for handouts. While this is certainly an oversimplification of a complex situation, I have heard variations on this same story so many times that I can't help but believe it is a common occurrence.

For Lucita's mother, Enet, the consequences of a polygynous marriage were severe. Lucita's father, Azibo, is a farmer. Enet was his first wife, but over the years Azibo took three more wives. Although the wives lived in separate houses, there was much gossiping. It's common for men to listen to the newest wife and disregard the wishes of an older wife. Because Enet was the first wife, Azibo gradually turned against her.

Each wife managed a small garden plot, a *dimba*, which supplied food for her and her children. Each wife was also expected to work Azibo's cash crop of tobacco. In return, each wife would be given fertilizer and seeds so they would be able to produce better yields in their own *dimbas*, but Azibo began withholding support from Enet. Eventually, she moved back to her home village.

Lucita's older sister was "very bright" and got selected to go to a national secondary school in Lilongwe. When he heard the news, Azibo said, "I don't believe in school. I'm not going to sponsor you. Just get married." Lucita's sister married. She had two children, but, for reasons I don't know, got divorced.

Lucita's older brother had also been selected into a good secondary school, but his father had said the same thing. "I will not sponsor you." Lucita realized the same would happen to her.

Life hadn't improved for Enet. Food was a problem, too, and because they had little to eat, she stopped Lucita from going to school so they could both take on piecework.

The following year, Lucita's uncle, Bomani, suggested Lucita come to live with him, so she could return to school. She was living with her uncle when she heard about APU.

This trend is confirmed by an extensive study done by the Malawi Human Rights Commission: "The first wife finds herself in a situation where she has to look after herself as well as fending for her children... Many husbands in such unions rarely communicate with their first wives except on a few occasions at night when they want to claim their conjugal rights. As such, it was learnt, conflicts between the wives and between husbands and wives, which spill over to the children from the different mothers, abound."[6] I have no doubt that there are polygynous marriages that work to the benefit of all parties, but they appear to be in the minority and more often to the benefit of the men rather than the women. Most women would like to see the practice banned.[7]

There are many cultural reasons for the practice. A husband might find that his first wife is infertile, or he may want more children than one wife can bear. Some men father illegitimate children and feel they should marry the mother. Other men see women as cheap labour, and some value wives and their children as status symbols. In other cases, a man might take on the responsibility of caring for the wives and children of deceased relatives. In these cases and others, women are often so desperate for support that they will accept a polygynous union. Occasionally, a man takes another wife as punishment for his first wife's, real or perceived, transgressions.[8] I can only assume that these situations do not end well.

As part of the recent study done by the Malawi Human Rights Commission, men were asked why they believed polygynous marriage should be preserved. Many of the men believed there was a shortage of men. They also believed the practice of having more than one wife meant the "men are well cared for and respected by the wives." Other men felt it was important to be able to exercise their "conjugal rights" while their other wife or wives were menstruating or if they had recently given birth.

There were many men who simply believed it was part of their culture, and they had a right to preserve it.[9]

During the same study, those opposed to polygyny were asked their reasons for opposing the practice. Not surprisingly, more women were against the practice than men, but some men spoke out too. As mentioned earlier, both men and women were of the opinion that first wives and their children were often neglected after the husband took more wives. Many women were unhappy that husbands rarely communicated with their first wives. Another reason that respondents believed polygyny was an undesirable practice was because of the practices it appears to perpetuate. Desperate women will sometimes employ witch doctors to curse or even kill their rivals.

People included in the study also expressed pragmatic reasons for abolishing polygyny. Many people realize that multiple partners can contribute to poverty, especially when a husband takes on more wives than he is able to support financially. Youth, in particular, stated they believed polygyny was contributing to the spread of HIV/AIDS and also contributing to the large number of orphans in sub-Saharan Africa.[10] All of these are legitimate concerns, but polygyny is a long-standing tradition throughout the country going back hundreds, if not thousands, of years.

After becoming president in 1964, Dr. Hastings Kamuzu Banda legalized polygyny.[11] While polygyny is widely practised in Malawi, it is not recognized under the civil marriage laws of the country. Currently, about 8 per cent of women with secondary or post-secondary education are in polygynous relationships, while 21 per cent of women with little or no education report being in polygynous relationships. Nine per cent of married men claim to be in polygynous relationships, but many polygynous unions are of an informal nature, and for these, there are no formal statistics.[12]

A young divorced woman living in poverty explains:

Men can't be satisfied with only one woman. That's why men have ziwenzi (girlfriends) in addition to their wives. Sometimes they have only one girlfriend and take another after they have broken up. But often they have more girlfriends at a time. But they do this secretly. They hide this from their wives. But also from their other girlfriends. Otherwise there would be war between the women.[13]

It's a sad story that many women share.

Polygyny has recently been accused of standing in the way of economic development. Many people in sub-Saharan Africa practise polygyny legally, but it's often practised illegally as well. The countries that do practise polygyny have several common characteristics. They all have a high fertility rate: 6.8 children per woman on average, as opposed to 4.6 in monogamous countries. There is a broad age difference between married men and women, 6.4 years instead of 2.8. They have a lower savings rate, 13 compared to 19 per cent of GDP, and that GDP rate is itself much lower; averaging C$1,037 instead of C$2,975.[14] While these are dramatic statistics, they downplay the cultural investment a people can feel toward an established way of life. Cultural paradigms are difficult to change, even when it appears change might be beneficial to all.

It has been said that banning the practice of polygyny would, on average, decrease a country's "fertility by 40%, [while increasing] the savings rate by 70% and [the per capita output] by 170%."[15] These are staggering numbers that give a great deal of credence to the antipolygyny movement, but as with every controversy, there are two sides.

In a recent backlash against "feminist" antipolygyny campaigns, Stewart Chipofya, of the northern Malawi tribe of Tumbuka, said, "These organizations should fight homosexuality, prostitution and not the legal and legitimate marriage of several wives." Sheikh Mohammad Uthman, secretary general of the Majlis Ulam Council of Malawi, agrees: "It bothers us much when instead of fighting outright evils in the streets such as prostitution and homosexuality; they oppose legitimate ways of enjoying conjugal rights."[16] But another campaign is underway.

OneLove is a multiregional campaign aimed at getting "us thinking and talking about our sexual behaviour in this time of HIV and AIDS." The campaign began in 2008 and is based on the premise that "having multiple concurrent relationships puts you and your loved ones at risk of getting infected with HIV." Across sub-Saharan Africa, OneLove's campaign seeks to question attitudes toward women and encourages people to think about how cultural patterns affect their sexual decision making.[17] With two such strong opposing views—one based on generations of tradition, the other based on human rights and health concerns—this debate will likely rage for some time to come. And although monogamous unions might be preferable to most women, even monogamous marriages can be less than ideal situations for women lacking an education.

Recently, past President Bingu wa Mutharika passed a bill that raised the age a girl can marry with parental consent from fifteen to sixteen years of age. Mutharika found himself surrounded by a storm of harsh criticism from a number of civil society groups. Mutharika defended his actions, saying, "Let the people and all stakeholders, including boys and girls, debate the issue and agree on whether the marriage age should be eighteen, twenty-one or twenty-five as some people are proposing. After the consensus, the matter will go back to parliament."[18]

While the ruling is an improvement over previous legislation, individuals like MacBain Mkandawire, executive director of Youth Net and Counselling, believe, "When our national assembly accepted that a girl of the age of sixteen can be married, we, in the child protection sector, saw our hard work to alleviate the challenged lives of girls taken aback several years. In all fairness, a girl at the age of sixteen is still a child."[19]

The controversy surrounding this new legislation appears fraught with inconsistency. The law seems to contradict the practice. On my trips to Malawi, I have heard of many young girls being forced or persuaded into marriage long before they reach fifteen, much less sixteen, years of age. But the confusion lies in the separation of practice from law.

Because many marriages take place as a result of traditional custom, instead of civil law, girls are often married at a very young age—sometimes they barely reach puberty—to men years or even decades their senior. Most often the reasons are financial. A girl might be "sold" to pay off family debts. In some cases, girls are forced to marry after the death of one or both parents.

Memory's cousin, Mwayi, lost her parents when she was thirteen. Mwayi's older stepbrother moved to a distant area and left Mwayi with a younger brother and sister to care for on her own. Eventually, Mwayi's brother and sister went to stay at a relative's house in Madisi, but no one wanted to adopt them.

The women from Mwayi's village began pressuring her to get married. "If you get married, you will have a husband, and you will be able to support your brother and sister," they said.

Mwayi's family found a man who was willing to marry her, and a hasty wedding was planned. There is a snapshot of Mwayi on her wedding day. She sits next to her new husband in her wedding dress. Her head is bowed, and her expression is sombre. She has done what she had to do.

The issue is not simply whether or not girls should marry. The real issue is that girls have few choices. They may be forced into marrying someone they don't want to marry, or they may decide to marry for lack of a better choice. Without education, girls' choices remain limited at best. Even with an education, jobs are scarce and low-paying. Benia, a young Malawian woman, graduated from post-secondary school a few years ago with a two-year secretarial diploma. When I met Benia, she worked fifty-six hours a week as a clerk at a local pharmacy. She earned K4,000 a month (now the equivalent of C$15 but at the time closer to C$25).

At the time, she was looking for another job, but there were few opportunities. With an unemployment rate of over 40 per cent, competition is brisk. Benia could not afford to purchase newspapers. She relied on word-of-mouth to learn about job openings, and her long hours made it difficult for her to apply for another job. This is the trap that Malawian women often find themselves in—if they are fortunate enough to be employed at all.

While twenty-five dollars may not sound like much (and it isn't), at least Benia was able to support herself. She earned far more working in the pharmacy than she could expect to earn taking on piecework. If she were to harvest beans or pull weeds in a neighbour's garden, she would be fortunate to earn fifty kwacha a day. She also knows that her experience in the pharmacy will eventually help her find a better, higher-paying job.

By being employed, Benia also gains self-respect. Men respect women who are educated and self-sufficient more than women, such as Mwayi, who must rely on their husbands to earn a wage.

Eunice

EUNICE WAS ONE OF THE FIRST GIRLS chosen to study at CEAG.[1] When I met her, she was running a preschool with Agness, but she had already endured many challenges throughout her short life.

Eunice was born in 1983: the third child of her father, Richard, but the first child for her mother, Yasinta. Yasinta was Richard's second wife. His first wife had borne two sons and died in childbirth. Then he married Yasinta.

Her father had hoped for a boy, so when Eunice was born, Richard divorced her mother and took a new wife. Not long after, the new wife was accused of witchcraft, and he divorced again.

He took Eunice's mother back the following year, but here the story becomes shadowed. I asked Eunice, "Was your mother happy to have him back?"

Eunice answered in a soft, reflective voice. "Most women, they are afraid of men. Whatever the man says, they can't disagree. My mother is just like that. Even if she knows what my father is doing is wrong, she can't say anything. Most women in the villages don't know they've got rights."

Once they were together again, Yasinta gave birth to a baby boy. "He's the one who saved their marriage," Eunice says, and giggles in embarrassment. Yasinta eventually gave birth to two boys and seven girls.

Eunice hopes for a different future for herself. At one time she had hoped to become a doctor, but instead she went to Phwezi Technical College, where she received a diploma in business. Although she believes in the power of education now, school wasn't always a good experience for her.

During President Banda's rule, parents had to pay school fees if they wanted their children to attend primary school. Students were also required to wear uniforms. Eunice's father didn't believe girls needed to go to school. "He didn't trust that girls would be successful with education. He thought that when they grew up, they would get married." He would not pay for Eunice's primary school fees, much less a uniform.

Eunice's older brothers went to school, but when Eunice tried to go too, the teachers said, "Go home."

"So I started hating school," confides Eunice. "But I started liking it in 1994 when the government changed to a multi-party system." That's when school became free for all.

If it had not been for CEAG, Eunice knows she would not have been able to go to secondary school. "It has done a very great deal in my life."

Although she had completed the JCES, once CEAG closed, Eunice despaired of completing secondary school. "It would have been very hard for me to find a job," she said, and she knew her father was unlikely to pay. She would have to get married.

It was through Memory and Christie's determination that Eunice was able to go to Phwezi to attend secondary and later post-secondary school.

Eunice earned a business diploma at Phwezi Polytechnic College and experimented with a number of small businesses: raising chickens, owning a tuck shop, and running a nursery school, which was where I met her in 2007. I saw Eunice again two years later. She had given up the business, but she had a good job as an outreach worker. She was married and had a little seven-week-old baby girl: Catherine. She had waited until she was twenty-five years old before she got married, and she came into the marriage on her own terms. She insisted that her husband go for HIV/AIDS testing before they married, and he had agreed.

14

The Dream Takes Shape

My time at APU has helped me to realize that women can do anything...I see a generation that is educated and employed. A generation that is able to send its children to school...I see a generation that will reach other people's lives and bring change.

—*Maness Samuel*[1]

I TOOK MY FIRST TRIP TO MALAWI in June 2007, flying from Canada with Christie Johnson and four students from Pearson College.[2] Christie was there to discuss the school and its construction with Memory and Henry. The students were there to learn about the Malawian people and their culture first-hand. Marie Abbott, Jacob Schweda, An Tran, and Evelyn Balsells had come together to form a youth chapter. Their intent was to host various fundraisers that would raise money for the construction of the school. They named their group the Yamba Youth Initiative—*yamba* means "to start" in Chichewa. We just called them the Yamba Kids.

We were scheduled to stay at Memory and Henry's house in Lilongwe for a few days; then we would catch a minibus to Kasungu, where we would visit Memory's village, and Marie, Jacob, An, and Evelyn would spend two weeks with host families to learn first-hand about the country. Memory was just shy of nine months pregnant at the time, and on the drive from the airport we learned that she and Henry had moved into a new house that morning. Their previous landlord had sold their last home without telling them. They found out they had nowhere to live when the new owners showed up at the door, expecting to move in.

Memory and Henry's "new" house was in Area 25 of the capital city. Each "Area" has specific characteristics. For example, Area 15 is middle class, made up primarily of public servants. Area 25, on the other hand, is a "high-density" area. It covers about one hundred square kilometres and is filled with many of the cities' unfortunates.

The United Nations recently released a report stating that Malawi is the fastest urbanizing country in the world. While only 16 per cent of Malawi's population now lives in urban areas, the United Nations estimates that this number will double by 2030.[3] Cities like Lilongwe are struggling to keep up with the growth. These growing pains are familiar to most developed countries. Think of Charles Dickens's descriptions of life in London's slums during the Industrial Revolution and you will glimpse life in Area 25.

There were children everywhere. Dressed in ripped Teletubbie shirts and dusty, well-worn pants, they played beside the road and in the gutters, forming ragged little bands of dust-covered waifs. When I walked outside, the brave ones laughed and ran after me. Others waved and smiled, dirty fingers in their mouths.

The young ones were always excited to see visitors, and their enthusiasm was genuine and infectious. They came to the road and called out, "Hello, hello." For some, this was all the English they knew. Others asked, "How are yoo-oo?"—putting the accent on the sing-song "yoo-oo." They were always excited to practise the little English they had learned at school or from their older brothers and sisters.

On our first day in the city, I took a walk through Area 25. Most of the roads were unpaved, rutted, dusty things. Except for the main arteries, they carried mostly foot traffic anyway, but because the roads were unpaved, there was rust-coloured dust everywhere. It coated the trees, the houses, the people.

The houses were made of brick or mud, with corrugated metal roofs weighed down with stones. Most of the houses in the area were small, not more than shacks lacking windows and doors. In one yard, a woman washed laundry under the trees. She had a little one tied to her back with a *chitenje*. She looked at me with suspicion as I passed—her eyes squinted against the sun. She was very young. I could see her hands moving expertly against the fabric as her eyes followed me down the road. Her house was like the others, stained red from the dust. A small window in the front had been boarded over with rough sticks, and a rectangle of torn cloth covered part of the doorway. The yard was packed earth with a few scattered trees. If this woman had hopes and dreams, I couldn't imagine what they were.

Some yards contained small shops. These tuck shops were pressed up to the edge of the road. They sold things like bread, toilet paper, and telephone cards. They were arbitrarily plastered with signs advertising Celtel and other products—arbitrary because these signs didn't always have a correlation to what the store sold. There were tailoring shops and open tables selling vegetables and fruits. Sometimes there was no more than a small stool with a single bag of charcoal waiting for a customer.

Despite the recent move and Memory's pregnancy, Memory and Henry welcomed us into their home. I had met Memory on her trip to Canada the previous year, but I was one of hundreds, so she didn't remember me. I'd seen photos of Henry, but this was my first time meeting him in person. I liked him. He was courteous and soft-spoken, but also intelligent, and I quickly learned that if I had a question about the country, he was the one to ask. Grace, Memory's youngest sister, lived in the house too. She was quiet, and when she spoke, she had a slight stutter, as if she was trying to speak too fast and couldn't quite manage.

Memory and Henry's house was brick with a metal roof and cement floors throughout. Next to the front door grew a lemon tree and basking lizards clung to the three-and-a-half-metre brick wall that surrounded the yard. There was a sliding metal gate that needed to be opened to drive a vehicle in or out of the yard. Next to the gate was a smaller pedestrian door that remained locked from the inside at night. At other times, people came and went: friends, former students, business associates, family. The house was continually abuzz with activity, and it seemed as though every few minutes I'd hear "Hell-o-o" from the kitchen door as someone new announced their entrance.

The kitchen was tiny, with a small stove and room for little else. These houses seemed to be built with the expectation that much of the cooking would be done outside—which it is, on a small charcoal stove. The dining area was small too. There was just enough space for a circular table and a fridge. The fridge was a luxury, but the power was off so much of the time that it was hardly ever used to keep things cold. It was used more as a cupboard, which was needed. There were no cupboards in the kitchen. Beans were kept in a large basket on the floor. *Nsima* flour was kept in a bag on top of the beans, and other food was stored wherever space was available. The sitting room was the largest room in the house, and it was in constant use. Visitors gathered on chairs or on the floor to eat and chat. There were three bedrooms, two toilets, and a small shower room. It was a typical, middle-class, Malawian home.

That evening, Memory and Christie sat at the kitchen table and discussed APU. They were still working on the details of enrollment. How would the girls be selected? Christie wanted to be sure that the girls who received scholarships would not be able to go to school any other way. Memory wanted to make sure they took a multiplicity of factors into consideration. "We must also see who is the girl's guardian. We should write the entrance exam in a way that we get to know the girl. Where is she coming from? How many are there in her family? Are both parents alive?"

I jumped into the conversation. "Could some of the CEAG parents have paid their daughters' school fees?"

"Oh yes," said Memory. "There was that case of Mesi. Mesi's father was quite wealthy. He could have sent Mesi to school."

"Well, you showed me that family, and all those girls who just didn't get a chance," added Christie.

"So it was good for Mesi to be at CEAG and have everything paid for," said Memory. "Now is the time when her father is realizing the importance of education. Now he is encouraging the younger girls, but the rest of the family is uneducated. We feel like with Mesi, we planted a seed. It will multiply."

I've heard this message from Christie too. There are still many people who do not recognize the importance of education—especially for girls. Memory and Christie hope that APU will have a ripple effect in the surrounding communities. By showing the value of schooling for a small number of girls and their families, people will begin to appreciate the value of education for all girls. That is the hope—and the dream.

The next morning we caught a minibus to Old Town—the old business district in Lilongwe. Minibuses pulled up to the corner near Memory and Henry's house every five or ten minutes. Starting at five o'clock every morning, I heard their calls. "Town," they yelled. "Town." And then they honked their horns. It even took on a rhythm: town, town, honk, town, town, honk.

If you've never seen a minibus, you might have the wrong mental image. A minibus isn't really a bus at all. It's more like a van converted to carry passengers—a maximum number of passengers. The bus we caught that morning had three rows, plus an extra seat behind the driver, which faced the rear. The buses are not supposed to carry more than four passengers per row, but that doesn't account for children, parcels, and, on one trip, a goat. The conductor gestured for us to get inside, where we were pressed tightly together on narrow, vinyl-covered seats. Altogether, there were twenty-eight people, of varying sizes, and one chicken crammed into that one small bus.

We went to a market in Old Town. If we hadn't been with Henry, I don't know how we would have found it. The market had grown up in the spaces between the buildings. In places there was room for no more than one person to pass between the stalls. At other times, the alleys of shops opened onto little courtyards crowded with bags of beans, baskets of rice, and vendors. Walking between the lanes of shops was like stepping into another world. Small makeshift stalls crowded together. Patterned skirts and white blouses swung from rope hangers. In the next shop, sandals were piled high under a makeshift awning, splashes of neon green, sunset orange, and banana yellow appearing in the shadows.

Further down, the lane opened into a small courtyard. Women sat on the packed, dry earth surrounded by baskets of potatoes, bags of beans, and piles of small, wrinkled onions. The beans were white, red, and black. The women called out. A man stepped in front of me. He carried a cardboard box heaped with bananas. He held up a large, spotted bunch, "70 kwacha," he said, nodding and smiling.

I shook my head, "No, thank you."

"70 kwacha," he insisted.

I smiled and shook my head again.

The market was a maze of alleys and courtyards. There was a man selling something that looked like a large gourd. I asked him what it was. "Baobab. 20 kwacha." And he handed me one. A baobab feels warm to the touch. It is covered in soft fur and rattles when you shake it. Henry told me to choose the one that rattled the most. Pregnant women suck the seeds to relieve morning sickness. I decided to buy one for Memory. Really, I bought it for myself. I wanted to see what was inside. I remembered, as a child, reading a story about a monkey who washed clothes under a baobab tree. I must have liked the sound of the word, "baobab," because it stuck in my head, and I've been fascinated by baobab trees ever since.

We turned down another alley. This one had rows of open tables. Men and women were selling papayas, garlic, and potatoes. I saw a man selling pineapples. They were divided into three neat piles. He saw me looking and pointed to the smaller pineapples, "50 kwacha," he said. He pointed to another pile, "75 kwacha." And, finally, to the third, "100 kwacha."

I chose one of the largest pineapples, "100 kwacha?" I asked. He nodded. It looked ripe and fresh. I was curious to find out if it tasted any different from the ones we got at home. At that time, there were about 130 kwacha to every Canadian dollar, so I rounded down, thinking one hundred kwacha was around eighty cents. That seemed good to me. I gave him the money and we moved on.

Down a narrow, makeshift alley, we found a big shop selling *chitenjes*—thousands of *chitenjes*. The shop was open along the front but dark inside. Women stood next to tables covered with multicoloured *chitenjes* displayed for sale. The fabrics were imported from Zambia and came in wonderful, magical patterns: giant orange flowers in full bloom, forests filled with birds, and abstract patterns. There were rich blues, vibrant yellows, and, my favourite—greens of all shades.

I bought two *chitenjes* for 250 kwacha each. One was a forest scene in green, the other depicted stylized birds and flowers on a blue sky. Marie found a *chitenje* with a map of Malawi on a cobalt blue background.

I looked for one like hers, but in all those piles of fabric, it seemed she had found the only one.

The airline had lost my luggage, so there were a few things I needed. Henry asked if we'd like to go to the market by the river. I was excited. I'd read about this market in a Malawi guidebook. Henry said it could be dangerous. It's not difficult to lose your purse in a place like this with crowds of people bumping into each other, and sometimes people get knifed.

We walked the short way to Lilongwe River. It was not the torrent it would become in the rainy season, but it held more water than it would in a couple months, when the river would slow to just a trickle. In years of drought, the riverbed nearly dries out, but that June it spanned a lazy seven metres.

There were stalls of all shapes and sizes about eighty metres from the riverbank. Henry said there had been stalls right up to the water's edge until the police cleared them out in an effort to cut back on crime. I bought a pair of used white socks, while Henry bartered for a watch for Jacob. I saw my first whites since we landed—two young women buying shoes. They looked out of place, but then I'm sure I did too.

After walking the length of the market, we decided to cross the river. The river was cross-hatched with a jumble of rough-hewn footbridges. We picked one. It swayed as we crossed. It looked like something out of an Indiana Jones movie. There was space between the boards, and I could see the tall grasses and the slow-moving water beneath my feet. The bridge looked like it could collapse at any minute, but at least there wouldn't be far to fall.

We were almost to the other side when we stopped. Henry was arguing with some men. We didn't learn what had happened until we were across the bridge.

Crossing the bridge was not free. The bridges have been built by local men who charged a toll—ten kwacha per person. Henry was arguing with the men because they wanted to charge twenty kwacha for each of the foreigners. Henry refused to pay the inflated price, so the men backed off and let us cross—nodding their heads and smiling big, white, angry smiles.

After returning to the house, I learned that three of the CEAG girls lived in Area 25, a brisk, five-minute walk from Memory and Henry's house. Eunice and Agness ran a private nursery school out of their home, while Mesi worked at a local shop and boarded in the house with the other girls. Later that evening, Agness and Eunice came by to talk to Christie. They had both taken out microcredit loans and were looking for some guidance on how to manage their money.

Business had not been easy. Both of the girls worked long hours for very little pay. What they did make was eaten up in rent and other expenses, so it was difficult for them to get ahead, much less make loan payments. Because she studied tailoring in school, Agness sometimes sewed garments to make extra money, and since she owned her own sewing machine, she was able to rent it out when she was not using it herself. Later, when I stopped by to visit the two girls, there was a boy, Isaac, sitting in the front yard in the shade of a small enclosure, his foot moving swiftly to operate the machine's treadle. Isaac purchased worn-out clothing cheaply and took the clothes apart, making them into new pieces. In Malawi, nothing goes to waste.

Even after completing two years at Phwezi Polytechnic, the girls had struggled. For awhile, they raised chickens, but the chickens were stolen. Later, they thought of opening the nursery school, and, although they had many children coming to the school, the parents were often reluctant to pay. They had also had their house broken into on a number of occasions.

Without a man in the house, the girls are seen as easy targets. Their house was old. The doors didn't have proper locks, and many of the bars on the windows were bent or broken. One night, thieves broke the window in their bedroom, and a man reached his arm in through the bars while the girls were sleeping. He couldn't get in. He was trying to grab something, anything. It terrified the girls, so much so that for awhile they employed a night watchman, but the two thousand kwacha a month was too much, and when I visited, they told me they barricaded themselves in at night, using old planks and other scraps of wood to block the doors and windows.

The girls were right to be frightened. Stories circulated throughout the city about gangs of thieves wielding machetes. In actuality, such gangs are uncommon, but it is not uncommon for small boys to be employed to squeeze through barred house windows. Once inside, they unlock a door to let their accomplice, or accomplices, into the house.

I spoke to Christie about the girls' problems after we got back to Canada. "It would be so easy to help them," she said. And she was right. What would it cost me to hire a night watchman for a year? Less than C$200. Not much, considering it would guarantee their safety. But ultimately it wouldn't change their situation. It would simply give them a small respite and take away their self-reliance. It would remove the opportunity for them to solve the problem on their own.

The next day, we left for Memory's home village. Memory had arranged for the Yamba Kids to spend time with host families. They would even go to school with their "host" sisters and brothers. This trip would also give Christie the chance to meet with the CEAG girls who still lived in the Kasungu area. Lucy, Memory's sister, would go with us and help us with translation. It's always preferable to travel with a native of the country.

Christie had arranged for a minibus to drive us from Lilongwe. There were enough of us to warrant the expense, and it would cut the travel time in half. The road from Lilongwe to Kasungu was well-paved and modern. Kasungu is north of Lilongwe along Highway One, the main route running from the northern to the southern tip of the country. If we were to continue driving north, we would eventually reach the Tanzanian border. Once we reached Kasungu, however, we turned off the highway and drove the last hundred kilometres on a series of rutted dirt roads.

There were a lot of people walking or riding their bikes along the side of the road, but Malawian drivers don't slow down or swerve to miss them. They frantically honk their horns. People, goats, and chickens all know enough to get out of the way—fast.

When we arrived at the village, we were met by a hoard of children—thirty or forty at least. Like everything else, the children were stained a dull rusty red, the same as the roads and trees and houses. The children hadn't all come from Kapwayi village. They came from the area surrounding the village too—all excited to see the *asungu*—"whites." It didn't take long for the number of children to double.

We gathered in the village. Lucy interpreted for us. She introduced us to the children and the other people who had come to greet us. For the children, she laid down the rules. No calling the visitors *asungu*. No asking for gifts. Once she was done, Christie took over.

Christie was wonderful with the children. She taught them "Bat and Moth." Christie chose two children who had played the game before. The bat and the moth stood in the middle, and the bat was blindfolded. We all joined hands to form a circle. Whenever the bat said, "bat," the moth would say, "moth." The bat tried to catch the moth. The bat stumbled around while the moth slipped out of the way. The children laughed so hard they could hardly stand. Their eyes sparkled. They squirmed. They twisted. They laughed with their whole bodies.

After the game, we settled into our accommodation. It was a mud house with a thatched roof and dirt floor: small but clean. There were two tiny bedrooms and an equally small sitting room. The house was built by Memory when she was still travelling back and forth to the village. Christie had stayed in this house on each of her trips back to the village. It was also used as a guesthouse for various relatives when they came to visit. The house was surrounded by a fence made from elephant grass, the tall grass that grows naturally in the fields throughout the country. Within the fenced yard was a newly dug pit latrine. I was glad to hear the pit was freshly dug. There would be no cockroaches poking their antennae up out of the hole at inconvenient moments.

Soon after we unpacked, visitors began to arrive. A grandmother came to see us. She was wizened and bent with arthritis. She wore a too-big,

Christie spent time drawing with the village children, 2007.

grey suit jacket over a flowered blouse. A brightly patterned *chitenje* was
tied around her waist. She asked us to call her *agogo*—grandmother.
With one hand clutching her back, she shook our hands and mimicked
pain. She was asking for medicine. She did this whenever visitors came.

Later, Memory's grandfather came to see that we were comfortable
and settled in.

Once again, Lucy acted as translator for Christie. Christie sat and
talked to Mr. Kapwayi for some time. Christie asked him many questions.

"How was the harvest?"

"The rain was enough."

"Did you try new crops?"

"The paprika was destroyed in the nursery."

He seemed like a kind and gentle man.

The next day, we went to visit Memory's grandmother's garden. It
was a ten-minute walk. On the way, we passed a group of boys. They had

dug a huge hole next to the trail. They were hunting for mice. There was a small pile of furry bodies next to the hole. Children often dig up mice to sell. Driving in from the airport, I saw a boy selling cooked mice. He was standing on the side of the road holding up his mice, skewered on a stick. Not all tribes eat mice, but it's common among the Chewa.

The Kapwayis grow maize, tobacco, and groundnuts (what we call peanuts). The maize harvest was over, but they were still cutting down the dry stocks. That's what Mr. Kapwayi was doing when we reached the garden, and he posed for pictures holding his machete high above his head. The groundnuts were Mrs. Kapwayi's responsibility.

After our trip to the garden, we visited Chiconde. She was one of the CEAG girls and ran a small nursery school in the village. She looked after over twenty children, all under school age. She was busy with the children when we got there but was happy to see Christie. She liked the children, but she was having trouble making ends meet. Mothers would bring their children some days and not others, so they refused to pay for the entire month's tuition. She also struggled because they expected her to serve the children tea with milk, but that was an added expense for Chiconde and she couldn't afford it. She promised to come for a visit later. She hoped Christie could give her advice.

After we said goodbye to Chiconde, Christie walked us over to the old CEAG site. Most of the buildings were still in good shape. One of the teachers' residences held a clinic. Another was given to the police to live in rent-free. This was meant to increase security in the village. The volunteer house that Audrey and Larry built had melted into the ground, gone without a trace. There was no sign of the chicken coop or the school garden either, but I saw the field from the photo that Christie showed during her presentation to the Stony Plain Rotary Club, the field where a pregnant Ivy and her two brothers sat picking termites one hot day many years ago.

On the way back to the village, we walked through Kalenga trading centre. It is a small trading centre. Young men sold produce, small fish, and cooked pork. Others milled about. Some were friendly, but not in a good way. It's difficult to explain the difference between "good" friendly and "bad" friendly, but I've come to understand in my short time in the country that the more "friendly" men usually want something: sponsorship, money, or marriage.

There was no way of telling where the trading centre ended and the village began. The one merged into the other. When we got back to the house, Lucy had lunch waiting for us. There was *nsima* and beans mixed with tomatoes and onions.

As I pressed the *nsima* into the relish, I watched a mama hen and her chicks pick at the ground. They wandered in the shade of the kaysha tree growing outside our house. The tree had large clusters of yellow flowers and leaves that looked a lot like the leaves of a mountain ash tree. There was a shrub-like plant growing on the other side of the fence too. I'd seen it used as a hedge plant in Lilongwe. It had big sweeping branches with feathered leaves and yellow trumpet flowers. I didn't know what it was called, but it was ubiquitous. It's been difficult to learn the names of trees and plants. Eunice says, "Only old people know the names of those things."

We went to the well to wash our clothes. The borehole well was drilled in December and had made a huge difference to the community. Until this year, both communities shared the well in the trading centre. This meant long line-ups, and many women were resorting to ground water, which was dangerous. The line-ups had also caused considerable friction between the two communities. Having the new well made many women's lives easier.

Next to the well were two large metal sinks built into a cement stand. The sinks were installed at the same time as the well. Each sink drained into a trench that ran along the ground. The villagers used maize cobs to plug the drains. The day after we arrived, at least twenty children gathered around to watch us wash our laundry. They crowded and pressed themselves around the sinks. They watched our every movement.

An older man also came to watch. He spoke English and gave us a play-by-play of how to wash the clothes. He critiqued and offered suggestions. He even gave us a demonstration. Then he asked me if I was married. Once I told him I was, he moved on.

Mr. Kapwayi came by for another visit. He is a calm, soft-spoken man. It's easy to see why he commands so much respect. He came dressed in a clean, pale-blue dress shirt with a well-worn collar and neatly patched black dress pants. He has quiet eyes deep set under strong eyebrows. His cheekbones are prominent, and although he has deep lines across his forehead, he has no other noticeable wrinkles. He's a tidy man with a white stubbled chin.

Mr. Kapwayi was born in Ndonda, but he settled here in 1973, and the village, Kapwayi, is named after him. When they moved here, there were only eight houses and the area was densely treed. By then, he and his wife had already been married for twenty years. At the time of our visit he was seventy-two. The couple have four children who are still living. They lost two boys, one at the age of one, the other at the age of three. Mr. Kapwayi didn't say how, and I didn't ask. He is well respected in the community and surrounding area. Christie explained that he will probably be made Group Village Headman, a highly respected position.

I asked him what he had seen in his lifetime. He told me that when they first came here, there were many animals: elephants, leopards, lions, buffalo, and antelope. Apparently, the lions were always eating people, and the villagers had to stand guard on their maize crops because the monkeys would come and take the silk from the maize in the gardens. But the baboons were the worst. They would start raiding the crops as soon as they were planted and continue right up until the time of harvest. In those days, they dug pits to catch animals for food, trapping buffalo, antelope, and zebra, but those are gone now.

In those days, poverty was more of a problem, he explained. People would only cover the lower half of their bodies. "Most parents didn't know the importance of education," he said. "Children spent their days playing and chasing mice." Mr. Kapwayi was once a teacher at a missionary school, where he taught reading and math. He believes strongly in the importance of education.

I asked him about the crops. In the past, they didn't need to fertilize and yet the crops were large. "Now," he said, "we fertilize and the harvest isn't as good." But this year the rain was enough, so the harvest was a good one.

Mr. Kapwayi and his wife grow three crops: maize, groundnuts, and *fodia* (tobacco). The maize and groundnuts are for consumption, but the tobacco is a cash crop. He hoped to make K15,000 (about C$118) that year. He was doing well to earn that much from a cash crop. It would go toward basic needs like fertilizer, food, and clothing.

In the afternoon, the host families came to pick up the Pearson students. Christie sat the families down and with the help of Lucy explained their responsibilities and the expectations of the students. The students would be attending school with their host sister or brother. In Malawi, people treat guests with great respect. Rather than have them work, it's usual for a guest to sit and do nothing. So Christie explained that the Pearson students would like to help in any way they could: cooking *nsima*, working in the garden, packing water, cleaning the house. The host families seemed to take their responsibilities very seriously, and the students were enthusiastic about the experience to come.

It looked like Evelyn was holding back some tears when she left, but I knew she'd be okay. She was adaptable. Marie was a very reserved person, but her host family spoke English, and that would eliminate the language barrier that the other students would encounter. An was so outgoing that I couldn't imagine anything fazing her. Jacob was sick when he left; he had come down with a cold the day before, and I wondered if he should be leaving. It would be a long walk to the village where he'd be staying.

In the evening, while Christie, Lucy, and I sat around the table playing cards, we heard a tiny trickling of dirt. It was the smallest of sounds. Christie thought it was wall erosion, but it kept on throughout the evening. When

I went to bed, I could see the termites working in the wall next to me. Usually you can just see little rivulets of clay running down the walls, but I could see the little guys right there through a hole in the wall. Every few seconds, a grain of dirt would fall with a little dribbling sound.

When I woke up in the morning, I was curious to see what progress they had made. I knew there had to be some since they'd kept me awake for a long time into the night, but I couldn't see the termites. The hole was closed over, and there was a little mound of clay against the wall by the foot of the bed. We moved the bed and pulled up the grass mat. Under the floor mat, the termites had built a metropolis of roads and freeways that extended right across the room. Later on, while we were out, Lucy and a woman from the village cleaned up the room and eradicated their work. The termites would have to start over.

I found out later that the house had been built on an old termite mound. Prior to construction, the mound had been dug out, but termites are tenacious, and they'll eventually raze the house to the ground. It's termites and rain that are ultimately the demise of these mud houses.

Between termites, mosquitos, and dogs I hadn't slept much that night. The dogs had been quarrelling outside, and one of them had a wickedly menacing growl. I had visions of tigers prowling around outside the fence.

I had woken at 3:30 AM. That's when the village started to come alive. I could hear a rhythmic pounding in the distance, not loud, but relentless. Later, I learned that women get an early start on the maize pounding because it takes so long to pound each batch, and it's difficult to work in the heat of the day. They pound the maize in a large, hourglass-shaped, wooden mortar called a *ntondo*, using a huge pestle called a *mus*. The pestle is well over a-metre-and-a-half tall and probably fifteen centimetres in diameter. They lift it as high as they can and bring it down with all their force on the maize in the mortar. It's exhausting work.

The next day, another CEAG girl came to visit. Cecilia arrived with Gift, a friend who was also visiting the village. Cecilia had taken a diploma in tailoring, but later she had decided to become a nun.

Evelyn learns to pound maize, 2007.

Gift is the son of the policeman living at the CEAG site. He wanted to be a priest, but first he was completing a degree in political science at Chancellor College in Zomba. He had some interesting ideas, and he was very well spoken. "People have to be empowered. I don't believe in hand-outs. Empower them with skills, so they become self-reliant," he said. I enjoyed our conversation, but I got the impression that he was hinting at sponsorship. It's the way things are here. I don't blame him.

After Cecilia and Gift left, Mr. and Mrs. Kapwayi came to eat lunch with us. We pulled the table into the middle of the sitting room and managed to cram enough chairs and benches around it so we all had a place to sit. We served them rice pilaf and scrambled eggs with relish made from tomatoes, green peppers, and onions. This is how scrambled eggs are prepared in Malawi. I think the Kapwayis enjoyed the meal. Mr. Kapwayi in particular liked the "spice for rice." At first I was worried he would find it too strong, but he kept shaking more and more onto his rice.

I liked the Kapwayis. They were honest, hard-working people, like a typical elderly farming couple living in Canada. They had experienced much hardship and continued to survive the challenges of daily life.

Mr. Kapwayi was respectful and thoughtful. He seemed quite touched that we would have lunch with him and was happy to eat with us. Mrs. Kapwayi also expressed her happiness that we were there. They didn't stay after we ate, but then it was difficult to talk for long with ;the language barrier.

After another day in the village, Christie and I returned to Lilongwe, leaving Lucy to keep an eye on the four Pearson College students. Christie was eager to get back to Memory and Henry's house. Memory was due to deliver her baby any day, and there was much to discuss about APU.

Back in Lilongwe, we drove out to the APU site. The site is not far from Lilongwe, but it took nearly an hour to drive the distance. After the perfectly spaced, gridded roads of Alberta, the rural roads of Malawi appear haphazard and disorderly. It's as if they have organically emerged, replacing existing walking paths and trails—maybe they have. Every year, the rains do their damage, turning the bumpy, washboard roads into barely traversable, washed-out tracks.

I sat crammed into the backseat of the school's latest purchase, a burgundy, late-model Toyota Hilux truck. The truck had spent more time with its engine exposed and one mechanic or another's backside protruding from under the hood than it had on the road since it was purchased earlier that month. I hoped we would make it to the school site. It would be a long walk home. Throughout our drive, Henry carried on a monologue, addressing the complications of building the school on a sandy site. Four-foot-deep trenches were filled with layers of cement, limestone, wet dirt, crushed brick, and more concrete—all the while he swerved to miss potholes, pedestrians, and cyclists. The truck bucked and weaved over the dirt road, sending clouds of the thick red dust, which I'd become so accustomed to, into the air. I rolled down my window, and as we bumped along, I snapped off a few quick shots of a goat grazing next to one of the grass-roofed mud huts that crowded the roadside. It took only a moment for the dust to get into the cab. It quickly coats the skin and grinds between the teeth.

Henry was the project manager at APU, but at the time of my first trip, he also held down a full-time career as a mechanical engineer at the local tobacco factory. Between meetings, phone calls, trips out to the site, and his night shift at the factory, I watched as the circles grew deeper and darker under his eyes. He'd been running on almost no sleep since I'd arrived, but still he wanted us to see the site. This was his passion, and he would ensure its success.

As he drove, he explained the school's construction. "After the foundation is in place, the walls will go up quickly." He honked the horn and jerked the steering wheel, just missing a man with a mountain of firewood strapped to the back of his bicycle. Henry released a quick, nervous laugh.

Even a year earlier, I couldn't have imagined I'd be travelling this dusty road on the other side of the world, surrounded by this foreign landscape— baobab trees, termite mounds, and the tall, elegant, elephant grass that swayed in the breeze. Until I'd met Memory, I'd had no real desire to travel to Africa, certainly not to diminutive Malawi, so far from the historic pyramids of Egypt or the bustling markets of Marrakesh. Until I'd met Christie, I'd been blissfully ignorant of the challenges these people faced. Here there was no social safety net, no food bank, no shelters, no old age pension—all the things we take for granted back in Canada.

The APU construction site was located on a plateau and the view was stunning. I could see scattered trees and rolling hills far into the distance. Nsaru village bordered the property on one side, very near Nsaru trading centre, and although I couldn't see it from where I stood, I knew that if I walked through the elephant grass in the opposite direction, I would come across Nsaru River.

The only completed building on the site was the storage shed. It was a necessary structure so the school didn't lose supplies. There was a full-time watchman who guarded the site and stayed in the shed. Two more watchmen joined him at night. Nothing had been stolen yet.

Construction was well under way on the first classroom block and dormitory, but because of the soil's composition, they were taking their time on the foundation. Thousands of fired bricks awaited the next stage of construction, which would begin within weeks. It was difficult to imagine that the school would be ready to open in a mere six months.

On the night of June 12, Memory went into labour. She had been up and walking around for most of the night, and at 4 AM, she was ready to go to the clinic. It had been arranged that Memory would have her baby at a private clinic. She didn't want to go to Lilongwe General, so she and Henry had been saving what money they could for the expense. Christie, Laura, and I didn't want to see her deliver the baby in a public facility either, so we pitched in too. It was a good decision. Later the following day, Memory gave birth to her first baby by Caesarian section.

Memory and Henry named their son Teloni, which means "let it be" in Chichewa. He was a healthy boy, and when we went to visit mother and son at the clinic, I saw he already had a full head of black, curly hair. At over four kilograms, he was a big boy.

Although she'd had a Caesarean section, Memory came home after just two days. Even so, she alarmed me with her energy. She must have had sleepless nights, but she would rise early and was kept busy throughout the day caring for Teloni, tending to chores, planning for the school, and greeting an endless succession of visitors. Even when her Aunt Inez came to help, Memory didn't slow down.

Inez is a lovely woman. Although she didn't speak English, she always had a smile for me. One day, I was holding Teloni in the sitting room and began to doze off. She gently took him from my arms and then smiled so I'd know she was simply helping. Another day, while I was hand-washing my clothes at the washstand, she came close to me and watched. I knew she thought I was doing it all wrong and wanted to help, but I didn't know how to communicate with her. Instead, I kept scrubbing, self-consciously aware that I was failing miserably. I would have made a terrible Malawian wife.

I often visited Agness and Eunice during the day. They were always happy to receive help with the children, so I joined them on several occasions. They cared for close to sixty children ranging in age from six months to five years of age. Although they had a third woman who came in to help for a few hours most days, it was an enormous task. The children were full of energy and required constant attention.

One morning, I went to help Agness with the children. Eunice was at a two-week nursery school training course, and Agness was desperate for another pair of hands. Agness taught the older children in the larger room at the front of the house, and I read to the younger children in a smaller room at the back. I read *Mr. Brown Can Moo! Can You?* I'd moo like a cow, and the children would moo back. I'd buzz like a bee, and the children would buzz too. Their small voices joined me, and we sang "Head and Shoulders, Knees and Toes." We all touched our heads, shoulders, knees, and toes, but I soon ran out of material.

When we were finished singing and reading, I took the children out into the yard. A grass fence surrounded the yard, so the children were easy to watch and couldn't run out onto the road. We threw a ball back and forth, and some of the children went into the backyard to relieve themselves. There was a single outside pit latrine, but it had no roof and no door, and it was nearly full. The children didn't bother with the latrine; they simply pulled down their pants or lifted their skirts and squatted in the dirt. Agness and Eunice would have liked to have a new latrine constructed, but it was beyond their means.

After I left Malawi, I heard they had an inspector stop by. He gave them a list of recommendations they needed to comply with. He informed the girls they should not be operating a preschool out of their home, but it would be impossible for the girls to afford a second house to live in. They hoped the inspector wouldn't return.

It was a cobbled-together existence. While the girls struggled to run a successful business, they were chronically short of money, and they lived in perpetual fear and uncertainty. But they were also resourceful and resilient. I had no doubt they would continue to improve their lives— *pang'ono pang'ono*.

Another day, I walked to the market to pick up fabric for Memory. I usually took Grace with me on these excursions, but today Grace was at school, so Danny offered to accompany me. He was going to the market to buy a broom.

On the streets, nearly everyone was friendly, but there was no question I was an outsider. As we neared the market, I saw more people on the streets chatting in groups, getting water from the public taps, or, like me, walking to the market. The children ran along the roadside, waving and shouting, "*Asungu, asungu.*" On these outings, I was careful not to carry anything of value. I always walked purposefully and acknowledged the people who passed me with a smile. I was always on guard.

We passed a group of women. One pretty young woman looked at me and smiled. "Hello, Madam," she said.

"Hello," I replied.

"Can you give me 20 kwacha?" she asked.

"No, I'm sorry," I said, as I smiled and kept walking.

"Fuck you, Madam," she yelled after me. "Fuck you."

Danny looked embarrassed and softly offered an apology. "That woman. She doesn't know."

It was a disturbing experience, and I wondered how much veiled animosity I might not be aware of in the crowds around me.

Indications of poverty were everywhere. Because there was no garbage pickup, much of the trash was found in the gutters that cut into the shoulders along the road. The gutters were meant to carry away the rains during the rainy season, but at that time of year, they were filled with garbage: bits of blue plastic, torn newspaper, maize husks, used condoms. Bricks tumbled into the street. An ancient cube truck stood on blocks in front of a house. The truck had been stripped down to its frame, now blue paint and rust in equal parts.

The market in Area 25 was more spread out than the market along the Lilongwe River, but the street was crowded with men and trucks and buses. The shops were set back from the road, with a second row of awnings and stalls built on the edge of the pavement. Some of the stalls appeared to be barely held upright. Under the crude awnings, men tended free-standing stoves, where they cooked chips or goat intestines in bubbling oil. Other hawkers walked down the road carrying boxes of bananas or bowls of fritters. Still others sat by the side of the road surrounded by baskets of beans or rice. It didn't take long for me to find a shop that sold fabric. While I chose a pattern, Danny left to find a broom. By the time I was ready to leave, Danny was there, and we walked back to Memory and Henry's house together with our purchases. This time without incident.

My trip to Malawi had been an enlightening one. I knew I would need to return if I were to begin to understand the country, its customs, and its people.

Patience

PATIENCE WAS ONE OF THE FIRST intake of students at *Atsikana Pa Ulendo*.[1] She is a bright and vibrant girl, outgoing and friendly, with an enormous smile that lights up her entire face.

While attending APU, Patience is living with her father and stepmother in the village adjacent to the school. Her father owns a teahouse and bakery in the nearby trading centre. It's a small, dark, one-room building that serves as a gathering place for local workers and merchants. I counted nine customers seated on the roughly constructed benches, their elbows resting on low wooden tables, when Grace and I went to look for her. Patience helps out at the teahouse when she's on holidays, but we were told she had already gone home for the day with her stepmother.

Before we left, Grace took me into the backyard, so I could see the bakery oven. It was a large outdoor oven, nearly two metres in height, constructed of bricks and mortar. A sheet of tin acts as an oven door. The tin is held in place with several large pieces of wood. A woman who was working in the yard pulled away the props so I could see the buns cooking inside.

Patience's mother left her husband after the second and third wives turned her husband against her. Her husband still expected her to work on his cash crop garden but stopped supporting her and their children. Out of desperation, when Patience was in standard six, Patience's mother returned to her home village, where she now lives in abject poverty. Because her mother is unable to support her, Patience lives with her father and his third wife, Merane.

It was a five-minute walk to Patience's home, where we found her working in the yard. We were invited into the family's small, crowded sitting room.

Patience went to fetch her stepmother from the other room, and we exchanged traditional greetings. *"Muli Bwanji,"* I said.

"Ndili bwino. Kaya inu?" Merane responded.

"Zikomo."

With the formal greetings completed, we sat down across from Patience, her stepmother, and, I presume, several siblings. It was a tight fit. Grace and I could barely squeeze our legs between the couch and table.

The house was a typical, small, two-room, mud home, and the tiny sitting room contained a set of the handmade wooden furniture that is common in Malawi: three chairs and a small couch with cushions covered in dark blue fabric and a wooden coffee table in the middle. The walls were dark with water stains, which gave the room an oppressive feel. The narrow plank door hung on one hinge, but the furniture set this house apart from its neighbours. Here was a family that had a little more than most.

The stepmother had just finished a day working at the teahouse. Sitting across from me, she looked gaunt and tired, aged long past her years. She carried a small boy on one hip, and as we spoke, he nursed disinterestedly at her breast.

I knew something of Patience's story, so I was surprised when she introduced her stepmother to me by saying in a sweet, almost simpering, tone, "This is my mommy. She protects me." I don't know how much English Patience's stepmother understands, but I am of the belief that this is Patience's way of surviving within the household.

When I asked Patience how many brothers and sisters she had, the explanation became quite complicated. There were brothers and sisters who lived in this house, and there were brothers and sisters who lived elsewhere. Some were siblings and some were half-siblings, but I was able to learn that there were three brothers and three sisters who lived in this house with their parents. Patience went on to explain that she had three moms. Polygyny is marked by these complex relationships.

Speaking through Patience, her stepmother said, "Best wishes."

I ask her if she thought girls should get an education, and she responded, "When the girls are educated, it is good because they can be independent." She went on to say that she was very happy when she saw Patience go to school because later she would be able to help her family. I knew this was not entirely the truth.

It began to grow dark, so Grace and I said our goodbyes and walked the short distance back to the school, trailed by a dozen ragged, boisterous children.

A few days later, when the girls returned from their holiday, Patience took me aside. She explained that she had to say those things in front of her stepmother but confided, "That one, she is troublesome." Her stepmother worried that Patience would steal her husband's affection, and she didn't like to see Patience receive recognition for her accomplishments.

When in private, she would admonish her husband. "Why do you buy these things for Patience? Why?"

Her father would respond, "It's my daughter. I can buy things that help her."

But Merane was insistent. "Don't buy things for her." Merane appeared to be a very unhappy, frightened woman.

Merane quit school to get married, and her oldest child is thirteen years old. She can be no older than her late twenties. Yet she looked haggard and beaten down. It seemed to me that it was not only the first wife who was hurt by these polygynous unions.

Patience told me, "I will work hard in school, so that one day I will have a good life, and I will be able to help my mother." I hoped Patience would be the one to break the cycle of poverty and suffering.

15
Atsikana Pa Ulendo

Under the powerful and inspiring
leadership provided by Memory
Mdyetseni, the director of APU...
[our] students are being empowered
to learn and to lead, to give of
themselves to their communities
and to share their knowledge
with others.

—*Christie Johnson*[1]

IN 2008, I visited Malawi for the second time.[2] It had only been a year since my last trip, but the school site had changed so much that it was nearly unrecognizable. Where there had been foundations, there were now buildings. The first classroom block, a long brick building, had risen from the earth. On the north side of the building, a cement-floored verandah ran the length of the building. The corrugated metal roof extended over the verandah, and under its shade, doors led into the building's three large classrooms. Because Malawi is south of the equator, the overhang protects the classrooms from the hard, tropical sun. In the rainy season, the verandah offers protection from the sky's frequent downpours.

One of the classrooms was being used as a communal teachers' office. Several wooden tables were pushed together under the windows, making a large workspace or eating area, depending on the time of day. There were benches on both sides of the tables. When parents came for meetings, they sat on one side and the teachers sat on the other, ready to discuss the girls' marks, attendance, or food contributions.

In one corner of the room stood sacks of maize. Some of the sacks had not been secured, so maize kernels had spilled to the floor. The maize would be cleaned up later and the sacks moved to their permanent storage room. Blue, vinyl-covered mattresses, each marked with a number, were stacked against one wall, nearly reaching the ceiling. When the girls came back from their break, they would each sign for a mattress and take it back to the dormitory.

The two classrooms were bright and new. Each contained forty desks, enough for eighty students in total: the first intake of APU students. With large windows on both the north and south sides, the classrooms were well lit, but cool, during the day. At night, the generator filled the space with an intense white light so the girls could spend time in their classrooms studying after dinner.

From the verandah, the land fell away to the north. A large garden held rows of small, but vibrantly green, maize plants. Beyond the garden were stands of banana trees and tall elephant grass. The grass hid the Nsaru

River, which I knew was a short walk down a dirt path. Further yet was the Africa savannah, grasslands spotted with acacia and sausage trees.

Just south of the classroom block, the land was being terraced for the next block of classrooms. The terracing was being done by hand, a painstaking process involving wheelbarrows, shovels, and sweat.

Next to the classroom block was a roughly constructed building, the temporary cafeteria. Inside, the dirt-floored room had been divided into three smaller areas: cooking, storage, and eating. The girls carried their plates up to a counter where they were served *nsima*, eggs or meat, and greens. They then took their meals and sat on the long, low, wooden benches that were arrayed in rows throughout the eating area. They balanced their plates on their laps and rolled the *nsima* with their hands, pressing it into the greens or relish until it stuck, chatting in happy voices as they ate.

With a pile of firewood pushed into the corner, an enormous caldron balanced on an open fire, using up most of the cooking space. The caldron was used to cook *nsima*, while smaller pots were used to cook relishes and greens. Off the cooking area, a small storage room held bags of beans and *nsima*. Like any area containing foodstuffs, it was under constant siege by rats and other vermin.

Further west still was the first dormitory. The building housed all eighty girls. The girls slept on bunk beds, ten to a room. They each had their own closet and mosquito net. For most of the girls, this was their first time sleeping off the ground. It was a treat and an adjustment.

South of the dormitory was the first teachers' duplex. Memory and Henry lived in one half. The other half had just been completed. No one lived there yet, but it would soon house one or more of the school's teachers.

Throughout the grounds, buildings were at various stages of construction—thankfully, it was the dry season. Later, the grounds would be sown with trees and grass seed. During the rainy season, the ground turned into a sea of mud, and the construction pits and ditches filled with water.

Newly formed bricks dry in the sun, 2008.

Nearly all the construction work was being done by hand. Thousands of bricks were at various stages of creation. I watched one man, clad only in rolled-up trousers, molding the bricks from clay. I asked, through a combination of hand gestures and English, if I could take pictures of the process and was happy when I found he spoke fluent English. He told me he could make about a thousand bricks in nine hours.

A pit had been dug and the soil loosened. To this he added water and dried grass. He used his feet and a small shovel to stir the mixture, stomping up and down, lifting his knees high and then plunging his feet back into the mud. Once satisfied with the consistency, he filled his molds and scraped off the excess in the same way one might level a measuring cup. He then flipped the mold over, and out popped two bricks laid out to dry in the baking sun.

Once the bricks had dried, they were stacked into a rectangular pyramid (one batch contained eighty thousand bricks). The workers leave spaces between the bricks along the bottom of the pyramid and fill these spaces with dried maize stalks and elephant grass. The workers slathered the entire structure with mud, and when the mud was dry, they set the pyramid on fire. The bricks burned through the night and into the following day. The firing process cured the bricks. They would last for decades.

It isn't just bricks that have been fired and laid since my last visit. Memory went through a gruelling selection process with the girls. She had sent out notices to surrounding schools and plastered Nsaru trading centre with posters inviting girls to attend entrance exams. The notices attracted 360 girls to Kabuthu Primary School, where the exams were to be held. This was far more students than Memory had expected. Since there was only space to accommodate seventy students at a time, they had to hold the examinations in five shifts. "Girls poured in from all directions," said Henry. "Some walked about fifteen kilometres; some were ferried by bike by fathers, uncles, brothers, you name them; and some came cycling on their own, carrying a friend at the back of the bike."

Memory later said about the scene at the school: "I was amazed to see the number of girls who managed to come. We had girls from thirty-four primary schools. Those exams took the whole day. The last group started their papers around 4:30."

Once the written exams were complete, Memory read all the papers and chose 120 girls to come for oral interviews. The exams were evaluated on academic merit, but the girls' life circumstances weighed heavily in the selection process too. Memory was able to contact the successful girls through their schools to let them know that they had made it through the first part of the process. Over the course of a week, Memory, her sister, Lucy, and Monica, a member of the Malawian APU board, conducted the oral interviews. The girls were asked about their family, their experiences at primary school, and their dreams for the future. Memory, Lucy, and Monica were looking for "teachable" girls, girls who showed potential but whose parents could not or would not pay their tuition.

Prisca recalled being selected for APU. "I was very happy to hear that I had been selected to *Atsikana Pa Ulendo* Secondary School because I knew that I had found a good school. When I reached home, I opened the door while jumping up and down with joy. My parents were also very happy, and they shouted with joy, 'Well done. Keep it up.'"[3]

I think back to the first time I heard Memory speak. "The world is made for the stubborn," she said. Many of the girls are stubborn. They need to be. I hope that with the help of Memory's stubbornness and determination, these girls will have a chance at a life in which they can make their own choices and pursue their dreams.

Whenever Memory has the opportunity to speak before an audience, she stresses the importance of education. She begins with these words: "Malawi is one of the smallest countries in Africa, but it has a lot of problems. You talk of poverty. You talk of hunger. You talk of HIV/AIDS. Many problems. And me, I strongly believe that the way out of all these problems is education."

Although it's impossible for the young girls who come to APU to fully grasp the power of education, they recognize something of its importance. Milika is one of the first intake of students. She recounted her fears when she went to write the entrance exam: "When I was in standard eight, I heard that at Nsaru there was a school. But...I was afraid because there I found many girls. They all wanted to write the exam too... The questions were simple, but also difficult. There were questions like, 'How do you avoid HIV/AIDS?'"[4]

Milika passed the entrance exam, and although her father was proud of her, she received a different reception from her friends: "My friends, they were sad with me. They said, 'How come Milika passed? Why not us?'"[5]

Like Memory and Milika, many of the girls have had to overcome the scorn of their peers, but for the most part, they are able to stay focused on the future. Maness, who received a scholarship at Pearson College in Victoria, British Columbia, was determined to go to a girls' secondary school, so much so that she chose to repeat standard eight. At the end of primary school, Maness was accepted into a co-education secondary school, but rather than accept, she rewrote her standard eight exams the following year. That year, she heard about APU and was accepted into the program. She recognized the potential of the opportunity and was grateful for the placement: "I am working hard so that I should have a bright future."

That doesn't mean the girls haven't had moments of rebellion; they are, after all, teenagers. One of the biggest challenges the girls faced in their first years at APU was learning English.

The Malawian curriculum requires students to start learning English in standard five, but this doesn't always happen—particularly in rural schools. At the end of form two, students must write their JCEs, and these exams are in English. If the students are not fluent in English by the end of form two, they will fail these exams. Yet, apart from a few greetings, most of the girls who came to APU knew almost no English. "Hello. How are you?" and "Good day, Madame," would not be enough to help them pass their exams.

To ensure that the girls learned English quickly, they were not permitted to speak Chichewa on the school grounds. This led to much complaining and even rebellion by a few of the students. Diliya wrote about her early days at APU: "It was very, very difficult for us because we had never spoken English before, and at first we were angry." A few of the girls got together and decided to rebel. "Myself and my friends started discussing this problems: 'Okay girls, you have listened to the rules that we mustn't speak Chichewa. What can we do?' Then I said, 'It's better to just go to the bush like we're going to read, and we can start speaking Chichewa there.'"

With their plan in place, the girls went back to their classrooms, but they came back to their agreed hideout every day to speak Chichewa. They continued to meet over the next few months, but Diliya realized that while many of her classmates were learning English, she and her friends were not. Diliya decided she wanted to learn English too. "Now, I was trying my best to speak English. My teacher was there to help me when I didn't speak well. Finally I spoke English, and my teacher made me leader of the entertainment for my good English, and we had a party for those who knew how to speak English. I am very happy using English as the language of communication at school."[6]

Although many of the girls struggled to learn English at first, once they had mastered the language, it became a source of pride. When the girls went home for school breaks, they would show their parents and teach their siblings how to speak English. The girls began to see that their hard work was paying off, and they worked even harder.

The school opened in 2008, but that was also the year the Ministry of Education transitioned to a new school year. Instead of classes starting in January, the school year would now begin in September. This shortened the school year for the first intake of students considerably and put pressure on the school to integrate another eighty girls within eight months of the school's opening. By September 2008, the school had doubled in size.

For Memory, managing the school was an ongoing challenge: at APU, 160 girls came to Memory asking for advice, 160 girls confronted life's challenges, and 160 girls struggled to learn. When I travelled back to the country the following year, I reacquainted myself with the first group of girls and met many of the second group of girls as well.

On one occasion, Memory and I went to meet with some of the students who were home on a break. We met with Chasazo at her home in a small rural village. Chasazo lives with her large extended family: parents, brothers, sisters, in-laws, and grandparents. Chasazo is more fortunate than many of the girls. Her parents are both alive and living together, and her family possesses more resources than many of the rural families I've met. They own four sheep, a cow, and ten ducks. They also have a bathhouse and a pit latrine, which they don't have to share with anyone else in the village.

When we went to visit, the family had just completed the harvest, and Chasazo proudly showed us their two full granaries. One structure was circular and the other square, but they were both made in, more or less, the same manner. Maize stalks had been woven through thin poles. Larger timbers supported the structure and a platform kept it off the ground. The structures resembled enormous upright baskets.

Chasazo also showed us her bedroom. She slept in a separate mud hut with her sisters. This is common. Once children reach adolescence, the boys and girls often sleep in separate buildings.

While Chasazo showed us around her home, an elderly man approached. He didn't speak English, but we were able to exchange greetings in the traditional fashion. Memory introduced us and asked him several questions. I didn't learn his name, but he was the leader of the local headmen—a headman of the village headmen, one could say. The elderly man had deep wrinkles running vertically through his forehead and a grizzled salt-and-pepper beard. With Memory translating, I learned that he supported girls' education. He explained that when the traditional village authority gathered together, he often spoke up in favour of encouraging boys and girls to go back to school. He also said he was looking forward to these boys and girls changing themselves and the country for the better.

With JCEs coming up, the girls needed to focus on exam preparation. The school didn't have electricity yet. They couldn't study in their dormitories; instead, they went back to their classrooms after dinner. The classrooms were lit by the generator that ran for a few hours every night, so the girls could prepare for exams. The following is taken from a poem entitled "Examinations," written by Diliya:

Can anyone tell me plainly?
Tell me why legless examinations
Lurk in the corners of classrooms
To pounce on little pupils and make them sad.[7]

Because so much academic significance is placed on national exams, the girls are under a great deal of pressure to succeed. During my stay, except on those occasions when Henry was unable to purchase gas in

Nsaru, the generator ran nearly every evening. Now—years later—the school has electricity, but in 2008, the school relied on an unpredictable gasoline supply.

Malawi is plagued by energy shortages of all kinds. In Lilongwe, there are electricity brownouts more evenings than not. Gasoline availability fluctuates. And perhaps the girls were relieved when gas was unavailable to power the lights, but the lights are vital to the girls' success. Nighttime comes at six o'clock sharp, and without power, the girls are unable to do their homework or review the materials they cover in class. The girls have learned that homework is part of succeeding at school.

I enjoyed the girls' humour and insight. Despite their dislike of examinations, they recognized that school and exams were the key to their future. The following is an excerpt from a poem written by Brandina entitled "School Journey":

When I started school
It was a long journey...
Like a big mountain
With thorns and stones
Difficult to climb.

Soon I will be at a college
Almost at the top of the mountain
Looking down at the foot
With pride and happiness
Making my own decisions
Deciding on my career.[8]

In 2009, the national pass rate for JCEs was at 67 per cent.[9] At APU, 100 per cent of the first intake of girls passed. This was an enormous accomplishment for the girls and served to bolster their confidence. If they could beat the national average, they could accomplish any goal, any dream. When Memory phoned Christie to tell her the good news, it was the middle of the night in Canada. There was singing in the background as the students rejoiced and sang. They had conquered another hurdle on their way to education and independence.

Two years of hard study later, the girls wrote their MSCEs. In 2011, 102,691 Malawian students sat for their MSCEs. Of those who wrote the exams, 56,273 passed, a 55 per cent pass rate. At APU, of the seventy-three girls who wrote the exams, only four failed; 95 per cent of the girls passed. Of the girls who failed, three returned to school later to improve their marks.

The MSCE is a difficult exam that encompasses all major subjects: mathematics, agriculture, biology, general science, and physical science. For those who excel, it can mean the opportunity to go on to university entrance exams and the chance to earn a scholarship at the University of Malawi, Mzuzu University, Chancellor College, or Bunda College. But positions are limited, and only the very brightest earn these placements. For those who fail the exams, it can mean going back to form three and trying again—an arduous path.

Blandina Diva is one of the first intake of girls. In 2012, I met with Blandina. She was living in Dawson Creek, British Columbia, on a scholarship to Northern Lights College. By then, she was a confident young woman, very different from the young girl I met in Malawi five years before, but she was still quiet and reserved. We spent a long time talking. I asked her why she believed in the importance of education:

> Girl's education leads directly to better reproductive health, improved family health, economic growth for the family and for society, as well as lower rates of child mortality and malnutrition. It is also a key in the fight against the spread of HIV & AIDS. If a girl is educated, she will get married at a later time, when she is fully grown, and she will have a small family as one way of reducing Malawi's population. If a girl had the opportunity to get education, she is likely to send her children to school to get a better quality of education.

The achievement of girls' right to education can address some of societies' deeply rooted inequalities, which condemn many girls to a life without quality education because of cultural and traditional values. If a girl is educated she does not follow the cultural and traditional values because some of the cultural beliefs interfere with girls' education.

Education provides girls with an understanding of basic health and family planning, giving them choices and the power to decide over their own lives and bodies. For example back home, those women who did not go to school have no say in the family apart from doing what the man decides. Women cannot even go for family planning if the man says no, and they do not have a choice on how many children they should have. It all depends on the man. But if you're educated you cannot allow such kind of things to happen to you because you have a voice and a choice on what to say.

We have many cases in Malawi of early marriages for those who did not go to school. If these young girls had a chance to get education there would not be many cases of early marriages.

In Malawi if girls do not have a chance to get an education they believe that there is no need. They can still be home with their parents apart from getting married. There is a traditional belief that says: if girls stay longer without getting married they will not find spouses because it will be that they are very old. So in order to avoid that, if they are not going to school, they just rush into early marriages.

The other thing is that many young girls in Malawi who are married think their husbands do not treat them fairly. There is nothing they can do apart from still sticking to their husbands and accepting the insult because they have kids, and they can't go because they fear there might be no one to help them look after their kids. While if the girl went to school and she sees that the husband is ill treating her, she does not hold the insult because she is independent, and she can live by herself with the kids without seeking any help from the husband. Most times girls who went to school are respected by their husbands because they know that their wives can leave.

The obvious answer to this question might be that everybody has the right to education, which has been recognized since the Universal Declaration of Human Rights (UDHR) in 1948. However, because of poverty, many people do not continue with their education.[10]

Despite all the reasons for a girl to continue her education, there are still many obstacles. "It is very hard for girls, more especially in rural areas, to receive an education. There are so many obstacles that these girls face," says Memory.

Over the last few years, I've come to believe that education is the answer to many of this country's problems, the world's problems. There are obvious reasons why this is the case. Education allows women to increase their incomes, thus allowing them to buy food and other necessities, but there are many other reasons why education makes a difference in women's lives. Because education increases a woman's earning power, it also empowers her, increasing her independence and sense of self-worth.

By empowering women, we create thriving, vibrant societies with healthier and better-educated citizens. United Nations Special Envoy for HIV/AIDS in Africa Asha-Rose Migiro believes that, while women remain underrepresented in most countries throughout the world, it is only through empowering this often marginalized portion of our population that we can effectively take on the challenges of peace building, poverty alleviation, and HIV/AIDS reduction.[11]

Blandina

I MET BLANDINA IN 2008.[1] That was the year my daughter, Nastassja, travelled to Malawi with me. Nastassja's place of work, Health Sciences Association of Alberta, had sponsored Blandina's four-year placement at APU, so she wanted to meet Blandina while she was in Malawi.

When we arrived in the country, the girls were on a break, and Nastassja would be leaving before they returned, so Memory drove us to visit Blandina and some of the other girls at their homes.

In rural Malawi, there are no street addresses and no telephones, so there was no way to call ahead and let her know we were coming. Memory only had the name of the trading centre where Blandina lived.

To reach her home, we drove over a series of seemingly random dirt roads, red dust billowing up from the tires of the red Hilux. James, one of the APU workers, had agreed to come with us. James is from the area and knows how to find the villages and trading centres that speckle the land. There were no road signs, and we often turned onto tracks that looked like nothing more than widened pathways plunging straight through the cornfields. When we reached the trading centre near Blandina's home, we stopped at a shop. The shop had a wide verandah where a small group of people stood chatting. Several children stood nearby eating sugarcane. They peeled back the outer skin with their teeth and watched as our truck pulled up. A woman with two identically dressed toddlers stood in the shade. Each girl wore a cream-coloured smock and held a maize cob in her hand. The little girls were twins, not something I'd seen in Malawi. When Memory went to ask directions, she also asked the mother if I could photograph her girls. I stepped out of the truck, and the girls simultaneously burst into tears and cringed behind their mother. Their mother yelled something in Chichewa, and I quickly retreated to the truck, feeling like a fool.

Memory learned that Blandina's family lived in government housing near the trading centre. It took no more than a few minutes for us to arrive at a series of identical buildings: small houses built from well-cured bricks, arranged in rows with the ubiquitous, corrugated tin roofs that one sees throughout Malawi. They were older homes, but well-built and durable—longer lasting than the thatch-roofed dirt houses that speckle the rural countryside.

As we slowed, a group of children ran up to the truck. When Memory asked if they knew Blandina, they pointed excitedly toward one of the nearby houses. A young girl was standing in the yard, washing her hair in a basin. It was Blandina.

Blandina is petite, with an enormous smile that shows off a wide gap between her front teeth. She was shy at first, but she welcomed us into her home once Memory explained the purpose of our visit.

Blandina is the youngest of seven children: two boys and five girls. Although most of Blandina's siblings have left home, her parents also care for two little boys, cousins who can no longer live with their mother since she remarried.

We sat down together in a small sitting room. Blandina had only been learning to speak English since she started at APU in January, so I spoke slowly and repeated myself often. Her voice was quiet and unsure. She told us that her parents were not home. Her mother had been suffering from back pain, so her father had taken her to the clinic. They would be back later that afternoon.

We sat in a small dark room with stained walls and a single tiny window, but it was clean and tidy, with flowered curtains and furniture typical to the area, a wooden-framed chair and loveseat with thick burgundy cushions similar to the ones I'd seen displayed by furniture makers in Lilongwe.

She told us she liked volleyball and that her favourite subject was English, but she struggled with math. She had a friend, Ellen, who helped her with the subject.

All the while we were chatting, children poked their heads in at the door, some were relatives and some were children from the area, grubby little children in bare feet with shirts that sagged at the shoulders but bright smiles that plainly indicated mischief and vitality. Blandina's oldest sister lived at home, but was out working at a shop. She had a small baby, but she was not married. One of her brothers was a primary school teacher. Her next sister was the third born in the family. She finished form four but failed her MSCE, but she was fortunate to be employed as a health care worker. Blandina's next sister went to form one but got married and had two children. The next brother lived with his older brother and was repeating form three. Blandina's fourth sister was in form four at another school.

Blandina appeared so shy that I was surprised when she asked Memory, "Madame, may I show them my report card?"

While she was out of the room, Memory explained that they chose Blandina to come to APU because she had a good attitude and none of her sisters had managed to complete form four. "Without a form four certificate it's difficult to find a job or proceed with your education."

Blandina brought back her report card and explained the results. She was strong in English and Chichewa, but struggled with math and history. Out of seventy-two girls, she placed number thirty-seven. I asked her what she would like to do once she finished school. "I want to be a nurse," she said. "I want to help people who are sick."

⊞ Four years later, Nastassja and I made the six-hour drive from Edmonton, Alberta, to Dawson Creek. Dawson Creek is a small community located in northeastern British Columbia along the Alaskan highway. With a population of less than twelve thousand people, Dawson Creek relies upon agriculture as its primary industry, with extra income generated through the retail sector by people travelling the highway. There is also some spillover from the oil and gas sector as oil patch workers frequent the community. Not far from the city, British Columbia's first wind farm, Bear Mountain Wind Park, sits high on the crest of a ridge overlooking a broad, green valley and the Kiskatinaw River. The wind farm holds thirty-four enormous wind turbines and offers another tourist attraction to the area. It seems like an unusual place to bring a young Malawian woman.

After completing form four, Blandina received a two-year scholarship to Northern Lights Community College, located in the centre of Dawson Creek, where she has been studying for the past eight months.

Not everything has gone well for Blandina since her arrival. She had expected to receive a two-year early childhood education diploma at the college, but she had trouble obtaining a visa before leaving Malawi and arrived in Canada late in the term. Once she arrived in Dawson Creek, further difficulties awaited her. A change in administration at the college caused confusion and even more delays. Blandina settled for a series of ESL classes and computer courses. I ask her if she would be able to receive a diploma or certificate while she is at the college, and she tells me she hopes she will be able to take a six-month health care assistant certificate in the fall.

Four years after our first meeting, Blandina still wanted to become a nurse, but that seemed unlikely now. Although her marks were good overall, she still struggled with math. Shortly after arriving in Canada, she found that she had passed her MSCE, but the math portion of her mark was not high enough for her to take a university entrance exam. "When I go back to Malawi, maybe I will have to go back to school for me to have mathematics on my certificate. Or maybe I will just apply for health care assistant in the community."

We sat at one of three Arborite tables in the Old Fashioned Bakery, a rustic building built to resemble a log cabin. It stands beside an old railway station turned museum along Alaska Avenue, the road you would take if you were travelling to Fairbanks, Alaska. It was the May long weekend, yet none of the coffee shops in the city were open. We thought the bakery would be a quiet place to talk. I asked Blandina, "Is health care assistant a good job in Malawi?"

"Yeah, it is, but not very good," she replied.

I've heard this way of expressing disappointment before, so I asked her, "Is the wage enough to live on?"

"No, but we just make it be enough."

I asked if she's disappointed by the outcome of her scholarship. "I don't feel disappointed because I understand that hope for the future is something difficult to come by, so whenever there is something little, we have to go for it because we never know. It may be a way of going where I want to be. Who knows? I would love to go back to school and become a nurse."

Since our first meeting, Blandina has grown up and developed confidence. Despite her misfortunes, Blandina kept her attitude upbeat. She called her stay in Canada her "biggest adventure," an adventure that has had its challenges.

The population of Dawson Creek is primarily white. Blandina says, "If you meet a black you are lucky." Even as we sat at our table in the bakery, I noticed many of the customers openly staring at her. While her skin colour set her apart, her accent was also confusing to people, and she knew that it further identified her as someone from a foreign country. But the people had been good to her here. It was the food and the weather that she found challenging. She spent the winter months hanging out in her dorm room, not wanting to brave the cold.

I was surprised to hear that she lost weight when she first arrived in the country. She missed *nsima* and found much of the food overly rich and foreign. In desperation, she tried making *nsima* in her small dorm room kitchen. "I cooked *nsima* using baking flour. It didn't work. I didn't even continue."

There had been other challenges too. "I went to Shoppers Drug Mart. I was looking for a face cream. I bought a scrub thinking that I've got a cream, so I started using it as a cream. It was a disaster. Ooh! My face was like maybe I'm burnt with fire. The top layer pealed off. I was just crying. I was not going anywhere." Blandina laughed. "You'll not even believe me. I did not take a picture."

Blandina had good experiences too. Just a few weeks before, she went fishing and caught a fish. "I was about to give up. That was the first time for me to fish." She took cooking and swimming lessons, and for the first time in her life, she saw bear and elk at the nearby game farm. She made new friends and learned about Canada's culture and its people.

Blandina returned home with a wealth of knowledge, experience, and confidence that will set her apart from her peers. Despite Blandina's concerns, Memory was certain that she would be able to get a job in Malawi's health care sector. The health care assistant certificate would qualify her to work at a clinic or in an outreach program advising women about nutrition or promoting HIV/AIDS awareness.

16
A Moral Universe

I do not pretend to understand the moral universe; the arc is a long one, my eye reaches but little ways; I cannot calculate the curve and complete the figure by the experience of sight, I can divine it by conscience. And from what I see I am sure it bends towards justice.

—*Theodore Parker*[1]

ATSIKANA PA ULENDO IS NOW A REALITY.[2] It is a distinguished school with 320 female students, four classroom blocks, a cafeteria, dormitories, science labs, and teachers' accommodation—a success.

Christie has fundraised tirelessly in Canada, while Memory and Henry have ensured that the school conforms to the highest of standards in Malawi. Memory has travelled to Canada on several occasions to help with the fundraising by speaking to dozens of service clubs, schools, and other groups.

Christie and Memory still work closely to ensure the success of the school: Christie as the executive director of APU-Malawi Education Foundation in Canada, and Memory as the director of the school in Malawi. Henry continues to work as project manager, and the two are now the proud parents of three little boys: Teloni, Trevor, and Tamandani.

In the fall of 2014, APU began operating a small primary school. The school serves the teachers that APU employs, as well as the surrounding community. It is an important service if APU wishes to attract qualified teachers. For a time, Teloni—Memory's oldest son—lived in Lilongwe during the week, so he could attend a primary school in the city. But he disliked leaving his parents, and having him board with family members became an intolerable hardship for the family. Teloni and his two younger brothers now attend APU's primary school.

Memory is also committed to her siblings. On my visits to the school, I became used to seeing Stephano, a quiet man, working on the campus. He is there still, working as a driver and a labourer for the school. Bodwin has tried to pass his MSCEs, but last I heard it was with limited success. Danny has taken numerous courses in mechanics and currently works at a garage in Lilongwe.

In 2010, Lucy married her fiancé, Chisomo Kaferantu. She had met Chisomo while living in Area 15. He is James and Esther's son. The

> *Memory, Henry, and their boys Teloni, Trevor, and Tamandani, 2014.*
[Photo courtesy of Memory Chazeza-Mdyetseni]

following year, Lucy gave birth to a boy, Wanga, meaning "mine" in Chichewa. Lucy had been scheduled to start her degree at African Bible College in August 2012, but before she could pay her tuition, she suffered a severe setback.

Lucy had been buying maize directly from the maize mills in Lilongwe and the surrounding area. She would purchase the maize for between K350 and K450 for a fifty-five-kilogram bag. She'd gradually accumulate maize at her home in Lilongwe until she had enough to take to the market. Then she'd hire a truck to transport the maize to the market in Lilongwe or Blantyre, where she would sell it to companies that make feed for livestock. She was usually able to sell the maize at the Lilongwe market for K18 per kilogram or in Blantyre for K22 per kilogram.

Lucy was doing well with her business until the woman she employed to sell her maize at the market fled to Zimbabwe with Lucy's investment: K400,000. That had been the money for her tuition. Lucy is back to brokering maize. "I am not planning to have another baby until I go to school first," she said.

In early 2012, Henry made his first trip to Canada. During his stay, he spoke to over 1,500 present and potential donors. He also downhill skied, ate his first Subway sandwich, and visited the famous West Edmonton Mall.

I spoke to Henry after he returned to Malawi. He told me, "I knew I was going to a developed country, but I didn't expect to see so much order. It was an overwhelming experience. It made me think: 'How long do we have to go before we reach this stage?'" On several occasions, he spoke about the quantity of food. "There was so much food around. At the same time, I'm just coming from home where we have no fuel. We have no money. I was confused in a way." I think back to the times I've returned from Malawi, and I can only imagine his confusion. Like Christie and Audrey before me, after spending time in a country where most people struggle for every meal, I've found returning to a country that thrives on excess a difficult adjustment. I have often felt emotions of anger, resentment, and an almost overwhelming pathos upon my return. But Memory and Henry continue to persevere.

On many occasions, Henry has spoken to me about his determination to help the people of his country. He believes that he can best serve the people of Malawi by offering them the opportunity of a good education. "We feel that if we can give the kind of education that teaches people to serve their country and be proud of their country, maybe we can start building a better future for ourselves and our children," he told me. "An educated nation is better because the people have the tools to solve their own problems, and we have so many problems."

To that end, Memory, Henry, and Christie began to discuss how they could best help the girls who were now graduating from APU. The class blocks were complete and the science labs were built, so it seemed possible to take APU to the next level. For some time, Memory, Christie, and Henry had discussed the future of the girls who would one day graduate from the school.

Christie, Memory, and Henry hope to add a teachers' training college to the school. Without the college, the majority of the girls will not be able to continue with their education once they complete their MSCEs. Adding a TTC to the school will give the girls the option of continuing to study for another two years, and a diploma from the college would qualify them to teach. Henry sees the college as a way of not only helping the girls but also contributing to the education of the next generation: "The girls would make very good teachers, people who are ready to make a difference in other people's lives."

Christie is also committed to adding a TTC to the campus: "I feel strongly that the entire premise of APU is that of empowering and enabling our students to become independent women, able to think for themselves and to take care of themselves and their future families. Most of our APU graduates will not have the chance of continuing with their education once they finish at APU, and without some form of tertiary education, the majority of them will end up back in a cycle of poverty and dependence." More than most Canadians, Christie understands the challenges these girls will face when they graduate from APU. "We will already have invested four years into our APU girls and want to keep them moving forward and upward. We see the addition of a teachers' training college as the one single solution that would have the greatest impact on the largest number of our graduates. We do not have the capacity to fundraise enough to give each girl a scholarship to the program of her choice, but we do feel that there is real energy and excitement amongst our supporters for the implementation of a teachers' training college on the APU Campus." Christie also recognizes that a TTC will not just benefit the girls, it will benefit the country. "The country of Malawi badly needs primary school teachers, particularly well-educated female teachers. Our girls badly need to be employed."

While there are already government-run TTCs operating in Malawi, there are not nearly enough placements within these schools to supply qualified teachers for the entire country. Both the public and the private sectors are looking for teachers. Girls graduating from a TTC would almost certainly gain employment. APU is currently fundraising for the college.

The TTC is still in the future, but many of the first intake of girls have already found jobs or moved on to post-secondary education. Maness Samuel, Angella Benjamin, and Blandina Diva all obtained scholarships at colleges in Canada. Killiness Champion, Selina Shisha, Dorah Banda, and several others were accepted into a government-run teacher training college in Lilongwe. They began their studies in September 2012. Upon graduation, Killiness was hired by APU to teach at their primary school. Evelyn Jekapu became a policewoman and works in Lilongwe. I've lost touch with Solstina, but I heard that she dropped out of university and is now married. Although Grace, Memory's sister, passed her MSCEs, she was not happy with the results. She decided to go back to secondary school to upgrade her marks. She is now studying education at Nkhoma University, and Memory has heard "good recommendations from her lecturers." Grace's teachers say, "She is a leader." Maria Nkhoma is volunteering for the Msakambewa community-based organization (CBO). The CBO runs twenty-three nursery schools and other community-service projects. Maria works as a secretary for the organization and teaches at the nursery schools. Although she volunteers her time, it's likely the position will be able to pay her in the future. Many of the first intake of girls have found employment or are continuing their education.

Subsequent intakes have set an even higher standard for the school. While the national pass rate stood at 54.8 per cent, every one of the 2014 APU graduating class passed their MSCEs.[3] Of the ninety students in the 2014 graduating class, thirty have been selected to attend Malawian universities and colleges—a breathtaking accomplishment.[4]

The school is a success story in Malawi as well as in the surrounding communities. "It's a beautiful school," people will say. Memory often hears talk about the school in the shops and markets of Lilongwe. Without knowing who she is, people will tell her, "If you've got a girl child, think about that school." Memory giggles like a schoolgirl as she relates this story. Her delight is tangible half a world away.

Many Rotary clubs have been instrumental in making the school a success, and the Stony Plain Rotary Club has been among the most supportive. Chuck Morrison, a long-time member of the club, became interested in the possibility of helping the girls through microcredit loans after hearing a presentation given by a member of the Rotary Action Group for Microcredit (RAGM). As the name implies, the group's "purpose is to provide global leadership to assist clubs and districts to participate in effective Microcredit programs."[5]

Chuck collaborated with several club members who had been inspired by the talk, and they formed a committee. They researched various microcredit programs throughout the world, but they soon came to the conclusion that World Vision would be the best NGO to partner with.

As the vision took shape, the committee proposed making loans available not only to the APU girls but also to their families and their communities. World Vision Canada liked the idea and decided to endorse the project.

In Malawi, World Vision uses the Finance Trust for the Self-Employed (FITSE) to broker its loans. In 2011, the institution sent a loans officer out to the school to look into the viability of setting up an office in the area. He met with Henry and the two toured the area, Henry showing him the school and the surrounding communities and trading centres. Henry offered him office space at the school, ensuring that the school would be at the centre of the project. The officer confirmed that they would move forward with the plan.

In the meantime, Chuck's committee had been raising capital for the project. The Stony Plain Rotary Club agreed to contribute $45,000 over two years, and Chuck was able to raise an additional $15,000 by speaking to other clubs. This money would supply the capital for the loans. The interest and a donation from World Vision would pay for loan management. World Vision has a record of high loan repayment, so with this capital, the project has the potential to run for many years.

The program doesn't just hand out money to its recipients, it offers training in marketing and basic banking. There is regular interaction between the loan recipients, and the loans officer supplies counselling on business and money management.

FITSE uses a "group lending methodology" they call solidarity groups. The groups consist of five to ten people who offer support to one another and guarantee each other's loans. They meet regularly to discuss their loans and share strategies for each other's business or agricultural success. The loans are payable over six to twelve months, and the repayment frequency can be weekly, biweekly, or monthly, depending upon the endeavour.[6]

The fund has three target groups: 1) the girls graduating from the school; 2) the parents of the girls at the school; and 3) the people of the villages from which the girls come.[7] So, directly or indirectly, the girls will benefit from the program.

One of the first recipients of funds was Abedi, the father of an APU student. He requested a loan of C$160 to buy seed, farming equipment, and four bags of fertilizer. Abedi said, "Our family has more than enough food this year to take us to the next harvest season, and I paid back the entire loan in only one harvest."[8] The profits from Abedi's cash crops ensure that his four children continue to go to school, and that his eldest daughter is given the school supplies she needs for her studies at APU.

Margret has also received support from the program. Margret is a subsistence farmer and the mother of one of the girls studying at APU. In the past, Margret has had difficulty making her harvest last from one year to the next. Her C$121 loan has allowed her to purchase fertilizer and groundnut and maize seed. She expects a large harvest will allow her to pay off her loan and revive her small grocery shop.[9] It is these small victories that offer hope to the women of Malawi.

Malawi has seen many changes in the past few years. During the 2009 presidential election, President Bingu wa Mutharika was elected to a second term of office, but it didn't take long for Mutharika to raise the ire of the Malawian people. The following year, he was accused of secretly purchasing a $13.26 million presidential jet. The purchase had been made the year before, but rumours circulated surrounding the purchase. Fahad Assani, spokesperson for the UDF, said, "The government and the head of state [are] quite insensitive to the people. Buying a presidential jet at this time just proves how irresponsible that decision can be."[10] The British government agreed, and as a result of the revelation, they reduced their budgetary aid by three million pounds.[11] The expulsion of British ambassador, Fergus Cochrane-Dyet, led to further strained relations, and Britain announced another $550 million in cuts over four years.

Cochrane-Dyet was expelled after a message to William Hague, the UK foreign secretary, was published on the *WikiLeaks* website. The message described Mutharika as "autocratic and intolerant of criticism." He also wrote, "[The] governance situation continues to deteriorate in terms of media freedom, freedom of speech and minority rights."[12]

Other organizations and countries also suspended aid as a result of the Mutharika Government's policies: the World Bank, the African Development Bank, the European Union, the United States, Germany, and Norway all cut or suspended aid between 2010 and 2011.[13] "Malawi has been put on a watch list. There is obviously an issue of credibility on the side of the government," said Alexander Baum, the head of the EU delegation to Malawi.[14]

Allegations against the Mutharika Government also included accusations of cronyism and corruption.[15] Beginning in July 2010, Mutharika's wife, Callista, was paid a monthly salary of K1.3 million for her role as the coordinator of safe motherhood—a salary that was questioned by many in the opposition and ultimately withdrawn at the beginning of 2012 due to pressure.[16]

Other questionable government policies were also at the heart of donor, and public, discontent. The government had been accused of arbitrary arrest and detention. This was particularly the case of Levi Nyondo, general secretary of the Livingstonia Synod of the Church of Central Africa, who was arrested on charges of sedition as a result of statements he made that were critical of the government. The 2010 Human Rights Report released by the US government also accused the Mutharika Government of threatening "to arrest journalists and to close newspapers that 'print lies.'"[17]

It didn't seem that the Malawian people blamed the donors for the reduction in aid. Friday Jumbe, leader of the UDF, said, "The President had displayed sheer arrogance by fighting the British who are our major donor."[18] The *Nation* newspaper came forward and labelled Mutharika a "Mr Know-it-All" and claimed he was "accountable for the UK aid mess."[19] Following the aid cutbacks, the government increased its value-added tax on essential goods, such as flour and salt—further angering its citizens.

The aid debacle was followed by fuel shortages throughout the country and continued anger among the Malawian population toward their government. Rising dissatisfaction with the presidency culminated in a series of antigovernment protests that took place in Mzuzu, Lilongwe, Blantyre, and other urban centres throughout the country in July 2011. At least eighteen people were killed during the two days of civil unrest.[20] Amnesty International reported, "at least three journalists have been severely beaten by police."[21] Dozens more were injured.

While protesters ransacked and burned government offices, looted shops, and demanded that Mutharika step down as president, the army and police cracked down, using tear gas and live ammunition. Noel Mbowela, a political analyst, said, "[The] people have been baptized and every time they see something bad, they will always go into the streets."[22] But later Mutharika warned against future protests, saying, "This time I'll go after you. Even if you hide in a hole, I'll smoke you out."[23] Further aid suspension followed the protests and the Mutharika Government's response.[24] It seemed that Malawi was slipping toward autocracy.

Relief came to the aid of Malawi's democracy in strangely serendipitous fashion the following year. On April 5, 2012, Dr. Bingu wa Mutharika collapsed and died from a heart attack at the age of seventy-eight. The founder of the ironically titled Democratic Progressive Party (DPP) did not live to finish his second term.[25]

The direction forward should have been self-evident, but Vice-President Joyce Banda had been expelled from the party in 2010 after "championing programs that are contrary to the party's agenda."[26] Fortunately, for Banda and the Malawian people, the impeachment process had not been carried through. The Constitution clearly called for the vice-president to replace the president, and although Mutharika had been grooming his brother, Peter Mutharika, as successor to the party leadership, the president's lack of popularity made it unlikely that his relative would be welcomed to power. "[Mutharika] was very unpopular. People were praying for his death," said former Attorney General Ralph Kasambara.[27]

Despite initial concerns of political upheaval, Joyce Banda was sworn in as Malawi's first female president two days after Mutharika's collapse. Henry spoke to me about the peoples' concerns: "We are relieved that

Mutharika is gone, but at the same time, Joyce Banda was not prepared for the presidency. It came too much too soon for her. As a result it's clear that she hasn't established where to start from. She was overwhelmed by the position itself, and she was preoccupied with her own political survival. She has gone in a different direction altogether, and it has brought a lot of confusion, a lot of mixed feelings."

Banda began by attempting to rebuild relations with the international community. "My government will work towards normalizing relations with our traditional partners."[28] In the first of many tough decisions to improve the country's international reputation, Banda allowed the overvalued Malawian kwacha to depreciate, a move that the IMF had recommended years before.[29] She quickly grew in popularity with her own people after deciding to give up the presidential jet and fleet of sixty Mercedes. "The proceeds can be used to provide basic services to Malawi's poorest people who urgently need help following the vital devaluation of the currency."[30] Banda also pledged to remove Malawi's ban on homosexuality, stating, "Indecency and unnatural acts laws shall be repealed."[31] Although she was able to temporarily halt the enforcement of antigay laws, it was unclear whether Banda would be able to follow through with her promise, but even her stance seemed to go some way to changing attitudes in the traditional country. Human rights lawyer, Wapona Kita, said, "She has done the right thing. The repeal of this bad law is long overdue."[32]

In spite of good intentions, political expedience won, and Banda was unable to execute her promise, conceding that the country was "not ready" to decriminalize homosexuality. However, in 2014, Malawi's High Court called for a moratorium on the arrest of people for same-sex acts while it completed a review of the country's antihomosexual laws.[33]

Although it ended a short two years after her election, Banda's presidency offered hope to women throughout the country. Not only did she serve as an outstanding role model but she had long supported women's health initiatives, girls' education, and gender equality, believing that access to education and health care for girls of all economic levels is vital to their economic future.[34]

Not long after Banda's ascendancy, international donors began to restore aid to the country. In July 2012, Malawi's largest donor, Britain, announced it would give the country an additional twenty-four million pounds to aid its economic recovery.[35] The United States has also restored a US$350 million aid program that is meant to help repair and overhaul the country's electricity grid.[36] It would seem that under Banda's leadership, Malawi could recover its reputation and improved the lives of its citizens. Banda explained, "I have a passion for helping people; this position of president will help me change the lives of many poor Malawians. I want people in future to look back and say, Malawi had a female president who did a lot for her people."[37]

Henry was not convinced though. "We've had some relief from the economic problems that we've had, but the same problems are now resurfacing," he explained. "So it's worrisome on that end. We need to sell things to get money, but there's nothing for sale. We need to commercialize agriculture. So that the larger amount of labour is put into industry. Without that, everyone farms two acres; they're only there to feed their own families. If everyone is farming two acres that doesn't feed the country; it only feeds the family. The government is still going in the same direction of giving subsidies for fertilizer. They are not finding a new solution to the problem. When I came to Canada, I saw those huge farms and every home has every kind of food you can imagine. Do we still go on with subsistence farming? There is nothing we can achieve with that."

In spite of high expectations, Joyce Banda was defeated in the 2014 election by DPP candidate Peter Mutharika. Mutharika is the younger brother of past President Bingu wa Mutharika and has a lengthy past in Malawian politics. He was foreign minister in his brother's government but was charged with treason in 2013 after allegedly plotting a coup— an allegation he continues to deny. Relations between Peter Mutharika

APU's 2014 graduating class. [Photo courtesy of APU]

and Joyce Banda had been turbulent, but after the election, Mutharika publicly stated, "I look forward to shaking hands with her to bury the past."[38]

Whatever the outcome of Mutharika's presidency, APU will continue to educate the girls of the country. Memory and Henry are committed to their vision. Christie is also committed to the project, but she wants to see it become independent, free from dependency on Canadian support. "I believe that like our students, APU itself needs to work towards independence," Christie explains. "I will know that we have truly succeeded only when the school is able to fully sustain itself independently from the need for outside donations."

For the school to be sustainable, Henry believes, "We need to get to a steady state where for the next 40 years we'll be able to provide decent education." While the school must work toward sustainability, it also needs to be adaptable. "Problems keep coming," Henry explains. "The country's problems keep changing." For the school to be effective, it must also grow to meet the needs of the community. To this end, Memory and Henry hope that one day they'll host a clinic. Like the school, a clinic would help to serve the needs of the community.

Christie's vision is in lockstep with those of Memory and Henry: " This is my vision. A school that is able to exist and thrive as a financially independent institution; a school that is known for academic rigour and excellence while empowering girls and women to assume roles of leadership in their communities and country. Most importantly, a school that is giving a voice to the voiceless and a choice to those who, without an education, will have no choices available to them other than early marriage, poverty and a life of hardship."

Despite traditional perception, educating girls serves a number of purposes that benefit families, communities, and society as a whole. Women with an education know more about reproductive health, nutrition, and hygiene than do women who lack schooling. They are also more likely to seek medical attention. This lowers infant and child mortality rates. Girls who have attended secondary and post-secondary school are less likely to become pregnant at a young age and are more likely to receive pre- and postnatal care when they finally decide to start a family—thus reducing the country's birth rate and infant mortality.

Educating women is their best protection against HIV/AIDS. Because education improves women's self-esteem, independence, and level of knowledge, they are less likely to engage in risky sexual activity. They are also much more likely to have the courage to ask their partners for HIV/AIDS testing before getting married. It was education that gave Eunice the determination to ask Owen for blood testing and the resolve to leave him when he refused.

With education comes confidence and self-esteem. Girls who develop a healthy sense of self-worth are more likely to develop healthy relationships with men. They are also far more likely to defend their rights and resist oppression. If girls like Ivy and Esnet had believed in their own worth, they would have been less likely to fall prey to the male predators who took their lives.

Lucita was one of the few girls from the first intake who performed poorly on her MSCEs. For a time, I only heard rumours about her situation, but when I spoke with Memory in May of 2015, she told me Lucita had recently contacted her. After leaving APU, Lucita had returned to secondary school, and this time, she had passed the government exams. I had grown close to Lucita on my trips to Malawi, so this news came as a relief. To me, this single, seemingly minor, success illustrates the immense impact that Memory and APU are having on the girls of Malawi. As a result of her experience at APU, Lucita—a reserved, shy, village girl—had the vision and the determination to go back to school after what must have felt to her like an insurmountable failure. As Memory spoke, tears filled my eyes, and I was overcome by the sense that this was a profound accomplishment—a moment worthy of celebration. Memory and APU have taught the girls to perceive life's possibilities; they now believe in themselves and their abilities. This knowledge will follow them through their lives, rippling through their families and their communities.

Education also increases a woman's ability to earn a living wage. Through employment, women gain economic independence, and with economic independence comes the ability to stand up for oneself. Women who do not need financial support from men can leave abusive relationships. Without the confidence she gained from education, Estel may have lacked the resolve to leave her fiancé, Malcom, before she became locked into a hurtful, harmful, "permanent" relationship. Once a woman is earning a living wage, she will often help needy relatives. Because of her education, Agness was able to build her mother a house, Memory was able to help her siblings attend school, and Lucita will one day help to support her little sister.

Through education and the power of learning, people are able to make sense of their worlds. Education assists in dispelling superstition and harmful cultural paradigms. Education will ultimately dispel the belief that girls are "worthless." Hopefully, it will also help women like Florence get the medical help they need rather than persecution based on ignorance and lack of knowledge. And an educated woman is far more likely to insist on her children completing their education, thus perpetuating the cycle of learning for future generations.[39]

Through education, girls become empowered and capable of solving their own problems. They are then more capable of becoming community leaders, like Memory. They begin to understand the value of helping others and of lifting people up rather than putting them down. They are willing to support those who strive to improve their lives by moving away from ignorance and poverty. When Maria Nkhoma decided to volunteer within her community, it could not have been an easy decision. "When women are fully empowered and engaged, all of society benefits."[40]

Educated women also become role models for the girls within their communities. Memory has certainly accomplished this. Many of the girls who first came to study at APU were incredulous when they learned their head teacher was a woman. And former President Joyce Banda has also given girls hope. She has shown that a woman can reach the highest office in the country.

After completing two years at Pearson College, Maness Samuel is now on full scholarship at Westminster College. Maness trusts in the power of education: "I really believe that education is important for girls because it gives us a voice, and it opens doors to many opportunities that will enable us to be independent and role models. Look at how many rural girls have been exposed to high school education just through Memory Chazeza."[41]

Memory is not only an inspiration and a role model for the women of Malawi, she stands as an example to us all. Memory is a visionary. She demonstrates what is possible given determination, perseverance, and the will to achieve an education.

Notes

Introduction

1. Memory Chazeza-Mdyetseni, spoken during her address at the Rotary District Conference in Spruce Grove, AB, 2006.

1 The Dream Becomes Reality

1. This chapter is based primarily on interviews with Memory Chazeza-Mdyetseni and Henry Mdyetseni, which took place during 2008 and 2009, both in person and by telephone.

Solstina

1. This account of Solstina is based on my interview with her at APU in 2008.

2 The Warm Heart of Africa

1. Martin Dugard, *Into Africa: The Epic Adventures of Stanley & Livingstone* (New York: Broadway Books, 2003), 36.
2. This chapter is based, in part, on author interviews with Memory Chazeza-Mdyetseni and Lucy Chazeza-Kaferantu in 2008 and 2009.

3.	D.D. Phiri, *History of Malawi: From Earliest Times to the Year 1915* (Malawi: Christian Literature Association of Malawi, 2004).

4.	Charles M. Good, *The Steamer Parish: The Rise and Fall of Missionary Medicine on an African Frontier* (Chicago: University of Chicago Press, 2004), 51.

5.	Phiri, *History of Malawi*, 64.

6.	Ibid., 39.

7.	Ibid., 72.

8.	Ibid., 73.

9.	Good, *The Steamer Parish*, 51.

10.	United Human Rights Council, *Genocide in Rwanda*, 2011, http://www.unitedhumanrights.org/genocide/genocide_in_rwanda.htm.

11.	Susan Dalgety, "David Livingstone: The mill worker who made an incredible journey to the heart of Africa," *The Daily Record*, September 17, 2009, http://www.dailyrecord.co.uk/news/uk-world-news/david-livingstone-the-mill-worker-who-1036829.

12.	Good, *The Steamer Parish*, 51.

13.	Ibid., 54.

14.	David Livingstone, *A Popular Account of Dr. Livingstone's Expedition to the Zambezi and Its Tributaries: And the Discovery of Lakes Shirwa and Nyassa 1858–1864* (South Carolina: BiblioBazaar, 2007), 220.

15.	Good, *The Steamer Parish*, 53.

16.	Phiri, *History of Malawi*, 74.

17.	Ibid., 113.

18.	Livingstone, *A Popular Account of Dr. Livingstone's Expedition*, 218.

19.	Ibid., 210.

20.	Ibid., 11.

21.	Kenneth P. Vickery, "Prelude to the 'Scramble for Africa,'" in *The African Experience: From "Lucy" to Mandela* (Chantilly, VA: The Teaching Company Limited Partnership, 2006).

22.	Dugard, *Into Africa*, 32.

23.	Andrew Ross, "Dr. Livingstone, I Presume?" *History Today*, July 2002, 21–27.

24.	Phiri, *History of Malawi*, 115.

25.	Ibid., 114.

26.	"Livingstonia Mission Archives, 1874–1934," Adam Matthew Publications, 2015, http://www.ampltd.co.uk/collections_az/Livingst/description.aspx.

27.	UNESCO, "Lake Malawi National Park," December 3, 2009, http://whc.UNESCO.org/en/list/289.

28. Central Intelligence Agency, "Malawi Geography 2009," *The World Factbook: Malawi*, 2010, http://www.theodora.com/wfbcurrent/malawi/malawi_geography.html.

29. Central Intelligence Agency, *The World Factbook: Malawi*, 2014, https://www.cia.gov/library/publications/the-world-factbook/geos/mi.html.

30. "Hastings Kamuzu Banda Facts," *Your Dictionary*, 2010, http://biography.yourdictionary.com/hastings-kamuzu-banda; "Hastings Banda," *New World Encyclopedia*, 2012, http://www.newworldencyclopedia.org/entry/Hastings_Banda.

31. Bakili Muluzi et al., *Democracy with a Price: The History of Malawi Since 1900* (Oxford: Heinemann Educational Publishers, 1999), 68.

32. Ibid., 70–71.

33. Ibid., 77.

34. Francine van den Borne, *Trying to Survive in Times of Poverty and AIDS: Women and Multiple Partner Sex in Malawi* (Amsterdam: Het Spinhuis Publishers, 2005).

35. "Idi Amin," About.com: 20th Century History, http://history1900s.about.com/cs/idiamin.

36. "Ex-President Banda's Apology," Hartford Web Publishing, http://www.hartford-hwp.com/archives/37/033.html.

37. Geoffrey York, "The cult of Hastings Banda takes hold," *The Globe and Mail*, May 20, 2009, http://www.theglobeandmail.com/news/world/the-cult-of-hastings-banda-takes-hold/article4273860/.

Lucita

1. This account of Lucita is based on my observations, as well as interviews with Lucita and Memory Chazeza-Mdyetseni at APU, Malawi, in 2008 and 2009.

3 Education for All

1. Anne C. Conroy, Malcolm J. Blackie, Alan Whiteside, Justin C. Malewezi, and Jeffrey D. Sachs, *Poverty, AIDS and Hunger: Breaking the Poverty Trap in Malawi* (London: Palgrave Macmillan, 2007), 187.

2. This chapter is based, in part, on author interviews with Memory Chazeza-Mdyetseni in 2007, 2008, and 2009, as well as my own experiences during my time in that country.

3. M.M. Mughogho, interview by author at Karonga, Malawi, May 2009.

4. Humza Yousaf, "Mary's Meals is helping to save lives," May 25, 2015, *Evening Times*, http://www.eveningtimes.co.uk/opinion/columnists/marys-meals-is-helping-to-save-lives-207921n.126944682.

5. Samer Al-Samarrai and Hassan Zaman, *Abolishing School Fees in Malawi: The Impact on Education Access and Equity*, MPRA Paper No. 130 (Munich: Munich Personal RePEc Archive, 2000), 2, http://mpra.ub.uni-muenchen.de/130/.

6. Ibid., 3.

7. Fredriksen Birger and Di Craissati, *Abolishing School Fees in Africa: Lessons from Ethiopia, Ghana, Kenya, Malawi, and Mozambique* (Washington, DC: World Bank, in collaboration with UNICEF, 2009), 163, http://www.unicef.org/publications/files/Aboloshing_School_Fees_in_Africa.pdf.

8. Brian Ligomeka, "Free Primary Education Backfires," *News from Africa*, November 11, 2009, http://www.newsfromafrica.org/newsfromafrica/articles/art_902.html.

9. Herman Kruijer, *Learning How to Teach: The upgrading of unqualified primary teachers in subSaharan Africa: Lessons from Tanzania, Malawi, and Nigeria*, April 2010, 60, http://download.ei-ie.org/Docs/WebDepot/EIResearch_Herman_Eng_final_med.pdf.

10. Esme Chipo Kadzamira, "Teacher Motivation and Incentives in Malawi" (Zomba, Malawi, Centre for Educational Research and Training, University of Malawi, 2006), 5, http://community.eldis.org/.59ee4573/Teacher%20motivation%20and%20incentives%20in%20Malawi.pdf.

11. Beatrice Debut, "Africa Struggles with Free Primary Education," *Agence France-Presse*, April 15, 2006.

12. Birger and Craissati, *Abolishing School Fees in Africa*, 167.

13. Mary D. Lugton, "Problematizing the Practicum," 2000, 4, http://people.umass.edu/educ870/teacher_education/Lugton-presrv.htm.

14. Debut, "Africa Struggles with Free Primary Education."

15. Birger and Craissati, *Abolishing School Fees in Africa*, 175.

16. Debut, "Africa Struggles with Free Primary Education."

17. Kadzamira, "Teacher Motivation and Incentives in Malawi," 6.

18. Ibid., 2.

19. Ibid., 15.

20. Emmie Chanika, "Male Teacher Sexual Abuse of the Girl Child in the School Context: A Case Study of Primary Schools in Chiradzulu District" (Report by the Civil Liberties Committee submitted to the Commonwealth Education Fund, July 2003).

21. Kadzamira, "Teacher Motivation and Incentives in Malawi," 14.

22. Ibid., 12.

23. Ibid., 9–10.

24. *Canadian Oxford Dictionary*, s.v. "IMF."

25. David Harvey, "Brief History of Neoliberalism," in *The World Beyond the Headlines Series* (London: Oxford University Press, 2007).

26. Paul Treanor, "Neoliberalism: Origins, Theory, Definition," http://web.inter.nl.net/users/Paul.Treanor/neoliberalism.html.

27. Naomi Klein, *The Shock Doctrine: The Rise of Disaster Capitalism* (Toronto: Vintage Canada, 2007), 17.

28. Anup Shah, "A Primer on Neoliberalism," *Global Issues*, June 1, 2009, http://www.globalissues.org/article/39/a-primer-on-neoliberalism.

29. Klein, *The Shock Doctrine*, 17.

30. Harvey, "Brief History of Neoliberalism."

31. James Raymond Vreeland, "The IMF and Economic Development," in *Reinventing Foreign Aid*, ed. William Easterly (Cambridge, MA: MIT Press, 2008), 355.

32. "What are the main concerns and criticism about the World Bank and IMF?" *Bretton Woods Project*, August 23, 2005, http://www.brettonwoodsproject.org/item.shtml?x=320869.

33. Action Aid, *Malawi: A Decade after FPE the teacher shortage persists* (Lilongwe, Malawi: Action Aid International, 2007).

34. "Changing IMF Policies to Get More Doctors, Nurses and Teachers Hired in Developing Countries," *Action Aid*, 2, http://www.healthworkforce.info/advocacy/IMF_HRH_ActionAid.pdf.

35. Ibid., 3.

36. Central Intelligence Agency, *The World Factbook: Malawi, 2014*.

37. Kadzamira, "Teacher Motivation and Incentives in Malawi," 5.

38. United Nations, "We Can End Poverty: Millennium Development Goals and Beyond 2015," http://www.un.org/millenniumgoals/bkgd.shtml.

39. Aidan Mulkeen, "Teachers for Rural Schools: A Challenge for Africa" (report prepared for the Ministerial Seminar on Education for Rural People in Africa Policy Lessons, Options and Priorities, Addis Ababa, Ethiopia, September 2005), 8–9.

40. UNESCO, "Malawi," *The Global Economy*, http://www.theglobaleconomy.com/Malawi/Student_teacher_ratio_primary_school/.

41. Government of Malawi, Ministry of Education, Science and Technology, *Education Sector Implementation Plan: Towards Quality Education: Implementing the National Education Sector Plan 2009–2013* (August 2009), 20, http://planipolis.iiep.UNESCO.org/upload/Malawi/Malawi_ESIP_FINAL.pdf.

42. Ibid., 21.

43. Ibid., 18.

44. World Bank, "Primary completion rate, total (% of relevant age group)," http://data.worldbank.org/indicator/SE.PRM.CMPT.ZS.

45. World Bank, "Malawi: Repetition rate in primary. Grade 3," https://www.quandl.com/data/WORLDBANK/ MWI_UIS_REPR_1_G3_F-Malawi-Repetition-rate-in-primary-Grade-3-Female.

46. Central Intelligence Agency, *The World Factbook: Malawi, 2014.*

47. Ruben D. Hango, "The Malawi Education System: Changes and Challenges 1994 to 2003," *Newsletter of the Scottish Malawi Network,* no. 45 (June 2003), accessed July 2009, http://www.malawi-update/org/index.php?issue_number=45&articleid=42.

48. Samer Al-Samarrai and Hassan Zaman, "The Changing Distribution of Public Education Expenditure in Malawi" (Africa Region Working Paper Series, No. 29, March 2002), 17.

49. Ibid.

50. Joseph Chimombo et al., "The SACMEQ II Project in Malawi: A Study of the Conditions of Schooling and the Quality of Education" (SACMEQ Educational Policy Research Series, SACMEQ, Harare, Zimbabwe, 2005).

51. Ibid., 34.

52. Ibid., 31.

53. Ibid., 32.

54. Ibid., 37.

55. Government of Malawi, Ministry of Education, Science and Technology, *Education Sector Implementation Plan,* 18.

56. Nils Blythe, "Hard Choices Over Food Versus Education in Malawi," *BBC News,* November 20, 2009, http://news.bbc.co.uk/2/hi/business/8369120.stm.

57. Chimombo et al., "The SACMEQ II Project in Malawi," 63.

58. Center for Social Concern, "News clippings with analysis from the major newspapers in Malawi," 2011, http://www.africamission-mafr.org/kanengo_sept11.pdf.

59. Emmanuel Chibwana, "2011 MSCE Results Out: 55% Pass Rate," *Zodiak Online,* October 19, 2011, http://zodiakmalawi.com/ZBS2012_BACKUP/ archive/2811-2011-msce-results-out-55-pass-rate.

60. Frank Namagale, "Malawi: MSCE, JCE Results Disaster," *Daily Times* (Blantyre), http://allafrica.com/stories/200203120003.html.

61. Lameck Masina, "Malawi Schools to Teach in English," *Aljazeera: Africa,* August 21, 2014, http://www.aljazeera.com/news/africa/2014/08/ malawi-schools-teach-english-local-debate-colonial-201482184041156272.html.

62. Ibid.

63. Diliya, "English as the Language of Communication," in *In Their Own Words: The Girls of Atsikana Pa Ulendo Tell Their Stories,* ed. Roberta Laurie (Edmonton: Prairie Dog Publishing, 2011), 79.

64. Chimombo et al., "The SACMEQ II Project in Malawi," 22.

65. Ibid., 23.

66. Ibid., 22.

67. Ibid., 39.

68. Birger and Craissati, *Abolishing School Fees in Africa*, 189.

69. Ibid., 188.

70. Excerpted from "Table 5.7: Survival Rates by Standard and Gender, 1990/91–2005," ibid., 189.

71. *Malawi School WASH 2008: A Status Report on Water, Sanitation, and Hygiene in Primary Schools* (Malawi Ministry of Education, Science and Technology, 2009), 13.

72. "Malawi: Enabling Policy Environment for WASH in Schools," WASH, 2011, http://www.washinschoolsmapping.com/projects/Malawi.html.

73. *Malawi School WASH 2008*.

74. Sally Pillitteri, "School Menstrual Hygiene Management in Malawi: More than Toilets," *WaterAid*, 2011, 6, http://www.ndr.mw:8080/xmlui/bitstream/handle/123456789/313/School%20menstrual%20hygiene%20managment%20in%20Malawi%20is%20more%20than%20toilets.pdf?sequence=1.

75. Monalisa Nkhonjera, "Improved Sanitation, Crucial to Girl-Child Education," *WaterAid*, March 8, 2011, http://malawi.wateraid.org/news/item/69-improed-santitation-crucial-to-girl-child-education.

76. Pillitteri, "School Menstrual Hygiene Management in Malawi," 10.

77. Ibid., 14.

78. "Sanitary Towel Project," *Sanitary Pads for Africa*, 2012, accessed 2012, http://www.sanitarypadsforafrica.org/project.htm.

79. Pillitteri, "School Menstrual Hygiene Management in Malawi," 17–18.

80. Ibid., 18.

81. Chimombo et al., "The SACMEQ II Project in Malawi," 188.

82. Ibid., 189–190.

83. Ibid., 201.

84. Birger and Craissati, *Abolishing School Fees in Africa*, 181.

85. United Nations, "Malawi," *UNData: A World of Information*, 2014, http://data.un.org/CountryProfile.aspx?crName=Malawi.

86. Birger and Craissati, *Abolishing School Fees in Africa*, 20.

87. Ibid., 25.

88. Ibid., 66–69.

89. Ibid., 39.

90. "Mutharika Gov't Education Challenges for 2010," *Nyasa Times*, January 4, 2010.

Shakira

1. This account of Shakira is based on my interviews with her at Nsaru and APU in 2008.

4   You Should Work Hard in School

1. Pascal J. Kishindo, "Recurrent Themes in Chichewa Verse in Malawian Newspapers," *Nordic Journal of African Studies* 12, no. 3 (2003): 329.

2. This chapter is based, in part, on the observations I made during my 2009 trip to Malawi, as well as author interviews with Memory Chazeza-Mdyetseni in Lilongwe in 2007 and in Kalonga and at APU in 2009, as well as with Sala in Lilongwe in 2007 and discussions with APU girls at APU in 2008.

3. USAID, *The Safe Schools Program: Student and Teacher Baseline Report on School-Related Gender-Based Violence in Machinga District*, Malawi, December 2007, http://hivhealthclearinghouse.unesco.org/library/documents/safe-schools-program-student-and-teacher-baseline-report-school-related-gender.

4. Ibid., 20.

5. US Department of State, *2007 Country Reports on Human Rights Practices*, http://www.state.gov/j/drl/rls/hrrpt/2007/index.htm.

6. Ibid.

7. Patrick Burton, "Suffering at School: Results of the Malawi Gender-based Violence in Schools Survey" (Crime & Justice Statistical Division, National Statistical Office, October 2005), x.

8. Emmie Chanika, for DAPP Child Aid Program, "Male Teacher Sexual Abuse of the Girl Child in the School Context: A Case Study of Primary Schools in Chiradzulu District" (Commonwealth Education Fund, July 2003).

9. Burton, "Suffering at School," 42.

10. Ibid., 32.

11. USAID, "Are Schools Safe Havens for Children? Examining School-related Gender-based Violence," September 2008, http://pdf.usaid.gov/pdf_docs/PNADM792.pdf.

12. Mercy Tembon and Lucia Fort, eds., *Girls' Education in the 21st Century: Gender Equality, Empowerment, and Economic Growth*, World Bank, 2008, 58–59, iteresources.worldbank.org/EDUCATION/Resources/278200-1099079877269/547664-1099080014368/DID_Girls_edu.pdf.

13. Maria Saur et al., *Nkanza, Listening to People's Voices: A Study of Gender-Based Violence, Nkanza in Three Districts of Malawi* (Zomba, Malawi: Kachere Series, 2005), 37.

14. Ibid., 38.

15. Ibid., 83.

16. Chiku Ndaferankhande, "Rescuing Girls from Retrogressive Traditions," in *Kamanga Zula! Stop Gender-based Violence* (Zomba, Malawi: Kachere Series, 2008), 63.

17. Saur et al., *Nkanza, Listening to People's Voices*, 33.

18. Limbikani Mhura, "Man Arrested after Assaulting Wife for Cooking Nsima without Relish," *Malawi Voice*, June 12, 2012, http://malawivoice.com/2012/06/12/man-arrested-after-assaulting-wife-for-cooking-nsima-without-relish-94806/.

19. Ndaferankhande, "Rescuing Girls from Retrogressive Traditions," 11–12.

20. Deogratias Mmana, "Moving Away from Hardcore Beliefs," *The Nation*, October 23, 2009.

21. Nicholas D. Kristof and Sheryl WuDunn, *Half the Sky: Turning Oppression into Opportunity for Women Worldwide* (New York: Alfred A. Knopf, 2009), 164.

22. UNFPA, "About Us," http://www.unfpa.org/about-us.

23. Ibid.

24. Burton, "Suffering at School," 16.

25. Tiyese, "Why Dogs Are Dangerous," in *In Their Own Words: The Girls of Atsikana Pa Ulendo Tell Their Stories*, ed. Roberta Laurie (Edmonton: Prairie Dog Publishing, 2011), 77.

26. Gina Porter et al., "Young people's transport and mobility in sub-Saharan Africa: The gendered journey to school," *Documents d'Anàlisi Geogràfica* 51, no. 1 (2011): 68, http://www.raco.cat/index.php/DocumentsAnalisi/article/viewFile/241960/324551.

27. Van den Borne, *Trying to Survive in Times of Poverty and AIDS*.

28. UNESCO Institute for Statistics, as supplied by *Index Mundi*, http://www.indexmundi.com/facts/malawi/primary-completion-rate.

29. Mr. Kapwayi, interview by author, June 2007.

30. Ibid.

31. Charles Banda, "Child sexual assaults irk women activists," *News from Africa*, December 2003, http://www.newsfromafrica.org/newsfromafrica/articles/art_2616.html.

32. "Women in Malawi Protest Attacks over Skirts, Pants," *Associated Press*, 2012, http://elitedaily.com/elite/2012/women-malawi-protest-attacks-skirts-pants/.

33. "Malawi: After Attacks, President Says Women Have Right to Choose Clothing," *New York Times*, January 19, 2012, http://www.nytimes.com/2012/01/20/world/africa/malawi-after-attacks-president-says-women-have-right-to-choose-clothing.html?_r=0.

34. "Women in Malawi Protest Attacks over Skirts, Pants."

Agness

1. This account of Agness is based on my interview with her at Lilongwe, Malawi, in 2007.

2. "Jehovah's Witnesses Claim Persecution in Malawi," *Ocala Star-Banner, Associated Press*, December 26, 1975.

5   I Should Be Buried

1. Memory Chazeza-Mdyetseni, interview by author at Mzuzu in 2009.

2. This chapter is based, in part, on author interviews with Memory Chazeza-Mdyetseni at Lilongwe in 2007 and Mzuzu in 2009.

3. John Douglas and Kelly White, *Spectrum Guide to Malawi* (Northampton, MA: Interlink Books, 2003), 92.

4. Global Initiative to End All Corporal Punishment of Children, *Corporal Punishment of Children in Malawi*, December 2010, http://www.endcorporalpunishment.org/pages/progress/reports/malawi.html.

5. Ibid.

6. USAID, *The Safe Schools Program*, 22.

7. Global Initiative to End All Corporal Punishment of Children, *Corporal Punishment of Children in Malawi*.

8. USAID, *The Safe Schools Program*, 23.

9. Ibid.

10. Ibid., 21.

11. Richard Record and Abdu Mohiddin, "An Economic Perspective on Malawi's Medical 'Brain Drain,'" *Globalization and Health,* December 1, 2006, 2, http://www.globalizationandhealth.com/content/2/1/12.

12. Reidar Oderth, *Migration and Brain Drain: The Case of Malawi* (Bloomington, IN: iUniverse, Inc., 2002).

13. Ibid., 54.

14. Record and Mohiddin, "An Economic Perspective on Malawi's Medical 'Brain Drain.'"

15. Ibid.

16. Ibid.

17. "100 Nurses Migrate Every Year," *Daily Times*, September 6, 2006, http://www.queensu.ca/samp/migrationnews/article.php?Mig_News_ID=3229&Mig_News_Issue=18&Mig_News_Cat=5.

18. Jane Elliott, "Saving Africa's dying from the 'Brain Drain,'" *BBC News Health,* September 25, 2010, http://www.bbc.co.uk/news/health-11327505.

19. Christine Gorman, "Malawi Halts Nursing Brain Drain," *International CNN.com/health*, July 30, 2009, http://edition.cnn.com/2009/HEALTH/07/29/malawi.nurses.shortage/.

20. Ibid.

21. Khumbo Kalua, "Reversing Doctors brain drain from Malawi," *My Best Days*, May 17, 2009, http://khumbokalua.blogspot.com/2009/05/reversing-doctors-brain-drain-from.html.

22. Ibid.

23. Record and Mohiddin, "An Economic Perspective on Malawi's Medical 'Brain Drain.'"

24. Ibid.

25. Mary Robinson, "British Hospitals Are Africa's Real Poachers," *The Independent on Sunday*, April 9, 2006.

26. Sharon LaFraniere, "For Girls in Africa, Education Is Uphill Fight," *New York Times*, December 23, 2005, http://www.nytimes.com/2005/12/22/world/africa/22iht-ethiopia.html.

27. Birger and Craissati, *Abolishing School Fees in Africa*, 176.

28. Molly Longwe, *Growing Up: A Chewa Girls' Initiation*, Kachere Theses no. 15 (Zomba, Malawi: Kachere Series, 2007), 42.

29. Malawi Human Rights Commission, "Cultural Practices and Their Impact on the Enjoyment of Human Rights, Particularly the Rights of Women and Children in Malawi" (Lilongwe, Malawi, 2006), 81.

30. Suzanne Leclerc-Madlala, "Intergenerational/age-disparate Sex: Policy and Programme Action Brief" (UNAIDS and RHRU, 2008).

31. Xanthe Scharff, "Primary School Is Not Enough: Proposal for Safe and Affordable Secondary School for Girls in Malawi," *Africa Policy Journal* 3 (Spring 2007), http://ageafrica.org/app/wp-content/uploads/2013/05/Scharff-Primary-School-is-not-enough-Article.pdf.

32. Leclerc-Madlala, "Intergenerational/age-disparate Sex," 2.

33. Central Intelligence Agency, *The World Factbook: Malawi, 2014*.

34. Van den Borne, *Trying to Survive in Times of Poverty and AIDS*, 31.

35. National Statistical Office, "Malawi Demographic and Health Survey 2010: Preliminary Report" (Zomba, Malawi, 2010).

36. Scharff, "Primary School Is Not Enough," 12.

37. Ibid.

Grace

1. This account of Grace Chazeza is based on my interviews with her, in person and via telephone, in 2007, 2008, 2009, and 2011.

6   What It Means To Be an Orphan

1. Wiseman Chijere Chirwa, "Social Exclusion and Inclusion: Challenges to Orphan Care in Malawi," *Nordic Journal of African Studies* 11, no. 1 (2001): 96.

2. This chapter is based, in part, on author interviews with Memory Chazeza-Mdyetseni at Lilongwe in 2007 and at APU in 2009.

3. "About SCOM," *SCOM Ministry Website*, 2009, http://scoministry.webs.com/aboutscom.htm.

4. Chirwa, "Social Exclusion and Inclusion," 98.

5. "CIA World Fact Book, 2004/Malawi," *Wikisource*, http://en.wikisource.org/wiki/CIA_World_Fact_Book,_2004/Malawi.

6. Central Intelligence Agency, *The World Factbook: Malawi*, 2014.

7. "HIV & AIDS in Malawi," *AVERT*, 2010, http://www.avert.org/aids-malawi.htm.

8. UNAIDS, "Malawi," http://www.unaids.org/en/regionscountries/countries/malawi/.

9. Ibid.

10. Stephen Lewis, *Race against Time: Searching for Hope in AIDS-Ravaged Africa*, 2nd ed. (Toronto: House of Anansi Press, 2006), 51.

11. Chirwa, "Social Exclusion and Inclusion," 100.

12. Brigitte Zimmerman, "Orphan Living Situations in Malawi: A Comparison of Orphanages and Foster Homes," *Review of Policy Research* 1 (November 2005): 2.

13. Grace Chazeza, "What Made Me Stop Eating Coconut Biscuits," in *In Their Own Words: The Girls of Atsikana Pa Ulendo Tell Their Stories*, ed. Roberta Laurie (Edmonton: Prairie Dog Publishing, 2011), 25.

14. Claire Ngozo, "Malawi: Rural Communities Jointly Care for Orphans," *IPS News*, March 15, 2010, http://www.ipsnews.net.

Chifundo

1. This account of Chifundo is based on my interviews with her at APU in 2008 and 2009.

7   Life in the Village

1. M.J. Maluleke, "Culture, Tradition, Custom, Law and Gender Equality," 2012, http://www.saflii.org/za/journals/PER/2012/1.html.

2. This chapter is based, in part, on interviews with Christie Johnson at Victoria, BC, in 2009, Memory Chazeza-Mdyetseni at Lilongwe, Malawi, in 2007, Audrey Kaplan-Entz at Edmonton, AB, in 2010, and Moses Nyama in Malawi in 2009.

3. Excerpted from "Malawi," in *Compendium of Elections in Southern Africa*, ed. Tom Lodge, Denis Kadima, and David Pottie (Johannesburg, South Africa: Electoral Institute of South Africa, 2002), 133–136.

4. Ibid.

5. J.W.M. van Breugel, *Chewa Traditional Religion* (Zomba, Malawi: Kachere Series, 2001), 217.

6. "Witchcraft Act Review Programme: Issues Paper" (Malawi Law Commission, April 2009), 16.

7. "Conference Report for the National Conference on Witchcraft Violence" (convened by the Commission on Gender Equality, Malawi, September 6–10, 1998), ix.

8. Ibid., 11.

9. Ibid., 14.

10. Van Breugel, *Chewa Traditional Religion*, 211.

11. Ibid., 238.

12. Pilarani Semu-Banda, "Witchcraft and Mob Justice in Malawi," *The Wip*, May 28, 2008.

13. "Conference Report for the National Conference on Witchcraft Violence," viii.

14. Ibid., xi.

15. Ibid., 19.

16. "Witchcraft Act Review Programme: Issues Paper," 6.

17. Ibid., 5.

18. "Conference Report for the National Conference on Witchcraft Violence," 35.

19. "Witchcraft Act Review Programme: Issues Paper," 14.

20. Gregory Gondwe, "Witchcraft Strife Storms Malawi," *Ground Report*, February 3, 2008, http://www.Groundreport.com/World/Witchcraft-Strife-Storms-Malawi/2854513.

21. Rune Blix Hagen, "The Witch-hunts on African Sorcerers" (Department of History, University of Tromsø, Norway, 2000), 3.

22. Ibid.

23. Semu-Banda, "Witchcraft and Mob Justice in Malawi."

24. Ibid.

25. "Cilic demand witchcraft bill," *Nyasa Times*, April 10, 2008.

26. Stella Twea, "Women as offenders—the social and legal circumstances of women who commit crimes: A case study of selected prisons in Malawi" (MA thesis, Southern and Eastern African Regional Centre for Women's Law, University of Zimbabwe, 2004), 31.

27. Ibid., 32.

28. Ibid.

29. Blix Hagen, "The Witch-hunts on African Sorcerers," 2.

30. Andrew Malone, "The albino tribe butchered to feed a gruesome trade in magical body parts," *Mail Online*, September 25, 2009, http://www.dailymail.co.uk/news/article-1215949/The-albino-tribe-butchered-feed-gruesome-trade-magical-body-parts.html.

31. Ibid.

32. Pilirani Semu-Banda, "On the Prowl for Private Body Parts," *The Wip*, March 17, 2007.

33. "Conference Report for the National Conference on Witchcraft Violence," viii–ix.

Florence

1. Chifundo, "The Day I Was Born," in *In Their Own Words: The Girls of Atsikana Pa Ulendo Tell Their Stories*, ed. Roberta Laurie (Edmonton: Prairie Dog Publishing, 2011), 33.

2. Mirriam, "How I Stopped Stealing Mangoes," in *In Their Own Words: The Girls of Atsikana Pa Ulendo Tell Their Stories*, ed. Roberta Laurie (Edmonton: Prairie Dog Publishing, 2011), 103.

3. Memory Chazeza-Mdyetseni, interviews by author at APU in 2008 and 2009.

8   Canadians Educating African Girls

1. Sellina, "Educate girls and fight AIDS," *Malawi Girls on the Move Atsikana Pa Ulendo News*, Fall 2007, http://www.malawigirlsonthemove.com/sites/default/files/newsletters/Newsletter_Oct_07.pdf.

2. This chapter is based, in part, on interviews with Christie Johnson at Victoria, BC, in 2009; Gordon Poultney at Spruce Grove, AB, in 2011, along with additional correspondence in 2013; Memory Chazeza-Mdyetseni at Lilongwe, Malawi, in 2007, and via telephone in 2010; Lucy Chazeza-Kaferantu at APU in 2009, and via telephone in 2010; and a joint interview with Memory and Christie during Memory's 2008 Canadian speaking tour.

3. Tamanda, "Atsikana Pa Ulendo," in *In Their Own Words: The Girls of Atsikana Pa Ulendo Tell Their Stories*, ed. Roberta Laurie (Edmonton: Prairie Dog Publishing, 2011), 125.

4. Raising Malawi, "About," 2012, http://www.raisingmalawi.org/pagers/about.

5. Joseph Giovannini, "Ground Breaking," *Architectural Digest*, October 2010, p. 44.

6. "Malawi: Madonna launches Malawi school contruction," *TendersInfo.*, Al Bawaba (Middle East) Ltd., 2009, HighBeam Research, March 26, 2010, http://www.highbeam.com.

7. "Malawi Officials Blast Madonna's School Plans," *Rolling Stone*, March 14, 2012, http://www.rollingstone.com/music/news/Malawi-officials-blast-madonnas-school-plans-20120314.

8.   David Smith, "Madonna's New Schools Pledge Angers Malawi Officials," *Guardian*, February 23, 2012, http://www.theguardian.com/music/2012/feb/23/madonna-schools-pledge-angers-malawi-officials.

9.   Ibid.

10. "Statement from Madonna," *Raising Malawi*, January 11, 2011, http://www.raisingmalawi.org/blog/entry/statement-from-madonna.

11. Smith, "Madonna's New Schools Pledge Angers Malawi Officials."

12. Ibid.

13. "Malawi Officials Blast Madonna's School Plans."

14. Nick Rockel, "Stephen Lewis is on a global mission for AIDS relief," *Globe and Mail*, November 9, 2010, http://www.theglobeandmail.com/report-on-business/stephen-lewis-is-on-a-global-mission-for-aids-relief/article1319684/.

15. Wendy Smith, *Give a Little: How Your Small Donations Can Transform Our World* (New York: Hyperion, 2009), 28–31.

16. Ibid., 28.

17. UNICEF, "The State of the World's Children," 2009, http://www.unicef.org/protection/SOWC09-FullReport-EN.pdf.

18. Ibid., 32.

19. National Research Council, *Social Dynamics of Adolescent Fertility in Sub-Saharan Africa* (Washington, DC: The National Academies Press, 1993), 148.

20. Ibid., 149–150.

21. Ibid., 150–151.

22. Pilirani Semu-Banda, "Health-Malawi: Help for Women with Obstetric Fistula," http://www.ipsnews.net/2008/10/health-malawi-help-for-women-with-obstetric-fistula/.

23. Ibid.

24. National Research Council, *Social Dynamics of Adolescent Fertility in Sub-Saharan Africa*, 150.

25. Pilirani Semu-Banda, "Beyond Witchcraft," *New Internationalist*, March 2009, http://www.newint.org/features/2009/03/01/fistula/.

26. Malawi News Agency, "Joyce Banda: Stop Stigmatizing Women with Fistula...2000 Cases in Malawi Yearly," July 19, 2012, accessed August 2012, http://www.maravipost.com/life-and-style/health/1346-joyce-banda-stop-stigmatizing-women-with-fistula...ffff-2,000-cases-in-malawi-yearly.html#.UDpgwqmhD8s.

27. IRIN Global, "Malawi: President Lifts Ban on Traditional Birth Assistants," October 11, 2010, http://www.irinnews.org/Report/90732/MALAWI-President-lifts-ban-on-traditional-birth-assistants.

28. Ibid.

29. National Research Council, *Social Dynamics of Adolescent Fertility in Sub-Saharan Africa*, 114.

30. "'Sense of Urgency' Needed to Cut Maternal Deaths, UNICEF Head Says," *Associated Press*, January 15, 2009, http://www.cbc.ca/news/health/story/2009/01/15/maternity-deaths.html.

Audrey

1. This account of Audrey Kaplan-Entz is based on my interview with her in Edmonton, AB, in 2010.

9   A Trip to the Lake

1. UNESCO, "Lake Malawi National Park," 2015, http://whc.UNESCO.org/en/list/289.

2. This chapter is based, in part, on personal interviews with Memory Chazeza-Mdyetseni at Lilongwe, Malawi, in 2007, in addition to a telephone interview in 2011, and personal interviews with Christie Johnson at Victoria, BC, in 2009.

3. Jacques Pepin, *The Origin of AIDS* (Cambridge: Cambridge University Press, 2011).

4. Ibid., 36.

5. Ibid., 162.

6. Ibid., 164.

7. Ibid., 10.

8. Ibid., 9.

9. Van den Borne, *Trying to Survive in Times of Poverty and AIDS*, 45.

10. Lewis, *Race against Time*, 4.

11. Stephen Lewis, "AIDS Pandemic can be Stopped, says Stephen Lewis," CAW/TCA, August 21, 2012, http://www.caw2012.ca/aids-pandemic-can-be-stopped-says-stephen-lewis/.

12. Lewis, *Race against Time*, 5.

13. Ibid., 15.

14. Ibid., 206.

15. UNAIDS, *Global Report: UNAIDS Report on the Global AIDS Epidemic*, 2010, http://www.unaids.org/globalreport/documents/20101123_GlobalReport_full_en.pdf.

16. Lewis, *Race against Time*, 206.

17. Anne C. Conroy et al., *Poverty, AIDS and Hunger: Breaking the Poverty Trap in Malawi* (London: Palgrave Macmillan, 2006), 34.

18. Central Intelligence Agency, *The World Factbook: Malawi*, 2014.

19. Tiyamike, "My Parents' Sickness," in *In Their Own Words: The Girls of Atsikana Pa Ulendo Tell Their Stories*, ed. Roberta Laurie (Edmonton: Prairie Dog Publishing, 2011), 147–148.

20. "HIV & AIDS in Malawi," *AVERT*, http://www.avert.org/hiv-aids-malawi.htm.

21. Van Kornegay, "Words and Deeds," July 31, 2004, http://www.worldmag.com/articles/9455.

22. Theatre for Change UK/Theatre for Change Malawi, "National Teacher Training HIV Baseline Survey," 2009, 4–5, http://hivhealthclearinghouse.UNESCO.org/library/documents/national-teacher-training-hiv-baseline-survey-malawi-2009.

23. "HIV & AIDS in Malawi."

24. "Malawi: Leader Offers Aids Policy and Reveals a Death," *New York Times*, February 11, 2004, http://www.nytimes.com/2004/02/11/world/world-briefing-africa-malawi-leader-offers-aids-policy-reveals-a-death.html.

25. UNAIDS, *Global Report*, 29.

26. "HIV & AIDS in Malawi."

27. Ibid.

28. Lewis, *Race against Time*, 56–57.

29. Ibid., 57.

30. USAID Malawi, "HIV/AIDS Health Profile," July 2012, http://transition.usaid.gov/our_work/global_health/aids/Countries/africa/malawi_profile.pdf.

31. UNAIDS, "Epidemiological Fact Sheets on HIV/AIDS and Sexually Transmitted Infections," 2004, http://data.unaids.org/Publications/Fact-Sheets01/malawi_en.pdf.

32. Angella, "What Is Wrong?" in *In Their Own Words: The Girls of Atsikana Pa Ulendo Tell Their Stories*, ed. Roberta Laurie (Edmonton: Prairie Dog Publishing, 2011), 150.

33. David Werner, with Carol Thuman and Jan Maxwell, *Where There Is No Doctor* (Berkeley, CA: Hesperian Health Guides, 1992), 279.

Chidothi

1. This account of Chidothi is based on my interview with her at Lilongwe, Malawi, in 2007.

2. Cecilia, "Someday, Something Exciting Will Happen," in *In Their Own Words: The Girls of Atsikana Pa Ulendo Tell Their Stories*, ed. Roberta Laurie (Edmonton: Prairie Dog Publishing, 2011), 65.

3. Ibid.

10 The CEAG Girls

1. Memory Chazeza-Mdyetseni, telephone interview by author, 2010.

2. This chapter is based, in part, on author interviews with Christie Johnson and Memory Chazeza-Mdyetseni during their Alberta speaking tour in 2007; with Memory Chazeza-Mdyetseni at Lilongwe, Malawi, in 2007; and with Christie Johnson at Victoria, BC, in 2009.

Estel

1. This account of Estel is based on my interview with her in Malawi in 2007.

11 Growing Up

1. Malawi Girls on the Move Secondary School Education Project, Grand Opening, http://www.malawigirlsonthemove.com/videos.

2. This chapter is based, in part, on personal interviews with Auralia at Mzuzu, Malawi, in 2009; with Lucy Chazeza-Kaferantu at Lilongwe, Malawi, in 2007, and at APU in 2009; with Maness Samuel at Victoria, BC, in 2011; and with Eunice at Lilongwe in 2007.

3. African Bible Colleges, "About," 2012, https://africanbiblecolleges.net/about/.

4. Kasupe Ministries, 2008, accessed July 2009, http://www.gencoo.be/drupal/node/75.

5. World Bank, "Data," 2015, http://data.worldbank.org/indicator/SI.POV.2DAY/countries.

6. Obinna Chima, "Africa: Experts Harp on Microcredit for Poverty Eradication," *This Day*, December 26, 2011, http://allafrica.com/stories/201112260222.html.

7. "Online Extra: Yunus Blasts Compartamos," *Bloomberg Businessweek Magazine*, December 12, 2007, http://www.businessweek.com/stories/2007-12-12/online-extra-yunus-blasts-compartamos.

8. Ibid.

9. Richard Rosenberg, "Is Microcredit Over-Indebtedness a Worldwide Problem?" http://microfinance.cgap.org/2011/11/07/is-microcredit-over-indebtedness-a-worldwide-problem/#more-3045.

10. Smita Premchander, *Multiple Meanings of Money: How Women See Microfinance* (Thousands Oaks, CA: Sage Publications, 2009), 222.

Basimati

1. This account of Basimati is based on my interviews with her, Christie Johnson, and Memory Chazeza-Mdyetseni in Malawi in 2007.

12 Quietly, Malawi Begins to Starve

1. Memory Chazeza-Mdyetseni, interview by author at Lilongwe, Malawi, in 2007.
2. This chapter is based in large part on my interviews with Memory Chazeza-Mdyetseni at Lilongwe and APU, Malawi, in 2007 and 2008, and with Christie Johnson at Victoria, BC, in 2009, as well as with Chrissy Phelani at APU, Malawi, in 2008.
3. Stephen Devereaux, "The Malawi Famine of 2002," *IDS Bulletin* 33, no. 4 (2002): 71.
4. Raphael Tenthani, "Malawi donors suspend aid," *BBC NEWS*, November 19, 2001, http://news.bbc.co.uk/2/hi/africa/1665141.stm.
5. "Famine stalks Southern Africa," *BBC NEWS*, February 19, 2002, http://news.bbc.co.uk/2/hi/africa/1830296.stm.
6. ActionAid, *Death by Starvation in Malawi: The link between macro-economic and structural policies and the agricultural disaster in Malawi*, June 13, 2002, 2, http://207.254.216.62/assets/pdfs/food_rights/Death_by_Starvation_Malawi.pdf.
7. Ibid., 3.
8. Ibid.
9. Ibid.
10. Devereaux, "The Malawi Famine of 2002," 74.
11. Raphael Tenthani, "Muluzi faces moving on," *BBC NEWS*, May 13, 2004, http://news.bbc.co.uk/2/hi/africa/3586807.stm.
12. Ibid.
13. "Malawi ex-leader Muluzi held on coup charge," *Reuters*, May 25, 2008, http://in.reuters.com/article/2008/05/25/idINIndia-33762420080525.
14. Raphael Tenthani, "Malawi's president rules his way," *BBC NEWS*, September 1, 2004, http://news.bbc.co.uk/2/hi/africa/3618948.stm.
15. Tenthani, "Muluzi faces moving on."
16. Devereaux, "The Malawi Famine of 2002," 76–77.
17. Roshni Menon, *Famine in Malawi: Causes and Consequences*, Human Development Report 2007/2008, http://hdr.undp.org/sites/default/files/menon_roshni_2007a_malawi.pdf.
18. Ezequiel Burgo and Heather Stewart, "IMF policies 'led to Malawi famine,'" October 29, 2002, http://www.theguardian.com/business/2002/oct/29/3.
19. Devereaux, "The Malawi Famine of 2002," 72.
20. Ibid., 73.
21. Ibid., 75.
22. Kelechi Nnoaham, "Pathology of a famine: The Malawi Example," *The Internet Journal of Rescue & Disaster Medicine* 7, no. 2 (2008), https://ispub.com/IJRDM/7/2/12463.

23. European Union Directorate-General for Humanitarian Aid, "Emergency assistance to the vulnerable groups suffering from food shortages in Malawi," October 19, 2005, http://ec.europa.eu/echo/files/funding/decisions/2005/dec_malawi_01000.pdf.

24. United Nations, "Malawi 2005 Flash Appeal," August 30, 2005, http://www.unocha.org/cap/malawi-2005-flash-appeal.

25. "Malawi leader declares disaster over food crisis," *ABC News*, October 15, 2005, http://www.abc.net.au/news/2005-10-16/malawi-leader-declares-disaster-over-food-crisis/2125414.

26. Ibid.

27. Irene Phalula, "Malawi Food Crisis Hits Women Hardest," *Africa Files*, http://digbig.com/4fprf.

28. Bill Corcoran, "Five Million Face Death as Famine Grips Malawi," *Guardian*, October 2, 2005, http://www.theguardian.com/world/2005/oct/02/famine.theobserver.

29. Phalula, "Malawi Food Crisis Hits Women Hardest."

30. Ibid.

31. Raphael Tenthani, "Top Malawi official blamed in decision to sell off grain reserves," *Associated Press*, August 31, 2004, http://www.highbeam.com/doc/1P1-98559603.html.

32. Ibid.

33. European Union Directorate-General for Humanitarian Aid, "Emergency assistance to the vulnerable groups."

34. Shakira, "The Death of My Brother," in *In Their Own Words: The Girls of Atsikana Pa Ulendo Tell Their Stories*, ed. Roberta Laurie (Edmonton: Prairie Dog Publishing, 2011), 139.

35. Seth Borenstein, "Dirt problem overlooked in global food crisis," *NBC News*, May 8, 2008, http://www.nbcnews.com/id/24524912/ns/technology_and_science-science/t/dirt-problem-overlooked-global-food-crisis/#.VWKSuRYx_8s.

36. Jocelyn Kaiser, "Wounding Earth's Fragile Skin," *Science* 304, no. 5677 (June 11, 2004): 1616–1618.

37. John Vidal and Tim Radford, "One in six countries facing food shortage," *Guardian*, June 30, 2005, http://www.theguardian.com/world/2005/jun/30/science.famine.

38. Charles Mkula, "Climate Change Affecting Malawi's Maize Production," *Malawi Voice*, March 29, 2012, http://www.malawivoice.com/2012/03/29/climate-change-affecting-malawis-maize-production-51308/.

39. Ibid.

40. Ibid.

41. World Bank, "Severe Droughts Drive Food Prices Higher, Threatening the Poor," August 30, 2012, http://www.worldbank.org/en/news/2012/08/30/severe-droughts-drive-food-prices-higher-threatening-poor.

42. Paul Collier, *The Bottom Billion: Why the Poorest Countries Are Failing and What Can Be Done about It* (New York: Oxford University Press, 2007), 71.

43. Celia W. Dugger, "Ending Famine, Simply by Ignoring the Experts," *New York Times*, December 2, 2007, http://www.nytimes.com/2007/12/02/world/africa/02malawi.html?scp=1&sq=ending+famine+simply+by+ignoring+the+experts&st=nyt&_r=0.

44. Morocco, Report written to Canadian donors and included in a longer report by Christie Johnson, "Memory's Famine Relief Efforts Continue," April 1, 2006.

45. Ibid.

Henry

1. This account of Henry Mdyetseni is based on my interview with him near Mzuzu, Malawi, in 2009.

13 A Global Perspective

1. World of Proverbs, http://www.worldofproverbs.com/2012/09/if-you-think-youre-too-small-to-make.html.

2. This chapter is based, in part, on my personal experience, as well as interviews with Memory Chazeza-Mdyetseni at Lilongwe, Malawi, in 2007, and at APU in 2008 and 2009, and interviews with Lucita at APU in 2008.

3. Malawi Human Rights Commission, "Cultural Practices and Their Impact on the Enjoyment of Human Rights," 78.

4. Van den Borne, *Trying to Survive in Times of Poverty and AIDS*, 72.

5. Ibid., 76.

6. Malawi Human Rights Commission, "Cultural Practices and Their Impact on the Enjoyment of Human Rights," 20.

7. Ibid.

8. Ibid., 19.

9. Ibid., 20.

10. Ibid., 21.

11. Van den Borne, *Trying to Survive in Times of Poverty and AIDS*, 32.

12. Ibid., 78.

13. Ibid.

14. Michele Tertilt, "Polygyny, Women's Rights, and Development" (Department of Economics, Stanford University, California, September 2005), 2.

15. Ibid.

16. Mallick Mnela, "Malawians Defend Polygamy," *Islam Online*, March 16, 2008, http://www.islamonline.net/servlet/Satellit?c=Article_C&cid=1203758094341&pagename=Zone-English-News/NWELayout.

17. OneLove, "Background," accessed October 2009, http://www.onelovesouthernafrica.org/index.php/background.

18. Claire Ngozo, "Sweet 16 Marriages Cause Controversy in Malawi," *Inter Press Service News Agency*, August 21, 2009, http://www.ipsnews.net/2009/08/rights-sweet-16-marriages-cause-controversy-in-malawi/.

19. Ibid.

Eunice

1. This account of Eunice is based on my interviews with her at Lilongwe, Malawi, in 2007.

14 The Dream Takes Shape

1. *Atsikana Pa Ulendo*, Fall 2012 newsletter, http://www.malawigirlsonthemove.com/sites/default/files/APU-Newsletter-Fall-2012.pdf.

2. This chapter is based primarily on the observations, experiences, and conversations of my 2007 trip to Malawi.

3. United Nations, "World Urbanization Prospects: The 2007 Revision," http://www.un.org/esa/population/publications/wup2007/2007WUP_Highlights_web.pdf.

Patience

1. This account of Patience is based on my interview with her at Nsaru, Malawi, in 2008.

15 Atsikana Pa Ulendo

1. Christie Johnson, "Life at the School," *Atsikana Pa Ulendo*—Girls on the Move, 2010, http://www.malawigirlsonthemove.com/life_school.

2. This chapter is based, in part, on my observations during my 2008 and 2009 trips to Malawi, personal interviews with Memory Chazeza-Mdyetseni and Henry Mdyetseni at APU in 2008 and 2009, and telephone interviews with Memory in 2010 and 2011 on Memory's Canadian speaking tour in 2010.

3. Prisca, "When I Was Selected at Atsikana Pa Ulendo," in *In Their Own Words: The Girls of Atsikana Pa Ulendo Tell Their Stories*, ed. Roberta Laurie (Edmonton: Prairie Dog Publishing, 2011), 67.

4.   Milika, "When I Wrote the Entrance Exam," in *In Their Own Words: The Girls of Atsikana Pa Ulendo Tell Their Stories*, ed. Roberta Laurie (Edmonton: Prairie Dog Publishing, 2011), 117.

5.   Ibid.

6.   Diliya, "English as the Language of Communication."

7.   Diliya, "Examinations," in *In Their Own Words: The Girls of Atsikana Pa Ulendo Tell Their Stories*, ed. Roberta Laurie (Edmonton: Prairie Dog Publishing, 2011), 155.

8.   Brandina, "School Journey," in *In Their Own Words: The Girls of Atsikana Pa Ulendo Tell Their Stories*, ed. Roberta Laurie (Edmonton: Prairie Dog Publishing, 2011), 152.

9.   Theresa Chapulapula, "JCE exam results best in 5 years," MTENDERE: *Malawi Teachers for Peace* (blog), December 7, 2009, http://mtenderekumalawi.blogspot.ca/2009/12/jce-exam-results-best-in-5-years.html.

10.   Blandina Diva, email correspondence, May 24, 2012.

11.   United Nations, "When Women Are Empowered, All of Society Benefits—Migiro," UN *News Centre*, November 16, 2007, http://www.un.org/apps/news/story.asp?NewsID=24698&Cr=women&Cr1.

Blandina

1.   This account of Blandina Diva is based on my interview with her in Dawson Creek, BC, in 2012.

16 A Moral Universe

1.   Theodore Parker, speech given before the Massachusetts Anti-Slavery Convention, January 29, 1858, https://www.goodreads.com/quotes/303285-i-do-not-pretend-to-understand-the-moral-universe-the.

2.   This chapter is based, in part, on telephone interviews with Memory Chazeza-Mdyetseni during the years 2012, 2013, 2014, and 2015, as well as a telephone interview with Henry Mdyetseni in 2012, a telephone interview with Lucy Chazeza-Kaferantu in 2012, and telephone interviews with Christie Johnson in 2012 and 2015.

3.   *Atsikana Pa Ulendo* (Malawi Girls on the Move) Education Project, *Facebook*, October 21, 2014, https://www.facebook.com/MalawiGirlsOnTheMove?fref=ts.

4.   *Atsikana Pa Ulendo* (Malawi Girls on the Move) Education Project, *Facebook*, May 13, 2015, https://www.facebook.com/MalawiGirlsOnTheMove?fref=ts.

5.   RAGM, "About RAGM," 2012, http://ragm.rotaryglobal.net/p/sp1/220/About_RAGM/.

6.   "A Semi-Annual Progress Report for Stony Plain Rotary" (World Vision, 2012).

7.   Chuck Morrison, interview by author, Spruce Grove, AB, 2012.

8.   "A Semi-Annual Progress Report for Stony Plain Rotary."

9. "Your Gift in Action in Malawi: An Annual Progress Report for Stony Plain Rotary" (World Vision, March 2013).

10. "Malawi's President Secretly Buys a Private Jet," *Newstime Africa*, 2010, http://www.newstimeafrica.com/archives/11294.

11. Ibid.

12. Mark Tran, "Explainer: Why are people demonstrating in Malawi?" *Guardian*, July 21, 2011, http://www.guardian.co.uk/global-development/2011/jul/21/malawi-anti-government-protests.

13. Ibid.

14. Michelle Dobrovolny, "EU to make decision on Malawi support next month," *Malawi Today*, May 27, 2011, http://www.malawitoday.com/content/eu-make-decision-malawi-support-next-month.

15. David Smith, "Malawi: Africa's 'warm heart' feels chill of creeping dictatorship," *Guardian*, February 15, 2012, http://www.guardian.co.uk/world/2012/feb/15/malawi-africa-creeping-dictatorship.

16. "Callista Mutharika under Malawi Police probe over 'wrongful self-enrichment,'" *Nyasa Times*, August 5, 2013, http://www.nyasatimes.com/2013/08/05/callista-mutharika-under-malawi-police-probe-over-wrongful-self-enrichment/.

17. US Department of State, Bureau of Democracy, Human Rights, and Labor, "2010 Human Rights Report: Malawi," April 8, 2011, http://www.state.gov/j/drl/rls/hrrpt/2010/af/154356.htm.

18. "Opposition Blames Mutharika for Aid Ban," *News24*, July 15, 2011, http://www.news24.com/Africa/News/Opposition-blames-Mutharika-for-aid-ban-20110715.

19. Ibid.

20. Godfrey Mapondera and David Smith, "Malawi protesters killed during anti-regime riots," *Guardian*, July 21, 2011, http://www.guardian.co.uk/world/2011/jul/21/malawi-protesters-killed-anti-regime-riots.

21. "Violence erupts during Malawi anti-government demonstrations," *Amnesty International*, July 20, 2011, http://www.amnesty.org/en/news-and-updates/violence-erupts-during-malawi-anti-government-demonstrations-2011-07-20.

22. Mapondera and Smith, "Malawi protesters killed during anti-regime riots."

23. Celia W. Dugger, "Malawi President Blames Protesters for Violence," *New York Times*, July 22, 2011, http://www.nytimes.com/2011/07/23/world/africa/23malawi.html.

24. Jamie Crawford, "US suspends some aid to Malawi over violence," *CNN*, July 26, 2011, http://articles.cnn.com/2011-07-26/world/us.malawi.aid_1_malawian-economy-mcc-protesters?_s=PM:WORLD.

25. Mobhare Matinyi, "Sad, bleak legacy of Malawi's Mutharika," *Citizen*, April 16, 2012, http://www.malawitoday.com/news/124533-sad-bleak-legacy-malawi's-mutharika.

26. Frank Jomo, "Malawi's Vice President Joyce Banda Expelled from Ruling Party," *Bloomberg*, December 13, 2010, http://www.bloomberg.com/news/2010-12-13/malawi-s-vice-president-joyce-banda-expelled-from-ruling-party.html.

27. Mabvuto Banda, "Malawi's President Mutharika Dead," *Reuters*, April 6, 2012, http://www.reuters.com/article/2012/04/06/us-malawi-president-idUSBRE83504E20120406.

28. Raphael Tenthani, "Malawi: Joyce Banda Shakes the System," *Africa Report*, June 27, 2012, http://www.theafricareport.com/index.php/20120627501814344/southern-africa/malawi-joyce-banda-shakes-the-system-501814344.html.

29. Ibid.

30. David Smith, "Malawi's Joyce Banda Discards Presidential Jet and Luxury Car Fleet," *Guardian*, June 1, 2012, http://www.guardian.co.uk/world/2012/jun/01/malawi-joyce-banda-discards-presidential-jet.

31. David Smith, "Malawi president vows to legalise homosexuality," *Guardian*, May 18, 2012, http://www.guardian.co.uk/world/2012/may/18/malawi-president-vows-legalise-homosexuality.

32. Ibid.

33. Colin Stewart, "It's official: Mo more Malawi arrests under anti-gay laws," July 14, 2014, http://76crimes.com/2014/07/14/its-official-no-more-malawi-arrests-under-anti-gay-laws/; Joseph Patrick McCormick, "Malawi to stop arresting people for having gay sex," *Pink News*, July 15, 2014, http://www.pinknews.co.uk/2014/07/15/malawi-to-stop-arresting-people-for-having-gay-sex/.

34. Lyndon Haviland, "The Debating Chamber—New Malawi President Joyce Banda offers hope for women," *AlertNet*, April 13, 2012, http://www.trust.org/alertnet/blogs/the-debating-chamber/new-malawi-president-joyce-banda-offers-hope-for-women/.

35. Elwin Mandowa, "Britain gives Malawi additional aid, Pres Banda says it came at right time," *Maravi Post*, July 17, 2012, accessed September 2012, http://www.maravipost.com/malawi-news/political/1329-britain-gives-malawi-additional-aid,-pres-banda-says-it-came-at-right-time.html#.UEj-MUKhD8s.

36. "US Restores $350 mln Malawi aid programme," *Reuters*, June 22, 2012, http://af.reuters.com/article/malawiNews/idAFL5E8HM1HE20120622.

37. Amanda Chiliro, "President Banda says PP to rule Malawi beyond 2014," *Nyasa Times*, August 12, 2012, http://www.nyasatimes.com/malawi/2012/08/12/president-banda-says-pp-to-rule-malawi-beyond-2014/.

38. "Malawi's Peter Mutharika Offers Joyce Banda Olive Branch," BBC *News: Africa*, June 2, 2014, http://www.bbc.com/news/world-africa-27669753.

39. World Bank, "Girls' Education," December 3, 2014, http://web.worldbank.org/WBSITE/EXTERNAL/TOPICS/EXTEDUCATION/0,,contentMDK:20298916~menuPK:617572~pagePK:148956~piPK:216618~theSitePK:282386,00.html#why.

40. United Nations, "When Women Are Empowered, all of Society Benefits—Migiro," November 16, 2007, http://www.un.org/apps/news/story.asp?NewsID=24698&Cr=women&Cr1.

41. Maness Samuel, email correspondence, September 10, 2012.

Index